The Big Ditch

Princeton University Press   *Princeton & Oxford*

THE BIG DITCH

How America Took, Built, Ran, and Ultimately Gave Away the Panama Canal

NOEL MAURER & CARLOS YU

Copyright © 2011 by Princeton University Press

Published by Princeton University Press,
41 William Street, Princeton, New Jersey 08540

In the United Kingdom: Princeton University Press,
6 Oxford Street, Woodstock, Oxfordshire OX20 1TW

press.princeton.edu

Library of Congress Cataloging-in-Publication Data

Maurer, Noel.
The big ditch : how America took, built, ran, and ultimately gave away the
Panama Canal / Noel Maurer and Carlos Yu.
p. cm.
Includes bibliographical references and index.
ISBN 978-0-691-14738-3 (hardcover : alk. paper) 1. Panama Canal (Panama)—
History. 2. United States—Foreign relations—Panama. 3. Panama—Foreign
relations—United States. 4. Imperialism—Economic aspects.
I. Yu, Carlos, 1970– II. Title.
F1569.C2M157 2011
386'.44—dc22
2010029058

British Library Cataloging-in-Publication Data is available

This book has been composed in Din Pro and Warnock Pro
Printed on acid-free paper. ∞
Printed in the United States of America
1 3 5 7 9 10 8 6 4 2

CONTENTS

LIST OF ILLUSTRATIONS

FIGURES

MAPS

LIST OF TABLES

PREFACE

ONE OF THE BEST THINGS ABOUT HAVING GREAT COLLEAGUES is that they recognize implications of your work in ways that had never occurred to you. This book began as a short social savings exercise. After we presented our preliminary results, Gavin Wright encouraged us to expand the analysis to include some of the linkages we had mentioned wholly offhandedly during our talk. Alan Dye further encouraged us to explore the political ramifications of the Panamanian-American relationship, and what it implied about the economic impact of American interventionism at home and abroad. At this point we realized we had a book on our hands. All that was left for us to do was to write it.

As the book grew, the number of people and institutions who contributed to it grew as well. At Harvard, Veronica Martini, Zac Pelleriti, and Juliana Seminerio provided irreplaceable support, without which we would have been unable to complete this book. In Panama, Carlos Mendoza gave us more help in locating people and archives than we could have possibly hoped for. We would also like to thank Celestino Araúz, Rubén Dario Carles, Osvaldo Heilbron, Carlos Alberto Mendoza, and Stanley Motta for taking the time to talk to us in Panama City. Special thanks go to the Autoridad del Canal de Panamá for their help with this project, particularly José Barrios Ng and Guillermo Chapman. In New York City, the librarians of the New York Public Library at the Stephen Schwarzman Building and the Science, Industry and Business Library were invaluable in their help locating historical materials. In Washington DC and College Park, Maryland, the staff of the

National Archives facilities must be praised for their detailed knowledge of their immense collection.

An earlier version of chapter 5 appeared as "What T.R. Took: The Economic Impact of the Panama Canal, 1903–1937," *Journal of Economic History* 68, no. 3 (September 2008): 686–721. Alan Dye, Steve Haber, Aldo Musacchio, and Kris Mitchener were willing to read and extensively comment on versions of the article and later drafts of the manuscript. We also have to thank Stanley Engerman, Eric Hilt, Rick Hornbeck, Claudia Goldin, Jonathan Liebowitz, Suresh Naidu, James Robinson, Peter Temin, Jeff Williamson, and the other participants in Harvard University's Economic History Workshop for their detailed comments and criticisms. Drafts of other portions of this book have appeared at various conferences and seminars over the last few years, including the Conference on the New Frontiers in Latin American Economic History, the Washington Area Economic History Seminar at the University of Maryland, and the Business History Seminar at Harvard. We thank the conveners of those seminars and conferences, as well as the audiences who provided much useful feedback. In particular, we owe special thanks to Lee Alston, Leticia Arroyo, Price Fishback, John Wallis, and William Summerhill for their comments and advice.

Most of the funding for this book came from the Harvard Business School. We would like to thank its dean, Jay Light, and our research director, Geoff Jones, for the generous support given to us during the writing of this book. We would also like to thank Geoff, in particular, for excellent advice about the overall argument of the book. In addition, the heads of the Business, Government, and the International Economy (BGIE) unit at HBS during the time this book was written, David Moss and Forest Reinhardt, gave a great deal of support, both intellectual and moral. Also at HBS, Niall Ferguson read and extensively commented on entire chapters, and Walter Friedman provided vital feedback on the book's theme. We would also like to thank our other BGIE colleagues for all their support and advice: Rawi Abdelal, Laura Alfaro, Diego Comín, Arthur Daemmerich, Rafael Di Tella, Catherine Duggan,

Lakshmi Iyer, Dante Roscini, Julio Rotemberg, Gunnar Trumbull, Matt Weinzierl, Louis Wells, and Eric Werker.

Numerous people gave generously of their time to help make this book happen. Their conversations and suggestions have enriched this book in many surprising ways. We would in particular like to thank Janie Chan, Kathleen Cioffi, Seth Ditchik, Joan Gieseke, and Dimitri Karetnikov at Princeton University Press. Jason Alejandro did an amazing job with the cover art. We would also like to thank the anonymous referees from Princeton University Press for their incisive reviews of an early draft of this book. Any flaws or errors that remain are of course our own.

We have dedicated this book to Amma Maurer, for her unfailing support while writing this book—including reading the entire manuscript on more than one occasion!—and to Carlos C. and Barbara Yu. Without their love and understanding, it would not have been possible.

The Big Ditch

ONE

INTRODUCTION TO THE DITCH

FROM A DISTANCE, IN NORTH AMERICA, THE PANAMA CANAL seems like an imperialist anachronism, a historical leftover from a discreditable and nearly forgotten chapter of U.S. history. Up close, however, it is immediately apparent that the Panama Canal is one of the world's great waterways, the highly efficient economic engine for a rather prosperous Latin American country. Both of these interpretations of the Panama Canal are correct. This book was written to reconcile these seemingly conflicting points of view.

There is a stylized narrative many Americans learn about the history of the Panama Canal. In the late nineteenth century, so the story goes, French private interests tried and failed to build a canal across the Isthmus of Panama. Amidst the wreckage of the French effort, President Theodore Roosevelt stepped in, unleashing America's industrial energy on the isthmus, and in the process accidentally inspiring the greatest palindrome in the English language. The Panama Canal became an unparalleled economic and strategic success, cutting the cost of ocean transport and permitting the U.S. Navy to dominate two seas for the price of one. President Jimmy Carter, however, mysteriously decided that the United States could no longer ignore the Panamanians. And so the Americans, controversially, at great risk, and with no gain to themselves, arranged to give one of their greatest engineering triumphs to the Panamanian people, whom they fully expected to squander it.

This standard story of the Panama Canal raises more questions than answers. The Isthmus of Panama might have enjoyed a uniquely privileged geographic location, but Panama remained a backwater for hundreds of years. The United States and Colombia were unable to negotiate an agreement on the Panama Canal to their mutual benefit, despite the obvious advantages for both nations. The Panama Canal project was a triumph of American engineering skill, but the reports of the time documented extensive delays, cost overruns, and management problems. The independent Republic of Panama remained an underdeveloped country, despite the presence of one of the world's major commercial arteries on its territory. The Carter administration gave into Panamanian requests that American administrations had ignored for decades and agreed to return the canal back to Panama in 1999. Finally, once Panama took back ownership of the canal, the waterway became phenomenally profitable despite the growth of alternative transport routes and fuelled a prolonged economic boom after decades of stagnation and relative decline. What explains these paradoxical outcomes?

Broadly speaking, this book is about the economics of American imperialism. "Imperialism," of course, has almost as many definitions as it has authors who have written about it. The most useful definition of "imperialism," we believe, is the use of state-enforced sanctions (or the threat of sanctions) by one political community to impose policies upon another political community.[1] As with any political institution, imperialism can be formal or informal. "Formal" imperialism follows rules laid down in constitutions or treaties, in which the government of the ruling community either exercises full sovereignty or exercises direct control over specific policy spheres in the subordinate community. "Informal" imperialism follows a less transparent but not necessarily less effective set of sanctions and rewards. (The line between the two is fuzzy; an example would be a treaty giving one country the right to intervene in the internal affairs of another under specific circumstances.) Imperialism can also be direct or indirect. When the government of the ruling political community is able to routinely impose its will upon *individual* members of the subordinate political community—most obviously, but not exclusively, through a formal colonial administration—then imperialism is direct. If the government of the ruling political community exercises its will through intermediaries, be they traditional tribal rulers or "sovereign" elected governments, then imperialism is indirect.

The literature on the economics of imperialism is long and distinguished. It has two general lacunae, however. The first is a relative lack of detailed case studies informed by quantitative analysis and economic theory. This is not to say that there is not a long and distinguished literature on the history of various imperial ventures. It is simply to say that with a few exceptions (such as Foreman's work on India), they do not engage in the explicit framing and formal testing of hypotheses. To the extent that they are informed by theory, the theories tend to be vague, ill-defined, and often left implicit. There are, of course, a number of large-N studies of imperialism that do engage in explicit hypothesis testing and are informed by economic theory. The unit of analysis in these studies is colonial governments (as in the cases of Ferguson and Schularick or Mitchener and Weidenmier) or imperial enterprises (as in the cases of Svedberg, Edelstein, and Davis and Huttenback).[2] These studies have greatly expanded our understanding of European colonialism, but they suffer from the specification problems common to all large-N studies. It is hard to use them to understand exactly how specific institutional arrangements created certain economic effects. Moreover, most of them tend to find (quite convincingly, for the periods that they study) that imperialism produced few benefits (if any) for the metropole but did create a beneficial "empire effect" for the colonies. What we do not know is whether these results are universal, or limited to the periods and empires studied by the authors.

Similarly, relatively little of the literature on economic imperialism deals with the difference between formal and informal empire in a modern context. (Mitchener and Weidenmier and Alfaro, Maurer, and Ahmed's work on the effects of U.S. policy in the circum-Caribbean are partial exceptions.) In 1961, David Landes concluded on remarkably little evidence, "Informal imperialism paid—in spite of occasional crashes and repudiations, if only because the use of power in such situations was minimal and the outlay of funds was based on essentially rational grounds. Formal imperialism, on the other hand, rarely paid."[3] Both types of imperialism considered by Landes, however, took place in an almost unrecognizable historical and institutional context. The subordinate political societies were often not organized as states. When they were organized into states, those states generally lacked Westphalian legal sovereignty, let alone significant access to modern military technology. Nor were these societies generally motivated by nationalism in the Western sense. Moreover, the dominant European colonizers were rarely characterized by democratic governments that periodically needed to win elections based on universal male suffrage, let alone universal suffrage. The question of the economic impact of old-style European imperialism is an important one for understanding how the world of the early twenty-first century emerged, but it offers only limited lessons for today.

America's imperial venture in Panama took place in a context that seems remarkably familiar to a reader from a century later, unlike the superficially similar (but actually quite different) Suez Canal project in Egypt. Despite the undemocratic nature of the regimes in the southern states, the general disenfranchisement of women, and the indirect election of the U.S. Senate, American politics circa 1903 were populist and democratic in a way instantaneously recognizable to a modern observer. The states of Latin America, like states today, enjoyed full Westphalian sovereignty (in theory), and despite their internal weaknesses they possessed modern national identities that governments could and did mobilize for their own purposes. The United States may have declared itself "practically sovereign upon this continent," as Secretary of State Richard Olney maintained in 1895, but it also faced foreign powers lurking in the wings who could potentially do it grievous damage, economically if not militarily. In short, President Theodore Roosevelt faced a context both domestic and external that more resembled that faced by the current leaders of powerful countries—be it Barack Obama, Lula da Silva, Vladimir Putin, or whomever it is that runs the European Union—than it resembled that faced by his European contemporaries.

The specific question that this book seeks to shed light on, then, is whether a relatively modern democratic nation, operating inside the strictures of Westphalian sovereignty, was able to leverage its ability to impose military and economic sanctions into sustainable economic gains. Conversely, why did that selfsame nation decide to withdraw from its imperial commitment a few decades later? Was it because of changing ideologies at home and changing power balances abroad, or was it because the economic value of its imperial venture had declined?

To answer these questions about America's imperial endeavor in Panama, we employed a form of the "analytic narrative" method pioneered by Bates, Greif, Levi, Rosenthal, and Weingast.[4] There is a vast and almost bewildering amount of economic, institutional, and historical data available about the Panama Canal. The analytic narrative allowed us to place these rich sources of information within a theoretical context to move forward from specific to more general conclusions, reasoning from the "thick" to the "thin," as the method's authors described it. In doing so, we borrowed the rational choice assumption that political actors seek to maximize their benefits in their interactions with others. This clarified several confusing points in the political history of the Panama Canal, such as the deliberate policy of the Colombian government to hamstring its own diplomats during its negotiations with the United States over the canal. As later events proved, this was a mistaken strategy for Colombia regarding the Panama Canal, but it was not an irrational one.

Within the narrative, we relied on quantitative techniques, many first developed by Robert Fogel. We especially borrowed from his social savings methodology in order to determine the economic value of the Panama Canal and examine the various policy options surrounding the canal at particular historical junctures. Fogel's simple yet powerful method of analysis compared the cost savings of a historical enterprise—in his case, U.S. railroads—to those of the next-best option that would exist in that enterprise's absence—in his example, a counterfactual network of canals and highways.[5] Fogel defined the difference between the two as the "social savings," e.g., the additional amount of economic activity created by the venture.

As an object of economic inquiry, the Panama Canal is obviously well suited for Fogellian methods. In addition, the Panama Canal has a wealth of "roads not taken" in its history, which allow us to evaluate the relative value (to the United States, the titular government of the isthmus, and others) of a variety of political options involving the canal. Finally, because of Panama's unique geographic location, we could compare the economic and historical effects of the modern Panama Canal to that of other isthmian transportation enterprises in earlier and later eras.

Panama enjoyed a privileged geographic location, but the basic question in its history has always been: who gets the economic rents generated from that geography? Would it be the people who occupied the land, the people who financed the infrastructure, or the people who used that infrastructure to move goods and people? The answer has historically been determined by three related factors: the value of the infrastructure to consumers (itself a function of the availability of good transport substitutes); the ability of those consumers to mobilize their government to defend their interests at a reasonable cost; and the symbolic power of ownership over infrastructure.

The Panama Canal was not the first transportation technology across the isthmus to reshape the world's economic geography. It was in fact the third. In the early Spanish colonial era, a trans-Panamanian road built by tens of thousands of slaves from Nicaragua allowed the Spanish to transport high-value silver from Peru to the Atlantic. Colonial Panama boomed—and native Panama dwindled—until competition from overland routes via Buenos Aires undercut the Panama route in the seventeenth century. A few centuries later, the process repeated itself. Just as the Spanish conquest of Peru unleashed a mass of precious metals heading east and a wave of prospectors heading west, so did the American conquest of California and subsequent gold rush. The Panama Railroad proved very profitable for its New York investors, until competition from the 1869 opening of the Transcontinental Railroad undercut it. Once the United States emerged as a transcontinental power, its geography and industrial economy ensured that its residents stood to benefit more from cheaper passage across the Isthmus of Panama than those of any other country. In that sense, it was inevitable that the United States would become involved in the politics of Panama. The question was what form such involvement would take.

The form of involvement taken by the United States in Panama proved to be a rather odd sort of imperialism. Washington employed a mix of strategies to take, build, and run the Panama Canal. In 1903, President Theodore Roosevelt used the threat of force against the Colombian government to permit local secessionists to peel the Panamanian isthmus away from Colombia. He then used the threat of force against the newly created Republic of Panama to take direct and *formal* control over the Canal Zone. Finally, he imposed indirect but formal rule over Panama (via Article 136 of the Panamanian constitution). Why did Roosevelt's administration choose the mix that it did?

The reasons were economic. The U.S. government under Roosevelt developed a set of political strategies that enabled it to expropriate most of the rents generated by Panama's geography through its imperial control of the Panama Canal. The Canal Zone drew a bright line around the canal, from which it was relatively easy to exclude Panamanian (and other potential foreign) competition from the provision of services or other ancillary operations. Article 136 provided a ready-made justification for intervention that could be wielded against domestic and foreign opponents. In addition, as part of the Panamanian constitution, it provided the occasional presence of American troops on Panamanian streets with an additional dollop of legitimacy—a vital thing in any foreign occupation. Limiting American involvement in Panama to excluding the Panamanians from the Zone and the occasional intervention freed the U.S. government from potential opposition at home.

The rents were enjoyed by a broad base of the imperial power's society—that is, the average American consumer. The cost of defending America's new Panamanian possession was small compared to these benefits. Unlike other empires of the era, the United States in Panama extracted significant value for its citizens. The flip side of this successful American venture into imperialism, of course, was a thorough lack of economic benefit for Panama, which captured essentially none of the rents from the Panama Canal. Neither did the American involvement in Panama lead to stronger political institutions, greater investment, nor lower borrowing costs for the Panamanian government. Rather, the major—but far from inconsiderable!—benefit from the American presence in Panama was an accidental spillover: the improvement in disease mortality rates caused by the public health programs the United States implemented during construction.

Why then did the United States choose to abandon its formal control over the Panama Canal in 1977—only to invade and overthrow the country's government in 1989? The answer to the first part of that question is simple: the strategic and economic value of U.S. ownership of the Panama Canal declined after World War II. The strategic benefits proved chimerical. The economic benefits fell as domestic cargoes made up less and less of the traffic through the canal, lured away by falling railroad and trucking costs. In addition, the industrialization of the West Coast meant that it consumed more and more of its own primary product production, leaving less to be shipped east via Panama. Moreover, falling transport costs meant that American agricultural exporters to Asia—who became the largest users of the canal by the 1970s—grew almost indifferent between shipping their grain south to the Gulf Coast and moving it west to Seattle. These changes in the users of the Panama Canal meant that Washington had less and less reason to fear that a Panamanian-owned canal would jack up transit rates at the expense of American consumers and producers. Rather, by the 1970s the primary burden of higher rates would fall on Asian exporters of inexpensive manufactured goods.

As the American interest in the Panama Canal declined, however, Panamanian political voice regarding the canal expanded. While American policy largely denied Panama economic benefits from the canal, increasing Panamanian national sentiment required the United States to channel compensating aid flows to Panama. At the same time, the long-term American workforce on the Panama Canal had captured the institutional administration of the canal, making it more inefficient and less profitable as a business enterprise. These two factors made the transfer of the Panama Canal from the United States to Panama mutually beneficial by the 1960s. The Panama Canal in Panamanian hands became more valuable to the United States than the Panama Canal in American hands. American nationalism, however, postponed the signing of any agreement to 1977.

Nevertheless, Washington's imperial role in Panama did not come to an end with the signing of the Carter-Torrijos treaties. Following the death of President Omar Torrijos in a mysterious plane crash, General Manuel Noriega rose to power. Noriega proved very useful to an American administration deeply concerned about Communist penetration of Central America. Noriega also proved to be spectacularly corrupt and even more spectacularly brutal. The result was an escalating conflict with Washington. The United States, however, did not contemplate a military invasion of Panama until Noriega made it clear he would interfere with the operation of the Panama Canal.

Noriega's 1989 overthrow by American troops ironically cleared the way for the end of America's imperial relationship with Panama. The two dictatorships of Omar Torrijos and Manuel Noriega had produced the side benefit of greatly weakening Panama's traditional patronage-based politics. (In Torrijos's case, the weakening of the old oligarchy was part of a deliberate reform strategy; in Noriega's it was merely a side effect of his attacks on anyone who threatened his political control or narcotics profits.) In the aftermath of the invasion, with the old parties needing to compete for votes on a far more open political market, Panamanian democracy began to thrive. After decades of dictatorship and despite the long-term effects of the American patron-client relationship, Panamanian voters were finally able to choose and dismiss candidates in favor of their own political and economic interests without fear of losing the benefits that came from membership in a particular political machine. Tampering with the Panama Canal for political gain (or even seeming to tamper with the Panama Canal for political gain) rapidly became the quickest way to lose support among the electorate. As a result, competitive politics led to a new Panama Canal Administration that ran the canal much more efficiently and commercially than the United States ever did. Consequently, the Panama Canal became an engine of growth for Panama for the first time in its history, and the presence of the United States receded into that of a distant neighbor, rather than one next door, or sometimes on the lawn. The 1999 handover of the Panama Canal to Panama marked the beginning of a new phase in the U.S. Panamanian relationship, one of mutual benefit through voluntary association—or, given the power difference between the two nations, a phase perhaps more accurately described as an "empire by invitation."

There has been little formal economic history written specifically about the Panama Canal. In writing this book, we found the topic nearly untouched, like the proverbial $50 bill left on the sidewalk. Even the basic question of the economic impact of the Panama Canal on the world economy produced wildly divergent opinions. Lebergott in 1980 believed the Panama Canal generated little to no benefits for the economic interests of the United States.[6] On the other hand, in 2004 Hutchinson and Ungo estimated that the Panama Canal paid for itself in a single year soon after its opening.[7] Unsurprisingly, this book argues that the economic benefits of the Panama Canal lie between these two poles.

The Panama Canal is richly documented in primary source material. The annual reports first issued by the Isthmian Canal Commission, later the governor of the Panama Canal, the Panama Canal Company, and finally the Panama Canal Commission are invaluable both as sources of economic data and as political documents for understanding the complex relationship of the Canal Zone administration with Washington. The creators of the Panama Canal were not shy about their accomplishments, and left considerable writing in their memoirs and correspondence about their intent. The U.S. Senate testimony in the debate regarding the construction of an isthmian canal is eye-opening, as are the Colombian diplomatic documents collected in the *Libro azul* concerning the canal and the rebellion in Panama.[8] The *Foreign Relations of the United States* provides a somewhat sanitized version of U.S. attempts to placate or ignore Panama in the decades before the handover of the canal. Finally, the U.S. National Archives have an immense amount of material pertaining to the Panama Canal, of which we have only used crumbs from a very rich plate.

We are not ashamed to admit that we have relied on Walter LaFeber's *The Panama Canal* and John Major's *Prize Possession: The United States and the Panama Canal, 1903–1979*, while writing this book to better understand the specific historic, diplomatic, and institutional situation of the Panama Canal. So too we have relied upon many authors about Panama itself, not least among them Conniff, Pearcy, Pippin, Zimbalist, and Weeks. Many of our findings have seemed almost serendipitous: in particular, Bonham Richardson's work on Barbadian history and Samuel Eliot Morison's maritime and naval histories led us down paths of research we would not have previously considered. Finally, we must mention two works that appeared during the writing of this book, Adam Clymer's *Drawing the Line at the Big Ditch: The Panama Canal Treaties and the Rise of the Right*, on the interplay between the domestic American politics of the 1970s and the handover of the canal to Panama; and Julie Greene's *The Canal Builders: Making America's Empire at the Panama Canal*, on the complicated and disturbing history of the foreign workers who built the Panama Canal for the United States.[9] Both Clymer and Greene made points that we wanted to make, but earlier and more thoroughly.

To recap, this book advances two arguments. One is a substantive argument about the nature of economic imperialism. We argue that the United States developed strategies that enabled it to leverage its military dominance into a far better economic outcome than it otherwise could have achieved. We also argue that the United States returned the Panama Canal to Panama when the economic benefits from *ownership* of the canal (if not necessarily the benefits of the canal's existence) sufficiently declined.

Moreover, America's indirect imperialism produced little in the way of institutional or economic development for Panama, which continued to be an authoritarian underdeveloped nation until the 1990s. The United States was instrumental in removing the blight of Manuel Noriega, but the robust democracy that emerged thereafter was *hecho en Panamá*, and had little do with the previous decades of U.S. intervention.

The other argument we make in this book is a methodological statement about history and the social sciences. The social sciences are fundamentally about the study of social processes—the ways that human beings interact and the institutions that structure those interactions over time. Thus, social scientists do not really have a choice regarding the use of history—their interest in change over time gives them little choice but to make historical arguments. The real choice for economists and political scientists is whether the historical arguments they make are supported by systematically gathered and carefully analyzed evidence, or whether they are supported by "stylized facts." We strongly support the former, and hope that this book provides at least a modest example.

TWO
BEFORE THE DITCH

Regarding Your Majesty's other command, that it be
seen where one sea can be joined with the other: this
counsel was given by a man of very scant intelligence,
who has travelled and understood little of this land . . .
I pledge to Your Majesty that I believe there is not a
prince in the world with the power to accomplish this.

—*Pascual de Andagoya, 1534*

The difficulty of accomplishing such a work, and
its utter inefficiency when accomplished, were . . .
apparent to all men, whether of common or
uncommon sense.

—*Charles Biddle, 1836*

CENTURIES BEFORE THE PANAMA CANAL WAS BUILT, COMMER-
cial traffic used the Isthmus of Panama to cross between the Atlantic and Pacific Oceans. In fact, Panama experienced *two* economic
booms in the pre-canal era. The first economic boom occurred
practically right after the Spanish established Panama City in
1519. A geopolitical event, the Spanish conquest of Peru, triggered
the boom. The sailing ships of the sixteenth century had a difficult time navigating the Strait of Magellan; there were only nine
successful passages of the Strait in the sixty years after Magellan's
discovery.[1] Peruvian silver therefore passed through Panama on its

way to Spain. As a result, the Isthmus of Panama became a major commercial center, although the hostile disease environment kept the population down.

The second economic boom on the Isthmus of Panama occurred in the middle of the nineteenth century. Just as in the first boom, a geopolitical event was the trigger: the American conquest of California. U.S. diplomacy obtained British and Colombian agreement to allow American private capital to build a railroad across Panama. Competing attempts across Nicaragua and the Isthmus of Tehuantepec in Mexico floundered on hostile geography and unstable politics. As a result, Panama boomed in the 1850s and 1860s, although again, the hostile disease environment on the isthmus took its toll.

Both booms came to an end for the same reason: competition. Overland commercial routes via Buenos Aires undercut the Panama route in the seventeenth century. The Spanish Crown attempted to maintain Panama's privileges via legislation, but ultimately failed. Similar events occurred two centuries later. The opening of the Transcontinental Railroad across the United States in 1869 undercut the Panama route, and both the Panama Railroad and Panama's commercial fortunes declined.

TRADE ACROSS THE ISTHMUS BEFORE COLUMBUS

Enough archaeological and textual evidence remains to sketch the outlines of how pre-Columbian societies used the Panamanian isthmus to bridge the oceans. Panama was home to extensive local exchange networks, although it remains debatable whether these networks represented commerce in the modern sense.[2] The natives of the isthmus traded pearls between the Islas de Perlas in the Pacific and the Caribbean coast, and salt between the extensive salt marshes on the Pacific coast and other locations along the isthmus. There was also an extensive trade in shells (most likely used as penis sheaths) and objects made of gold and *tumbaga*, a gold-copper alloy known in the indigenous Caribbean as *guanín* and later called "base gold" (*oro bajo*) by the Spanish.[3]

Pre-Columbian Panama also enjoyed trading contacts with Mesoamerica. The conquistador Pascual de Andagoya recorded a group of "Chuchures," who had come by canoe from the direction of Honduras, spoke "with a language different from that of the other Indians," and possessed a small colony near the Chagres River. (The colony was on the later site of the Panamanian town of Nombre de Díos.) The Chuchures were most likely Mayan traders.[4] They proved no better to resist the area's disease environment than later European settlers. Their numbers rapidly decreased, and as Andagoya grimly concluded, "Of these few none survived the treatment they received after Nombre de Díos was founded."[5]

The accounts of the earliest Spanish arrivals provide more evidence of Panamanian trade links between North and South America.[6] In 1525, the Spanish navigator Bartolomé Ruyz encountered a raft off the Pacific coast of Colombia. Its passengers carried embroidered clothing and jewelry to exchange for red-colored shells.[7] Ruyz's description of the shells matches those of the thorny oyster (genus *Spondylus*), called *mullu* in Quechua.[8] This genus of oyster is not typically found in the cooler waters of the Peruvian coast. Rather, its range extends from Central America north to the Gulf of California. Ornaments of *Spondylus* shell have been found in archaeological contexts in Panama.[9]

THE FIRST CANAL PROPOSALS

In 1501, the explorer Rodrigo de Bastidas sighted Panama. Columbus landed near Nombre de Díos in late 1502 and explored the northern coast. Subsequently, a series of Spanish expeditions tried and failed to find a natural passage between the Atlantic Ocean and the seas to Asia. Finally, in 1513, Vasco Núñez de Balboa, acting on reports from local villages, launched the expedition that finally crossed Panama and established that it was indeed a narrow isthmus that could potentially be bridged. A permanent settlement followed in 1519.

The first proposal for a canal across Panama appeared in 1529, prompted by the difficulty of land transport across the isthmus.

Álvaro de Saavedra Cerón, one of Balboa's lieutenants, "proposed to open the land of Castilia del Oro and New Spain from sea to sea." Saavedra's goal was to ease travel from Europe to the wealth of Asia. A canal, he wrote, would mean that ships "might sail from the Canaries unto the Malucos, under the climate of the zodiac in less time and with much less danger than to sail about the Cape of Bona Sperança or by the strait of Magelan."[10] (Saavedra died that same year on an exploratory mission to find winds that would allow sailing across the Pacific from west to east.)[11]

Saavedra proposed four possible canal routes. The first ran "from Panama to Nombre de Díos, being 17 leagues distance," very close to the modern Panama Canal route. The second crossed the Darién "from the Gulf of S. Michael to Urabá, which is 25 leagues." The third passed "through Xaquator [the San Juan River], a river of Nicaragua, which springs out of a lake three or four leagues from the South Sea [Lake Nicaragua]." Saavedra's fourth and final proposal ran "from Tecoantepec through a river to Verdadera Cruz, in the Bay of the Honduras," across the Isthmus of Tehuantepec.[12] Saavedra's four routes, in different permutations, appeared repeatedly in canal proposals and counterproposals for the next 350 years.[13]

Charles V responded enthusiastically to the possibility of a Panamanian canal. He sent three expeditions down the Chagres River to scout possible routes between 1529 and 1533. The third expedition returned a positive report from Gaspar de Espinosa: "The Chagres can be made navigable at a very small cost. . . . A channel for navigation could be dredged."[14] The report prompted Charles V to order the provincial governor to dredge the Chagres and report on "the ways and means to be employed to cut open the land and unite the South Sea with the river" including "what difficulties might be caused by the tides of the sea and the elevation of the land, what it would cost in money, how many men would be required, how much time it would take, and what hills and valleys would be encountered."[15]

Spanish administrators in Panama, realizing the impossibility of a canal project given the technologies of the time, were notably less enthusiastic than the royal government in Madrid. Governor Francisco de Barrionuevo passed off the responsibility for carrying out the king's orders to his aide, Pascual de Andagoya.[16] Andagoya wrote back to the king on October 22, 1534. He was absolutely scathing about Espinosa's report on the feasibility of a canal. "Regarding Your Majesty's other command, that it be seen where one sea can be joined with the other: this counsel was given by a man of very scant intelligence, who has travelled and understood little of this land. . . . I pledge to Your Majesty that I believe there is not a prince in the world with the power to accomplish this."[17]

Spanish observers again proposed canal projects in 1552, 1600, and 1620, but nothing came of them.[18] They simply were not feasible given the available technology. In fact, by 1590 canal pessimism had taken on a theological dimension. José de Acosta, a Jesuit natural philosopher familiar with the Americas, wrote, "I think that such a plan is useless. . . . I believe that no human power is capable of tearing down the strong and impenetrable mountain that God places between the two seas, with hills and rocky crags able to withstand the fury of the seas on either side. And even if it were possible for men to do it I believe it would be very reasonable to expect punishment from Heaven for wishing to improve the works that the Maker, with sublime prudence and forethought, ordered in the fabric of this world."[19]

PANAMANIAN ROAD-BUILDING AND THE DEPOPULATION OF CENTRAL AMERICA, 1519–36

The Spanish, completely aware of the geographic possibilities of Panama, soon felt the limitations of land transport across the isthmus. In 1525 the royal government under Governor Pedro Arias resolved to build two roads across Panama. The first one directly connected Panama City on the Pacific coast with Nombre de Díos on the Atlantic. The government officially called this route the Calle de Santo Domingo, but it became commonly known as the Camino Real. The second route covered fifteen miles from Panama City to the Chagres River at Las Cruces, from which goods could then be ported to the Caribbean coast. This route became known the Camino de Cruces. The Camino de Cruces was eight feet wide, raised one to three feet above the ground, and fully paved in the Roman style.[20]

Building these roads was no small feat. In 1525, Peter Martyr d'Anghiera, the official chronicler of the Council of the Indies, reported, "Between the colony of Nombre de Dios, situated on the north sea, and that of Panama on the south sea, extend mountains covered with virgin forests which are impassable because of great rocks towering to the very heavens. . . . This road across the isthmus was, therefore, laid out at the cost of the King and the colonists, nor was the expense small. Rocks had to be broken up, and wild beasts had to be driven from their lairs in the forests."[21]

Panama itself lacked the labor required to build the roads. European diseases had devastated Panama's small indigenous population.[22] The tropical Panamanian climate, meanwhile, dissuaded Spaniards from migrating to the isthmus in significant numbers.[23] The isthmus received only 590 colonists between Balboa's expedition in 1513 and the founding of Panama City in 1519, and an additional 958—overwhelmingly male—colonists between 1520 and 1539.[24]

The "solution" to Panama's labor ills came from Pedro Arias "Pedrarias" Dávila, Panama City's governor. In 1522, Pedrarias sent a relative, Gil González Dávila, on an exploratory mission northward into Central America.[25] González soon made contact with two settled kingdoms in the areas which are now western Nicaragua and the northwest part of Costa Rica: their rulers were named Nicoya, for whom the Nicoya Peninsula in what is now Costa Rica is named, and Nicatlnauac, which became "Nicarao" to the Spanish. González named this new country Nicaragua, literally Nicarao's Water, after Lake Nicaragua.

The Nicaraguan kingdoms practiced a combination of serfdom and slavery. Slaves were taken in several ways. The wives and children of tributary subjects who fled the territory of their kingdom could be converted into slaves if caught. In addition, Nicaraguan kingdoms punished theft and poaching in protected hunting and fishing grounds by enslavement. Finally, slaves were commonly taken as booty by the victorious side in war.[26]

Pedrarias quickly realized the commercial potential of Nicaragua's labor institutions. He promptly attempted to arrest his cousin, forcing González to flee to Santo Domingo. Pedrarias then organized a colonizing mission under Francisco Hernández de Córdoba, who established settlements in Nicaragua at Granada and León. In 1524, González returned from Santo Domingo, precipitating a civil war between the two Spanish factions. The "War of the Captains" did not definitively end until 1528, when Pedrarias assumed the governorship of Nicaragua.[27]

The Spanish shipped the first Indian slaves from Nicaragua to Panama in late 1526. The first group consisted of captives taken by the Spanish in war, but the Spaniards soon turned to purchasing slaves from the local kingdoms.[28] By 1529, five ships were engaged full-time in shipping slaves. The Spanish Crown and Pedrarias's successor as governor of Panama jointly owned one ship. Pedrarias himself owned a second. Francisco Pizarro—who would begin the conquest of Peru in 1530—owned two more in partnership with Diego de Almagro. The royal treasurer, Alonso de Cáceres, owned the fifth. Ponce de León, meanwhile, had contracted the construction in Nicaragua of a sixth ship to engage in the trade.[29]

The Crown banned the taking of slaves as captives in 1530, but the ban had no effect because the trade consisted mostly of slaves purchased from other Indians. Circa 1531, slaves could be had for a pittance. A Nicaraguan slave cost between two to five pesos at a time when four pesos bought 1.5 bushels of corn, 3.3 gallons of oil, 4.3 gallons of wine or vinegar, 21 pounds of cassava, or 25 pounds of salted meat.[30] Slave prices in Nicaragua rose to between six and seven pesos as more and more slaves were purchased and shipped to Panama, but the monopsony power held by the provincial governor—who issued slave export licenses—placed an effective lid on prices. It is impossible to determine what the market price of slaves would have been in the absence of export licenses, but a

notary in Granada complained that Governor Francisco de Castañeda forced him to sell the governor slaves worth as much as fifteen pesos for only seven.[31]

How many slaves did the Spanish transport to Panama from
Nicaragua? We know that there were six vessels engaged in the
trade in 1530.[32] By 1535 the number of ships on the Panama run
had risen to seventeen.[33] Most of the ships departed from the Gulf
of Nicoya, although Realejo grew in importance as the trade went
on.[34] A typical round-trip voyage took sixteen to twenty days.[35]
The ships were classed as caravels, which ranged between 50 and
200 tons.[36] For comparison, the ships on the Indies route averaged
150 tons.[37] Manifests survive for six vessels, which carried an average of 183 people.[38] These ships, however, may have been particularly large. The typical Dutch slaver of the seventeenth century
carried 1.67 slaves per ton (admittedly for a much longer journey), which would imply a carrying capacity of only 84 slaves for a
50-ton vessel.[39]

Table 2.1 presents annual estimates of the Nicaragua-Panama
slave trade assuming an average of 84 embarked slaves per trip.
The estimates stop in 1536, when the Crown banned the trade
following a report that 350 slaves had died in a ship packed with
400.[40] Illicit slaving continued into the 1540s, however, and the
trade only stopped with the virtual depopulation of the Nicaraguan highlands.[41] Some sense of the scale of the depopulation can
be taken from the 1548 tribute assessment for Nicaragua, which
found only 11,343 tributary households.[42] Even at an optimistic value of 5 people per household, that means that the Spanish
could find only 58,000 people left in the province, by which point
roughly 99,000 people had been forcibly deported. (See table 2.1.)
Nicaragua had been depopulated.[43]

The Nicaraguans did not significantly increase Panama's permanent population. Most of them either died or travelled home
overland—a few may have been sold onward to Peru after Pizarro
completed the conquest of the Inca Empire in 1535. By 1607,
Panama's population had grown only to 29,000 people, a sixth of
whom resided in the capital.

TABLE 2.1
Minimum Estimate of the Nicaragua-Panama Slave Trade, 1527–36

	Ships on Panama run	Annual trips. per ship	Total trips	Slaves embarked	Cumulative embarkations
1527	2	12	24	2,016	2,016
1528	5	12	60	5,040	7,056
1529	6	12	72	6,048	13,104
1530	8	12	96	8,064	21,168
1531	10	12	120	10,080	31,248
1532	12	12	144	12,096	43,344
1533	14	12	168	14,112	57,456
1534	16	12	192	16,128	73,584
1535	17	12	204	17,136	90,720
1536	17	6	102	8,568	99,288

Source: See text. We assume a linear increase in the number of ships engaged in the trade between 1529 and 1534. Our estimation procedure follows David Radell, "The Indian Slave Trade and Population of Nicaragua during the Sixteenth Century," in *The Native Population of the Americas in 1492*, ed. William Denevan (Madison: University of Wisconsin Press, 1976), using different data and assumptions in order to bias our estimates downward.

In addition to the depredations of the slave trade, the growth of Panama as a transit center had a second negative effect on the demographics of Central America: its centrality to the American trade of the Spanish Empire also made it an ideal nexus for long-distance contagion. For example, the historic pandemic of 1529–31—probably pneumonic plague—appears to have had its start in Panama.[44] By the time the Crown stopped the slave trade, Nicaragua's relentless population decline was already well on its way to making it unprofitable.

CROSSROADS OF EMPIRE: PANAMA AT ITS FIRST PEAK, 1550–1671

The decline of the Nicaraguan slave trade did not lead to decline in Panama's position as the commercial center of the Spanish Empire in South America. In fact, once the roads were completed, by the mid-sixteenth century, Panama's importance grew.

Panama initially grew as a conduit for royal silver from Peru. The Spanish government taxed Peruvian mining output (at 20 percent of gross output, the famous "fifth") and used the resulting revenues to finance military and other activities in Europe. In the absence of international payment mechanisms, however, that silver needed to be physically transported to Europe in order to be spent.

The Spanish Empire organized the silver shipments around the regular sailing of fleets from the peninsula to four designated American ports: Cartagena, Veracruz, Havana, and Portobelo in Panama.[45] Once the fleet arrived at Cartagena, the "southern fleet" (which plied the Pacific Ocean, then still called the Great South Sea) would sail from Peru to Panama City. The southern fleet discharged the silver at Panama, from which the Spanish then transported it by land across the isthmus to Portobelo. At Portobelo, the royal fleet would pick up the silver and take it to Spain.[46] Between 1581 and 1660, fully 31 percent of all the royal revenue generated by the viceroyalty of Peru passed through Panama on its way to Madrid. (See table 2.2.)

The fleets carried privately owned silver in addition to the government's revenues. Private parties in Peru sent this silver through Panama either to remit it to Spain or, more likely, to purchase imported merchandise at the Portobelo trade fairs. Private flows of silver through Panama, therefore, represented a rough estimate of the annual value of goods entering the isthmus. (See table 2.2.) Textiles made up the overwhelming bulk of imports, by value, followed (in order) by wine, oil, aguardiente, and iron products.[47]

Panama also became a center for trading African slaves. Over the course of the seventeenth century, the annual flow of Africans passing through the isthmus numbered approximately 3,500.[48] Most of the slaves were sold onward to the viceroyalty of Peru.[49] Panama's own African population grew rather slowly. Nevertheless, by 1607 slaves made up 70 percent of the capital city's 5,702 inhabitants.[50] Free blacks made up an additional 8 percent.[51] In addition, escaped slaves formed sizeable (but uncounted) maroon colonies in the Panamanian countryside.

TABLE 2.2
Average Annual Silver Flows through Panama (Pesos), by Quinquennia,
1551–1660

	Royal treasure shipped from Peru	As % of total royal revenues from Peru	Registered private silver exported from Panama
1551–55	149,387		986,551
1556–60	135,358		799,900
1561–65	42,960		1,165,584
1566–70	164,365		1,414,122
1571–75	170,118		928,716
1576–80	787,950		1,966,721
1581–85	388,153	15	3,818,700
1586–90	60,000	2	2,859,916
1591–95	160,000	5	4,785,141
1596–1600	295,498	9	4,406,848
1601–5	1,095,930	31	3,074,819
1606–10	1,625,494	46	3,957,056
1611–15	1,953,389	56	3,188,656
1616–20	1,277,524	36	3,854,395
1621–25	647,523	20	3,241,281
1626–30	1,445,114	44	3,967,770
1631–35	1,144,935	31	2,686,404
1636–40	1,447,861	40	1,957,752
1641–45	2,670,530	67	2,092,098
1646–50	1,723,816	43	1,836,205
1651–55	1,256,520	34	933,602
1656–60	749,656	20	416,778

Source: Christopher Ward, *Imperial Panama: Commerce and Conflict in Isthmian America, 1550–1800* (Albuquerque: University of New Mexico Press, 1993), tables 2 and 3, 8–9, citing Alfredo Castillero Calvo, *Economía terciaria y sociedad, Panamá siglos XVI y XVII* (Panama City, 1980), 51–57. Total royal revenues generated by Peru from John TePaske and Herbert Klein, *Royal Treasuries of the Spanish Empire in America* (Durham, NC: Duke University Press), 1:284ff.

THE *TRAJÍN*

Cargoes crossed Panama over two routes. The eight-foot-wide cobblestone-paved Camino de Cruces ran north from Panama City to the town of Cruces on the Chagres River. The Spanish built bridges over permanent creeks and rivers—the Puente del Rey still spans the Río Abajo—but the road's builders made no attempts to bridge all the various small seasonal streams that crossed the route. As a result, it was frequently blocked during the rainy season. Cruces itself was little more than a collection of warehouses, docks, about fifty houses, and a church.[52] Goods arrived by mule train and were transferred onto small flat-bottomed boats called "bongos." A pilot and about twenty slaves crewed the bongos, which were pushed down the shallow river by poles. The bongos then travelled east along the coast to Portobelo.[53]

The Camino Real was far more difficult than the Camino de Cruces. The paved portion ascended six hundred feet into the mountains north of Panama City, crossed the Chagres and Boquerón rivers, and then passed through a hilly section where it narrowed to three feet with five-hundred-foot drops on either side.[54] The road then got worse as it passed through the Santa Clara Mountains. It became "so narrow and steep, in many places almost perpendicular, that we were obliged to ascend climbing with our hands and feet. . . . We sank up to our knees in mud . . . and at other times the whole party seemed to be lost in the windings of the road, cut deep into the side of the mountain."[55] Very large mule trains—collectively called the *trajín*—travelled over the precarious trail. A typical convoy consisted of twenty-four trains of fifty mules each, each train handled by twenty-four specially trained slaves. Each mule carried roughly two hundred pounds.[56] In 1540, when the Camino Real was finally finished, it generally took four days to cover the fifty-mile route.[57]

Labor shortages negatively affected the Camino Real. Slave prices increased a hundredfold in the decades following the end of the Nicaraguan trade: by the 1590s, Peruvian slave prices reached 450 pesos for a healthy adult male, and Panamanian prices followed suit.[58] As a result, a 1569 report complained that neither the Panamanian provincial government nor the viceroy of Peru could afford to keep sufficient slaves in Panama to properly maintain the route. Seventy years later, a priest complained that that the Camino Real was a "terrible road, worse than any I have ever seen anyplace I've been."[59] The price gap grew between the Camino Real

MAR DEL NORTE
(ATLANTIC OCEAN)

Nombre De Dios

Portobelo

Venta de Capirilla

RIO BOQUERÓN

CAMINO
REAL

RIO CHAGRES

Venta de Chagres

Venta de Cruces

CAMINO
DE CRUCES

Panama

MAR DEL SUR
(PACIFIC OCEAN)

RIVER ROUTE - - - - - - -

LAND ROUTE ————

0   10   20 Miles

Map 2.1:   Colonial Spanish routes across Panama, ca. 1600.

and Camino de Cruces routes. (See table 2.3.) Travel times across the isthmus doubled by 1700.[60]

If the Camino Real was bad and getting worse, why didn't merchants abandon it in favor of the Camino de Cruces? The Spanish could not adequately defend the riverine and coastal portions of the Camino de Cruces. Bandits, freebooters, and international pirates preyed on the lucrative traffic, and the Panamanian coast provided numerous safe havens for them to escape government retribution. The San Lorenzo fort wasn't built until 1575, but British raiders destroyed it in 1671 and again in 1740. Worse still, the fort could not protect the bongos as they travelled twenty-five miles along the shore between the mouth of the Chagres and Portobelo. Spanish bullion, therefore, stuck to the Camino Real, along with high-value items like pearls.[61]

Panamanian transport costs rose relative to other routes for two additional reasons. The first was ecological: mules could not be bred successfully in the Panamanian climate. As a result, the more traffic grew, the more the isthmus needed to import mules from elsewhere, chiefly El Salvador, Nicaragua, and Honduras. The mules travelled overland down the Pacific coast to Panama. Imports plateaued around one thousand animals per year by the mid-seventeenth century.[62] Moreover, although corn was generally available on Panama's southern coast, animal feed on the north coast needed to be imported from Cartagena.[63] Mule importation, it turned out, did not benefit from economies of scale.

The second reason for increasing costs was economic: the muleteers organized and increasingly exerted monopoly power over

TABLE 2.3
Ratio of the Cost of Mule Transport Prices via the Camino Real to the Cost via the Camino de Cruces

1547	1.7
1612	2.8
1662	3.6

Source: Christopher Ward, *Imperial Panama: Commerce and Conflict in Isthmian America, 1550–1800* (Albuquerque: University of New Mexico Press, 1993), 64, table 9.

transport across the isthmus. Panamanian officials did little to foster competition, since they were directly involved with the trade and profited from exorbitant transit rates. As a result, the Panamanian muleteers became wealthy. The value of Panama City's 332 residential structures reached an astounding (for the time) 906,440 pesos in 1607.[64] Christopher Ward concluded in his book on colonial Panama that the collusion between mule owners and local officials to maintain monopoly profits was "the genesis of a Panamanian sense of identity."[65]

The combination of these three factors—poor roads, imported inputs, and low competition—meant that trans-isthmian transits cost much more than other mule routes in Spanish America. (See table 2.4.) It cost thirteen times as much per unit weight to travel the fifty miles along the royal road from Panama City to Portobelo as it cost to take cargo five hundred miles from Potosí to Huancavelica. Even more astoundingly, mule transport across Panama cost *forty-seven* times as much as the Acapulco-to-Veracruz mule route in Mexico.

TABLE 2.4
Per-Mile Cost of Various Mule Routes in the Americas, circa 1650

	Miles	Days	Cost to move 100 lbs. (pesos)	Cost per mile per 100 lbs. (pesos)
Panama–Portobelo via Camino Real	62	8	874	14.1
Panama-Portobelo via Camino de Chagres	16	4	81	5.0
Huancavelica–Potosí (Peru–Bolivia)	875	57	963	1.1
Mendoza–Santiago (Argentina–Chile)	276	19	634	2.3
Punta Arenas–Cartago (Chile)	83	5	74	0.9
Acapulco–Veracruz (Mexico)	464	30	139	0.3

Source: Table 2.3 and Christopher Ward, *Imperial Panama: Commerce and Conflict in Isthmian America, 1550–1800* (Albuquerque: University of New Mexico Press, 1993), 231 n. 67. Camino Real transit time from Omar Jaén Suárez, *La población del Istmo de Panamá* (Madrid: Agencia Española de Cooperación Internacional, 1998), 130.

The decline of the Panama *trajín* had three causes. The first cause was Spain's growing military weakness. Spanish colonial territory was much more porous to foreign incursions than it appeared on a map, and Spanish wealth presented foreign powers (and even private citizens) with tempting targets. In famous raids, the English privateer Henry Morgan sacked Portobelo in 1667 and the city of Panama in 1671. The Royal Navy again destroyed Portobelo in 1739, as part of its prosecution of the War of Jenkins' Ear.

The second was the slow collapse of the Peruvian silver economy. The Potosí mines peaked around 1610. Other mines came on line, but Peru's overall silver production declined 83 percent between 1611 and 1714.[66] Royal income from Peru declined commensurately. As silver output and royal income fell, so did the Peruvian transit trade through Panama.

The third factor in Panama's commercial decline was competition. Goods could be more cheaply smuggled via the Río de la Plata and carried overland to Peru. (See table 2.4.) Spanish policy, however, was to maintain Panama's central position in American trade. The reason was that centralized control in Panama made it easier to control smuggling and helped maintain the profits of the influential merchants who controlled the Portobelo trade fairs. It was even proposed in 1613 that Buenos Aires be depopulated in order to return Panamanian trade to its former vitality.[67]

Needless to say, Buenos Aires was not abandoned. Illicit trading to Peru continued, mainly via the Buenos Aires–Tucumán route. With the dissolution of the Iberian Union in 1640, more routes were opened to Peru by Portuguese merchants who could no longer trade at Portobelo.[68] (See figure 2.1.) By 1739, after Admiral Vernon's destruction of Portobelo during the War of Jenkins' Ear, the fair system slowly collapsed.[69] The annual number of ships docking at Panama fell to ten in 1750–59 and six in 1760–69, before recovering to thirteen in 1770–79 and seventeen in 1780–93. The volume of trade remained similarly depressed. In 1761–70, the annual average value of gross imports was only 108,071 pesos.

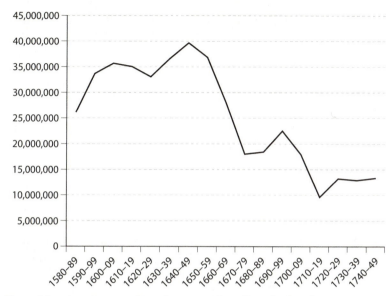

Figure 2.1: Average annual royal revenues from Peru, by decade, pesos.
Source: John TePaske and Herbert Klein, *Royal Treasuries of the Spanish Empire in America* (Durham, NC: Duke University Press), 1:284ff.

This figure rose to 158,494 pesos in 1771–80 and 271,786 pesos in 1781–90, far below the volumes registered during the halcyon days of the seventeenth century.[70] (See table 2.2.)

Ultimately, in 1778 the Bourbons allowed free trade within the empire. Vessels from Peru freely sailed to Europe via the Straits of Magellan—ship technology having improved since the sixteenth century—and the Buenos Aires transit trade came out of the shadows. The economy of the isthmus would remain depressed for the next century.

Independence from Spanish rule did not reverse Panama's economic decline. When Simón Bolívar's army took Bogotá in 1819, the Spanish viceroy fled to Panama. After the viceroy departed to campaign in Ecuador, Panama declared independence under the control of Colonel José de Fábrega. Doubtful about the viability of an independent Panama, Fábrega guided the new republic into Bolívar's great Colombian federation.

Panama failed to benefit from the growth of trade between the Atlantic and the Pacific in the 1830s and 1840s. British and American sailing ships had mastered the Cape Horn route in the late eighteenth century.[71] As a result, the growth of a trade in hides (called "California banknotes") between the ranchers of Alta California and tanneries and shoe factories in New England travelled the same route, bypassing Panama.[72] By 1840, Panamanian customhouses yielded almost no revenue. The Isthmus of Panama slid into obscurity.[73]

THE CANAL IDEA REVIVES

Panama's decline into obscurity did not last—its geographic position was too key for that. The German polymath-explorer Alexander von Humboldt revived the idea of a canal across the Panamanian isthmus in his writings in 1811. Humboldt examined nine routes in the Americas for a feasible interoceanic route, beginning with a plausible-sounding but nonexistent passage across the Continental Divide on the Columbia River, and ending with a Patagonian alternative to the Straits of Magellan. Humboldt devoted the largest part of his discussion, however, to the Panamanian isthmus.[74]

Humboldt reasoned that a Panamanian passage would have little value for direct trade between Europe and Asia. "Every nation which wished to trade in this way would be dependent on the masters of the isthmus and canal; and this would be a very great inconvenience for the vessels dispatched from Europe. Supposing then that this canal were cut, the greatest number of these vessels would probably continue their voyage around Cape Horn."[75]

Humboldt anticipated instead that an isthmian canal would be useful for trade between the Pacific coast of the Americas and Europe or the United States. (When Humboldt wrote, the United States was an Atlantic power only.) Goods along these routes, he remarked, "would cross the isthmus at less expense, and in less danger, particularly in time of war, than in doubling the southern extremity of the new continent."[76] He concluded, "Should a canal of communication be opened between the two oceans, the productions of Nootka Sound and of China will be brought more than 2000 leagues nearer to Europe and the United States."[77]

Humboldt foresaw that because of the rough Panamanian terrain, a sea-level canal would be impracticable, and the idea "ought to be completely abandoned." He argued, however, that the alternative of a "system of sluices" (or "subterraneous galleries") would provide only a partial solution because they could accommodate unseaworthy flat-bottomed boats. As a result, cargo would need to be transferred to special barges at each end of the canal.[78]

Humboldt ended his discussion of a Panamanian canal on a prophetic note. Only after the building of a canal, he wrote, "can any great changes be effected in the political state of Eastern Asia, for this neck of land, the barrier against the waves of the Atlantic Ocean, has been for many ages the bulwark of the independence of China and Japan."[79] It was a bold prediction of importance for a land whose economy, as Humboldt noted, still suffered from a lack of mules.[80]

The geography of Panama also fired the imagination of Simón Bolívar. In his famous Jamaica letter of 1815, Bolívar enthused, "How beautiful it would be if the Isthmus of Panama could be for us what Corinth was for the Greeks!"[81] In 1824, Bolívar wrote that "if the world had to choose its capital, the Isthmus of Panama would be indicated for this august destiny." Under Bolívar's auspices, the city of Panama would host the Amphictyonic Congress, to discuss the formation of a league of American republics, in the summer of 1826.[82]

On November 29, 1827, Bolívar commissioned captains Maurice Falmarc, the Swedish temporary commander of the engineering corps in the isthmus, and John Augustus Lloyd, a Briton, to survey the isthmus with regard to the best possible route for a canal or a road.[83] The task was difficult, not least because their survey coincided with General José Sardá's governorship. Sardá, a political enemy of Bolívar's, refused to assist the two men, denying them funds and allowing them to be attacked by bandits.[84] Nonetheless, the survey was finished in 1829, and Lloyd presented his (somewhat inconclusive) results to the Royal Society in London in November.[85] Bolívar would abdicate a few months later, before his death from tuberculosis, and the Colombian government collapsed soon after.

The idea of a canal across the isthmus also sparked the imaginations of the greatest minds of Europe. Goethe, dining with his friend Eckermann on February 21, 1827, gave a prescient impromptu extension of Humboldt's analysis. Foreseeing the growth of great commercial cities on the Pacific coast of North America, he mused, "I should wonder if the United States were to let an opportunity escape of getting such a work in their own hands . . . it is absolutely indispensable for the United States to effect a passage from the Mexican Gulf to the Pacific Ocean and I am certain they will do it. Would that I might live to see it!—but I shall not."[86]

ENTER THE AMERICANS

Little did Goethe know that some Americans were already trying—and failing—to put his idea into action. William Duane, a Spanish-speaking Philadelphia lawyer, visited Gran Colombia in 1822 and 1823 to pursue compensation claims against the Colombian government on behalf of his clients. Along the way, he became taken with "the grand work of the strait of Panama, to effect which I have made proposals to the Colombian government (sustained by capitalists)—and which, if accomplished, as I know it is practicable, would render the communication between the two oceans as free and more secure than the passage of the straits of Sunda or Gibraltar." Given Duane's somewhat adversarial relationship with the Colombian government, however, Bogotá was not willing to grant him a concession.[87]

In 1830, Gran Colombia fragmented into Ecuador, Venezuela, and New Granada. In 1833, the government of New Granada announced that it was welcome to canal proposals from European governments.[88] On May 29, 1835, New Granada granted a canal concession to a French citizen, Charles de Thierry.[89] Thierry turned out to be a fraudster.[90] He declared himself the "Sovereign Chief of New Zealand," and he only learned that New Granada had granted him a concession while reading the August 25 edition of the *Sydney Morning Herald* in Tahiti.[91]

In response to the Thierry concession, Senator John Clayton of Delaware proposed that the United States negotiate with the governments of Central America and New Granada to secure the rights to a future canal. "If, in completing such a work, fifty or a hundred millions (aye, one-half the money vainly expended in attempting to discover the Northwest Passage) should be expended, it would be a cheaper outlay, and render more benefits to the world, than an equal expenditure in any other enterprise that had ever been or could be undertaken by man."[92] President Andrew Jackson appointed Colonel Charles Biddle, from the prominent Philadelphia banking family, to negotiate with the governments of Central America and New Granada.[93]

Biddle decided to skip Central America and proceeded directly to Panama. When he arrived in Panama City on December 1, 1835, he found Thierry's backers disillusioned, but enthusiasm for a canal project remained quite high. Biddle also noticed separatist sentiments among the Panamanian elite. It was an open secret, Biddle wrote, that overtures had "been privately made by influential men to place the Isthmus under the protection of the British Government, and that such a course . . . [had] been declined by the English from an apprehension of giving offense to the United States."[94]

Biddle travelled on to Bogotá on March 13, 1836. The entire Panamanian congressional delegation travelled with him. The provincial governor, José de Obaldía, was considered very persuasive in both Spanish and English, and helped pave the way for Biddle's entry into New Granadan political circles.[95] John Steuart, an idealistic American businessman living in Bogotá in 1836, wrote of Biddle's effort. "The only question has ever been, is the thing practicable? Now that its practicability had been most fully and clearly demonstrated, and a capital of many millions was ready to put to a test of this practicability, *not* a doubt ever lingered in the breast of a single intelligent citizen of Panama but that government would accede with scarcely a debate on the question. . . . All would be completed without costing them a single thought, while they would merely sit by and receive a rent, exceeding, no doubt, the whole of the present state revenue. A city would arise on the present isolated site of Panama not surpassed by any in the commercial world."[96]

Legislative opposition to Biddle's plan took several forms: an almost Jacksonian resistance to internal improvements, spurious overvaluations of Panamanian land, xenophobia, support for Thierry's proposal, and the fear that a developed trans-isthmian route would make New Granada a ripe target for conquest.[97] Meanwhile, a "native" group of citizens of Bogotá—including Scottish and Irish expatriates, who ran the local saltworks—put together their own proposal, offering better terms to the New Granadan government.

Biddle managed to obtain a concession for a road or railway across Panama, and steam navigation rights up the Chagres.[98] He did not, however, obtain the rights to a Panamanian canal. This bothered Biddle not at all, since his brief trip up the Chagres and across the isthmus had convinced him that a canal would be both hard to build and useless in operation. "The difficulty of accomplishing such a work, and its utter inefficiency when accomplished, were . . . apparent to all men, whether of common or uncommon sense."[99]

President Jackson was furious at Biddle's lack of accomplishment. Not only had he failed to obtain a canal concession; he had disobeyed orders and ignored Central America entirely. When Biddle arrived in New York, the State Department formally repudiated him for gross insubordination. (It was perhaps fortunate that Biddle died on December 21, 1836, before he could face Jackson's full wrath.)[100] Biddle also managed to make enemies in New Granada. Upon leaving Bogotá, Biddle's enemies ensured that he received *macuquinas* for his expenses, crudely hammered silver cobs of dubious content. "Gentlemen, we have nearly finished our long and unpleasant business," said an angry Biddle. "I pray you, do not let me part with you under the same impressions as when we first became acquainted; pay me in *Christian coin*, or, if you will insist upon my carrying such adulterated trash as this to Cartagena, be so good as to furnish the necessary number of jackasses for its transportation." The New Granadan government interceded and compensated Biddle in gold, but a bad taste remained.[101]

Unfortunately for Bogotá, dealing with Washington was the best of its bad options. Given French interests on the isthmus, British interests in Nicaragua's Mosquito Coast (where New Granada also had a historical claim), and a Dutch proposal for a Nicaraguan canal, New Granada sought a counterweight to Europe in the United States. New Granadan fears of European expansion increased in 1845, when two British steamship companies organized a through service for passengers and baggage from Britain to the west coast of South America through the Panamanian isthmus.[102]

When Benjamin Bidlack, the new American chargé d'affaires, arrived in Bogotá to negotiate a new commercial treaty on December 1, 1845, he was astonished to hear the New Granadans propose that the United States become the privileged guarantor of the neutrality of the Panamanian isthmus.[103] It would be "dangerous to let the golden opportunity pass," Bidlack wrote to Secretary of State Buchanan.[104] Bidlack, operating without proper authority, hammered out a treaty with the Colombian foreign minister in late 1846. Article 35 of the resulting Bidlack-Mallarino Treaty stated, "The government of New Granada guarantees to the government of the United States that the right of way or transit across the Isthmus of Panama, upon any modes of communication that now exist, or that may be hereafter constructed, shall be open and free to the government and citizens of the United States." In turn, "the United States guaranty positively and efficaciously, to New Granada, by the present stipulation, the perfect neutrality of the before mentioned Isthmus, with the view that the free transit from the one to the other sea may not be interrupted or embarrassed in any future time while this Treaty exists; and in consequence, the United States also guarantee, in the same manner, the rights of sovereignty and property which New Granada has and possesses over the said territory."[105] The treaty would expire twenty years from its date of final ratification.

The Bidlack-Mallarino Treaty met with skepticism in Washington, where some senators argued that Article 35 constituted an alliance with New Granada. In response, Bogotá sent a large delegation to Washington, led by former president Pedro Herrán, to advocate the benefits of unlimited access to the Panama route. Herrán (and President Polk) was persuasive—the Senate ratified the treaty twenty-nine to seven on June 3, 1848.[106] Bogotá hoped that the Bidlack-Mallarino Treaty would encourage other powers to form similar agreements with New Granada, guaranteeing "universal neutrality" for the isthmus.[107] This did not occur, however, and the United States became the sole foreign protector of the neutrality of the Panamanian isthmus.

THE GOLD RUSH AND THE ISTHMUS OF PANAMA

31 miles by railroad! Safety and speed! No sickness!
No river travel!

—Advertisement for the Panama Railroad,
Pacific Mail, 1854

In the aftermath of the Mexican-American War, the acquisition of California whetted further interest in the United States in the Central American isthmus. Without a telegraph line across the continent, regular communication with this new territory was crucial. To avoid the uncertainties and delays of the Cape Horn route, Congress authorized contracts for an American steamship mail service from New York and New Orleans to Chagres, and from Oregon to Panama City. William Henry Aspinwall, a partner in New York's largest import-export firm, bought the contract for the Oregon route. It was a shrewd and daring decision on Aspinwall's part. The decision astounded his associates, who believed Aspinwall to be soundly conservative in matters of finance.[108]

The 1849 gold rush honed American interest in Panama to a fine edge. The Forty-niners and the Argonauts—seekers of a homespun Golden Fleece—sought a faster journey to the California gold fields. They were willing to pay a premium for speed. In 1849, 6,489 passengers reached San Francisco by way of Panama, compared to 15,597 by way of Cape Horn. By 1850, 13,809 had taken the Panama route, while only 11,770 arrived by way of Cape Horn.[109] By 1853, the number of arrivals in California via Panama reached 15,502, while the number departing rose to 10,533.[110] Relative to the population of the new territory, these numbers were large. Over the course of the 1850s, net migration over the Panama route contributed no less than 21 percent of California's total population growth.[111] (See table 2.5.)

In short, Aspinwall was in the right place at the right time. When his first ship arrived in Panama City from California, on January 17, 1849, the first few hundred Forty-niners to cross the isthmus were already waiting.[112] Business was so heavy that Aspinwall would jokingly complain to a friend, "What a snarl I am in from this California fever. I am half ruined by postage and have hired two clerks to answer letters, and these have proved so inadequate that I have had to resort to circulars."[113]

Not to be outdone, in August 1849, a former New York ferryman named Cornelius Vanderbilt—not quite yet the richest man in America—obtained the rights from the Nicaraguan government to build a canal across Nicaragua, and whatever land and water carriage might be necessary to complete it.[114] Vanderbilt's company had to complete the work within twelve years, but in the meantime the company would have a monopoly over steamship travel on the San Juan River or Lake Nicaragua.[115] In August 1850, Vanderbilt sent an agent, Orville Childs, to Nicaragua to plan the canal route. Childs had worked on the Erie Canal enlargement and brought with him a team of fourteen engineers: the result was a serious plan for a lock canal with a seventeen-foot draft. The canal's route would run along the San Juan River to Lake Nicaragua, and

TABLE 2.5

Passengers by the Isthmian Routes, 1848–69

	NY–SF via Panama	NY–SF via Nicaragua	Total NY–SF	SF–NY via Panama	SF–NY via Nicaragua	Total SF–NY	Total Panama	Total Nicaragua	Total
1848	335	—	335	—	—	—	335	—	335
1849	4,624	—	4,624	1,629	—	1,629	6,253	—	6,253
1850	11,229	—	11,229	7,770	—	7,770	18,999	—	18,999
1851	15,464	1,305	16,769	14,189	3,666	17,855	29,653	4,971	34,624
1852	21,263	10,851	32,120	11,845	6,552	18,397	33,108	17,403	50,511
1853	17,014	11,595	28,609	10,232	12,362	22,594	27,246	23,957	51,203
1854	18,445	13,128	31,573	10,808	10,461	21,269	29,253	23,589	52,842
1855	15,412	12,397	27,809	10,397	8,615	19,012	25,809	21,012	46,821
1856	18,090	6,092	24,182	12,245	7,270	19,515	30,335	13,362	43,697
1857	13,343	1,443	14,786	11,627	1,555	13,182	24,970	2,998	27,968
1858	20,596	—	20,596	8,030	—	8,030	28,626	—	28,626
1859	23,567	—	23,567	17,682	—	17,682	41,249	—	41,249
1860	16,257	—	16,257	11,213	—	11,213	27,470	—	27,470
1861	17,765	—	17,765	6,671	—	6,671	24,436	—	24,436
1862	17,328	562	17,890	5,959	538	6,497	23,287	1,100	24,387
1863	15,237	2,531	17,768	8,470	2,225	10,695	23,707	4,756	28,463
1864	20,643	1,145	21,788	12,671	2,125	14,796	33,314	3,270	36,584
1865	13,150	5,646	18,796	16,506	5,948	22,454	29,656	11,594	41,250
1866	22,889	5,312	28,201	12,450	7,589	20,039	35,339	12,901	48,240
1867	20,540	7,762	28,302	10,355	5,689	16,044	30,895	13,451	44,346
1868	38,680	1,713	40,393	18,243	484	18,727	56,923	2,197	59,120
1869	25,488	—	25,488	9,448	—	9,448	34,936	—	34,936
Total	387,359	81,482	468,847	228,440	75,079	303,519	615,799	156,561	772,360

Source: David I. Folkman, *The Nicaragua Route* (Salt Lake City: University of Utah Press, 1972), 163; John Haskell Kemble, *The Panama Route: 1848–1869* (Berkeley: University of California Press, 1943), 254.

Note: 1869 figure estimated from data through June 30.

then down to Brito on the Pacific coast via a series of locks. The plan estimated the cost of a canal to be $31.5 million, or $673 million in 2009 dollars.[116]

Vanderbilt travelled with Childs to Nicaragua, and personally led the first party across the route: up the San Juan River—infested by sandbars, rapids, and crocodiles—to Lake Nicaragua by shallow draft steamboat; across the lake by larger steamer; and finally a mule ride to the town of Rivas to await a steamer to San Francisco.[117] Unfortunately, his canal effort quickly failed for the simple reason that British investors believed that a seventeen-foot draft was too shallow to be a commercial success. They believed that deepening the canal sufficiently to accommodate deepwater vessels would at least triple the costs, and so refused to invest.[118]

Nevertheless, Vanderbilt succeeded in building a successful transport business. He replaced the mule ride to Rivas with a stagecoach to San Juan del Norte on the Pacific.[119] Then, as it became increasingly clear that he would be unable to get the financing for a canal, he managed to convince the Nicaraguan government to separate the canal concession from his steamship monopoly . . . in exchange for $20,000 in bribes, and an agreement to pay the Nicaraguan government a rent of $10,000 per year plus 10 percent of the line's profits.[120]

In 1852, after some significant blasting of rocks to clear rapids along the San Juan River and the construction of a road on the Pacific side, he began a combined steamer-stagecoach-steamer service from New York and New Orleans to San Francisco.[121] Steamers would enter the San Juan River at Greytown, Nicaragua, which at the time consisted of sixty thatched huts populated by a group of Americans and local Miskito Indians. The town was under British control. "The English authorities consisted chiefly of negroes from Jamaica," disapprovingly observed one American.[122] At Greytown, passengers changed to a shallow-bottomed steamship, which would travel up the San Juan River and across Lake Nicaragua to a small wharf called Virgin Bay, near the town of Rivas. They would then take a stagecoach over a macadamized road to San Juan del Sur, where they would transfer to another steamer to San Francisco.[123]

To start his operation, Vanderbilt had to face down the British Empire.[124] He travelled again to Nicaragua on June 14, 1851. At Greytown, British officials demanded that the ship obtain their permission to enter the San Juan. Vanderbilt's lieutenant responded that "the only way to prevent us is to blow us out of the water." Vanderbilt successfully called the local authorities' bluff, but his ship promptly ran aground, and it required the aid of sailors from the HMS *Bermuda* to free it.[125] Vanderbilt confronted a more serious threat from the British on his line's inaugural later that year. On November 21, 1851, the British port collector rowed out from Greytown and demanded fees from Vanderbilt's ship. "I cannot nor will not recognize any authority here," said Vanderbilt, "and I will not pay unless I am made by force." This time, to Vanderbilt's surprise, the British used just that: the HMS *Express* sailed to within a quarter mile, and fired a shot "over the forecastle, not clearing the wheelhouse over ten feet." The captain of the *Express* then demanded that Vanderbilt's ship anchor. Vanderbilt went ashore and paid the $123 in transit fees.[126]

THE CLAYTON-BULWER TREATY

The confrontation between Vanderbilt and the British government demonstrated the blurriness of the line between private enterprise and foreign policy in Central America. The British had a de facto protectorate over Nicaragua's Mosquito Coast, and extensive trade interests throughout the region. It appeared to most observers that whichever power that could exert political control over an interoceanic canal in the region would gain the opportunity for enormous profit.

The British ambassador in Washington, Sir Henry Bulwer, sought to defuse tensions. Bulwer had a history of resolving transit disputes—in 1838, he played the key role in fixing the details of the Treaty of Balta-Liman, which opened the Ottoman Empire to British trade and guaranteed free transit through the Bosporus and

Dardanelles for British vessels.[127] Bulwer had a perfect complement in John Clayton of Delaware, now Zachary Taylor's secretary of state. Clayton favored an isthmian canal, but opposed it being the property of any single nation.

Bulwer correctly assessed that the U.S. Senate was in no mood for a confrontation with Britain over Central America. He composed a draft treaty in which the British government disavowed any plan to "occupy, or fortify, or colonize, or assume or exercise any dominion over Nicaragua, Costa Rica, the Mosquito coast, or any part of Central America," provided that the United States did the same. Clayton immediately gave his support to Bulwer's initiative. Both countries signed the treaty on April 19, 1850, and the Senate quickly ratified it.[128]

The Clayton-Bulwer Treaty proved its value in Vanderbilt's two confrontations with British authorities at Greytown. The first time, the *Bermuda*'s captain refused to support the claims of the local British agents to control access to the river. The second time, when word reached the British cabinet of the confrontation, Foreign Minister Lord Granville wrote to Washington: "Her Majesty's Government have no hesitation in offering an ample apology for what they consider to have been an enfraction of Treaty engagements." They then recalled both the Greytown consul and the British viceroy in Central America, Frederick Chatsfield.[129] The treaty in effect pledged Great Britain to support the U.S. commitment to protect Panamanian neutrality. "Neither the one nor the other will ever obtain or maintain for itself any exclusive control over the said ship canal." Other nations could enter the agreement by request, but the United States remained the ultimate guarantor.[130] This would set the stage for the United States' later actions on the Panamanian isthmus.

THE PANAMA RAILROAD

Aspinwall had larger plans in Panama than a steamship route. A railroad across the Panamanian isthmus would serve as a feeder into his Pacific shipping line, and strengthen communication with the rest of the United States. He employed surveyors to find the best path for the railroad in early 1848.[131] The next step was to negotiate with the New Granadan government for the concession rights.

Once again, the French had been there first. In 1845, a group of French capitalists formed the Compagnie de Panama, and in 1847, its representative, Mathew Klein, obtained a ninety-nine-year concession from Bogotá to build a railroad across the isthmus. Fortunately for Aspinwall, a revolution and financial crisis in France meant that the Compagnie was unable to pay its security deposit, and New Granada cancelled the agreement on July 2, 1849.[132]

The collapse of the Compagnie de Panama and the opening of the Clayton-Bulwer negotiations provided Aspinwall the opportunity he needed to put his railroad plans into action. He incorporated the Panama Railroad Company on April 13, 1849, selling its first $1 million tranche of stock in June.[133] The company only managed to sell half its issue to the public—its directors had to subscribe to the rest.[134] The next step was to sign an agreement with the New Granadan government. The celebrated Latin American traveler John Stephens, Aspinwall's friend and the vice president of the railroad, negotiated for Aspinwall. (Stephens proved to be a very good friend indeed; he injured himself badly falling off his mule on his way to Bogotá.)[135] The contract gave the New Granada government 5 percent of the gross receipts from international mail contracts, promised that domestic New Granadan mail would be carried gratis, and transferred 3 percent of the railroad's dividend payments to Bogotá.[136] At the end of twenty years, the New Granadan government would have the option to buy the road for $5 million.[137] Stephens and the New Granadan government signed the agreement on April 15, 1850; the New Granadan Congress ratified it on May 29.[138]

Construction began in December 1850, around the small American settlement in Navy Bay on the Caribbean coast. In little over a year, Navy Bay became a flourishing small town, replacing Chagres as the terminus for American steamer traffic. At the ground-laying ceremony for the offices of the Panama Railroad—the first brick building in the settlement—the New Granadan minister to the United States, Victoriano de Diego Parédes, proposed the town be named Aspinwall. The New Granadan government repudiated Parédes's proposal, instead naming the town Colón.[139]

The Panama Railroad Company ran into the same problems with labor scarcity that had bedeviled Spanish road-builders three centuries before. With passing Forty-niners willing to pay them more for less arduous labor, local Panamanians were unwilling to work at the price the railroad was willing to pay. Of course, contemporary American observers tended to fit this perfectly rational behavior into the prejudices of their time. One company historian wrote, "The native population, composed of a mongrel race of Spanish, Indians, and Negroes, were too indolent and unaccustomed to labor to be depended on to any great extent."[140]

In order to obtain cheap labor, the railroad contracted foreign workers. They first turned to Americans stranded in Panama. The company offered them a dollar a day and a free ticket to California (worth approximately $110) at the end of their contract.[141] Unfortunately for the company, American laborers were not cost-effective, when they could be had at all. The company offered a dollar for a ten-hour day ($25.28 in 2009 dollars, using the CPI). A dollar a day was 15 percent higher than unskilled wages in the northeastern United States, but only 29 percent of the $3.48 per day available in California.[142] The company rapidly concluded that American labor cost too much.

The company then turned to Chinese contract labor, beginning with 705 workmen brought over on the Yankee clipper *Sea Witch*, operated by Aspinwall's New York trading firm. Despite special provisions of tea, rice, and opium (none of which were common at the time in Panama), the workers did not thrive. Suicide among the Chinese workers ran rampant, and the Chinese proved to have even less immunity to tropical diseases than the Americans. Approximately 80 percent of the Chinese workforce perished or deserted, and destitute Chinese beggars became a common sight in Panama City.[143] Ultimately, the railroad brought in 5,000 West Indians, largely Jamaicans, as well as hundreds of Irishmen and New

Granadans from Cartagena.[144] In a country with a population of only 138,000 as of the 1852 census, the migration would permanently change the demographic texture of Panama.[145]

Construction of the single-track line was neither easy nor simple. The company built a camp at Gatún, on the banks of the Chagres River. By October 1851, the workers had finished the tracks between the camp and Colón. Construction then proceeded along the banks of the Chagres: by July 1852 the road reached Barbacoas, halfway across the isthmus, where the company intended to bridge the river. Unfortunately, a flood washed out the bridge in April 1853. Undaunted—for reasons that will be made clear—the company pushed on, bridging the Chagres in May 1854 and opening the line as far as Gorgona. The last eighteen-mile link to Panama City was not finished until January 27, 1855, two years behind schedule and $1.5 million over its $5 million budget.[146] Service across the entire line opened on February 17, 1855.[147] Even then, however, the road was not finished. The company continued to build four strategically placed sidings and additional tracks at both ports, replace pine ties with more durable lignum vitae ties, construct repair and machine shops, and purchase new rolling stock. According to company records, the ultimate cost came to $8 million by the time construction ceased in 1858, a full 60 percent over budget.[148]

Why were the Panama Railroad's directors so sanguine in the face of setbacks and overruns? The answer is simple: quite by accident, the railroad began to generate revenue long before it was complete. In November 1851, when the road only reached as far as Gatún, two steamers arrived during a violent storm. The boats were unable to land near the town of Chagres, as planned, and instead discharged their passengers at Colón. The passengers—over one thousand of them—demanded to be taken the seven miles to Gatún over the railroad. Company officials had no passenger cars available, but they recognized opportunity when they saw it and placed the California-bound migrants on flatcars.[149] So avid were many Argonauts to cross the isthmus that they paid to ride—and allegedly, even to walk—over whatever tracks that had already

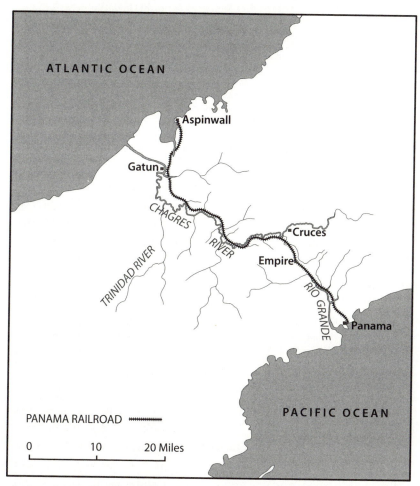

Map 2.2: The Panama Railroad, 1862.

been laid.[150] All the railroad needed to do to generate revenue was
to offer them a faster and relatively more comfortable transit for
part of the way across. Gross receipts through 1854 exceeded a
million dollars.[151]

The Panama Railroad was a massive undertaking by the standards of its day. The $8 million expended on construction by 1858
was the equivalent of $162 million in 2009, adjusted for inflation
using the U.S. GDP deflator. $162 million, however, does not give

an adequate idea of the project's relative scale, since the GDP of the United States increased much more rapidly than inflation in the intervening 150 years. In 1858, $8 million represented 0.2 percent of American GDP, the equivalent of $28.5 *billion* relative to the size of the U.S. economy in 2009.[152] For the 1850s, this was a big project, three times the relative scale of the Golden Gate Bridge.[153]

The Panama Railroad's contract with New Granada expired in 1870. For that reason, in 1867 the Panama Railroad negotiated a new contract with the government. The new contract extended the railroad's franchise until 1966, at which point it would revert to the government without compensation. The company, in turn, had to pay Colombia—as New Granada had been renamed in 1863—$1 million up front and agree to an annual rent of $250,000 in addition to the government's 3 percent share in the dividends.[154]

Proponents of the Panama Railroad Company had another purpose besides making money. In 1849, the superintendent of the U.S. Naval Observatory, Matthew Fontaine Maury, explained to Representative John Rockwell of Connecticut that the railroad would pave the way for a canal "by showing to the world how immense this business is."[155]

Did the Panama Railroad succeed in "showing to the world how immense this business is"? The Panama Railroad was a rather profitable undertaking by the standards of any day, albeit nowhere near as profitable as most historians believe. The company paid its first dividend in 1852, and continued to pay dividends until Ferdinand de Lesseps's Compagnie Universelle du Canal Interocéanique purchased it in 1881. The average total return on Panama Railroad stock between 1853 and 1880 was 13.7 percent, substantially higher than the average 8.4 percent return earned on all stocks listed on the New York Stock Exchange over the same period.[156] Calculated a different way, the Panama Railroad generated an internal rate of return of 13.1 percent between 1849 and 1881, from the moment of its first construction outlays to its purchase by the Compagnie Universelle. (The internal rate of return is the discount rate at which the net present value of a series of cash flows is equal to zero.) While not extravagant, 13 percent was a healthy rate of return, especially in an era where inflation (using the CPI) averaged a little less than 1 percent per year.

In 1877, the Compagnie Universelle du Canal Interocéanique sent Lucien Wyse, a French lieutenant, to Panama to investigate a route for an isthmian canal. Wyse determined that the Panama Railroad travelled over the only feasible route, but the Panama Railroad's charter gave it the right to veto any canal built using its right of way. The railroad's stock price immediately began to rise,

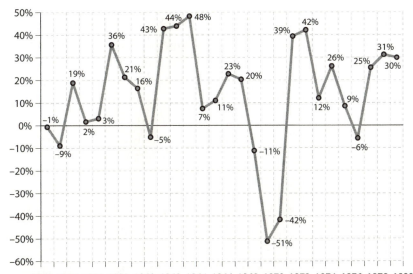

Figure 2.2:   Average annual return on Panama Railroad stock, 1853–80.
Source: Price data from the NYSE History Research Project at the International Center of Finance of the Yale School of Management, available at http://icf. som.yale.edu/nyse/downloads.php. Dividend data from the same source, except for the following periods: 1852–61 from company statements published in F. N. Otis, *Illustrated History of the Panama Railroad* (New York: Harper and Brothers, 1862), app. B, 61–71; 1871 from E. Taylor Parks, *Colombia and the United States, 1765–1934* (New York: Arno Press, 1970), 273; 1874 from "Panama and Pacific Mail," *New York Times*, December 11, 1874; 1875 from "Railroad Notes," *New York Times*, April 5, 1875; 1876 from "Panama Railroad Dividend Passed," *New York Times*, April 5, 1876; and 1878–80 from *Hearings before the Senate Committee on Interoceanic Canals*, H.R. 3110, 57th Cong. (Washington, DC: GPO, 1902), 217.

and it soared further when Wyse travelled to New York in 1879 to negotiate with the directors.[157] The Panama Railroad's directors and the French managers of the new canal project ultimately decided on a sale price of $250 per share, in addition to a special dividend of $41, and the purchase went through in 1881.[158]

The Panama Railroad would have been rather less profitable for its investors if it had not been for the Compagnie Universelle. Panama Railroad stock was relatively risky. (See figures 2.2 and 2.3.) Some risks were political. In 1867, for example, the Colombian government (as mentioned previously) demanded a $1 million up-front payment and imposed $250,000 in annual rent on top of its 3 percent share in the dividends. Other risks were economic. In 1869, the first U.S. transcontinental railroad opened, the competition cutting into the Panama Railroad's effective monopoly over intercoastal traffic. The real blow to the company, however, was

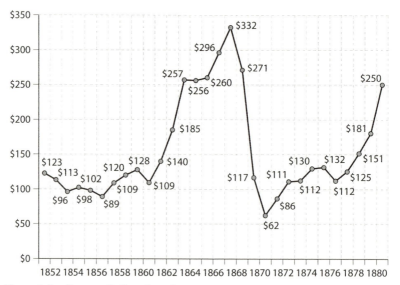

Figure 2.3:   Panama Railroad stock price, 1852–81.
Source: NYSE History Research Project at the International Center of Finance of the Yale School of Management, available at http://icf.som.yale.edu/nyse/downloads.php. Prices are annual averages, except for 1881, which is the closing price. The annual average for that year was $235.

self-inflicted. Its management got into a contractual dispute with the Pacific Steam Navigation Company over the division of passenger and freight revenues. In 1870, therefore, the steamship company decided to abandon the isthmus and began taking people and cargo by way of Cape Horn.[159] As a result, Panama Railroad stock plunged 81 percent. (See figure 2.3.) The Panama Railroad managed to contract with other steam lines and pay dividends over the rest of the 1870s, and its stock price recovered somewhat, but investors who purchased the stock anytime after 1863 would have lost money (including dividends) had they sold it before the Compagnie Universelle began to negotiate for the railroad in 1877.

A ROAD NOT TAKEN? THE TEHUANTEPEC SHIP RAILWAY

> Nowhere on the globe is there a healthier or more equable climate.
>
> —*Simon Stevens, president of the Tehuantepec Railway Company*

In 1880, the American engineer James Buchanan Eads proposed a radical solution to the problem of interoceanic transport. Almost forgotten today, Eads was considered one of the great engineers of his era. Originally from St. Louis, Eads made his fortune in the 1850s salvaging wrecked steamboats, using a diving bell suspended from a riverboat of his own design. During the Civil War, Eads was instrumental in building the Union's river-going ironclad fleet, a key part of the Union's Anaconda Plan to strangle the Confederacy along its waterways.[160] After the war, Eads designed the first bridge over the Mississippi at St. Louis. It was an engineering tour de force: the world's first steel arch bridge and the longest arch bridge ever built. Designed far beyond its requirements, the Eads Bridge is still in use carrying both cars and the trains of the St. Louis Metrolink.[161]

In 1880, Eads's background in ship and bridge design led him to propose a "ship railway" across the Isthmus of Tehuantepec in

Mexico. Ships of several thousand tons would enter a floating dry dock and be cradled onto a solidly designed four-hundred-foot-long railway carriage that would be pulled by a team of powerful locomotives. The carriage would run on multiple parallel tracks of standard gauge, relying on the ship's own rigidity for stability. The length of the carriage would require the track to have no curves with a radius of less than twenty miles. At five points on Eads's proposed route across Mexico, sharp bends would be necessary; Eads proposed an ingenious system of turntables floating on pontoons in giant basins. At the other side, the carriage would enter the dry dock and the ship would be released. Eads estimated the travel time across Tehuantepec at sixteen hours.[162] It would make Tehuantepec "the Centre of the World's Commerce."[163]

Less hyperbolically, some boosters of the Tehuantepec Ship Railway claimed that, unlike an isthmian canal, "no really new or startling engineering problems present themselves."[164] Eads estimated the ship railway would cost $75 million.[165] In 1880, President Porfirio Díaz of Mexico gave Eads a concession to build his railway. It provided one million acres in land grants, tax exemptions, and a quarter-mile right-of-way.[166] It promised Eads a profit guarantee of $1.25 million per year—contingent on a guarantee of $2.5 million from the United States.[167]

Unfortunately for Eads and the ship railway, the money was not forthcoming from private investors, the Mexican government, or the U.S. Congress. Eads travelled to Washington several times in order to lobby the U.S. Congress for the necessary funds. He came very close to success in 1885, when a bill made it out of both houses, only to have it die in conference. Exhausted from lobbying, Eads died in 1887 while visiting the Bahamas on his doctor's orders.[168] The Tehuantepec Ship Railway died with him.

While Eads pursued his dream, the Mexican government granted several concessions for more typical railroads across the Isthmus of Tehuantepec. The first project took thirteen years to build 193 miles of track, through the efforts of six different consortia, including the Mexican government itself, which directly invested $19 million in the project.[169] Officially inaugurated on

Map 2.3: The Eads Ship Railway and the Tehuantepec Railroad.

October 15, 1894, the railway was found to be unfit for transport.[170] An engineering survey reported, "The embankment is completely flooded, no part of it is well-ballasted, and the rolling stock is truly the worst."[171]

In 1898, Porfirio Díaz's pet British industrialist, Sir Weetman Pearson, received a contract to modernize the Tehuantepec Railroad and to establish functional ports at its terminals. Of the 845 railway bridges that had been previously built, 833 of them had to be reconstructed or replaced entirely. The roadbed needed to be continuously treated with herbicides to prevent vegetation from encroaching. Sharp curves and steep grades were made more gradual. A harbor at Salina Cruz on the Pacific had to be built from scratch. A sandbar blocking the river port at Coatzacoalcos on the Atlantic was removed using a technique Eads had used on the Mississippi: two converging concrete jetties were built at the mouth of the river, causing the faster current to erode the bar. [172] Pearson's contract with the Mexican government guaranteed him a return of 6 percent on his investments. The Mexican federal government would take all profits in excess of that, and the ports and railroad would be turned over to the state in 1953.[173]

The single-track line officially reopened on January 23, 1907, at a ceremony in Salina Cruz witnessed by President Díaz himself.[174] Díaz declared it "one of the greatest events in the past decade of Mexico's history," predicting "a great future for the new transcontinental line."[175]

The Tehuantepec Railroad proved to be extremely expensive. By 1904, two years before its reconstruction was complete, the Mexican government had spent $30.7 million (U.S.) in construction subsidies.[176] As a result of an agreement with the United States that allowed transcontinental cargoes to traverse Mexican territory without paying Mexican tariffs, the Mexican government spent an additional $10 million on special customs and defense installations.[177] In addition, Pearson invested by 1903 $1.0 million of his own money in the railroad, $2.5 million in the Caribbean port at Coatzacoalcos, and $3.0 million in the Pacific port at Salina Cruz.[178] The Tehuantepec National Railroad Company took out a

$9.7 million loan in London in 1905, and a second $1.9 million in 1908.[179] Finally, Pearson spent an estimated additional $4.0 million in Coatzacoalcos and $9.0 million in Salina Cruz to finish the ports.[180] The total cost of the project, including ancillary defense and port construction, came to $71.8 million. Converted into 2009 dollars using the U.S. GDP deflator, the total cost of the Tehuantepec National Railroad was $1.3 billion, 8.3 times the cost of the Panama Railroad.[181]

Although the Tehuantepec Railroad was an expensive and difficult undertaking by the standards of the early twentieth century, it is clear that Eads's proposed Tehuantepec Ship Railway represented a venture an order of magnitude more difficult. Though the costs of a purely speculative engineering project are difficult to determine, we can use the known costs of the Tehuantepec National Railroad to set a lower bound on its construction. If a single-track line across Tehuantepec ultimately cost $71.8 million, then it is unlikely in the extreme that the proposed ship railway, requiring multiple tracks for its function, would have cost as little as $75 million.

In addition, there are several reasons to believe that Tehuantepec's geography would have made the ship railway impossible at *any* cost. Pearson's retrofitting of the Tehuantepec Railroad straightened the railroad's original crooked path, yet the course of the railroad line still required two horseshoe curves and a tunnel through the Chivela Pass near the Pacific. It is unclear how nineteenth-century technology could have blasted a tunnel large enough to allow the passage of a steamship. Worse yet, the line abruptly descended toward the Atlantic after the Chivela Pass, reaching a 3 percent downward grade—160 feet to the mile—a dangerous descent for any cargo carried on multiple tracks.[182] In addition, the Chivela Pass is the only major gap in the southern Sierra Madre and funnels cold air from the north. This causes wind jets known as the *tehuano*, noted by Humboldt in the early nineteenth century.[183] Trains caught in a tehuano could suffer head (or tail) winds of twenty to forty knots with occasional gusts of hurricane force.[184] Such winds were problematic for regular railroad carriages; they would have been devastating for ships travelling on multiple tracks.

ONWARD TO THE DITCH

Panama's second great economic boom ended as competition whittled away the Panama Railroad's advantage. The U.S. Railroad Act of 1862 gave a federal charter, land grants, free right-of-way, and loan guarantees to the Union Pacific Railroad Company in order to build a transcontinental railroad. The Union Pacific joined the Central Pacific at Promontory, Utah, on May 10, 1869. By the time the Compagnie Universelle du Canal Interocéanique bought the Panama Railroad in 1881, it had become common to traverse the United States overland in only eight days. Over the rest of the century, four more transcontinental links would be built in the United States, one in Canada, and one (if not a very good one until 1907) in Mexico, with Panama's precocious transcontinental railroad bringing up the rear. As in the late Spanish colonial era, political decisions combined with new technologies served to attenuate Panama's geographic advantage.

This time, however, Panama was not fated to slide into obscurity. The reason was technological. The major industrial powers believed that an isthmian canal was finally within reach. Between 1870 and 1875, the United States government sent a series of expeditions to Panama and Nicaragua to scout possible locations for an isthmian canal. These expeditions were followed by Lucien Wyse's expeditions in 1876 and 1877.

Of course, the technological changes that made a canal seem possible did not guarantee that one would be built. Eads's proposed Tehuantepec Ship Railway is a perfect example of the overreach of nineteenth-century technological optimism. Nor did technology guarantee that a canal would be built in Panama. A number of political and practical barriers still needed to be overcome before the world would see the Big Ditch.

THREE

PREPARING THE DITCH

*You succeeded at the Suez by a miracle. Be satisfied
with accomplishing one miracle in a lifetime, and not
hope for a second.*

*—Charles de Lesseps to his father, Ferdinand, about a
new canal venture in Panama*

FROM THE PERSPECTIVE OF THE EARLY TWENTY-FIRST CEN-
tury, the Panama Canal stands as a singular accomplishment, a
triumph of smokestack technology and muscular diplomacy. To
its contemporaries, however, the Panama Canal as we know it
was the sole survivor of a bewildering array of failed proposals,
failed counterproposals, failed treaties, and one major failed attempt at construction. For economic historians, these failures are
an invaluable source of data for understanding the institutional
and economic constraints that had to be overcome to build a project that would primarily benefit the United States across territory
controlled by independent Latin American republics.

An isthmian canal might have been technologically feasible by
the second half of the nineteenth century, but it was by no means
inevitable. The same French entrepreneurs who had created the
Suez Canal turned their attention to Panama in 1877. After a decade and hundreds of millions of dollars, their effort failed. A mis-
guided attempt to dig a sea-level canal not only drove up costs, but
the dirt piled up on the sides of the excavation created malarial
swamps that sent death rates soaring. In 1888, the French canal

company went bankrupt, nearly dragging the French economy down with it.

The United States did not remain inactive during the prolonged failure of the French effort. The U.S. government and American entrepreneurs made several attempts to build a canal across Nicaraguan territory, all of which also failed. Nicaragua's geography was even less forgiving than Panama's, and Nicaragua's politics were far more precarious. Internal instability and external conflicts with Costa Rica turned a difficult mission into an impossible one.

No isthmian canal might have been built at all had it not been for the geopolitical shock of the American victory in the Spanish-American War. The war convinced American politicians that the United States needed to be able to shift vessels quickly between the oceans. The resulting acquisitions of Hawaii and the Philippines only reinforced that conviction. The American government began serious study of various isthmian routes in 1899. Once it became clear to the Roosevelt administration that Nicaragua was not a feasible option, it redoubled its efforts to take control of the French assets in Panama and restart construction. Unfortunately for the United States, the Colombian government refused to cooperate. Colombian diplomats demanded at least as good a deal as the country had obtained from the French, or that the Americans had previously offered Nicaragua.

Theodore Roosevelt, famously impatient, would not delay building a canal simply to aid the Colombian government. In addition, many prominent Republicans were financially vested in a Panama route through their ties to the French company that held title to the work already completed on the isthmus. Roosevelt therefore refused to entertain Colombian counteroffers. Instead, his administration engineered Panama's secession from Colombia and used America's military prowess to force the Panamanian government into signing a far better deal for the United States than Washington could have otherwise negotiated.

The newly independent Republic of Panama agreed to the new terms with thousands of U.S. troops on Panamanian soil. The agreement granted the United States a far higher share of the Panama Canal's economic benefits than any previous agreement on the table. Not only did the United States reduce its payments for the use of Panama's geographic assets, it succeeded in getting Panamanian taxpayers to subsidize some of the overhead costs of canal construction and operation. In other words, contrary to a large literature on the wages of empire, Theodore Roosevelt managed to make imperialism pay.

A FRENCH INTERCONNECTION

Ferdinand de Lesseps was not the person one might have expected to have created one of the world's greatest works of civil engineering, the Suez Canal. He had not been trained as an engineer. Rather, he started out as a rising star in the French diplomatic service, serving in Tunisia, Egypt, Holland, Spain, and Italy. He resigned from the service in 1849, after the French government rejected the terms of a truce that he had helped negotiate with Garibaldi's Roman Republic to allow for the return of the pope to Rome.

De Lesseps's time in Egypt fired his imagination about the possibilities of a canal at Suez and developed his contacts with the Egyptian government. In 1854, he used his personal connection with Sa'id Pasha, the ruler of Egypt, to obtain a concession to construct a canal. The concession granted the Compagnie Universelle du Canal Maritime de Suez ownership of the canal for ninety-nine years from its opening, gave the Egyptian government a 15 percent stake in the project, and required that 2 percent of the profits be distributed among the employees.[1] The Egyptian government paid $58,200 to finance the initial feasibility study.[2] De Lesseps failed to convince either the French or British governments to officially support the project, but he did manage to sell a bit over 207,000 shares—52 percent of the equity—to more than twenty-one thousand small investors in France. The Egyptian government purchased another 45 percent. Overall, the Compagnie de Suez raised $24.2 million.[3]

Funding in hand, de Lesseps's company began digging in 1859.[4] The Egyptian government promised to provide free labor in the initial contract, but in 1863 it abolished the corvée, depriving de Lesseps of his promised unpaid workers. (The Egyptian government also took back ownership of lands that had been promised the Compagnie de Suez.) In order to compensate for the resulting rise in labor costs, the company brought in steam engines and mechanized excavation equipment. In 1864, the Compagnie de Suez also took the Egyptian government to international arbitration over its failure to provide the promised corvée labor, among other alleged contract violations. The arbitration took place in France, under the auspices of the French head of state, Emperor Napoleon III. Not surprisingly, Napoleon III ordered the Egyptian government to pay an indemnity of $16.3 million, to be paid in sixteen installments between 1864 and 1879.[5]

The indemnity payments failed to satisfy the project's voracious demand for cash. The machinery purchased in response to the loss of forced labor alone cost $11.6 million and consumed $2.3 million in fuel every year.[6] In 1867, the company raised an additional $5.9 million in the bond market. (It tried and failed to issue $19.5 million.) The French government arranged to force the Egyptian government to move up the payment schedule on its indemnity, demanding payment in full in 1869. It also authorized a lottery in France to fund Suez Canal construction.[7] The lottery raised $13.6 million. In addition, the Egyptian government contributed an additional subsidy of $5.8 million, financed through a loan collateralized by the dividend payments from the government's share in the canal.[8] The company also made a $1.6 million profit on the sale of lands granted it by the Egyptian government.[9] Finally, the Compagnie de Suez raised $15.9 million through short-term borrowing.[10]

The Suez Canal opened in 1869, but at a final cost of $81.8 million, 2.2 times the project's initial projection.[11] The Compagnie de Suez would go on to suffer from financial troubles, and the canal itself needed to be widened and deepened only seven years after its opening. The Suez Canal's financial and engineering troubles did not, however, blunt de Lesseps's reputation. World opinion lionized him after his triumph in Egypt. De Lesseps, in turn, looked for new challenges to meet.[12]

A canal across Panama was the obvious choice. In late 1877, de Lesseps sent Lieutenant Lucien Napoleon-Bonaparte Wyse, a grandnephew of Napoleon Bonaparte on leave from the French Navy, to scout potential canal opportunities in Panama. After a cursory survey, Wyse crossed from Buenaventura on Colombia's Pacific coast to Bogotá in eleven days on horseback, a difficult route of several hundred miles, breaking his spurs and sustaining himself on balls of chocolate. The reason for the rush was Wyse's desire to conduct and conclude negotiations with the outgoing Colombian administration before it left office.[13] Wyse succeeded in his mission.

The Wyse Concession gave the French canal company a ninety-nine-year concession from the moment the canal began operations, after which it would be turned over to the Colombian government. In return, it promised Colombia an annual payment of $250,000 once the canal entered operation, in addition to the $250,000 annuity already provided by the Panama Railroad Company. The agreement also granted Colombia an increasing share of the enterprise's gross revenues: 5 percent for the first twenty-five years, 6 percent for the subsequent quarter century, 7 percent for the third quarter century, and 8 percent for the final twenty-four years of the concession.[14]

In early 1879, Wyse travelled to New York in order to negotiate the purchase of the Panama Railroad Company. The president and majority owner of the Panama Railroad, Trenor Park, was a shrewd Vermonter who made his fortune litigating in the California gold fields. Park cheerfully offered to sell his stock for $200 a share—at a time when Panama Railroad shares averaged $94 on the open market. For reasons that remain unclear, Wyse accepted.[15]

Agreements with the Colombian government and the Panama Railroad in hand, de Lesseps called a special congress in Paris on May 15, 1879, to organize his new venture. He calculated that he would be able to build a sea-level canal across Panama for $209 million, excluding interest costs and the cost of the Panama Rail-road.[16] He forecasted maritime traffic of six million tons a year, enough to generate $18 million in annual toll revenues (with tolls set at $3 per ton) and $8.4 million in profit.[17] The seven Americans at the congress abstained from voting. One of them, William Johnston, later wrote that de Lesseps had "packed and manipulated [the congress] so as to run through hastily."[18]

The project immediately ran into financial difficulties. An attempt at a direct issue of shares in Paris failed miserably.[19] After a scouting mission to Panama, de Lesseps returned to France. He reduced his estimate of the cost of an isthmian canal to $102 million.[20] He travelled to New York and established a lobbying committee there.[21] Finally, he returned to Paris and raised $60 million in capital for the Compagnie Universelle du Canal Interocéanique, almost exclusively from 104,345 small French and Spanish investors, most of whom purchased five shares of stock or less. Women purchased nearly a sixth of the issue, a rarity for the time.[22]

Cash in hand, de Lesseps went back to New York in 1881. His intention was to finalize the purchase of the Panama Railroad. Unfortunately, the Panama Railroad's directors raised their price to $250 per share and demanded a special $1 million bonus for themselves.[23] De Lesseps had little choice but to agree. The total cost of the purchase came to $17 million—$4.2 million more than de Lesseps anticipated.[24] In their last days in control of the company, the Panama Railroad's directors declared a $41 special dividend that extracted $2.9 million out of the company. An additional $6.4 million went to underwriting fees, remuneration to de Lesseps's backing syndicate, and publicity for the proposed canal.[25] It would prove to be an inauspicious financial start for the project.

CONSTRUCTION OF THE FRENCH CANAL

De Lesseps planned to build a sea-level canal across Panama. The technical challenges were immense. Mud slides dictated that the walls of the canal had to be dug at an angle much lower than the planned forty-five degrees, greatly magnifying the amount of earth that had to be moved.[26] To prevent the claylike soil removed from the cut from collapsing during the rainy season, the French dumped the spill in nearby valleys.[27] This had the twin side effects of exacerbating mud slides during the rainy season—since the fill blocked natural watercourses—and creating malarial swamps that impeded the French enterprise's efforts to reduce mortality rates among its employees. Moreover, the sea-level design required one set of locks to be built regardless—tides on the isthmus are twenty feet higher on the Pacific side than on the Atlantic. Currents without a lock would average 4.5 knots. Worse yet, the currents would vary with the tides, making navigation difficult.

Mortality ran exceedingly high during the French construction efforts. (See table 3.1.) Between the insect-borne diseases of malaria and yellow fever, diseases of poor hygiene such as typhoid fever and dysentery, and other misfortunes such as sunstroke, snakebite, and industrial accidents, at least 22,189 workers died.[28] Philippe Bunau-Varilla, an engineer under de Lesseps directing the excavation of the Culebra Cut, estimated "for every eighty employees who survived six months on the Isthmus one could say that twenty died."[29] American observers estimated that one-third of the labor force at any given time was sick, and the *New York Tribune* reported that chief resident officials of the project had an 83 percent mortality rate.[30] Particularly hard-hit were the French technical and administrative staff, who died by the dozens.[31] The predominantly West Indian construction workforce fared little better.[32]

The French construction efforts precipitated a temporary boom in Panama. Wealthy Panamanians established businesses supplying the French canal project and its workers. The revenues of the Panamanian provincial government rose from an average of $300,000 during the 1870s to a peak of $1.3 million in 1889.[33] Rents in Panama City rose between 1880 and 1885 by a factor of 3.5. (See table 3.2.) Passenger loads on the Panama Railroad rose 48-fold between 1880 and their peak in 1888, while cargo loads rose 2.2 times over the same period.[34]

TABLE 3.1
Death Rates during French Canal Construction in Panama

	Number of employees	Disease deaths	Death rates per 1,000	
			Canal employees	Cities of Panama and Colón
1881	967	58		
1882	1,998	125		
1883	6,941	423		
1884	17,436	1,231	70.6	100.2
1885	15,784	1,095	69.4	109.7
1886	15,193	954	62.8	105.2
1887	16,873	1,038	61.5	121.4
1888	13,993	604	43.2	90.2
1889	1,938	91	46.8	56.1
1890	913	30	32.8	42.1
1891	870	37	42.9	42.9
1892	796	22	27.6	38.6
1893	717	19	26.4	40.8
1894	805	17	21.1	37.3
1895			24.4	38.4
1896	2,715	79	29.1	43.0
1897	3,980	127	31.9	48.5
1898	3,396	73	21.4	40.9
1899	2,499	57	22.8	57.4
1900	2,000	69	34.5	55.8
1901	2,000	36	18.0	50.6
1902	1,449	33	22.7	98.8
1903	940	33	35.1	56.0

Source: Omar Jaén Suárez, *La población del Istmo de Panamá* (Madrid: Agencia Española de Cooperación Internacional, 1998), 505–6, 543.

In 1888 the French gave up trying to build a sea-level canal—Alexander von Humboldt laughing from his grave—and redesigned their project around a series of locks designed by the famed French engineer Alexandre Gustave Eiffel.[35] Unfortunately, by that point the Compagnie had already sunk $193.6 million into the project.

The capital markets expressed skepticism about the project from almost the very beginning. Practically every bond issue paid

TABLE 3.2

Property Values and Rents in Panama City, U.S. Dollars

	Total property value	Average property value	Average rent
1875	1,670,564	2,073	140
1880	2,069,222	2,741	185
1885	3,570,188	3,962	639
1890	4,423,993	2,941	251
1895	4,177,413	3,208	141

Source: Omar Jaén Suárez, *La población del Istmo de Panamá* (Madrid: Agencia Española de Cooperación Internacional, 1998), 519.

a higher effective interest rate than the one before. The Compagnie also faced increasing difficulty in marketing its bonds. The public purchased less of each issue than the previous one. The March 1888 issue faced particular problems. De Lesseps only managed to place 26 percent of the bonds, at an effective interest rate of 9.0 percent. Worse yet for the Compagnie Universelle, it had to use $14 for every bond sold in the 1888 issue to fund the amortization of previous bond issues.[36] (See table 3.3.) By 1888, the company had raised $244.8 million from the capital markets, including its $57 million initial public offering in 1880. Despite such prodigious feats of fund-raising in the face of investor skepticism, the Compagnie managed to spend money even faster, through a combination of disguised transfers from the Panama Railroad and accumulating accounts payable, as a later parliamentary investigatory committee was to discover.[37]

The Compagnie's March 1888 bond issue failed dismally. (See table 3.3.) De Lesseps pleaded for help from the French government. If the public did not subscribe to the bond issues, he said, "the enterprise must be abandoned, and a foreign nation would, for a morsel of bread, get a gigantic work which was nearly finished."[38] He managed to get an emergency bill through the National Assembly that allowed him to structure a new bond issue as a lottery. Each year, three bonds would win a cash price of FFr500,000

TABLE 3.3

Compagnie Universelle du Canal Interocéanique Bond Issues

	Number of bonds issued	Par value	Sale price	Sale price minus cost of issue	Uptake	Effective interest rate	Total amount raised
September 1882	250,000	$ 97	$ 85	$ 60	100%	8.1%	$ 14,939,613
October 1883	600,000	$ 96	$ 55	$ 53	100%	5.5%	$ 34,244,263
September 1884	387,387	$ 96	$ 64	$ 57	82%	6.7%	$ 18,232,901
April 1886	362,613	$ 96	$ 53	$ 41	39%	9.4%	$ 5,757,838
August 1886	500,000	$ 191	$ 86	$ 81	92%	7.1%	$ 37,212,723
July 1887	500,000	$ 192	$ 85	$ 79	52%	7.3%	$ 20,415,614
March 1888	350,000	$ 193	$ 75	$ 51	26%	9.0%	$ 4,577,528
May 1888*	na	na	na	na	na	5.0%	$ 4,173,044
June 1888**	2,000,000	$ 77	$ 58	$ 51	42%	6.1%	$ 43,135,185

Source: Calculated from data in Gerstle Mack, *The Land Divided* (New York: Knopf, 1943), 356–57, 361. Franc-dollar exchange rates from the Global Financial Database, available at http://www.globalfinancialdata.com/.

* On May 14, 1888, the Compagnie Universelle borrowed $5.8 million from Crédit Lyonnais and the Société Générale for a period of 111 days, pending the lottery bond issue of June 8 to June 26. The consortium charged the Compagnie Universelle an astonishing $1.6 million in fees and commissions.

** The June 1888 bond issue was a lottery bond, in which each bond would receive cash prizes selected at random. The cost of the issue does not include the cost of making future lottery payouts.

(US$96,488), three more bonds FFr250,000, six bonds FFr100,000, twelve bonds FFr10,000, another twelve bonds FFr5,000, thirty bonds FFr2,000, and 300 bonds FFr1,000. Unfortunately, the chance of winning a prize did not induce the investing public to take up the bond issue in the required amounts. De Lesseps barnstormed the country, trying to convince buyers to no avail. Finally, on December 14, 1888, the Assembly refused to pass a bill allowing the Compagnie Universelle to suspend its debt payments and continue operating.[39] On February 4, 1889, it formally went into receivership.[40] Work on the canal practically ceased by late March.[41] The collapse outraged the French public, and many of the backers went to prison. Final expenditures ran to $276.8 million.[42] The trauma ran so deep that the expression "Quel Panama!" came to mean "What a mess!" in French slang.[43]

In an attempt to keep the project alive, in 1890 Lucien Wyse negotiated a new contract with the Colombian government. Bogotá agreed to give a new company a new concession, provided that work restarted on the canal by February 1894 and was completed, or at least ongoing as of February 1904. In addition, the Colombian government received $1.93 million and a 7.7 percent equity stake in the enterprise.[44] The Compagnie Nouvelle du Canal de Panama, or the New Panama Canal Company, was incorporated on October 20, 1894—slightly after the deadline set by the Colombian government, which accepted the delay. The receiver and contractors received most of the new shares, although a good portion went to shareholders in the old company who purchased the new shares as a condition to avoid prosecution.[45]

The New Panama Canal Company continued some spotty construction efforts—excavating some 11.4 million cubic yards between 1889 and 1902, on top of the 66.7 million yards dug before 1889—in order to keep the Colombian government from taking over its properties under its concession. It also continued to operate the Panama Railroad, but the canal project remained essentially dead. Even in its afterlife, the canal effort sparked a major bribery scandal in France, causing one of de Lesseps's sons to be briefly imprisoned.[46] De Lesseps himself died shortly afterward in 1894, at the age of eighty-nine.[47]

REENTER THE AMERICANS

The United States remained an interested party in an isthmian canal. Although American demand for a high-speed isthmian route rapidly ebbed after the connection of the Central Pacific and Union Pacific railroads into a single transcontinental North American line in 1869, the obvious commercial potential for regular maritime traffic through an isthmian canal remained. In the minds of many Americans, there was no reason why the United States should not be involved. In 1878, the same year Wyse received his concession from the Colombian government, a Wall Street banker, Frederick Kelley, estimated that an isthmian canal would save world shipping $48 million per year, of which $36 million would accrue to the United States.[48] Two years later, President Rutherford Hayes declared before Congress, "The policy of this country is a canal under American control. . . . Our merely commercial interest is greater than that of any other country."[49]

Hayes's successor, Chester Arthur, believed that the French canal needed to be matched by an American canal. In 1884, he dispatched Secretary of State Frederick Frelinghuysen to negotiate a canal treaty with the Nicaraguan government. President Adán Cárdenas appointed his predecessor, Joaquín Zavala, to represent Nicaragua. The agreed-on treaty gave a joint canal administration authority over a 2½-mile-wide zone, including control over all port facilities, sanitary works, railroads, and telegraph lines, as well as freedom from Nicaraguan taxes or duties. Management of the canal would be entrusted to a six-member board, half of whom would be appointed by the Nicaraguan government. Nicaragua would also retain civil jurisdiction "in times of peace" over its citizens within the Zone. In return for joint control, the United States pledged "perpetual alliance between the United States of America and the Republic of Nicaragua, and the former agree to protect the integrity of the territory of the latter." In addition, the treaty granted Nicaragua one-third of the profits from the canal and its ancillary operations after "maintenance and improvement, if found necessary, of the works, including the salaries of the Board of Managers and all officers and others employed."[50]

President Arthur's reformist Democratic successor, Grover Cleveland, disliked the treaty's commitment to a taxpayer-funded canal, disliked the permanent alliance with Nicaragua, and disliked the casual way it dismissed terms of the 1850 Clayton-Bulwer Treaty. President Cleveland, therefore, chose not to submit it to the U.S. Senate.[51] Ironically, Cleveland himself found it necessary to dispatch troops to Panama during his first year in office to protect American interests and fulfill U.S. obligations under the Bidlack-Mallarino Treaty of 1848. In 1885, President Rafael Núñez of Colombia attempted to replace elected provincial governors with appointed officials.[52] This provoked a series of revolts. In March, Núñez removed most Colombian troops from Panama City in order to suppress fighting elsewhere. Perhaps predictably, on March 16 a former governor of Panama named Rafael Aizpuru seized the opportunity to expel the remaining skeleton force from Panama City and proclaim a coup d'état. Colombian troops in Colón left that city and promptly expelled Aizpuru, and their commander, General Gónima, proceeded to declare himself provincial governor.[53]

The departure of Colombian troops from Colón opened the way for Congressman Pedro Prestán to raise a ragtag militia and seize control of the city. Prestán immediately ordered a supply of arms from dealers in the United States, which arrived on March 29. The U.S. government, however, banned the export of weapons to Colombia under the provisions of the Neutrality Act of 1838.[54] In accordance with American policy, the agent of the American steamship line carrying the weapons, working with the local U.S. consul, refused to release them to their Colombian buyers. At that point Prestán detained the agent, the superintendent of the Panama Railroad, the U.S. consul, and two naval officers on leave from an American warship docked in Colón. Prestán threatened to kill the hostages if the weapons were not released. The consul ordered the captain of the warship, Theodore Kane, to hand over the arms. Order in hand, Prestán released the hostages, but Captain Kane did not release the weapons. Prestán once again nabbed the steamship line's agent. At that point, Kane ordered two platoons of U.S. Marines to storm the city. Prestán retreated from Colón on March 31, where he ran into a platoon of Colombian troops—their actual loyalty was not clear—advancing from Panama City.[55] Poorly armed and unwilling to engage regular troops, Prestán's forces retreated back to Colón and proceeded to burn the town down to the ground. Thousands were left homeless.[56] Monetary losses ran between $12 million and $15 million, and insurance policies were rendered void, "as the town was fired by rebels."[57] Forces loyal to Aizpuru, meanwhile, reoccupied Panama City while Gónima's troops battled Prestán outside Colón. The Panama Railroad closed, its tracks cut. Prestán retreated once again, this time into the countryside.[58]

The violence prompted President Cleveland to dispatch more troops to Panama from New York and Pensacola. The forces from Florida arrived on April 10; by April 15 there were more than 1,200 U.S. Marines off Colón. Once the American commander secured permission from Bogotá to disembark and establish order, the marines landed. They quickly crossed the isthmus and on April 24 assaulted Panama City, where they occupied the city's armories, established checkpoints, and assumed control—for precisely one day. After extracting a promise from Rafael Aizpuru not to fight within the city or establish barricades, the United States turned control of the city back over to the rebel force on April 25.[59]

President Cleveland wanted American forces to act as mediators: he had no desire to occupy Panama, let alone annex the place. When Colombian forces arrived on April 28, the American commander brokered Aizpuru's peaceful surrender. Commander Rafael Reyes took command of the province on behalf of President Núñez. Núñez, for his part, succeeded in replacing Colombia's elected provincial governors with his own appointees. Cleveland described the intervention in his subsequent State of the Union address on December 8, 1885. "Desirous of exercising only the powers expressly reserved to us by the [Bidlack-Mallarino] treaty, and mindful of the rights of Colombia, the forces sent to the isthmus were instructed to confine their action to 'positively and efficaciously' preventing the transit and its accessories from being 'interrupted or embarrassed.' The execution of this delicate and responsible task necessarily involved police control where the local authority was temporarily powerless, but always in aid of the sovereignty of Colombia."[60] The United States lodged damage claims of $3.75 million against the Colombian government, half of which was on behalf of the French-owned Panama Railroad. Colombia rejected the claims and refused arbitration. After six fruitless years of trying to collect, the U.S. government abandoned its claims in 1891.[61]

THE NICARAGUA OPTION

In 1887, the Cuban-American representative of the Nicaraguan Canal Association, Commander Aniceto García Menocal, negotiated a concession with the Nicaraguan government to build a transoceanic canal. The failure of the French effort in Panama was growing obvious, and the Nicaraguan Canal Association believed the time was ripe to begin a competing project. The resulting contract granted the Maritime Canal Company the exclusive right to build a canal, exemption from taxes and tariffs during its construction, and the help of the Nicaraguan government in using its powers of eminent domain to acquire property along the route. In return, the Maritime Canal Company agreed to grant Nicaragua 6 percent of "all shares, bonds, certificates, or other securities" issued to finance the construction of the canal and $150,000 in upfront payments.[62]

The contract, however, was complicated by the fact that the Nicaraguan route ran along the Costa Rican border. In an ironic inversion of later political sentiments, the Costa Rican government strongly opposed an American presence on the border. An earlier

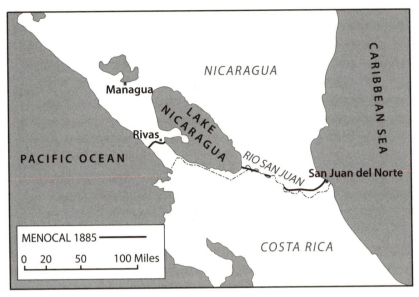

Map 3.1:   The Nicaraguan proposal.

protocol granted both Nicaragua and Costa Rica an interest in any canal constructed along the San Juan River.[63] An arbitration commission headed by President Cleveland negated Costa Rica's right to a share of canal revenues, but agreed that the country had a veto over construction and the right to demand unspecified compensation from any canal venture.[64]

The company's plan was to build a dam along the San Juan River that would have "practically converted the river from the lake to the dam into an arm of the lake," extending Lake Nicaragua forty miles to the east. The company would then dig a separate canal about twenty miles from the dam to San Juan del Norte, on the east coast. On the western side of Lake Nicaragua, a lock canal would be built between Rivas and Brito on the Pacific.[65]

Construction began in 1887, on the hope that a satisfactory arrangement could be made with Costa Rica. The Maritime Canal Company negotiated an agreement with Costa Rica the next year and received a federal charter from the U.S. Congress in 1889.[66] Within a year, the company excavated one and one-half miles of canal and built eleven and one-half miles of parallel railroad. The company used the railroad to ship in supplies and, as importantly, ship out excavated materiel. It purchased seven dredges, two tugboats, twenty lighters, and a machine shop from the bankrupt French operation in Panama and shipped them to Nicaragua.[67]

Unfortunately, the Nicaragua attempt ended in failure in 1893. Expenses proved higher than expected—particularly because the southern portion of the flooded area of the San Juan turned out to need large embankments in order to contain the water from the dam. The Maritime Canal Company's bond issues failed, and the U.S. Congress voted against loan guarantees in 1891. The next year, it voted against taking an $80.5 million equity stake in the enterprise.[68] Congress's reticence should not be surprising. In 1892, $80.5 million came to 0.5 percent of America's GDP, the equivalent of $71 *billion* in 2009. In 1893, the company failed, having spent only $6 million on construction.[69]

Not to be dissuaded, Nicaragua signed another concession in 1898. The new concession paralleled the Menocal Contract, but with $500,000 up front, in addition to the $150,000 already paid under the previous contract. In addition, Nicaragua's share in the canal was increased to 8 percent.[70] The new company, however, failed to start work on the project. Neither private financing nor a new agreement with Costa Rica was forthcoming.

THE STRATEGIC IMPERATIVE

As with the Spanish conquest of Perú and the American conquest of California, a major geopolitical event would prove key to making an isthmian project a reality. In this case, it was the United States' two-front war with Spain, which convinced many in the American government that a better way was needed to move warships between the Atlantic and Pacific oceans. The stormy sixty-eight-day voyage in 1898 of the American battleship *Oregon* from San Francisco to Key West symbolized American concerns. Although it is not clear that the *Oregon* was ever in serious danger—commercial steamships routinely navigated the route—the ship had a rather exciting voyage that captivated the public. American newspaper readers nervously awaited any scrap of information on her whereabouts during the two-month journey.[71] Her commander later recounted, "Just after we entered the Straits, a violent gale struck us. The thick, hurrying scud obscured the precipitous rockbound shores, and with night coming on, it seemed inadvisable to proceed. . . . That forenoon a heavy snowstorm chased us through the narrowest reaches of the Straits, which in some places are scarcely more than a mile in width. With sheer cliffs on either hand and fathomless depths below, there could be no pause or hesitation in this exciting race, and I think there was no man on board that did not feel the thrill of it."[72]

Lyman Cooley, the former chief engineer of the newly built Chicago Sanitary and Ship Canal, thought that the military benefits of an isthmian canal would be cheap even with a $100 million price tag. "As a bluff, if nothing more, the Nicaragua Canal in operation today would be worth $100,000,000 to this Government. . . . Suppose, at the least, it costs $54,000,000 to construct this canal, or at the most $133,000,000, what would that amount to in view of the fact that at the present moment every city on the Pacific coast could be destroyed by a hostile fleet before any battleship of ours could even round Cape Horn? When we could reach the ruins of San Francisco the enemy would be at Hawaii."[73]

The Spanish-American War also provided a window of opportunity for the United States to renegotiate the Clayton-Bulwer Treaty. Shortly after the war's end, Secretary of State John Hay broached the subject with the British. Within a month, Hay and Julian Pauncefote, the British ambassador, had put together a draft of a new treaty. It allowed the U.S. government to construct and operate a transoceanic canal in Central America, as long as it promised to keep the canal open to commercial use by all countries without discrimination.[74]

By 1899, the McKinley administration and Congress both turned their attention to planning an isthmian canal. Democratic senator John Morgan of Alabama sponsored a bill to support a canal through Nicaragua. Coincidentally, Morgan owned shares of the bankrupt Maritime Canal Company, which would be compensated for the work it had already accomplished.[75] (Equally coincidentally, Morgan introduced several bills to legalize lynching and deport black Americans to tropical countries.)[76]

On the opposite side of the political aisle, a lawyer and lobbyist for the New Panama Canal Company, the Brooklyn-born William Cromwell, donated $60,000 ($1.3 million in 2009 dollars, using the GDP deflator) to the Republican Party on his company's behalf. Senate Republicans filibustered Morgan's bill, and a compromise appropriated $1 million—$22.9 million in 2009 dollars—to fund the Isthmian Canal Commission, charged with determining the best route for a canal.[77]

RETURN TO PANAMA

The first year of the new century, 1901, saw the opening of the Pan-American Exposition in Buffalo, New York. The official logo of the exposition depicted two women as the personification of the Americas—blonde North America and brunette South America—holding hands in friendship across the two oceans. Famous in its time, it appeared on all manner of souvenir items from the exposition. (See figure 3.1.) A century later, the essayist Sarah Vowell commented about the logo: "Miss South America smiles, unaware that two years later, the U.S. Navy would swoop in and hack her arm off at the elbow so that cargo ships could sail through the blood of her severed stump."[78]

Vice President Theodore Roosevelt addressed the crowd at the dedication ceremony, to much applause. "We of the two Americas must be left to work out our own salvation along our own lines . . . among ourselves each nation must scrupulously regard the rights and interests of the others, so that instead of any one of us committing the criminal folly of trying to rise at the expense of our neighbors, we shall all strive upward in honest and manly brotherhood, shoulder to shoulder."[79]

Figure 3.1:   The Pan-American Exposition logo.

President McKinley was unable to make the dedication ceremony, but he did attend the Exposition. His September visit started
well.[80] Unfortunately, while attending the Exposition on September
6, an unemployed factory worker from Cleveland, Leon Czolgosz,
shot the president in the stomach.[81] On September 14, McKinley
died. Theodore Roosevelt, who had been incommunicado on a trip
in the Adirondack Mountains, quickly boarded a special chartered
train to Buffalo, where he took the presidential oath of office.[82]

McKinley's death did not slow the pace of isthmian canal efforts. The Isthmian Canal Commission filed its report on November 16, 1901, and the Senate ratified the revised Hay-Pauncefote
Treaty on December 16, 1901. The Isthmian Canal Commission
recommended the Nicaragua route. Its reasons were neither technical nor political—both of those factors pointed in Panama's direction—but rather budgetary: the New Panama Canal Company
demanded too much for its properties, an "unreasonable" $109
million. The commission estimated their worth at $40 million.
When factoring in the cost of the New Company's properties, the

commission's estimated cost for the Panama plan exceeded its Nicaraguan estimate by nearly $64 million.[83]

Philippe Bunau-Varilla spotted the opportunity to make the deal of a lifetime. Bunau-Varilla had directed excavations under de Lesseps. When the Compagnie Universelle went bankrupt, French magistrates accused him of fraud and ordered him to purchase $400,000 in shares of the New Panama Canal Company.[84] Bunau-Varilla spent most of 1900 and early 1901 in the United States, lobbying for the Panama route. His greatest accomplishment during that trip was restraining himself from slapping Senator Morgan in the face, and he sailed back to France in April.[85] The Isthmian Canal Commission's report, however, galvanized him to sail back to New York in November. He arranged a meeting with Republican senator Mark "Dollar" Hanna of Ohio, the Republican Party's chief fixer and a backer of the Panama route. In a lengthy interview, Hanna explained the political situation in detail to Bunau-Varilla. A bill to fund a Nicaraguan canal would be presented to Congress at the beginning of its next session, January 7, 1902. The New Panama Canal Company needed to drop its price quickly if it were to overtake the Nicaraguan bill in Congress.[86]

Quickly travelling to Paris, Bunau-Varilla convinced the company's new director-general, Marius Bô, to reduce its price from $109 million to $40 million. Bunau-Varilla argued that the New Company's concession from the Colombian government was slated to expire in 1904, after which its shareholders would receive nothing. On January 4, 1902, Bô cabled the Isthmian Canal Commission about the lower offer. Bô also sent official telegrams to President Roosevelt and Secretary of State Hay and publicized the offer in the press.[87]

The resulting legislative machinations in Congress were complicated, but ended with a clear victory for the Panama route. On January 9, a bill passed the House of Representatives in an overwhelming 308 to 2 vote in favor of the Nicaragua route. An amendment allowing the president to select the canal route failed with a vote of 206 to 41 against. One week later, President Roosevelt called for another meeting of the Isthmian Commission to discuss the New Company's offer. On January 18, the commission stated, "The unreasonable sum asked for the property and rights of the New Panama Canal Company when the Commission reached its former conclusion overbalanced the advantages of that route, but now that the estimates by the two routes have been nearly equalized, the Commission can form its judgment by weighing the advantages of each and determining which is the more practicable and feasible." The commission clearly concluded that the most practicable and feasible route "is that known as the Panama route."[88] On January 28, 1902, Republican senator John Spooner of Wisconsin introduced an amendment authorizing the president to purchase the assets of the New Company for $40 million—as long as a satisfactory agreement could be arranged with Colombia. [89]

THE COLOMBIAN POSITION

The turn of the century was an inauspicious time for Colombia. The destructive civil conflict later known as the War of a Thousand Days began in the fall of 1899, when Liberal generals revolted against the Conservative government. Almost a year into the conflict, Conservative factions became dissatisfied with President Manuel Antonio Sanclemente's prosecution of the war. On July 31, 1900, Vice President José Manuel Marroquín, a Conservative former university rector, placed President Sanclemente under house arrest and assumed the presidency.[90] Marroquín faced both Liberal armies and a split among the Conservatives over the conduct of the war. Worse yet, the increasingly chaotic and generalized nature of the violence had caused the coffee industry to collapse, and the country fell into hyperinflation as the government printed money to fund its war effort.

On May 9, 1901, the Isthmian Canal Commission asked the new Colombian minister to the United States, Carlos Martínez Silva, for his opinions on a draft canal agreement. The commission's draft included the permanent cession of a band around the canal ten miles across, including the cities of Colón and Panama, and the payment of a fixed rent for the use of the territory. Martínez sent the commission's note to Bogotá, urging that the Colombian government should reject the cession of either city, impose a time limit on the concession, and insist upon a percentage of the revenues rather than a fixed rent.[91] Bogotá chose not to reply.[92]

President Marroquín realized that Colombia enjoyed a good negotiating position with regard to the isthmian canal, despite his country's dire condition. First, Conservative armies had routed the Liberals a few days before he assumed power, at the battle of Palonegro on May 26, 1900. The victory did little to halt the violence, but it removed the possibility that Marroquín's government would be forcibly overthrown. Second, the French concession was scheduled to expire in 1904, after which all properties would revert to the Colombian government. If Colombia could simply delay an agreement with the United States until then, the Colombian government would receive the $40 million promised the New Company for its properties.[93] Finally, Costa Rican opposition made it unlikely that a Nicaraguan canal could be constructed without significant outlays to satisfy the government of President Rafael Yglesias, who went so far as to declare that Costa Rica would need to amend its constitution in order to allow the construction of an American canal.[94] President Marroquín's strategy, therefore, was to stall. His preferred method of stalling was to keep his representatives in Washington entirely in the dark about his preferences or intentions.

The Colombian president of course ran a risk with this Fabian strategy. The United States could intervene militarily at a time of its choosing, and Marroquín did not reckon with the new American president's legendary impatience.[95] Already in October 1901, the United States had dispatched three warships to Colombian waters, and between November 20 and December 4 U.S. Marines briefly occupied Colón and Panama City at the request of the province's governor.[96]

The House vote to approve a Nicaragua route on January 9, 1902, and Bogotá's refusal to provide any concrete instructions, finally caused Martínez to crack. "The past six months," he wrote, "have been virtual torture for me; pressed and harried day after day at various critical moments categorically the propositions of the Government of Colombia. I have had to resort to every manner of delay without compromising the outcome of the negotiations. To maintain this equilibrium, this indefinite procrastination, was no longer possible when the House of Representatives voted, almost unanimously, the bill in favor of Nicaragua. . . . In these circumstances, realizing I had not a moment to lose, I resolved to prepare a complete project of a Treaty. . . . On the very day on which I intended to present the project to the Secretary of State I received your telegram in which I was ordered to await instructions before contracting commitments."[97]

In February 1902, the Colombian government replaced an exhausted Martínez with José Vicente Concha, Marroquín's former secretary of war.[98] Concha was known in Colombia as a fair-minded intellectual, but Concha spoke no English, had little diplomatic experience, and in fact had never left Colombia before.[99] Concha was ordered to obtain the best terms possible without giving up Colombian sovereignty over the Isthmus of Panama.[100] Bogotá gave Concha few specific instructions, but it did lay out a minimum request: up-front payments of $7 million and an annual rent of $600,000, although Concha's instructions allowed him to defer rent negotiations until later.[101]

THE AMERICAN NEGOTIATIONS WITH COLOMBIA

On March 6, 1902, the Colombian government gave the United States minister to Colombia, Charles Hart, a list of the considerations under which it would be willing to discuss a treaty. Colombia was to be sovereign over the isthmus. The zone for the canal was to be policed by Colombian nationals paid for by the United States. A percentage of the tolls was to be given to the Colombian government at rates better than or equal to the terms provided by the Wyse Concession. Hart immediately cabled the State Department with this information, but Hart's message was delayed for eleven days by interruptions in the telegraph line.[102]

On March 13, 1902, after weeks of testimony, the Senate Committee on Interoceanic Canals reported favorably on the pro-Nicaragua bill and unfavorably on the pro-Panama Spooner amendment. Bogotá believed that American intentions to build in Nicaragua were hollow, and cabled Concha on March 17. "We ought not to be hurried by threats, intrigues; the Panama Canal will be made in any case, the Nicaraguan way being more difficult and costly."[103] On the same day, Hart's message arrived in Washington.[104]

On March 18, Secretary of State Hay cabled back to Hart, stating that the Colombian terms were "entirely inadmissible."[105] On March 22, Philippe Bunau-Varilla met with Concha in Washington, to inform him what he considered the maximum indemnity to Colombia should be: a $10 million cash payment, plus the current annuity paid by the Panama Railroad to the Colombian government, $250,000. Bunau-Varilla calculated the net present value of the indemnity for Concha: $14 million.[106] (The exact discount rate or time horizon Bunau-Varilla employed is not known; however, we calculate an extremely similar number later in this chapter.)

On March 24, the Colombian foreign minister mailed Concha the considerations under which the Colombian government would be willing to discuss a treaty. These included the same provisions given to Hart: complete Colombian sovereignty, a percentage of the gross revenues, and a subsidy from the United States for the costs of policing the canal.[107] Concha, however, did not receive Bogotá's instructions until April 26, eight days after Hay and Concha came to a tentative agreement.

On April 18, after a month of intense negotiations with Secretary of State Hay and the New Panama Canal Company's lawyer, William Cromwell, Concha agreed on the terms of what would be called the Hay-Concha Memorandum. The Hay-Concha Memorandum differed at several key points from the foreign minister's instructions. The United States kept the power to police the Canal

Zone, while Colombia renounced its claim to any share of the canal tolls and its right to tax any activity involved with the canal. Article 35 of the Bidlack-Mallarino Treaty remained in full effect, limiting Colombian sovereignty and providing diplomatic justification for continuing American military interventions on the isthmus. Colombia would receive $7 million up front, with a fixed rent to be determined within fourteen years of the signing of an agreement.

When Concha received Bogotá's instructions on April 26, he immediately realized how thoroughly he had been played by both sides. Colombia clearly wanted no agreement at all before the New Company's concession expired in 1904, whereas the United States had no intention of deviating from its initial terms. Concha immediately tendered his resignation, but Bogotá instructed him to remain at his post.[108]

Meanwhile, the debate in the U.S. Senate over the canal route continued through June. In May, Mount Pelée erupted on Martinique, killing over twenty-five thousand people.[109] Bunau-Varilla used this opportunity to send each senator a Nicaraguan stamp depicting a large smoking volcano overlooking an active port.[110] Meanwhile, Senator Hanna marshaled the diplomatic and engineering evidence in favor of a Panama route. A motion was proposed on June 19 to substitute the minority report in favor of Panama for the majority report in favor of Nicaragua. It passed, 42 to 34, with 12 abstentions. The Spooner Act then passed the Senate with a vote of 67 to 6.[111] President Roosevelt, for his part, showed few signs of respecting either Colombian sovereignty or its offered terms. "Why cannot we buy the Panama isthmus outright instead of leasing it from Colombia?" Roosevelt wondered to Secretary of State Hay on August 21. "It seems to me to be a good thing. I think they would change their constitution if we offered enough."[112]

On September 17, 1902, in response to unrest on the isthmus, the United States sent U.S. Marines to guard all trains crossing Panama and stationed warships off both terminals. Under increasing pressure to concede the Americans' points, Concha stormed out of the negotiations. "In no case," wrote Concha, "for any human reason, will I sign any treaty with the government of the United States while its troops continue to occupy Colombian territory against every principle of justice and in violation of a public promise."[113] In Bogotá, Foreign Minister Felipe Fermín assured the United States that Concha was "subject to great nervous excitement."[114]

Embittered, ostracized by his fellow diplomats, and given contradictory instructions from Bogotá, Concha left Washington on November 28.[115] After his departure, Cromwell, who had become something of a confidant to Concha during their April meetings, joked to Secretary of State Hay that Concha "was taken aboard the ship in a straitjacket."[116] Concha would later write, "Colombia stands mutilated today through crime and force by a foreign government that renounced its tradition of honor in order to play the role of pirate."[117]

The Colombian secretary of the legation, Tomás Herrán, was left in charge of the negotiations. Herrán, the son of the former Colombian president, had accompanied his father during his successful lobbying of the U.S. Senate regarding the Bidlack-Mallarino Treaty, and later attended Georgetown University. Unfortunately, he was unfamiliar with the previous negotiations and under severe pressure from both Bogotá and Washington.[118] In short, he was out of his league. After several high-pressure meetings with Secretary of State Hay and the New Panama Canal Company's lawyer Cromwell, Herrán received a cable from his government on January 16, 1903, insisting that he obtain a final offer from Secretary Hay as soon as possible. On January 21, Herrán received the expected ultimatum from Hay, which implied that Herrán's refusal to sign on American terms would cause the Americans to build the canal in Nicaragua instead. The following day, Herrán signed a treaty in Hay's home, with Cromwell attending. As a keepsake, Hay gave Cromwell the pen used to sign the treaty.[119]

Unsurprisingly, the Hay-Herrán Treaty granted essentially all of the Americans' demands. In fact, Cromwell had helped write the new agreement. The United States received a six-mile zone within which it could deploy troops with Colombia's consent, construct a canal, and control public health. Colombia also renounced its rights to a share of the revenues under the Wyse Convention and the $250,000 annuity paid by the Panama Railroad, in return for $10 million and a new annual payment of $250,000 that would begin in 1912. In addition, the United States would pay for all water and sanitation works built in Colón and Panama City.

The treaty's terms did not go down well in Bogotá. Minister Fermín resigned on January 24, shortly after the arrival of the news of Herrán's signing.[120] Public opinion and the Bogotá press ran strongly against the treaty, as did nearly all factions not associated with Marroquín. One letter to the editor in a Colombian newspaper humorously proposed the United States simply annex Colombia to settle the competing questions of sovereignty and unequal advantage once and for all. The editor dryly responded, "There are some to whom it has occurred to seek the annexation of the United States . . . *to Colombia*. What a solution!!!"[121]

The State Department, on the other hand, believed Colombian intransigence was all about money.[122] This point of view was certainly Roosevelt's, who constructed an elaborate mythology about Colombian "blackmailers."[123] Infuriated by the Colombian senate's opposition over the treaty's legitimacy, Roosevelt instructed Secretary Hay on July 14, 1903, to "[m]ake [the U.S. response] as strong as you can. . . . Those contemptible little creatures in Bogotá ought to understand how much they are jeopardizing things and imperiling their own future."[124] On August 12, the Colombian senate rejected the treaty, despite Roosevelt's implicit threat of force and the fact that U.S. Marines had twice intervened on Panamanian soil in the past two years. Of the twenty-seven members of the Colombian senate, twenty-four voted against the treaty and two abstained. The ostensibly pro-canal Senator José Domingo de Obaldía of Panama missed the vote, later claiming to have been too ill to attend.[125]

DIPLOMACY'S END

President Roosevelt erupted at the news of the Colombian senate's refusal to ratify the treaty. "We may have to give a lesson to these jackrabbits."[126] This was not merely the knee-jerk reaction of a petulant man-child. Roosevelt had legitimate worries about the Nicaraguan route. On technical terms, it appeared far easier to finish digging the Culebra Cut in Panama than to construct dams and build much longer and (on the Pacific side) steeper—lock canals. Dredging the San Juan River looked even less feasible.[127]

To add financial injury to Roosevelt's sense of insult, the Colombian senate proposed a counteroffer in early September: $20 million for the canal concession, an additional $10 million for the rights to the Panama Railroad, an annual payment of $150,000, and a continuation of the Panama Railroad's $250,000 annual rental.[128] The counteroffer infuriated the U.S. president. On September 15, an incensed Roosevelt wrote to Hay, calling the Colombians "foolish and homicidal corruptionists."[129]

A Republican expert on international law at Columbia University, John Bassett Moore, provided a plausible-sounding legal loophole to justify an American intervention in Panama. He suggested that the Bidlack-Mallarino Treaty, which committed the United States to protect Colombian sovereignty in Panama but had been used to justify three previous interventions in Panama, made the United States the "responsible sovereign" on the isthmus.[130]

On October 9, Bunau-Varilla returned to the United States from Paris and met with President Roosevelt. He left convinced that the president would support an uprising in Panama.[131] On October 16, Bunau-Varilla met with Hay. Bunau-Varilla opined that Panama was ripe for revolution. "That is unfortunately the most probable hypothesis," Hay replied. Hay then informed Bunau-Varilla, "Orders have been given to naval forces on the Pacific to sail towards the Isthmus."[132]

Bunau-Varilla received Hay's thinly coded message. On September 23, 1903, Bunau-Varilla met with Manuel Amador, the chief physician for the Panama Railroad and a leader of the Panamanian independence movement, in room 1162 of the Waldorf-Astoria in New York. Bunau-Varilla wrote Amador a check for $100,000 in order to organize a new revolt. In return, Amador promised to appoint Bunau-Varilla the new republic's representative in Washington.[133] Bunau-Varilla informed Assistant Secretary of State Francis

Loomis that the revolution was scheduled for November 3. Roosevelt ordered gunboats to be in position when the declaration was made.[134] On November 2, the Navy Department sent the following order to American ships in Panama: "Prevent landing of any armed force with hostile intent, either government or insurgent. . . . Government forces reported approaching the Isthmus in vessels. Prevent their landing, if in your judgment this would precipitate conflict."[135]

On November 6, 1903, Panama declared its independence. After reading an official proclamation in Colón, cables went to Washington, which Secretary of State Hay acknowledged two hours later. Colombia landed four hundred soldiers at Colón, but a contingent of U.S. Marines from the *Nashville* dissuaded them from attacking rebel positions. There was one fatality: a Colombian gunboat killed a sleeping Chinese man when it fired shells at Panama City.[136] The *Nashville* was shortly followed by the *Dixie, Atlanta, Maine, Mayflower, Prairie, Boston, Marblehead, Concord,* and *Wyoming*.[137] President Theodore Roosevelt would ebulliently declare in his autobiography, "No one connected with the American government had any part in preparing, inciting, or encouraging the revolution."[138]

As promised, President Amador appointed Bunau-Varilla Panama's official agent in Washington, giving him instructions to negotiate a new canal treaty with the United States.[139] In turn, Bunau-Varilla negotiated a treaty that granted the United States every one of its demands.[140] The resulting Hay–Bunau-Varilla Treaty gave Panama none of the proceeds from the sale of the New Panama Canal Company. Nor did it permit Panama to impose any taxes or "contributions or charges of a personal character" upon the canal, its subsidiary companies including the Panama Railroad, or its employees. The United States also gained the exclusive right to apply and enforce laws within a twenty-mile-wide zone around the canal—not including Panama City and Colón—and the unilateral authority to extend the Zone to any lands that the United States might find "necessary and convenient for the construction, maintenance, operation, sanitation and protection of the said Canal or of any auxiliary canals or other works." The treaty also required Panama to pay the entire capital and operating costs "of any works of sanitation, such as the collection and disposition of sewage and the distribution of water in the said cities of Panama and Colón." In other words, the United States would bring modern sanitation to Panama, but unlike the offer made to the Colombians, the Panamanians would have to pay for it.

In return for all this, the United States gave Panama an up-front payment of $10 million. The treaty also cancelled the $250,000 annual rent previously paid by the Panama Railroad. The United States would begin paying a new $250,000 annuity in 1913.[141] These were, in fact, the same terms that Concha angrily rejected in 1902.

Panama was not to receive most of the up-front payment. The United States turned over the $10 million to J. P. Morgan, which invested it on Panama's behalf. J. P. Morgan placed $6 million in Manhattan real estate and $2.8 million in various New York banks.[142] This became the basis for Panama's so-called Constitutional Fund, which remained active until 1950.[143] (It is strange to consider that had the fund not been liquidated, Panama might today own much of New York City.)

Unsurprisingly, the Panamanian delegation to the United States disavowed this new treaty—delegation member Federico Boyd allegedly struck Bunau-Varilla across the face at the news of the agreement. When the terms of Bunau-Varilla's treaty reached Amador in Panama City, Amador told Bunau-Varilla that the rest of the provisional government would need to be consulted before the treaty could be ratified. Bunau-Varilla replied to Amador that the United States would pull out its troops and come to terms with Colombia if Panama City did not ratify. In turn, Secretary of State Hay threatened "grave consequences" if Panama failed to ratify the treaty immediately. The Panamanians quickly ratified the new treaty, despite the lack of a Spanish translation.[144] When the Panamanians wrote a constitution for their new republic the following year (1904), the United States insisted upon Article 136, which stated that "the government of the United States of America may intervene . . . to re-establish public tranquility and constitutional order."

THE WAGES OF FORCE

The United States clearly used its military leverage—force and threats of force—in its negotiations with Panama. A skeptical reader might argue that it is unclear whether American threats and force resulted in Panama getting a worse deal. Fortunately, *six* comparable deals regarding an isthmian canal had been on the table at various times before the Americans intervened to secure Panama's independence. The terms of those counterfactual deals can be evaluated and compared to the historical outcome.

The first deal is the 1878 Wyse Concession negotiated with the French, which involved neither military force nor the threat of force. The second is the Hay-Herrán Treaty, signed by the United States but rejected by the Colombian senate. Unlike the Wyse Concession, the Hay-Herrán Treaty involved the threat of military intervention: the United States sent its marines to occupy the Panama Railroad when Colombia's representative at the treaty talks refused to accept the U.S. terms. The Colombian government overwhelmingly rejected the Hay-Herrán Treaty, in spite of the American intervention and the possibility that the canal might be built in Nicaragua instead. Minister Concha negotiated a third deal with the United States, although it is not clear if the Colombian government would have accepted its terms. In addition, the Colombian government made a concrete counteroffer to the United States, the terms of which we evaluate as a fourth deal. These voluntary agreements incorporated the possibility that an isthmian canal could be constructed along the Nicaragua route instead of across Panama, albeit at substantially higher cost.

In addition to the Colombian agreements, Americans also negotiated two agreements with Nicaragua to construct an isthmian canal, neither of which involved military force or the threat of force, and both of which the Nicaraguan government accepted.

The first was the 1884 Frelinghuysen-Zavala Treaty. That treaty gave the United States freedom from Nicaraguan taxes or duties within a 2½-mile-wide zone, including control over all port facilities, sanitary works, railroads, and telegraph lines. The treaty, however, granted the Nicaraguan government one-third of the revenue from the canal (including railway, telegraph, and other ancillary operations) after expenditures on "maintenance and improvement."[145] Exercising his constitutional privilege, President Grover Cleveland chose not to submit this treaty to the United States Senate.[146]

The second was the 1898 revision to the Menocal Contract of 1887. Under the Menocal Contract, named for the Cuban-American who negotiated the agreement, the private Maritime Canal Company would construct and operate an interoceanic canal along the San Juan River. The Nicaraguan government agreed to exempt the company from all taxes and tariffs during construction and to use its powers of eminent domain to acquire property along the route. In return, Nicaragua would receive a 6 percent share of "all shares, bonds, certificates, or other securities" issued to finance the construction of the canal and $150,000 in up-front payments.[147] In 1898 Nicaragua renegotiated the contract to provide an additional $500,000 in up-front payments, and Nicaragua's share in the proposed project was upped to 8 percent. In addition, the renegotiated contract granted the Costa Rican government $150,000 up front and a 1.5 percent share in the canal project.[148] These agreements incorporated the possibility that the Panama route was a viable competing route for the canal.

THE GOOD, THE BAD, AND THE UGLY

The United States leveraged its military force into Panamanian acceptance of the Hay–Bunau-Varilla Treaty. But what, if anything, did the United States gain from its leverage? The Hay–Bunau-Varilla Treaty can be compared to the aforementioned six historical alternatives, ranging from the most generous to the United States

TABLE 3-4

Alternate Isthmian Canal Agreements

	HBV (actual)	Hay–Herrán	Concha proposal	Menocal Contract	Wyse Concession	Colombian Senate offer	Frelinghuysen-Zavala
Initial payment to host country	$10 million	$10 million	$7 million	$800,000	Zero	$20 million	zero
Payment to host country for French assets	Zero	Zero	Zero	Not applicable	Zero	$10 million	Not applicable
Continues rent from Panama RR?	No	No	Yes	Not applicable	Yes	Yes	Not applicable
Annual payments to host country: First 9 years	Zero	Zero	$600,000	9.5% of profits	5% of revenues	$150,000	33% of profits
Next 16 years	$250,000	$250,000	$600,000	9.5% of profits	5% of revenues	$150,000	33% of profits
Next 25 years	$250,000	$250,000	$600,000	9.5% of profits	6% of revenues	$150,000	33% of profits
Next 25 years	$250,000	$250,000	$600,000	9.5% of profits	7% of revenues	$150,000	33% of profits
Final 24 years	$250,000	$250,000	$600,000	9.5% of profits	8% of revenues	$150,000	33% of profits
Reversion to host country?	Never	After 99 years	After 99 years	After 99 years	After 99 years	After 99 years	Never
Responsibility for sanitary works?	Host country	U.S.	U.S.	U.S.	U.S.	U.S.	U.S.

Source: Hay–Bunau-Varilla, Hay–Herrán, Frelinghuysen-Zavala, and Menocal Contract from the original texts. Wyse Concession from David G. McCullough, *The Path Between the Seas* (New York: Simon and Schuster, 1977), 66–67. Concha proposal from Diego Uribe Vargas, *Los últimos derechos de Colombia en el Canal de Panamá* (Bogotá: Facultad de Derecho, Ciencias Politicas y Sociales y Empresa Editorial, Universidad Nacional de Colombia, 2003), chap. 11; and William Scoullar, The Blue Book of Panama (Panamá: Imprenta nacional, 1917), 116–17. Colombian Senate proposal from Dwight Miner, *The Fight for the Panama Route* (New York: Columbia University Press, 1940), 327–28.

(the Hay-Herrán Treaty) to the most restrictive (the Colombian senate counteroffer). Table 3.4 summarizes the key features of each proposal. The estimates in table 3.5 use the historical earnings and expenses of the Panama Canal under its American administration to calculate the NPV in 1903 of counterfactual payment flows to the host government, using the rate on high-grade ten-year U.S. corporate bonds as the discount rate. The net present value of the Hay–Bunau-Varilla Treaty turns out to be almost exactly the $14 million that was the maximum amount Bunau-Varilla told the Panamanian government it could expect from the United States.

For the purposes of valuing the reversion of the canal to its host country, table 3.5 assumes that the Americans would return the canal in good-but-unimproved condition in 2002, discounting its construction cost back to 1903. In the case of the Colombian senate counteroffer, the $10 million that the New Panama Canal Company would have paid Colombia in 1904 was subtracted from the 2002 value of the canal.

The numbers are striking. The net present value of the Hay–Bunau-Varilla Treaty is less than half the value of an agreement based on the Hay-Herrán Treaty, *to which the United States had already agreed and whose terms already incorporated a military threat.* It is barely more than a third of the NPV of agreements based on either the Concha proposal or the Wyse Concession. Even without taking into account the value of the canal's reversion to the owner of the isthmus, the Hay-Herrán Treaty would have offered benefits worth 33 percent more than what Panama actually received, while an agreement based on the Wyse Concession would have offered 81 percent more, the Concha proposal 77 percent more, and the senate counteroffer 203 percent more. Contracts based on the two Nicaraguan agreements, also without including the value of the canal reversion, would have offered 79 percent or 122 percent more than Panama in fact received, even without considering the value of the 2002 reversion.

How much did the United States benefit from its military leverage? The benefit to the United States is the difference between

TABLE 3-5

NPV in 1903 of Alternate Isthmian Canal Agreements

	Initial payment	NPV of income stream	NPV of canal reversion	NPV of Panama Railroad	Value of sanitary works	TOTAL
Hay–Bunau-Varilla	$10.0 m	$4.2 m	—	—	—	$14.2 m
Hay–Herrán	$10.0 m	$4.1 m	$14.3 m	—	$4.8 m	$33.2 m
Concha proposal	$7.0 m	$7.7 m	$14.3 m	$5.6 m	$4.8 m	$39.4 m
Menocal Contract	$0.8 m	$14.3 m	$14.3 m	$5.6 m	$4.8 m	$39.8 m
Wyse Concession	—	$20.2 m	$14.3 m	$5.6 m	—	$40.1 m
Senate offer	$30.0 m	$2.8 m	$14.1 m	$ 5.6 m	$4.8 m	$57.3 m
Frelinghuysen-Zavala	—	$68.8 m	—	—	$4.8 m	$73.6 m

Source: Hay–Bunau-Varilla, Hay–Herrán, Frelinghuysen-Zavala, and Menocal Contract from the original texts. Wyse Concession from David McCullough, *The Path Between the Seas* (New York: Simon and Schuster, 1977), 66–67. Concha proposal from Diego Uribe Vargas, *Los últimos derechos de Colombia en el Canal de Panama* (Bogotá: Facultad de Derecho, Ciencias Políticas y Sociales y Empresa Editorial, Universidad Nacional de Colombia, 2003), chap. 11; and *Libro Azul*, 116–17. Colombian Senate proposal from Dwight Miner, *The Fight for the Panama Route* (New York: Columbia University Press, 1940), 327–28.

TABLE 3.6
Cost Difference to U.S. of Various Counterfactual Agreements Relative to Hay–Bunau-Varilla

Counterfactual	% of U.S. GDP	2009 dollar equivalent, billions	% of canal construction cost	% of estimated cost	% of high estimate of Panama's GDP	% of low estimate of Panama's GDP
Hay-Herrán	0.07	10.3	4.3	13.2	49	117
Concha proposal	0.10	13.7	5.7	17.5	65	155
Menocal Contract	0.10	13.9	5.8	17.7	66	157
Wyse Concession	0.10	14.1	5.8	17.9	67	159
Senate offer	0.17	23.4	9.7	29.9	111	265
Frelinghuysen-Zavala	0.23	32.3	13.4	41.3	153	366

Source: See table 3.5. Panamanian GDP in 1903 was estimated in two ways. The first method took 1946, the first year for which there are reliable GDP estimates, and assumed that real per capita GDP in 1903 was exactly the same. That is to say, it assumed no intensive growth in Panama over the entire forty-three-year period. The nominal GDP per capita in 1946 was then deflated using an index of import prices and multiplied by Panama's 1903 population. The low estimate regressed a time series of Central American GDP from Victor Bulmer-Thomas against imports of capital goods, exports, and government revenues. Panama's 1909 GDP was then estimated using the coefficients from the Central American regression. The 1903 GDP was then estimated assuming 2 percent per capita growth in 1903–9.

the amount the United States paid to Panama under the Hay–Bunau-Varilla Treaty and the amounts that the United States would have paid under a freely negotiated agreement. As a percentage of American GDP, the benefits were *relatively* small—the equivalent of $10.3 billion to $32.3 billion in 2009. (See table 3.6.) As a percentage of the actual ex post cost of canal construction, they were substantially higher. As a percentage of the ex ante estimated cost of the canal, they were higher still, and as a percentage of Panamanian GDP, the estimates bordered on astronomical. For example, relative to the agreement Colombia negotiated with the French in 1878, American coercive diplomacy under Theodore Roosevelt extracted as much as *1.6 times* Panama's estimated annual GDP.

In fact, table 3.6 significantly underestimates the value of the isthmus. It was American strategic policy to keep the canal tolls roughly revenue neutral, charging tolls just high enough to cover the canal's costs and the operating expenses of the Canal Zone government. In fact, the United States would not raise canal tolls until 1974. With a more aggressive toll policy, the net revenue of the Panama Canal would have been substantially higher. A privately operated canal, or one managed by a joint commission, would have had every incentive to maximize profits, or at least maximize them more than the United States actually did. Thus, under the Wyse Concession, the Frelinghuysen-Zavala Treaty, and the Menocal Contract, the operator of the canal would have almost certainly charged higher transit rates than the U.S. government chose to charge, and the revenue stream enjoyed by the Panamanian government would have been commensurately higher.

BIRTH OF A ZONE

In 1915, Roosevelt looked back on his creation of Panama and the Panama Canal with satisfaction. It would be an understatement to call him unrepentant. "To talk of Colombia as a responsible power to be dealt with as we would deal with Holland or Belgium or Switzerland or Denmark is a mere absurdity. The analogy is with a group of Sicilian or Calabrian bandits; with Villa and Carranza at this moment. You could no more make an agreement with the Colombian rulers than you could nail currant jelly to a wall—and the failure to nail currant jelly to a wall is not due to the nail; it is due to the currant jelly. I did my best to get them to act straight. Then I determined that I would do what ought to be done without regard to them."[149]

Roosevelt's words are a sharp reminder that the international norms of the period were strongly hierarchical. "The people of Panama were a unit in desiring the Canal and in wishing to overthrow the rule of Colombia. If they had not revolted, I should have recommended Congress to take possession of the Isthmus by force of arms. . . . When they revolted, I promptly used the Navy to prevent the bandits, who had tried to hold us up, from spending months of futile bloodshed in conquering or endeavoring to conquer the Isthmus, to the lasting damage of the Isthmus, of us, and of the world. I did not consult Hay, or Root, or anyone else as to what I did, because a council of war does not fight; and I intended to do the job once for all."[150] Offering financially fair terms to a tertiary power like Panama, or even terms consistent with previous offers, was not a policy priority for Roosevelt.

As pugnacious as Roosevelt's actions were in Panama, they did not represent the maximally imperialist course of action for the United States. Roosevelt's brief military intervention in favor of a minor Colombian separatist movement pales in comparison to the 1898 annexation of Hawaii, Puerto Rico, and the Philippines. Why didn't the Roosevelt administration use the Panamanian rebellion as a pretext for annexation? Three reasons immediately come to mind.

First, the domestic political climate in the aftermath of the 1898–1902 Philippine War was extremely unfavorable with regard to further formal colonization. That conflict created a great deal of domestic opposition, despite being fought by a small volunteer army; the close-run 1900 presidential campaign was fought almost entirely on the issue of the war. The legacy of the war was very much alive in 1903—in fact, American soldiers were still involved in combat operations in the Muslim territories of the island of

Mindanao. It would have been politically difficult for Roosevelt to push annexation through Congress in the face of any amount of active Panamanian opposition.

Second, by 1903 it had already proved impossible to keep Puerto Rico outside the American tariff wall, and pressures to extend the custom union to the Philippines were growing. (Congress would in fact bring the Philippines inside the U.S. tariff wall in 1909 and create a full customs union in 1912.) Annexing Panama would have provoked opposition from congressional districts that produced products with which Panamanian producers could have potentially competed: notably, sugar and cattle. The same domestic political calculations that prevented Cuba's annexation would have made Panama's annexation difficult, to say the least. The fiscal cost of administering Panama as a formal territory would not have been particularly great, but the domestic political cost would have been quite large.

Third, and most importantly, direct annexation by the United States would have violated the country's treaty agreements with Great Britain. By 1903, the United States was powerful enough to pay the costs of violating a treaty with Britain, but there would still have been a cost to pay. Woodrow Wilson later balked at paying that cost when Britain protested something as minor as America's proposed Panama Canal toll policy; it is unlikely that even as nationalist a figure as Theodore Roosevelt would have confronted the United Kingdom over something as serious as the annexation of Panama.

President Roosevelt ultimately figured out a way for the United States to enjoy most of the benefits of annexation without violating treaty agreements with Great Britain. The establishment of the Canal Zone effectively cut off the Panamanian economy from most of the possible benefits that could flow from the creation of an interoceanic waterway on its territory. Article 136 gave the United States a pretext to intervene should events in Panama threaten the sanctity and separation of the Zone. More importantly, Article 136 also ensured that no other power would be able to claim a pretext to intervene without asking Washington first. Should any other government intervene on the isthmus without requesting that the United States handle the issue, no matter how justified the reason, Washington would have no need to guess its intention. It could safely assume that the intent was to threaten the Canal Zone. Moreover, should Washington choose to intervene itself, it would gain *some* additional legitimacy among the Panamanian population by being able to claim *domestic* constitutional justification. There was, therefore, no reason to risk a confrontation with the sole global superpower of the first decade of the twentieth century.

Rightly or wrongly, an isthmian canal became a political imperative once the United States annexed the Philippines in 1898. Private attempts to build isthmian canals in Panama and Nicaragua failed, ultimately, because private investors were not willing to undertake large-scale and prolonged efforts in an unpredictable foreign environment without a government guarantee. The United States, through the actions of Theodore Roosevelt, provided that guarantee. The American politicians, of course, who provided the needed guarantee to the canal project did not do so in order to benefit the world or the isthmus. Rather, it was an American plan, made for American interests, and any benefits to the larger world were for the most part incidental. A frustrated President Roosevelt used the military and financial power of the United States to obtain a better deal *for the United States*, not the world. Had Roosevelt been concerned with the world, he could have waited until 1904 to negotiate with Colombia.

Does imperialism pay? The American interventions that led to the creation of the Panama Canal certainly did. The dividends gained by the United States by its actions in Panama were at least equal to the additional rents Panama would have gained under a deal similar to the Wyse Concession over the smaller rents it received under the terms of the Hay–Bunau-Varilla Treaty. In fact, American willingness to use military force produced even larger gains for the United States beyond the strictly monetary terms of the treaty, since a price-discriminating canal operator could have captured far more revenue than the United States could have captured operating the canal as a revenue-neutral utility. To sum up, in the particular case of the Panama Canal, it seems that not only did imperialism pay, but it appears to have paid quite well.

FOUR

DIGGING THE DITCH

The great bit of work of my administration, and from
the material and constructive standpoint one of the
greatest bits of work that the twentieth century will
see, is the Isthmian Canal.

—President Theodore Roosevelt

THE CONSTRUCTION OF THE PANAMA CANAL WAS A VERY LARGE
project in a very small economy. It created a management night-
mare. It ran significantly over budget by any standard. It generated
interest groups that captured canal policies to their own ends. It
magnified the sins of the time: the American administration imported a Jim Crow system of racial discrimination during its construction where none had previously existed, and it locked Panamanian firms and workers out of the construction boom. In one
very disturbing episode, the American administration even engineered the removal of a sitting Panamanian president because of
his race.

Despite this, the Panama Canal represented two great gains for
Panama. The first was the canal itself. The Panama Canal may have
come in behind schedule and over budget, and Panama may have
enjoyed few of its direct benefits for more than a half century, but
the canal itself was still an engineering marvel that revolution-
ized maritime commerce. The second was the American effort to
eliminate malaria and yellow fever in the Canal Zone. The American military epidemiologist William Gorgas ran the single largest

tropical public health effort in history until that date so that the labor force building the Panama Canal would not be decimated by disease, as it had during the private French attempt.

In addition, the Panama Canal project catalyzed the development of the West Indian island of Barbados. Barbados provided most of the labor to build the Panama Canal. Remittances sent back by Barbadian labor on the canal increased living standards on the island, fueling the growth of a small middle class and the financial system, while emigration to Panama raised Barbadian nominal wages by a quarter. Today Barbados is one of the richest countries in the Western Hemisphere, and ranks among the industrialized nations in terms of human development. The roots of this accomplishment date back to the island's role in the construction of the Panama Canal.

THE MANY COSTS OF THE PANAMA CANAL

The American effort to build the Panama Canal began in 1904. The first ship sailed through the canal in 1914, ten years and $326 million later—a considerable increase over the $144 million originally planned.[1] In fact, the canal would not be fully open to commercial traffic for another six years. Landslides shut it down for most of 1915 and 1916, and then again briefly in 1917 and 1920.[2] Strikes hit the canal in 1916 and 1917. World War I practically closed it to commercial traffic, and work continued on clearing dangerous hills, fixing locks, and finishing all the ancillary construction required by the canal. The Panama Canal finally opened to civilian traffic on July 12, 1920, after an additional six years and $53 million.[3]

By the time all was said and done, the construction of the Panama Canal cost 2.0 times its initial estimate, after adjusting for inflation. The overruns exceeded those on the Massachusetts Turnpike (1.1), the Hoover Dam (1.1), the Erie Canal (1.5), the Bay Area Rapid Transport system (1.6), and the Washington Metro (1.8), although the Panama Canal's construction overruns do compare favorably to the Miami Metrorail (2.1), Boston's infamous Big Dig (2.9), and the Brooklyn-Queens Expressway (5.1).[4]

Obviously, the United States did not set out to build the Panama Canal a decade late and double over budget. The Americans hoped that their $40 million purchase of the New Panama Canal Company's assets in Panama would greatly speed construction. Sadly, that did not turn out to be the case. The French had excavated seventy-eight million cubic yards, but most of those excavations had been designed for a sea-level canal and proved useless for the American effort. (In fact, most of the French excavations sank below Lake Gatún when the Americans dammed the Chagres River.) The Panama Railroad proved to be in such bad condition that the Americans needed to rebuild it twice: once to handle the initial excavations, and then again when Lake Gatún drowned much of the original route. The New Company owned most of the city of Colón, but its buildings were so dilapidated and disease-ridden that the Americans built a practically all-new town, Cristóbal, across Limón Bay. About the only substantial savings that the Americans received from their purchase of the French assets were some old dredges that could be repaired or reconstructed for $500,000 less than it would have cost to purchase new equipment.[5]

MANAGEMENT MISSTEPS

There are three diseases in Panama . . . yellow fever, malaria, and cold feet.

—*John Stevens*

The first few years of construction of the Panama Canal proved to be a management foul-up of the first order. The Isthmian Canal Commission tried to supervise construction from Washington. This would have been a bad idea with the communications technology of the first decade of the twenty-first century; it was an unmitigated disaster with the communications available in the first decade of the twentieth. Shipments arrived late, or piled up on docks with no means to unload them.[6] By 1905 the *New York Times* was complaining that the Isthmian Canal Commission was on track to have spent $66 million by the end of the year, with "no dirt flying."[7] In response, Theodore Roosevelt sacked the first commission. The replacement commissioners selected a civilian railroad engineer from Maine, John Stevens, to go to Panama to supervise the construction of the canal. The same Brooklyn lobbyist who had greased Congress's wheels in approving the Panama route for the canal, William Cromwell, convinced Stevens to take the job. Stevens accepted on condition that he "was not to be hampered or handicapped by anyone, high or low."[8]

Stevens arrived in Panama in early 1905. He approached the construction of the canal more systematically than the early, almost random efforts. His first task was to replace railroad "lines which, by the utmost stretch of the imagination, could not be termed railroad tracks."[9] With his typical style, he wrote, "The only claim for good work . . . was that there had been no collisions for some time. A collision has its good points as well as its bad ones—it indicates that there is something moving."[10] Unfortunately, Stevens had to deal with shifting design plans back in Washington. A board convened by President Roosevelt on June 24, 1905, came back with recommendations for four different lock-canal designs and one sea-level plan. After several months of squabbling, it decided on a lock-canal plan on February 19, 1906, which Congress approved on June 29.[11]

Political infighting continued on the new Isthmian Canal Commission. Theodore Roosevelt travelled to Panama in November 1906—not coincidentally right before the midterm elections and during the worst part of Panama's rainy season—returning convinced that it was time to junk the multiple-member commission and put one person in charge.[12] The results of the closed bidding for construction contracts only reinforced that decision: the commission invited bids on the entire project on October 9, 1906—and rejected all four bids in January 1907.[13] Stevens resigned on April 1, 1907, amid rumors of conflict.[14]

Roosevelt replaced Stevens with Colonel George Washington Goethals.[15] Goethals was a cold, withdrawn man of many prejudices, including ones both common and uncommon for the time.

He disdained blacks and loathed obese people, with the exception of William Howard Taft, who was "the only *clean* fat man he had ever known."[16] Goethals moved to the Canal Zone and required the other members of the Isthmian Canal Commission to follow him. He definitively rejected the government's plan to contract construction to the private sector. He established clear chains of command and authority, delegating authority whenever possible but personally investigating and inspecting all aspects of the construction effort. At the same time, however, he eschewed all military overtones, banning salutes and military uniforms, in order to keep up relations with his overwhelmingly civilian professional workforce.[17]

Goethals quickly moved to neuter the Isthmian Canal Commission. "The whole definition of a board is applicable to the Commission, namely, it is long, narrow, and wooden," said Goethals.[18] Goethals persuaded Roosevelt to sign an executive order in January 1908 that gave him sweeping authority over the entire canal project, including the right to fire commission members. Secretary of War William Howard Taft had doubts about the legality of granting the chief engineer control over the commission, which was technically governed by civil service rules and had been created by an act of Congress.[19] "That order is not in accordance with the law on the subject," he told Roosevelt. "Damn the law, I want the canal," replied the president.[20]

Goethals continued to fight to cement his control over the project. The first challenge came from the head of the Department of Civil Administration, Maurice Thatcher, who proposed that the U.S. government create an elected civil government in the Panama Canal Zone, with the aim of promoting permanent settlement. "We must have courts . . . I would like to see an American civil population here," Thatcher told Congress. "These Americans would come here to live, make their homes here, and they would prefer to live under the dominion of the American government, under American laws."[21]

Thatcher's plan to create civil government in the Canal Zone would have had dramatic consequences for the future. The Zone would have accrued a truly permanent population, possibly in large numbers, who would have been able to own private property, enjoy the jurisdiction of American courts, and vote for their own elected government. Under such circumstances, it is difficult to imagine the U.S. Congress *ever* returning the Canal Zone to Panama, with far-reaching implications for Panamanian economic development and U.S. relations with Latin America.

Goethals mobilized a strong lobbying effort to kill the proposal to give the Canal Zone a civil government. "Introduce the franchise, and we'd go to pieces," he wrote. His lawyer, Judge Frank Feuille, wrote that the Zone should be "like a large corporate enterprise," for the "management of a great public work, and not the government of a local republic." Taft, now president, backed Goethals. The Panama Canal Act of 1912 cemented Goethals's control over all aspects of the canal enterprise, at least until the end of construction, when the Isthmian Canal Commission would shut down. In the interim, the act effectively abolished private ownership of land inside the U.S. Canal Zone.[22] The Panama Canal Act's stipulations would far outlast the end of construction—in fact, they would last until the Republic of Panama took back jurisdiction over the Canal Zone.

A MAN, A PLAN, A CANAL

With his new congressional authority in hand, Goethals successfully carried out the new plan for a lock canal, although delays and cost overruns would still beset the project. The new plan involved the creation of an artificial lake eighty-five feet above sea level, filled by damming the Chagres River with two parallel stone walls filled with earth and clay. The dam slipped on three occasions and attracted some controversy; its construction, however, proceeded mostly on schedule.

The need to build lock canals on each end of the Panama Canal, however, caused delays and cost overruns. On both sides, three locks lifted ships eighty-five feet. Ships going up would enter the locks, which would then be filled with water to lift the ship. When the water level on both sides of the lock reached the desired level, the ship would then move forward into the next lock. Roughly 10 million cubic yards of rock needed to be excavated to make room for the locks; the structures then required an additional 4 million cubic yards of concrete to build. Government employees excavated the locks, but private contractors built the 59,000 ton steel gates the locks required. The gates rapidly fell behind schedule, due to a combination of "strikes, shipwrecks, interference by the Commission, and other 'acts of God.'"[23]

The new plan also called for an artificial channel called the Culebra Cut—also known as the Gaillard Cut, after the Army Corps of Engineers major who supervised its construction—which sliced southeast from Lake Gatún to a set of three locks, to take ships down to the Pacific. The Cut proved to be one of the most challenging parts of the project. One hundred and two Milwaukee-built steam shovels moved 400 to 600 cubic yards of dirt per hour, working sixty machine-hours per week.[24] Landslides slowed the work. For every 5 cubic yards of dirt that the Americans extracted, another yard slid back in from the hills lining the route. When all was said and done, the Americans excavated 110 million cubic yards to build the Cut, of which 25 million had been the result of landslides.[25] Recurring landslides along the Cut would keep the Panama Canal from fully opening to commercial traffic until 1920. Between the ostensible "opening" of the canal in 1914 and the actual opening in 1920, the Americans spent an additional $52.6 million on construction.[26] (See table 4.1.)

In order to be able to ship out the vast amounts of dirt generated by the construction of the Panama Canal, the Panama Railroad was rehabilitated, expanded, and in some places, entirely reconstructed. The Isthmian Canal Commission repaired the original line and double-tracked it along its length. Since Lake Gatún would cover most of the original line's route, however, an entirely new rail line needed to be constructed. The new line was built between May 1907 and May 25, 1912.[27] Reequipping the line added $4.2 million to the construction cost; relocating it cost an

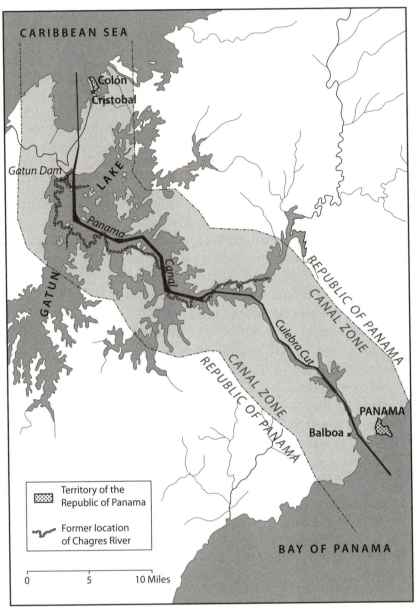

Map 4.1: The Panama Canal at the beginning of 1914. Later that year, the United States would cede to Panama a small corridor running northeast from Panama City.

additional $7.8 million. In addition, the U.S. government found itself on the hook for paying off $2.3 million of Panama Railroad bonds, for a total additional cost of $10.1 million—$168 million in 2009 dollars.[28]

DEFENDING THE BIG DITCH

Defense costs also drove up the cost of the Panama Canal. The initial American proposal for the Panama Canal envisioned no special expenditures to defend the canal from attack. The Isthmian Canal Commission believed that the canal was essentially indefensible, reasoning that "a small party of resolute men, armed with a few sticks of dynamite, could temporarily disable it without great difficulty." Additionally, it was argued, should enemy fleets dominate the Caribbean, the Panama Canal would be strategically worthless. Rather than liberating the United States from the need to build a two-ocean navy, defending the Panama Canal would require an even greater number of ships than before, supported by extensive and expensive land installations. The commission, therefore, recommended a policy of neutrality with regard to the canal.[29]

While it was unlikely in the extreme that the Theodore Roosevelt administration would agree to the neutralization of the Panama Canal, the United States did not formally reject the possibility until William Howard Taft became president in 1909. The Taft administration rejected neutralization in its characteristically tactful and mollifying way. The president's Panama Fortification Board ordered two six-inch guns installed as "as a formal and technical challenge to those . . . who may chance to deny the right of the United States to fortify."[30] Congress initially resisted. No funds were appropriated for canal defense until 1911. Ultimately, however, the Taft administration got its way, and Congress approved defense construction that the Panama Fortification Board estimated would cost $12.5 million.[31]

U.S. military needs in the Canal Zone steadily expanded. Initial plans called for three forts on the Atlantic side of the canal, and two on the Pacific. The coastal batteries would include several fourteen-inch and six-inch guns, and one sixteen-inch gun on the Pacific. In 1912, Goethals took the management of defense construction away from the U.S. Army and put it under his son, Lt. George Goethals. The number of fortifications grew; by the time the United States entered World War I, there were nine operational forts at each end of the canal.

Advances in military technology drove the expansion in military spending. For example, no sooner had shore batteries been installed than officers revealed that they could be outranged by the newest naval guns. Congress approved their replacement and modernization. Then Germany's naval deployment of U-boats convinced the Navy Department that the United States needed a submarine base at Coco Solo on the Atlantic, and a smaller auxiliary base on the Pacific side of the canal.[32] Congress approved the project. The use of airplanes during the Mexican Revolution and then World War I made it clear that the United States would need to build air bases and air defense in the canal; by 1920, the United States was in the midst of finishing France Field.[33] By 1921, defense-related capital expenditures had reached $41.4 million, more than three times the 1912 projection. Even when adjusted for inflation, the cost of defense-related construction multiplied by a factor of 2.4 over the initial estimate.[34]

In addition to the cost of construction and defense, the Panama Canal also incurred an interest cost on the bonds Congress issued to pay for construction. Congress also needed to finance the Panama Canal's operating losses between 1914, the year the *Ancon* first passed through the canal, and the year the canal fully opened to commercial transits, 1920. Using the rate on ten-year government bonds (most of the Panama Canal issues were ten-year bonds), the total interest cost on the Panama Canal in 1903–21 came to $175.9 million. (See table 4.2.) All in all, the Panama Canal ran over the initial estimate presented to Congress by a factor of 3.3 in nominal terms, including the $40 million for the New Panama Canal Company assets. In real terms, the overruns were slightly less, at 2.0.

TABLE 4.1
Nominal Panama Canal Costs and Revenues during Construction, in Millions of Dollars

	Construction*	Fortification	Operation and maintenance	Revenues	Net cash flow	Interest cost
1904–5	4.01				(4.01)	0.06
1906	18.02				(18.02)	0.67
1907	17.42				(17.42)	1.33
1908	28.91				(28.91)	2.24
1909	38.43				(38.43)	3.68
1910	85.63				(85.63)	6.66
1911	33.05	1.92			(34.97)	8.00
1912	34.18	2.81			(36.99)	9.29
1913	36.22	4.87			(41.09)	10.93
1914	30.28	1.12	0.17	0.01	(31.55)	12.25
1915	26.69	2.64	5.36	4.34	(30.35)	13.26
1916	11.59	0.53	8.30	2.56	(17.86)	13.91
1917	5.79	9.08	8.19	5.81	(17.25)	15.44
1918	2.90	2.46	7.72	6.41	(6.66)	15.34
1919	2.90	4.52	7.81	6.32	(8.91)	20.48
1920	2.74	5.33	8.32	8.94	(7.46)	22.98
1921**	1.80	6.13	11.08	12.04	(6.97)	19.33
Total	380.55	41.41				175.87

Note: The exact annual allocation of construction expenditure in 1917–20 has been estimated by the authors.

* Construction expenses include the $38.7 million paid (in installments) to the New Panama Canal Company for its assets and the $10 million paid to Panama.

** 1921 was the Panama Canal's first full year of commercial operation and open passage to civilian vessels.

TABLE 4.2
Total Panama Canal Start-Up Costs, in Millions of Dollars

	Payment to Panama	Payment to New Panama Canal Company	Construction	Fortification	Interest	Total
Nominal	10	39	332	41	176	598
2009 dollars	250	970	5,218	506	2,252	9,197
2009 equivalent proportion of GDP	5,480	21,219	124,508	10,578	48,117	209,905

Source: See table 4.1. GDP deflator and nominal GDP from Louis Johnston and Samuel Williamson, "What Was the U.S. GDP Then?" MeasuringWorth, 2010, available at http://www.measuringworth.com.

THE PANAMA CANAL AND ITS DISCONTENTS

People get kill and injure almost every day and all the
bosses want is to get the canal build.

—Constantine Parkinson, Barbadian canal worker

The construction of the Panama Canal created enormous disturbance for much of Panama's population. The Americans flooded
the Chagres River basin—home to 20,000 people, fully 8 percent
of the country's population at the time—to form Lake Gatún. The
flooding inundated dozens of historic towns and villages. Moreover, the Panama Canal Act of 1912 extinguished all private property rights in the flooded areas.[35] Some residents of the region
moved to the new waterline to establish new settlements, and the
Panamanian government relocated a few to the Pacific coast.[36] The
American Canal Zone administration, however, evicted most of
them at a cost of $2.3 million.[37] By the end of the 1930s, only 8,000
people remained in the Chagres basin.[38]

The labor force used to construct the Panama Canal did not
come from Panama. In part, this was because of the Panamanian
population's small size. Only 50,000 people lived in Panama City
and Colón in 1904, out of 263,000 people on the isthmus. In comparison, at its employment peak in 1913, the Isthmian Canal Commission employed over 44,000 workers—more than a *quarter* of
Panama's economically active population.[39] Wage rates would have
skyrocketed even had that many people been interested in killing
themselves to dig a big ditch—which few were. American observers, perhaps unsurprisingly, interpreted Panamanian reluctance to
take canal construction jobs as a sign of the low quality of local labor.
As General Hains of the Army Corps of Engineers opined in 1904,
"The native Isthmian will not work. He is naturally indolent; not
over strong; has no ambitions . . . he prefers to take it easy, swing-
ing in a hammock and smoking cigarettes."[40] Regardless of the reason, ultimately only 357 Panamanians worked as contract labor on
the canal, and even fewer held salaried positions.[41] (See table 4.3.)

TABLE 4.3
Panama Canal Contract Laborers, New Hires

	1904	1905	1906	1907	1908	1909	1910	1912	1913	Total	Proportion
Barbados	404	3,019	6,510	3,242	2,592	3,605	—	—	528	19,900	44.1%
Spain	—	—	1,174	5,293	1,831	—	—	—	—	8,298	18.4%
French West Indies	—	2,733	585	4,263	—	—	—	14	—	7,595	16.8%
British West Indies	—	—	2,443	—	—	—	205	928	—	3,576	7.9%
Italy	—	—	909	1,032	—	—	—	—	—	1,941	4.3%
Colombia	—	1,077	416	—	—	—	—	—	—	1,493	3.3%
Greece	—	—	—	1,101	—	—	—	—	—	1,101	2.4%
Cuba	—	—	500	—	—	—	—	—	—	500	1.1%
Panama	—	334	10	13	—	—	—	—	—	357	0.8%
Costa Rica	—	244	—	—	—	—	—	—	—	244	0.5%
Other	—	—	102	—	—	—	—	—	—	102	0.2%
Total	404	7,407	12,649	14,944	4,423	3,605	205	942	528	45,107	

Source: Annual Report of the Isthmian Canal Commission (1914), 294. No new laborers arrived in 1911.

If Panamanian labor could not be had at a competitive wage, the obvious alternative was to obtain low-wage workers from the same source as the earlier French canal effort: Jamaica. The rub was that Jamaican officials remembered the disaster that was the repatriation of Jamaican workers after the French canal effort collapsed in 1889—the crown colony wound up paying to bring them home.[42] As a result, the Jamaican government insisted the Americans guarantee repatriation costs for any and all workers. That ended the idea of using Jamaican labor; ultimately, only 47 worked on the canal.[43]

The United States then turned to Barbados. The first groups of Barbadians to arrive, however, proved too malnourished to accomplish their assigned tasks. "Not only do they seem to be disqualified by lack of actual vitality, but their disposition to labor seems to be as frail as their bodily strength."[44] Governor Stevens himself wrote, "I have no hesitancy in saying that the West Indian Negro is about the poorest excuse for a laborer I have ever been up against in thirty-five years of experience."[45]

Unhappy with the Barbadians, U.S. authorities attempted to hire Chinese contract laborers. Chinese workers had been tried during the construction of the Panama Railroad back in the 1850s. The chairman of the Isthmian Canal Commission, Theodore Shonts, stated in 1906, "We wish to get strong men from the rice fields of Southern China. . . . We want the work done, and we find the West Indian negroes are not what is needed."[46] In a perfect storm of opposition, the Chinese government refused to comply with the commission's request, American unions condemned the idea, and the Panamanian press denounced the commission for attempting to break Panama's anti-Chinese exclusionary laws.[47] The United States quietly dropped its plan to use Chinese labor.[48] Instead, the commission decided to supplement West Indian labor with contract labor from Spain.[49]

LABOR UNREST AT THE PANAMA CANAL

The Canal Zone recruited its first five hundred Spanish workers from Cuba in 1906.[50] The effort was a success, but Cuban planters resisted losing their immigrant workforce. Cuban opposition caused the Americans to recruit later tranches directly from Spain, primarily Galicia. The canal administration appeared unable to decide if the Spanish were white or nonwhite, one American manager writing in 1906, "The point that I have always maintained is that in deciding whether or not a white foreigner, or semi-white foreigner (Dago) should be put on a gold basis is the fact as whether or not they would take . . . a trip to the States every year."[51] An executive order in 1908 spared later Canal Zone managers from that decision, and relegated all Spanish workers to what was called the Silver Roll.

With the mass hiring of nonwhite contractors, the Americans decided to create a tiered workforce for the construction of the canal. Skilled American jobs went on the "Gold Roll," while other jobs went on the "Silver Roll." A tiered workforce was nothing new; the French used a similar system during de Lesseps's years.[52] The terms reflected the type of currency canal workers received: Americans were paid in gold dollars, while locally recruited labor received Colombian silver pesos.[53] The Americans changed the accounting system to dollars on April 1, 1909, but the disbursing department continued to collect silver from whatever origin to pay Silver Roll workers.[54] Sometimes the Canal Zone ran out of coins, requiring shipments of fractional silver from the United States, as in 1912.[55] In 1918, the Americans finally switched over completely to American currency, but the Gold and Silver designations remained.[56]

When the system began, hundreds of skilled blacks worked on the Gold Roll, both American and West Indian, and several thousand Spaniards, Italians, and Greeks labored on the Silver Roll.[57] (See table 4.3.) The flexibility in the American payroll system was slowly removed. In 1905, transfers between rolls were prohibited, and by the end of 1906, all Gold Roll blacks who were not United States citizens were demoted to the Silver Roll, with the exception of some civil servants in positions of authority over other West Indians and a few exceptional workers.[58] On February 8, 1908,

President Roosevelt closed the Gold Roll to non-Americans.[59] Four days later, the general manager of the Panama Railroad, Hiram Slifer, wrote to Major Gaillard: "I have been endeavoring to transfer all Negroes from the Gold to the Silver roll. Under the former operations of the Panama Railroad this question was not given very much attention. . . . The situation, however, is getting to be somewhat awkward, as we have divided the Gold from the Silver employees in our commissary." Three days later, the commission clarified its position: "It is the policy of the Commission to keep employees who are undoubtedly black or belong to mixed races on the Silver rolls."[60] Under Panamanian protest, the Gold Roll was reopened to Panamanian nationals in December of that year, but remained closed to any other group save white American citizens.[61]

The commission entirely removed higher-status jobs from the Silver Roll. Some West Indians on the Silver Roll had been employed as railroad engineers, machinists, boat pilots, wiremen, or other skilled positions. American unions protested, and in 1908 the Canal Zone administration put into place regulations restricting skilled jobs to American journeymen. In practice, canal administrators demoted the West Indians in those jobs to more menial assignments, while hiring Gold Roll employees at higher wages to do exactly the same work.[62] As an inducement to get West Indian workers to switch voluntarily (or quit), the Americans capped West Indian wages at 50¢ an hour.[63]

The Spanish on the Silver Roll received twice the rate of West Indian labor.[64] Spanish workers required a higher inducement to leave the *madre patria* than impoverished West Indians, whose island economies were in near collapse around the turn of the century. The Americans were willing to pay the higher wages because the Spanish were physically stronger and more robust than the first groups of West Indians hired by the Isthmian Canal Commission. The Spanish, however, were also the heirs to Spain's militant labor tradition. Spanish workers started the first major strike on the canal in 1907. The United States initially used Italian workers to break the 1907 strike, but the Canal Zone was only able to attract a total of 1,941 Italians in 1906–7, after which they received no more. The Spanish remained militant.

Spanish militancy led the Canal Zone to replace Spanish workers by any means necessary. The solution was to increase the productivity of Barbadian workers to Spanish levels. Barbadians arrived at the Canal Zone malnourished and weak, but their work ability rapidly improved with access to a complete diet and sufficient calories. Goethals cut the workday from ten hours to nine in 1907, which reduced exhaustion. He also required all workers to purchase three full meal tickets every day. Previously, many Barbadian workers had chosen to subsist on sugarcane in order to save more money to send home. "If they starve themselves," wrote two American journalists, "they can save a great deal . . . some of the men try hard to save; buy 2 cents bread, 2 cents sugar, and go to work all trembly and can't lift a thing."[65] Skimping on food was understandable, considering that meal tickets cost 9¢ ($1.98 in 2009 dollars, using the CPI) and the workers earned only 68¢ for a nine-hour day, but it was terrible for their health and energy levels.[66] Finally, American foremen learned how to work with the West Indians, which basically meant treating them with some modicum of respect.[67]

The issue of productivity resolved, the United States turned back to Barbadian labor in order to restrain the Spanish workforce, playing one group off against the other. As one foreman wrote, "I could keep them both on their metal by rivalry between the two."[68] The result, unsurprisingly, was hostility between the two groups, culminating in an all-out riot between Spanish and Barbadian workers in 1909.[69] The Americans ceased hiring Spanish workers that same year. (See table 4.3.) The Spanish did not go quietly. A violent wave of strikes rocked the canal in 1911 and 1912. The strikes ended with the complete replacement of Spanish labor by West Indians, mostly from Barbados.[70]

The Barbadians were not immune to labor unrest. Between 1914 and 1917, the cost of living for Silver Roll employees rose 65 percent, while average monthly Silver Roll wages rose only 11

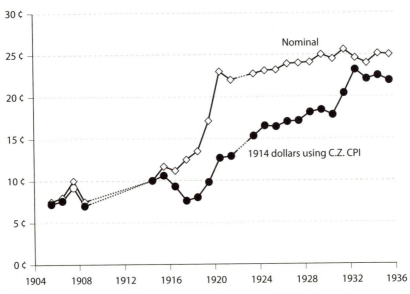

Figure 4.1:   Average Silver Roll wages per hour, cents (U.S.). *Source*: See table 4.4.

percent, to $30. (See figure 4.1.) As prices began to accelerate in 1916, President Woodrow Wilson affirmed an executive order that all canal employees should receive free rent. Canal Zone governor Chester Harding rescinded that order for the Silver Roll.[71] In the face of declining real wages, large-scale layoffs, and a deliberate lack of rent relief, the West Indian workers went on strike. In response, Harding threatened to occupy Panama City and Colón unless the Panamanian government broke the strike. Panama obliged by breaking up gatherings and deporting strike leaders.[72]

Further strikes of canal workers followed in 1919 and 1920. Harding again pressured Panama into breaking the strike with the threat of military occupation of Panama City and Colón.[73] West Indian workers and their dependents were deported from the Canal Zone into Panama, their possessions evicted and stacked in the streets.[74] Panama then banned strike meetings immediately following the 1920 strike. The Panamanian government went on to ban the immigration of non-Spanish-speaking blacks in 1926.[75]

Panama received no quid pro quo for their actions. Neither Harding nor his successor, Jay Morrow, agreed to hire more Panamanians on either the Gold or Silver rolls.

The strikers accomplished at least some of their goals, as the Canal Zone substantially raised nominal wages in 1919 and 1920, allowing Silver Zone employees to more than make up for the purchasing power lost in the postwar inflation. (See figure 4.1.) Unfortunately, the fired strikers were never hired back. The Silver Roll workforce fell by 55 percent between 1920 and 1922 as the Panama Canal shifted from construction to commercial operation. (See table 4.4.)

RACIAL DISCRIMINATION

Blacks had been present on the isthmus since the days of Balboa. By 1904, their descendants formed a substantial fraction of the Panamanian population. An additional West Indian–descended, English-speaking, Protestant *antillano* population dated from the 1850s. The *antillano* community began when some of the Jamaican workforce remained after the building of the Panama Railroad.[76] The end of de Lesseps's project added roughly six thousand more West Indians to the Panamanian cultural mix—the Jamaican crown colony government repatriated only seven thousand of the thirteen thousand left stranded by the financial collapse.[77]

The Canal Zone system required a degree of physical separation from Panamanian society, a difficult undertaking for a region that bisected the country right next to Panama's two largest cities. Governor Goethals decided to depopulate the Canal Zone of its nonemployees. Goethals was blunt about his motives. "I did not care to see a population of Panamanians or West Indian negroes occupying the land, for these are non-productive, thriftless and indolent. They would congregate in small settlements, and the cost of sanitation and government would be increased materially."[78] The drop in the "other" population of the Canal Zone between 1912 and 1916 (see table 4.4) underrepresents the population decline, since an influx of American and West Indian dependents partially

TABLE 4.4
Canal Zone (CZ) Labor and Price Statistics, 1904–35

	Average Silver Roll hourly wages					Work week	Average annual level		
	Nominal	1914 dollars using CZ CPI	2007 dollars using U.S. CPI	CZ CPI	U.S. CPI		Gold Roll	Silver Roll	Other CZ residents
1904							46	700	
1905	7.5¢	7.2¢	$ 1.48	104	88		2,705	14,250	
1906	8.0¢	7.6¢	$ 1.54	105	90		3,811	15,604	
1907	10.0¢	9.2¢	$ 1.82	109	94		4,513	18,912	
1908	7.5¢	7.0¢	$ 1.41	107	92		4,556	20,486	
1909							4,336	21,997	
1910							4,629	25,334	
1911							4,356	23,617	
1912							4,227	25,339	33,244
1913							3,916	27,064	26,421
1914	10.0¢	10.0¢	$ 2.14	100	100		3,867	22,662	19,851
1915	11.7¢	10.6¢	$ 2.07	110	101		3,643	19,935	17,919
1916	11.2¢	9.3¢	$ 1.66	120	110		3,169	17,571	10,708
1917	12.5¢	7.6¢	$ 0.98	165	132		3,391	17,185	12,469
1918	13.5¢	8.0¢	$ 1.00	170	155		2,975	14,975	15,854
1919	17.1¢	9.8¢	$ 1.19	175	179		2,836	13,736	15,795
1920	23.0¢	12.7¢	$ 1.51	180	207		3,943	13,976	9,541
1921	22.0¢	12.9¢	$ 1.61	171	185		3,506	10,035	17,836

Year									
1922				153	173		2,553	7,623	
1923				146	176		2,583	8,418	20,922
1924	23.1¢	16.5¢	$ 2.53	140	176	55	2,810	8,701	20,792
1925	23.2¢	16.44¢	$ 2.49	141	181	54	2,885	9,385	22,212
1926	23.9¢	17.0¢	$ 2.59	140	183	53	2,879	9,940	22,570
1927	24.0¢	17.1¢	$ 2.61	140	179	53	2,936	10,467	23,661
1928	24.1¢	18.1¢	$ 2.91	133	177	52	3,038	10,884	23,391
1929	25.0¢	18.4¢	$ 2.90	136	177	52	3,225	12,487	23,134
1930	24.5¢	17.8¢	$ 2.76	138	172	52	3,344	11,780	23,113
1931	25.6¢	20.4¢	$ 3.47	126	157	51	3,276	10,624	24,343
1932	24.6¢	23.2¢	$ 4.67	106	141	54	3,148	9,120	26,663
1933	24.0¢	22.1¢	$ 4.34	109	134	52	3,028	9,575	29,802
1934	25.1¢	22.5¢	$ 4.33	111	138	52	2,934	9,086	30,248
1935	25.0¢	21.9¢	$ 4.11	114	142	52	3,087	9,365	27,803

Source: 1905–19 wage levels "Minutes of the Silver Rate Board," January 15, 1920, in Panama Canal Commission 2-D-40/B, record group 185, National Archives, and *Collins Report*, July 10, 1921, in Panama Canal Commission 2-D-40. 1920–35 wage levels from *Annual Report of the Governor of the Panama Canal Zone* (various). Panamanian CPI for 1914–35 from *Annual Report of the Governor of the Panama Canal Zone* (various). Pre-1914 CPI estimated by authors using an import price index and rental data from the *Gaceta de Panamá* (various), and weights from the 1914 Canal Zone index. C.Z. employment, 1904–5 and 1921–39 from John Major, *Prize Possession*, app. A (Cambridge: Cambridge University Press, 1993). 1906–20 employment from data in *Annual Report* (1920), 232. Other population of C.Z. calculated from U.S. Census Bureau, *Fourteenth Census of the United States: 1920* (Washington, DC: GPO, 1921–22), 1:691 for 1912–16; and James Simmons, *Malaria in Panama* (Baltimore: Johns Hopkins Press, 1939), 87 thereafter.

compensated for the drop in the Panamanian population of the Zone. The Silver Zone workers who refused to live in segregated barracks remained in poor-quality tenements in Colón on land owned by the Panama Railroad.[79]

In addition to the Zone's separation from the rest of Panama, the American administration imposed segregation *within* the Zone. Segregation affected daily life at the most basic levels. As mentioned, blacks (and Spanish "semi-whites") were denied employment on the Gold Roll. The administration also segregated public services. Public schools, for example, were open to all dependents of canal employees, but only white students had the option of taking a full standard American high school curriculum. Blacks were automatically shunted into vocational training. In 1919, West Indian teachers earned half as much as their Gold Roll counterparts; by 1929, this figure had dropped to less than a third.[80] Annual expenditures were $29 for black students, $100 for white.[81]

Black Americans hired after 1908 received a modified version of the Silver Roll contract. Their pay was somewhat higher than the West Indians, and they received sick and home leave benefits, but they were denied access to Gold Roll clubs, eateries, or housing. Few were willing to travel to Panama in order to work under such onerous conditions. In 1912, there were only 69 black Americans working in the Canal Zone. By 1928, that number had declined to 23 out of a total American workforce of 3,038.[82]

In effect, an American system of racial discrimination and control was transplanted into Panamanian society. It should be noted that this system was largely a creation of Northerners. Only a third of the American employees in the Canal Zone were from the American South.[83] The primary instigator of the system, George Washington Goethals, had grown up in Brooklyn. It is more than slightly ironic that the military epidemiologist William Crawford Gorgas, an Alabaman and the son of a Confederate general, was possibly the major official most sympathetic to blacks within the early canal administration.

Separate did not mean equal under American rule: health outcomes in the Canal Zone varied dramatically across racial lines.

During the first years of construction, black mortality from infectious disease hit astounding levels. In 1906, the Isthmian Canal Commission employed 21,441 nonwhites over the course of the year. (Many of the workers did not work a full year; thus the total number of people who worked for the canal over the course of the year was higher than the average level of employment reported in table 4.4.) Fully 1,024 of them died during that same year. Mortality dropped precipitously in 1907, however, and by 1908 nonwhite death rates stabilized around 7.8 per 1,000 employees through the 1930s. White deaths rates, however, averaged only 4.8 per thousand after 1908. (See figure 4.2.)

The disparity between the races in the Canal Zone carried over into infant mortality. The rate for blacks living within the Canal Zone was twice as high as for whites, despite a long-term drop for both populations.[84] More surprisingly, the infant mortality rate for

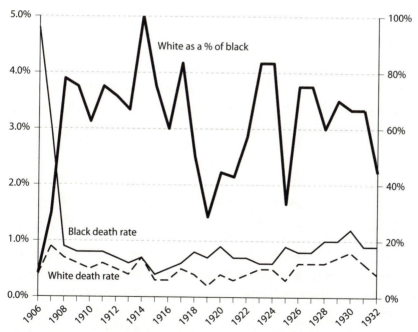

Figure 4.2: Annual disease mortality rates among canal employees, by race, 1906–32. *Source*: James Simmons, *Malaria in Panama* (Baltimore, MD: Johns Hopkins Press, 1939), 91, 92, 104.

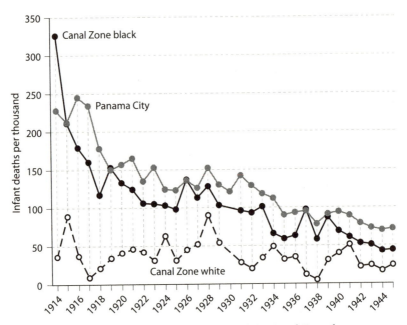

Figure 4.3: Infant mortality in Panama City and the Canal Zone, by race, 1914–46. Source: *Annual Reports* (selected years).

black Canal Zone residents was little better than the rate for the residents of Panama City, who had no access to the Canal Zone's modern (if segregated) hospitals. (See figure 4.3.)

THE MENDOZA AFFAIR

Discrimination against blacks did not stop at the border of the Canal Zone. The strangest instance of American racial politics on the isthmus followed the death of President José de Obaldía in March 1910. Obaldía's designated successor as president, Carlos Mendoza, was a popular member of the Liberal Party and the country's first justice minister. Mendoza also happened to be of mixed African ancestry.

Mendoza's assumption of the Panamanian presidency sent the Americans into a racial panic. While the chargé of the French legation admired Mendoza's "affability and honorable nature,"[85] the chargé of the American legation, George Weitzel, hurriedly wrote to Secretary of State Philander Knox that Mendoza had "a racial inability to refrain long from abuse of power."[86] The outgoing American minister to Panama, Reynolds Hitt, added that the white Panamanian oligarchy would never accept a president "partly of African descent."[87]

Reynolds Hitt may have been projecting his own prejudices onto the Panamanians: in July 1910, the Liberals under Mendoza managed to win twenty of the twenty-eight seats in the National Assembly, guaranteeing Mendoza's confirmation as president in September. After the results were published, the first secretary of the American legation, Richard Marsh, wrote a series of over-heated missives to Secretary of State Knox, claiming that "the objection to Mendoza . . . is of course the fact that he is half negro [*sic*] while his wife is a full negro."[88] Marsh added that Mendoza's "appeal to racial equality and negro solidarity is already having an unfortunate effect on the country."[89] In Marsh's opinion, Mendoza was dangerous because he had "perhaps the strongest personality in Panama," deriving his support from "the lowest and ignorant classes," but whose "political genius has linked to his cause certain influential whites," who might in the future "create a spirit of patriotism and unity in the country."[90] For good measure, Marsh added to Knox that Mendoza himself had "two mistresses . . . and is credited with numerous illegitimate children."[91]

On August 4, 1910, Marsh met with Governor Goethals— Marsh, like Goethals, had been in the Army Corps of Engineers— and Mendoza's chief political enemy, Santiago de la Guardia of the Conservative Party, to discuss their common Mendoza problem. They believed the Panamanian constitution provided the perfect rationale to prevent Mendoza's upcoming election. Under Article 82, "a citizen who has been elected President may not be re-elected for the following term; nor may he have exercised the Presidency inside 18 months before the election." Since Mendoza was already acting president, they reasoned, he could not be legitimately confirmed as president by the National Assembly in September. Moreover, Article 136 stated that "the government of the United States of the America may intervene . . . to re-establish public tranquility and constitutional order." De la Guardia, therefore, proposed that the United States prevent Mendoza's election in order to maintain Panamanian constitutional order.[92] The constitutional reasoning was dubious, because Article 82 referred to *popular* elections, not the legislative selection of someone to carry out the term of a sitting president. The next presidential election was not due until 1912. That did not stop the American legation from announcing on August 22, 1910, that it would consider Mendoza's confirmation to be unconstitutional.[93] Four days later, Mendoza withdrew his candidacy and retired from office. The resulting *New York Times* story was clear about the racial subtext involved in Mendoza's resignation: "Negro Candidate for Acting President of Panama Republic Retires."[94] Federico Boyd took over the presidency for four days before handing it over to Pablo Arosemena.

The subsequent Panamanian outcry forced Washington to cashier Marsh, who complained bitterly to Secretary Knox about "all the wild rumors circulated by the negro element in Panama about me."[95] Upon learning the details, President Taft, who had been led to believe that events in Panama were a standard constitutional crisis, thought "the attitude of the United States has been grossly misrepresented" due to Marsh, calling him "fresh and insubordinate"—but the precedent had been set.[96] The United States had prevented a person from assuming political power in Panama simply because of his race, and the United States would continue to have the power to vet Panamanian presidential hopefuls. Mendoza died in 1916 at the age of sixty, before having a chance to test the legitimacy of nonconsecutive presidential terms under the Panamanian constitution. Mendoza's *New York Times* obituary did not mention his race.[97]

THE SANITATION CRUSADE IN PANAMA

Prior to the American construction of the Panama Canal, the disease environment in Panamanian cities was notoriously bad. Panama City suffered a mortality rate of 66 deaths per thousand people in 1904—1 in 15—while Colón had a slightly healthier rate of 50 deaths per thousand, or 1 in 20.[98] Panama's cities were in effect demographic sinks, requiring continual immigration to maintain their population.

The extremely high death rates from disease during the failed French canal construction attempt worried the Isthmian Canal Commission. Unlike its dilatory efforts in digging the canal, the commission began its public health campaign almost immediately, on June 30, 1904, under the management of Colonel William Gorgas, who had supervised the disease control and sanitary efforts in American-occupied Cuba. Gorgas estimated that over 22,000 people died during the French construction, mainly from yellow fever, at a rate of 240 per thousand. Death rates had run even higher among French nationals, who had never been exposed to the disease. If the same ratios held for the American effort in Panama, Gorgas calculated, yellow fever would claim 3,500 people yearly.[99]

A recent breakthrough in understanding the etiology of yellow fever made it possible to control the disease. Carlos Finlay, Walter Reed, and their associates in Cuba discovered that yellow fever was carried by a specific mosquito vector, later identified as the species *Aedes aegyptii*. Reed confirmed Finlay's mosquito hypothesis using human volunteers, including American servicemen, Spanish immigrants to Cuba, and an U.S. Army nurse from New Jersey, Clara Maass, who died after volunteering for a second infection. Before Finlay and Reed, the general wisdom held that yellow fever was a "filth disease," transmitted through fouled bedding and clothing.[100] Once the proper etiology of yellow fever was understood, yellow fever was almost totally eradicated from Havana in the space of a few months. In 1900, there were 310 deaths from yellow fever; in 1901, there were only 18.[101]

Cleansing yellow fever from Panama proved more difficult than in Cuba. Gorgas originally believed that the small size of Panama City, with only twenty thousand residents in 1904, would make it possible to eradicate the *Aedes* mosquito by fumigation. Three attempts, 120 tons of insect powder, and several high-profile American deaths from yellow fever later, Gorgas realized this was not going to work.[102] In the spring of 1905, the full measures developed in Cuba against the *Aedes* mosquito were put into practice—officials covered, screened, or oiled all places where clear freshwater could collect and permit the mosquito to breed. The incidence of yellow fever dropped immediately. By December 1905, the Isthmian Canal Commission could claim that "yellow fever has been virtually extirpated from the Isthmus."[103] Gorgas recorded the last case in Panama City on November 11, 1905, and the last case in Colón on May 17, 1906.[104] Death rates in Panama City and Colón dropped dramatically in 1906 and 1907. (See table 4.5.)

Following the conquest of yellow fever in Panama, the Sanitary Department turned its attention to malaria.[105] While the mortality rate was significantly lower for malaria than for yellow fever, its rate of incidence was far higher: in 1906, 82 percent of all canal workers took sick from malaria.[106] In addition, unlike yellow fever, which conferred immunity to its survivors, malaria could be reacquired.

Malaria in Panama would be substantially more difficult to bring under control than yellow fever. While both diseases were transmitted by mosquitoes, the life cycles of the mosquito species differed in significant details. The *Aedes aegyptii* mosquito, which carries yellow fever, required clear freshwater to breed and had a limited range of flight in the open air. It easily transmitted disease in urban areas, particularly ones with poor drainage, but it was also easy to eradicate. The *Anopheles* mosquito, on the other hand, ranged for hundreds of yards and bred in freshwater protected by algae and grass.[107] Gorgas's antimalarial efforts therefore needed to be extended to suburban and wilderness areas around the canal.

Gorgas was a thorough man. Under his orders, all tall grass was cleared and all pools of standing water were drained within two hundred yards of individual houses in the Canal Zone. Where this was impossible, workers sprayed oil to kill the mosquito larvae. Where oiling failed, Gorgas applied a specially designed larvicide, made in the Ancon Hospital laboratory from carbolic acid detergent. It poisoned waters oil failed to reach.[108] The Sanitary Depart-

TABLE 4.5
Death Rates from Infectious Disease in Panama, per Thousand

	National	Panama City	Colón	Rural	Canal Zone
1903	21.0	50.0	56.0	16.0	
1904	20.7	50.0	50.2	15.8	
1905	20.4	65.8	49.5	13.4	
1906	20.0	44.8	51.4	15.4	39.3
1907	19.7	34.5	39.2	16.8	24.1
1908	19.6	34.8	26.3	17.3	8.7
1909	19.4	25.4	22.6	18.5	7.5
1910	19.3	31.7	26.3	17.3	7.5
1911	19.1	31.3	26.4	17.2	7.7
1912	19.0	29.3	24.4	17.4	6.4
1913	18.7	31.9	24.2	16.4	5.2
1914	18.3	34.5	25.2	15.3	7.0
1915	18.0	29.9	21.8	15.6	4.1
1916	17.6	29.0	28.2	14.8	4.6
1917	17.3	28.1	26.3	14.5	5.7
1918	17.3	21.4	23.6	16.0	7.1
1919	17.3	19.7	21.9	16.5	6.2
1920	17.3	21.4	21.2	16.3	7.4
1921	17.3	22.1	17.3	16.5	5.7

Source: James Simmons, *Malaria in Panama* (Baltimore: Johns Hopkins Press, 1939), 92; and Omar Jaén Suárez, *La población del Istmo de Panamá* (Madrid: Agencia Española de Cooperación Internacional, 1998), 505–6.

ment used 700,000 gallons of oil and 124,000 gallons of larvicide every year in the areas of treatment.[109]

The effects of Gorgas's antimalaria campaign were almost as substantial as the elimination of yellow fever. Malarial incidence fell from 821 per thousand canal employees in 1906 to 215 per thousand in 1909.[110] Malarial death rates for canal employees fell from 11.6 per thousand in 1906 to 1.2 per thousand in 1909. In the entire area covered by the campaign—the Canal Zone, Panama City, and Colón—malarial death rates decreased from 16.2 per thousand in 1906 to 2.6 per thousand in 1909.[111] The decline in the incidence of malaria accounted for approximately 40 percent of the total mortality decline in Panama City and Colón between the periods 1900–1904 and 1910–14. In short, the Panama Canal produced a major spillover of public health benefits for the Panamanian population: the eradication of urban yellow fever and the control of malaria.

A skeptical reader might argue that yellow fever would have been eliminated from Panama on a roughly similar timetable without the American presence. This seems unlikely. The Americans effectively eradicated the mosquito that transmitted yellow fever in urban Panama by 1906. Ecuador failed to accomplish this until 1919—yellow fever was endemic to the Guayaquil area—and outbreaks continued in Brazil, Colombia, and Venezuela into the 1920s. Colombia's last urban outbreak of yellow fever occurred in 1929.[112] Malaria eradication programs, meanwhile, did not produce significant drops in mortality in Mexico until the 1950s.[113]

How much of the drop in disease mortality in Panama was due to the American public health campaigns? Table 4.5 presents overall disease mortality rates for Panama City, Colón, and the rest of the country. It also presents the death rate for canal employees. Mortality rates outside the Zone and the port cities remained fairly constant after 1906. Table 4.6 presents a simple counterfactual of what Panama's mortality rates would have been in the absence of the American antimalaria program. This counterfactual assumes that death rates in Panama's port cities would experience an extra 10.4 deaths per thousand compared to their historical rates, an amount equivalent to the recorded drop in the malaria death rate among canal employees. It also assumes that net migration to the cities would remain the same.

In the counterfactual scenario, Panamanian mortality rises above its 1900–1904 levels. Although mortality in the cities drops (due to the elimination of yellow fever, which is not affected in our counterfactual scenario), it is not enough to offset the increase in the cities' share of the overall Panamanian population. The American antimalarial campaign decreased Panamanian mortality from disease by approximately one-quarter, or one life in two hundred.

Panama's pre-1903 mortality rates from infectious disease appear to have been somewhat lower than countries with similar

TABLE 4.6
Comparative Death Rates from Infectious Disease, per Thousand

	Panama City	Colón	Rest of Panama	All Panama	Canal Zone	Costa Rica	Venezuela	Cuba	All-Panama counterfactual
1885–89		96.5			56.7				
1890–94		40.3			30.2				
1895–99		45.6			25.9				
1900–1904	65.8	62.3	16.1	21.0	27.6	24.0	29.1	23.7	21.0
1905–9	41.1	37.8	16.2	19.7	23.5	25.5	29.8	23.3	24.0
1910–14	31.7	25.3	16.9	19.0	9.3	23.7	28.3	21.4	23.2
1915–19	25.6	24.4	15.3	17.3	6.8	25.1	29.7	22.2	22.1
1920–24	21.8	19.3	16.4	17.3	8.7	22.8	26.0	19.3	23.1

Source: Panama, *Gaceta de Panamá* and *Estadística Panameña* (various). Costa Rica, Brian R. Mitchell, *International Historical Statistics: The Americas 1750–2000* (New York: Palgrave Macmillan, 2003), 68; Venezuela and Cuba, 84–85.

disease environments. In the period between 1900 and 1904, for example, mortality rates in Panama were 11 percent lower than Cuba—where the United States spent a great deal on disease control in 1898 through 1902. Panamanian mortality rates were also 13 percent lower than Costa Rica and 28 percent lower than Venezuela. In contrast to the prevailing opinion of the time, Panama's climate was relatively healthy; Panama's cities were not.

The final contribution of the canal effort to Panama's public health came from the American construction of water and sewage works in the cities of Panama and Colón. Clean water technologies, such as water filtration and chlorination, caused half the reduction of overall mortality in the United States between 1900 and 1936, and three-quarters of the reduction of infant mortality in the same period.[114] Their arrival in Panama had similarly dramatic effects.

In 1905, the United States built a sixteen-inch pipe from the Ancon reservoir to supply Panama City with fresh water.[115] By 1906 it had finished a functional waterworks and sewage system for Panama City.[116] In 1903, Panama Railroad employees living in suburban Colón gained access to piped water from the Mount

Hope reservoir. In 1907 the United States enlarged the system to include the entire city of Colón.[117] In 1914, the United States finished a water purification plant for the Colón waterworks.[118] The next year it finished a companion plant for Panama City.[119] In fact, the U.S. government provided Panama with water filtration plants before most major *American* cities adopted the technology.

The United States may have brought new sanitation technology to Panama—but it made the Panamanians pay for it. The United States charged the cost of construction to the Panamanian government, plus interest.[120] In 1946, the United States finally turned the waterworks and sewage systems over to Panama, as part of a wartime agreement. The remaining unamortized debt came to only $669,226—Panamanian taxpayers having shelled out $4.1 million (not including interest) for sanitary works.[121] In 2009 dollars, using the GDP deflator, Panama spent roughly $97 million for American-built sanitary works.

Here the limits of counterfactual analysis become apparent. The benefits of the American-built waterworks can be attributed to the United States *only* if one believes that the United States accelerated the construction of the works compared to what the province of Panama would have achieved under Colombian rule. Pipes and modern sewers reached Bogotá in 1888, and the city built its first chlorine treatment plant in 1920, only five years after Panama City.[122] Medellín opened its first treatment plant in 1925.[123] Barranquilla received modern waterworks and sanitation in 1929.[124] The implication is that the U.S. presence brought waterworks to Panama sooner than they would have otherwise arrived, but Panama City was an important entrepôt and the provincial government controlled substantial revenues, even as part of the Colombian republic. In the absence of strong evidence about municipal policy on the isthmus in this counterfactual scenario—unlike the evidence that an American presence was required for the eradication of yellow fever and malaria on the isthmus—the most we can say about the benefit of American intervention in terms of access to potable water is the famous Scottish verdict: not proven.

The construction of the Panama Canal had greater economic impact on the island of Barbados than on Panama itself. By the end of the nineteenth century, Barbados, the most easterly of the Windward Islands, had become a backwater. According to the census of 1891, the population consisted of 15,613 whites, 122,717 blacks, and 43,976 people of mixed race.[125] An unmodernized British sugar colony, its small sugar estates continued to use windmills to grind cane and open pans to crystallize sugar. The Barbadian sugar industry, in other words, was a far cry from the modern mills of Cuba, which used steam power and the vacuum process for its sugar.[126]

A largely rural society of gentry and tenants, at first glance Barbados might have seemed to be a bit like the Wessex of Thomas Hardy's novels, albeit with more heat and humidity. The reality on the ground was far harsher. Subsidized European beet sugar caused sugar prices to crash during the "bounty depression" of the late nineteenth century. As a result, the financial system of the British West Indies essentially collapsed between 1884 and 1899, as the merchant houses that had provided both working and long-term capital to the sugar industry disappeared. The sugar price and resulting financial collapse drove down living standards, as plantation jobs dried up and imports (especially of food) became scarce. The Colonial Office was overwhelmed by reports of hardship.[127]

The British government established a royal commission in 1897 to report on the parlous state of the West Indian economy. Barbados especially worried the commission, because of its high population density. The vast majority of the black population consisted of tenants who rented small plots from nearby plantations and worked the main estate under the "located labor" laws that *required* labor from tenant farmers as a condition of tenancy.[128] The laws provided the plantations with a supply of cheap labor, even by West Indian standards; as early as 1884, the Barbadian colonial government worried about the backward production methods preferred by planters with access to practically free labor.[129]

In 1900, a male Barbadian agricultural worker on the open market earned 24¢ per day, at a time when farm laborers in the South Atlantic region of the United States—the poorest part—earned 36¢.[130] A craftsman in Barbados might earn twice that, a female agricultural worker less.[131] Child labor was common, at an average wage of 3¢ per day. The 1897 royal commission reported that falling wages and high unemployment meant that "the effort to keep the children at school is not so great as it was years ago."[132] Barbadians had traditionally emigrated to other islands when the economy slowed, but the general collapse of labor demand throughout the British West Indies as a result of the "bounty depression" left Barbados without emigration as a safety valve.

Low wages meant that undernourishment ran rampant. Barbados operated on a food deficit, growing sugar to buy food, and the small gardens of its tenants failed to make up for the lack.[133] As a result, infant mortality was shockingly high, even by the standards of the British West Indies. In 1900–1904, for example, Barbados registered an average of 282 infant deaths per 1,000. In comparison, Jamaica registered 171 and Trinidad only 162.[134]

In fact, despite its orderly reputation, Barbados appeared to be on the brink of collapse by the turn of the century. Its revenues chiefly came from import duties on food. The colonial government, facing bankruptcy, raised tariffs in 1896, which had the result of worsening the problem of undernourishment.[135] Unrest boiled over in 1898, when the outbreak of war between Spain and the United States in the context of a local drought sent the price of bread in Bridgetown up 20 percent. Hundreds of people organized a "potato raid" against a plantation. Three weeks later, someone shot and killed the speaker of the Barbadian assembly (and a major planter) as he rode home in his buggy from the capital. The island might have erupted had a hurricane not struck a week later, "wash[ing] away all concerns except those of immediate survival."[136] In 1899, London approved an unprecedented relief grant of £194,000 (£19.5 million in 2009 pounds, or £155 *million* as a constant share of the United Kingdom's GDP) to prop up its Barbadian dependency. It also hurried the negotiation of a reciprocity agreement with the United States that permitted the entry of Barbadian sugar at 1.4828¢ per pound, 12 percent below the prevailing rate.[137] Unfortunately, in May 1902 the United States allowed the free entry of Puerto Rican sugar, and the following year Congress signed a treaty permitting Cuban sugar to enter at 20 percent below the prevailing rate. Whatever advantage Barbadian sugar might have had was lost.

The Panama Canal's insatiable demand for labor came as a godsend for Barbados. The island's legislature responded to the inquiries of the Isthmian Canal Commission by amending the Emigration Act of 1904. The amendment allowed labor recruiters on the island as long as they posted bonds that would be used to pay for repatriation should the terms of the employment contract be violated. It also imposed a fine of £1 ($4.85) against any recruits who accepted a contract and then refused to leave. A standard contract in 1904 offered a pay rate of 75¢ day, free board (albeit in barracks), free medical care, and a free return trip to Barbados.[138] Ultimately, the Canal Commission recruited 19,900 Barbadians, nearly half its contract labor force.[139]

Recruiting took place in Trafalgar Square, in Bridgetown, conveniently near the main police station. Agents went out into the crowd to interview and select potential workers. A doctor then checked the potential workers, selecting those who would receive a contract. In 1907, Arthur Bullard described the scene as follows:

Several policemen kept the crowd in order and sent them up into the recruiting station in batches of 100 at a time. . . . As the men came up, they were formed in a line around the wall. First, all those who looked too old, or too young, or too weakly, were picked out and sent away. Then they were told that no man who had previously worked on the canal would be taken again. . . . Then the doctor told them all to roll up their left sleeves and began a mysterious examination of their forearms. He saw that a few men had been vaccinated by him already, and these were sent away. One protested that a dog had bitten him there. Then, he went over the whole line again for trachoma, rolling back their eyelids and looking for in-flammation. Seven or eight fell at this test. Then he made them strip, and went over them round after round for tuber-culosis, heart trouble, and rupture. . . . About 20 of 100 were left at the end.[140]

The selected migrants reported back to the docks a few days later. After a second medical examination and a check to ensure that every emigrant had a number that matched the one on their contract, they boarded the steamers, where they had to find deck space and food for themselves during the twelve-day voyage to Colón.[141] According to a report presented to the Barbados Legislative Council, the atmosphere on the docks was fairly hostile toward the ruling class. The crowds would "abuse whites and aggressively denounce them" before boarding.[142]

The anger was understandable, given the economic and political situation the emigrants were leaving. Ironically, the departure of so many angry young men gave plenty of leverage to those who stayed behind. One prospective emigrant was heard telling his co-workers, "Why you don't hit the manager in the head and come along with we?"[143] His coworkers refrained from assaulting the manager, but there was a wave of plantation labor disputes, and the following song became fairly common:

> We want more wages, we want it now
> And if we don't get it, we're going to Panama
> Yankees say they want we down there
> We want more wages, we want it now[144]

In addition to the contract laborers, an additional 25,000 Barbadians emigrated to Panama on their own.[145] A passage cost roughly £2 10s., or $14, no small amount for impoverished Barbadian families.[146] The 1911 census of Barbados recorded 39,760 *net* departures for Panama since 1901, and an estimated 2,000 more left between 1911 and the end of organized labor recruitment in 1914.[147] The ultimate emigration was substantially higher. In 1901, Barbados had a population of 195,558. In 1921, it had a population of only 156,744. Extrapolating from existing birth and death rates, the population of the island should have been 220,412 in 1921, implying a net outmigration of 64,000 people. (See table 4.7.)

Unsurprisingly, these high levels of emigration caused labor shortages. When planters began to complain in 1906, Governor Gilbert Carter refused to appoint a commission of inquiry. The reason that he gave was the remittances from the overseas workers had markedly improved the economy, especially for the poorer tenant farmers.[148] That same year, the Barbadian parliament passed a bill giving the governor the power to halt emigration. A pair of angry public demonstrations prompted Governor Carter to take the extraordinary measure of publicly proclaiming that he had no intention of using his new powers. The parliament then demanded that he appoint a commission of inquiry into emigration; he refused. Five years later, in 1911, Carter retired and returned to Britain. The new governor, Leslie Probyn, appeared to bow to planter pressure by declaring a ban on labor recruiting for Panama—but

TABLE 4.7
Barbados Population Statistics

	Population	Annual growth rate
1841	122,198	
1851	135,939	1.1%
1861	152,727	1.2%
1871	162,042	0.6%
1881	171,860	0.6%
1891	182,867	0.6%
1901	195,558	0.7%
1911	172,337	−1.3%
1921	156,744	−0.9%
1946	192,800	0.8%
Low counterfactual 1946	258,260	0.6%
High counterfactual 1946	319,947	1.1%

Source: Velma Newton, *The Silver Men: West Indian Migration to Panama, 1850–1914* (Kingston: University of the West Indies, 1984), app. I, 198–99. 1901 population from the 1911 edition of the *Encyclopedia Brittanica*, 28:545.

he took no action to enforce it. The canal recruited 528 workers in 1913, before it ceased organized transport of workers.[149]

TRANSFORMING THE ISLAND

The mass emigration reshaped Barbados. First, since contracted labor tended to be overwhelmingly male, the sex ratio of men to women on the island dropped from 80.1 percent in 1891 to 69.4 percent in 1911 and 67.9 percent in 1921. In the thirty to forty age group, the sex ratio bottomed out at 39.2 percent in 1921.[150] The absolute population of the island dropped from 195,558 in 1901 to 172,337 in 1911, and then plunged to 156,744 in 1921. As late as 1946, the population had only reached 192,800, rather less than the 258,260 who would have lived on the island had its 1861–91 population growth rate continued unabated.[151] (Barbados did not in fact reach that population level until 1990.) The 1861–1901 growth rate, however, already included significant emigration. Had the population increased between 1901 and 1946 at the rate of natural increase, then Barbados would have housed 319,947 people in 1946—although higher death rates from worsening malnutrition would have likely lowered that number somewhat.[152]

Second, Barbadian wages for unskilled male workers rose as emigration gathered pace. By 1910, the American consul in Bridgetown reported that agricultural workers received 30¢ per day, a 25 percent rise in nominal wages over the 1900 level.[153] Moreover, unpaid labor (due to the located labor laws) basically disappeared. To deal with the shortages and rising male wages, planters began to employ tenant women in the cane fields.[154] They also began to substitute capital for labor. In 1910 there were no modern sugar centrals on the island—instead, windmill-powered presses wasted upwards of 30 percent of the raw material.[155] By 1921, in contrast, nineteen modern sugar centrals had entered operation.[156] (See figure 4.4.)

The direct effect of remittances was relatively small in terms of bolstering living standards. In 1906, when Carter declared their importance, they came to 73¢ (U.S.) per inhabitant per year; call

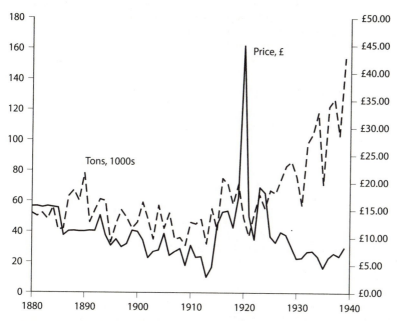

Figure 4.4:   Barbados sugar exports, 1880–1940. *Source*: Brian R. Mitchell, *International Historical Statistics: The Americas, 1750–2000* (New York: Palgrave Macmillan, 2003), 297–98, 527, 531.

it three days' wages. Contemporary estimates of the total inflow varied between $34,600 and $121,000 annually, or 20¢ to 70¢ per person.[157] Those estimates, however, appear to have been low. Estimates derived from records of money orders from Panama give a slightly larger number: $1.75 per inhabitant of Barbados per year in 1906–14. (See table 4.8.)[158] That number amounts to a bit more than a week's labor for a male worker at 1910 wage rates. Remittances allowed Barbados to cover its chronic trade deficits, but they did not directly raise living standards by more than a few percentage points.

The indirect effects of "Panama money," on the other hand, were huge. First, it bolstered the growth of smallholders. In 1897, an estimated 8,500 small proprietors held a bit less than 10,000 acres. By 1912, 13,152 smallholders owned plots.[159] Assuming that the average size of holding remained constant, this represented

TABLE 4.8
Remittances from Panama to Barbados, 1906–20

	Postal orders from CZ	Money remitted through post	Money declared upon return	Total	Remittances per inhabitant, US$
1906	3,613	£ 7,509	£ 18,800	£ 26,309	$ 0.73
1907	19,092	£ 46,160	£ 26,291	£ 72,451	$ 2.02
1908	26,360	£ 63,210	£ 21,864	£ 85,074	$ 2.38
1909	31,179	£ 66,272	£ 14,820	£ 81,092	$ 2.28
1910	31,059	£ 62,280	£ 20,604	£ 82,884	$ 2.33
1911	24,968	£ 51,009	£ 14,032	£ 65,041	$ 1.83
1912	28,394	£ 56,042	£ 12,773	£ 68,815	$ 1.96
1913	31,851	£ 63,816	£ 19,342	£ 83,158	$ 2.39
1914	22,619	£ 39,586	£ 16,449	£ 56,035	$ 1.65
1915	14,210	£ 22,874	£ 6,666	£ 29,540	$ 0.85
1916	11,241	£ 17,539			
1917	10,430	£ 15,194			
1918	8,777	£ 12,680			
1919	7,747	£ 12,591			
1920	5,782	£ 9,173			

Source: Bonham Richardson, *Panama Money in Barbados, 1900–1920* (Knoxville: University of Tennessee Press, 1985), 144, 157, 165.

an increase in smallholder ownership of 5,500 acres, or over 22 square kilometers, 5 percent of the land area of Barbados. (Had the average size risen, the transferred area would have been greater.) By 1929, the number of smallholding households had further increased to 17,731. Land ownership on the island remained astoundingly concentrated, but the percentage of Barbadians who lived in property-owning households rose from 18 percent in 1897 to 40 percent by 1929.[160] The rise in property ownership prompted the first wave of black political activism, including the election of blacks into the parliament, which was restricted by property and income qualifications.

Second, remittances supercharged the growth of the Barbadian banking sector. (See table 4.9.) Barbadians opened 16,094 new accounts in government savings banks between 1906 and 1913, while deposits increased 88 percent.[161] By 1920, deposits per person had surpassed $11. These figures gave Barbados a level of financial penetration roughly 47 percent of contemporary Spain and 66 percent of contemporary Italy.[162] This was a very high level of financial penetration for such a poor country, and prefigured Barbados' emergence as a regional banking center a half century later.

Third, "Panama money" prompted the emergence of a Barbadian social insurance state. The "friendly society" served as a form of insurance pool. For a weekly fee of ten to twelve pence, the societies provided their members with sickness insurance, unemployment insurance, death benefits, free scholarships to household members, and an annual "bonus." In 1901, there were 101 societies; between 1907 and 1910 a further 110 were founded, peaking at 260 in 1920. Their membership grew from 13,933 in 1904 to

TABLE 4.9
Barbadian Savings Bank Statistics, 1901–20

	Number of depositors	New accounts	Total deposits (pounds)	Total deposits (dollars)	Deposits per inhabitant
1901	13,457		97,161	473,174	$ 2.67
1902	13,566	1,308	105,226	512,451	$ 2.90
1903	13,936	1,341	113,462	551,425	$ 3.12
1904	14,212	1,625			
1905	14,773	1,464	117,395	571,714	$ 3.26
1906	15,308	1,764	138,839	673,369	$ 3.85
1907	16,193	2,465	153,452	745,777	$ 4.28
1908	17,793	2,212	195,745	953,278	$ 5.48
1909	18,696	1,973	216,278	1,053,274	$ 6.08
1910	19,576	2,124	233,010	1,132,429	$ 6.55
1911	20,185	1,931	295,912	1,438,132	$ 8.34
1912	20,683	1,909	261,602	1,274,002	$ 7.46
1913	20,572	1,716	253,013	1,232,173	$ 7.29
1914	20,881		209,339	1,032,041	$ 6.16
1915	20,393		193,646	921,755	$ 5.56
1916	19,973		203,731	971,797	$ 5.91
1917	13,110		254,790	1,212,800	$ 7.45
1918	12,639		262,270	1,248,405	$ 7.74
1919	12,647		303,734	1,345,542	$ 8.42
1920	13,057		496,479	1,817,113	$ 11.48

Source: Bonham Richardson, *Panama Money in Barbados, 1900–1920* (Knoxville: University of Tennessee Press, 1985), 144, 157, 165.

46,207 in 1920. The 1921 census found that 156,312 people lived in households belonging to a friendly society. That was 94 percent of the population. Alongside the friendlies were the "landships," which provided similar services along with ceremonial drills and uniforms modeled on the Royal Navy. Infant mortality continued to lag the rest of the Caribbean until the 1950s, but the societies aided a huge increase in literacy, to 93 percent by 1946.[163]

In short, remittances financed the creation of a middle class, a relatively large banking system, a social insurance scheme, and a big increase in educational attainment. Eventually the government took over the latter two functions, but in a context of fairly high expectations and a politically mobilized population. The Panama Canal project had utterly transformed Barbados.

FIVE

CROSSING THE DITCH

The canal cannot be a paying concern for any country
except the United States, and for the United States it is
a paying concern, not from a commercial standpoint—
it will therein be a loser, but on account of its Navy.

—*Spencer Dickson, British vice-consul to Colombia*

Huh! Is that all we got for nine years' work and half a
billion dollars?

—*Harry Franck*

THE PANAMA CANAL WAS AN ENGINEERING MARVEL. Many
people also predicted the Panama Canal would be an economic
marvel. Nearly all the early boosters and promoters of an isthmian
canal believed that a canal would be a godsend for world commerce. In 1903 the British vice-consul in Colombia presented a
Colombian estimate of the canal's economic value to the U.S. Congress. It concluded that an isthmian canal would produce benefits
worth $1.2 billion when capitalized, or 4.7 percent of United States
GDP at the time.[1]

Other observers were not so optimistic about the Panama Canal's economic utility. The costs and efforts that went into the canal's construction were heroic, but heroism does not pay the bills.
The same British vice-consul who provided Congress with the Colombian estimate stated, "The canal cannot be a paying concern

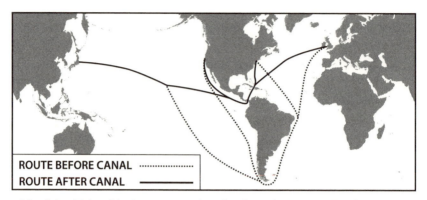

Map 5.1: Major shipping routes with and without the Panama Canal.

for any country except the United States, and for the United States it is a paying concern, not from a commercial standpoint—it will therein be a loser, but on account of its Navy."[2] From this point of view, the military and strategic benefits of the Panama Canal were the most important.

The economic boosters of the canal turned out to be correct, despite the delays and overruns during the Panama Canal's construction. The Panama Canal prompted large drops in the cost of transportation relative to the next-cheapest historical alternatives: steamships around Cape Horn or railroads across the United States. It freed up immense resources for economic growth, more than enough to justify its construction costs and its defense costs.

The benefits, however, were not evenly distributed. American producers, consumers, and transporters captured the lion's share of the canal's transport costs savings. Outside the United States, only Chile and Japan benefitted to any great extent. Income also shifted within the United States: California and the Pacific Northwest benefitted at the expense of the South.

THE PANAMA CANAL: TRANSPORTATION COST SAVINGS

The Panama Canal's chief benefit to world trade came from shortening the effective distance between ports. In the absence of the canal, trade between the East Coast and the West Coast of the

United States had three options: travel via transcontinental rail-road; travel by ship to Mexico or Panama for transfer via the Te-huantepec or Panama railroads, followed by another ship; or travel by ship around the southern tip of South America.[3] Cargoes travel-ling between Europe and the western coast of the Americas faced a similar set of options in the absence of the canal. (See table 5.1.) The canal had little impact on shipping distances between Europe and Asia, or between Europe and Australia, which could go through the Suez Canal or around the Cape of Good Hope.

Did the drop in distances prompted by the Panama Canal lead to an equivalent drop in freight rates? After all, it is possible to imagine a scenario in which the shipping lines captured all of the benefit from the opening of the canal, rather than passing those benefits on to consumers. Alternatively, it is possible to imagine a world in which the fixed cost of loading and unloading freight was so high that it overwhelmed any distance-related decrease in the marginal cost of running a ship. Neither scenario, however, appears to fit the reality. Saif Mohammed and Jeffrey Williamson

TABLE 5.1
Representative Distances of Shipping Routes, Miles

	Shortest alternative	Via Panama Canal
U.S. routes		
U.S. East to U.S. West	13,277	6,146
U.S. East to Canada West total	14,054	6,925
U.S. East to South America West total	8,512	5,515
U.S. East to Asia total	16,746	11,471
U.S. East to Australasia total	12,762	10,573
U.S. West to Europe total	13,841	7,825
Non-U.S. routes		
Europe to Canada West	13,251	8,602
Europe to Australasia	11,514	12,250
Europe to South America West	11,841	7,192
Europe to Asia	10,465	13,148
Mexico East to South America West	9,088	4,785

Source: Distances.com, "World Ports Distances Calculator," www.distances.com.

compiled a series of shipping rates between selected ports in the early twentieth century. In 1920, when the Panama Canal first opened to commercial traffic, real freight rates between Britain (Liverpool) and the West Coast of the United States (Portland, Oregon) dropped 27 percent. In 1921, the canal's first full year of operation, real shipping costs dropped another 35 percent. Much of the initial decline appears to be a return to normalcy from the elevated freight charges caused by the First World War, but by 1922, shipping costs had fallen 31 percent below their prewar average. The cost of transporting cargoes between New York and Asia dropped 18 percent, and the cost of transporting cargoes between California and Europe dropped 25 percent.[4] If the drop in freight rates in 1921–22 was due to the opening of the canal, which reduced costs by cutting travel distance, then the *per-mile* transportation cost should not have changed when the canal opened. Part of the cost of transporting a ton of cargo is fixed and does not change with distance: loading and unloading, warehousing, insurance, docking fees, and so on.[5] After stripping out estimated fixed costs, real per-mile costs on international routes did not change between 1921 and 1922. (See table 5.2.) This is consistent with the hypothesis that the drop in international freight rates was entirely due to the Panama Canal–caused reduction in the distances that ships needed to travel.

Freight rates on U.S. domestic routes did not show this pattern. Rather, intercoastal freight rates on U.S. domestic routes dropped dramatically, falling by a third when the Panama Canal opened, before *rising* in the Great Depression. Why did per-mile freight rates behave differently on domestic and international routes? The answer is that international rates, unlike domestic ones, were set in a competitive market. International shippers earned few rents before the Panama Canal opened; freight rates between certain destinations dropped because the effective distance between them dropped. Domestic shipping, however, came under the auspices of the Jones Act of 1920. Under the Jones Act, the United States required that all shipping between American ports be carried by

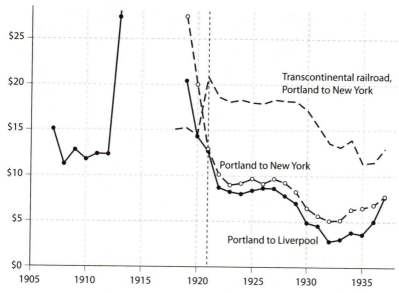

Figure 5.1: Transportation freight rates, constant 1925 dollars per ton. *Source:*
Pre-1915 water rates from Saif I. Shah Mohammed and Jeffrey G. Williamson,
Explorations in Economic History 41 (2004): 172–203, table 2. The 1919 and
1920 water rates from Portland to New York are from Arthur Rockwell, "The
Lumber Trade and the Panama Canal, 1921–1940," *Economic History Review* 24,
no. 3 (1971): 149. The 1921–37 water rates from Portland to New York are from
Rockwell, app. VIII, assuming a conversion factor of 679,000 board-feet per
ton. Railroad freight rates are from Rockwell, app. VII. We converted all rates
into 1925 dollars using the U.S. GDP deflator available at EH.net, "How Much Is
That?" eh.net/hmit.

American-flagged vessels, and the government played a role in
setting rates. The resulting lack of competition meant that domestic maritime freight rates were higher and behaved very differently
than international rates.

The opening of the Panama Canal triggered intense competition among domestic shippers in three interrelated ways. First, it
prompted the entry of the U.S. government into the provision of
shipping services. At the end of World War I, the U.S. Shipping
Board wound up with over two thousand vessels that had been
commissioned for the war. Rather than scrap them or sell them

en masse, Congress allowed the Shipping Board to commission merchant lines. These ships came on line after the war ended, and by 1923 the federal government operated 58 percent of the country's steam shipping.[6] Political pressure quickly forced the Shipping Board out of the intercoastal trade, but it continued to sell its lines to "to owners who intend to upset co-operative efforts toward rate stability."[7] Second, the Panama Canal Act of 1912 effectively prevented shipping lines that were owned by railroad companies from using the waterway; it also banned companies using the Panama Canal from negotiating or setting intercoastal shipping rates in violation of the antitrust laws. These provisions greatly increased the

TABLE 5.2

Transportation Freight Rates, Constant 1925 Cents per Ton-Mile

	(a) International	(b) U.S. intercoastal	(c) (a) ÷ (b)
1907	0.08¢		
1908	0.06¢		
1909	0.07¢		
1910	0.06¢		
1921	0.07¢	0.15¢	46%
1922	0.07¢	0.10¢	64%
1923	0.06¢	0.09¢	70%
1924	0.06¢	0.09¢	65%
1925	0.06¢	0.10¢	64%
1926	0.07¢	0.09¢	74%
1927	0.07¢	0.10¢	67%
1928	0.06¢	0.09¢	61%
1929	0.05¢	0.08¢	60%
1930	0.04¢	0.11¢	40%
1931	0.05¢	0.11¢	46%
1932	0.04¢	0.13¢	28%
1933	0.05¢	0.14¢	32%
1934	0.05¢	0.16¢	35%
1935	0.05¢	0.15¢	31%
1936	0.07¢	0.16¢	45%
1937	0.11¢	0.16¢	66%

Source: Noel Maurer and Carlos Yu, "What T. R. Took: The Economic Impact of the Panama Canal, 1903–1937," *Journal of Economic History* 68, no. 3 (2008): 686–721, table 4.

TABLE 5.3

Transport Costs per Ton before and after the Opening of the Canal,
1921 Dollars

	Cost without canal	Cost with canal	% reduction
U.S. routes			
U.S. intercoastal	12.66	8.57	32
U.S. East Coast to British Columbia	13.22	9.13	31
U.S. West Coast to Europe	13.06	9.77	25
U.S. East Coast to Asia	15.14	12.37	18
U.S. East Coast to South American West Coast	9.26	8.12	12
U.S. East Coast to Australasia	12.29	11.73	5
Non-U.S. routes			
Mexico East Coast to South American West Coast	9.67	7.60	21
Europe to South American West Coast	11.64	9.32	20
Europe to British Columbia	12.64	10.32	18

Source: Calculated from data in Noel Maurer and Carlos Yu, "What T. R. Took: The Economic Impact of the Panama Canal, 1903–1937," *Journal of Economic History* 68, no. 3 (2008).

intensity of competition, even absent the government's entry into the business. Before the war, the railroads had controlled 61.9 percent of regular line tonnage on the Atlantic and 19.8 percent on the Pacific.[8] Lastly, the opening of the Panama Canal meant that "the best of our privately owned merchant fleet deserted foreign trade routes and entered the protected trade between the Atlantic and Pacific coast."[9] In short, the political economy of domestic shipping in the United States meant that the opening of the Panama Canal prompted a drop in shipping rates above and beyond the reduction in the seagoing distance between New York and California. The cost of moving material between California and New York dropped a full 32 percent.[10] (See table 5.3.) The Panama Canal generated a transportation revolution.

The cost of shipping goods through the Panama Canal depended on several physical factors, such as distance, tonnage, and fuel. One factor, however, was determined purely by human agency: tolls. The United States, as the proud new possessor of the Panama Canal, faced an economic choice in setting canal tolls. Should it attempt to maximize its benefits of canal ownership by discriminating between American ships and those of other nations? Or should it run the canal "for the benefit of the world" and engage in price neutrality? Ultimately, the United States chose to charge the same price per ton to all ships crossing the Panama Canal, regardless of nationality or route.

The decision to pursue a policy of toll neutrality was politically controversial inside the United States. In fact, Congress initially mandated the reverse. The Panama Canal Act of 1912 stated that the canal would charge *no* tolls for intra-U.S. traffic, a rather extreme form of price discrimination. The international nature of Panama Canal commerce, however, brought diplomatic pressure to bear on this policy. The British government protested that allowing intra-U.S. traffic toll-free use of the canal would violate the terms of the Hay-Pauncefote Treaty, which allowed the U.S. government to construct and operate a transoceanic canal under the condition that it kept the canal open to commercial use by all countries without discrimination.[11] President Taft was not sympathetic to the British position. "The British protest," he wrote, "is a proposal to read into the treaty surrender by the United States of its right to regulate its own commerce in its own way and by its own methods."[12] Taft's position, unsurprisingly, was politically popular. During the 1912 presidential campaign, both of Taft's opponents—Woodrow Wilson for the Democrats and Theodore Roosevelt for the Progressive Party—declared their support for the Panama Canal Act.[13] It passed the Senate 47 to 15, including an additional provision that extended the toll exemption to American-owned ships engaged in foreign trade.[14]

Once elected, however, President Wilson changed his stance.

At a private preinauguration dinner meeting, former secretary of state Elihu Root and former ambassador to Great Britain Joseph Choate pointed out the dangers of discriminating between foreign and American shipping to the new president-elect. "This has been an illuminating discussion," said Wilson. "I knew very little about this subject. I think I now understand it and the principles that are involved. When the time comes for me to act, you may count upon my taking the right stand."[15] What Root and Choate had pointed out to the president-elect was that an American refusal to abide by the terms of the Hay-Pauncefote Treaty brought with it the possibility of British retaliation. In a game of tit for tat, Britain might refuse to renew the Arbitration Convention, which required the United Kingdom to take disputes between itself and the United States to a special court in The Hague rather than make its own unilateral decisions. More prosaically, the British might interfere with American policy in Mexico.[16] Wilson also had a domestic justification for toll neutrality. He did not want to subsidize the railroad companies which owned most of the country's transcontinental maritime trade, and who would therefore reap most of the benefits from toll-free canal traffic. As Secretary of State William Jennings Bryan put it, "If we are to give bounties to coastwise vessels for one reason, we will be asked to give bounties to some other corporations for reasons equally as good: and the party's power to protect the public treasury will be paralyzed."[17]

Wilson succeeded in having the Panama Canal Act repealed on June 15, 1914.[18] The vote was contentious but decisive—247–162 in the House and 50–35 in the Senate.[19] The new bill fixed tolls between 75¢ and $1.25 per ton, and mandated that they would apply equally to all ships. The only permitted variation in tolls per ton stemmed from the size of the passing ship.[20]

THE SOCIAL RETURNS FROM THE PANAMA CANAL

The Panama Canal attracted no small share of doubters, since it ran years behind schedule and massively over budget. Engineering problems bedeviled the project, as did labor shortages and high mortality. In addition, the canal required significant expenditures on fortification and defense. Canal construction in 1903–20 coincided with several revolutions in military technology, and canal fortifications multiplied from simple shore batteries to include airstrips, air defenses, minefields, and antisubmarine defenses. The Americans solved these problems, but at a high cost. By the time all was said and done, the Panama Canal cost more than twice Congress's initial projections.

Was the Panama Canal worth the expense? To answer this question, a method is needed to quantify the benefits the canal provided to world shipping. Robert Fogel's classic social savings analysis of American railroads in the nineteenth century provides just such a method. To determine the economic effects that railroads had on the economic growth of the United States, Fogel asked how many additional resources would have been consumed had all the goods that the railroads transported needed to be shipped by other means. He also compared the cost of building the railroads to the cost of a hypothetical expanded canal network. By comparing the difference between the historical and the counterfactual cases, Fogel was able to estimate the "social savings" railroads brought the United States over and above an expanded network of canals and roadways.[21]

In order to calculate the aggregate social savings that the Panama Canal provided to the world, it is first necessary to estimate how much it cost to transport freight through the Panama Canal. In addition, it is necessary to estimate the comparable cost to transport that freight in the absence of the Panama Canal, either by taking a longer steamship route or (in the case of intercoastal traffic) by using the transcontinental railroads. In other words, the first step is to calculate how much more it would have cost to move the same amount of goods had the Panama Canal been suddenly shut down in any given year, a method that the economist Paul David once jokingly referred to as "economics by strategic bombing force."[22]

Since the counterfactual cost of moving freight by alternative means is in fact *counter*factual, an estimate of costs which did not take place, it is important to use as pessimistic of assumptions as possible in estimating those costs. In that way, the results will be biased against the hypothesis that the Panama Canal produced significant social savings. The resulting estimate will provide a strong lower bound to the "real" social savings caused by the canal.

Four pessimistic assumptions, therefore, underpin the counterfactual analysis. The first assumption is that the opening of the Panama Canal did not reduce the fixed cost of shipping. This is corroborated by the claims of contemporary observers that the opening of the Panama Canal would not affect insurance rates.[23] If the opening of the Panama Canal did in fact reduce the fixed cost of shipping, then the estimated social savings from the Panama Canal will be *lower* than the actual social savings. The second assumption is that all reductions in per-mile shipping costs after 1921 were caused by improvements in shipping technology or drops in the cost of inputs such as fuel and labor, and *not* the opening of the canal. To the extent that the Panama Canal catalyzed technological improvements in shipping, then the estimated social savings from the Panama Canal will also be *lower* than the actual social savings. The third assumption is that there were no savings in inventory costs due to lowered time in transit. This assumption is clearly unrealistic, but ignoring inventory savings further pushes down the estimated social savings. The final assumption is that intercoastal cargoes would have been shipped via transcontinental railroad in the absence of the Panama Canal. The reason for this assumption is that transcontinental freight rates were lower than transcontinental shipping costs before the opening of the canal. (See figure 5.1.) Using the higher intercoastal shipping costs instead of railroad rates would artificially inflate the estimate of social savings. Instead, the assumption of railroad rates lowers the estimated social savings further.

As calculated, therefore, the basic social savings estimate from the Panama Canal will consist of the sum of the cost savings for cargo plus the profit and interest payments remitted back to the U.S. Treasury. For all cargoes save intercoastal U.S. shipping, the social savings will equal the difference in the number of ton-miles that needed to be shipped multiplied by the cost per ton-mile. (See table 5.2.) The Panama Canal administration collected tonnage and route data on all cargoes passing through the canal. The administration aggregated the data into eleven routes, recording tonnage separately for each direction. For each aggregated route, representative distances were calculated with and without using the Panama Canal, selecting specific city pairs on the basis of anecdotal evidence from the official reports.[24] Given the negligible distance reduction caused by the Panama Canal along the Europe-Asia and Europe-Australasia routes, and the small volume of cargoes they moved through the Panama Canal, no savings were attributed to the Panama Canal on those routes. In effect, the method weighted each route by the volume of cargo passing through the canal and the difference in the distance created by its opening.

The calculation of the social savings for U.S. transcontinental cargoes required a slightly different method. For most intercoastal cargoes, the transcontinental railroad is a cheaper counterfactual than shipment around Cape Horn.[25] (We can see historical evidence of this in the small volumes of trade between U.S. Atlantic and Pacific ports around Cape Horn or through the Strait of Magellan after the opening of the first Transcontinental Railroad.[26]) It is relatively straightforward to subtract the cost of shipping a ton between the coasts via the Panama Canal from the cost of transporting a ton via transcontinental railroad.[27] Multiplying that difference by the total amount of intercoastal freight transported via the Panama Canal then gives the total cost savings produced by the canal.

Table 5.4 works through a sample social savings calculation for 1921. In its first full year of commercial operation, the Panama Canal carried nearly nine million tons of cargo between the oceans. The lion's share of the cargo has the East Coast of the United States as either origin or destination. Already the cost savings from using the Panama Canal over the transcontinental railroads or the Cape Horn route were significant: over $27 million in 1925 dollars. Of

TABLE 5-4A

Representative Social Savings Calculation for 1921 (1925 Dollars)

Route	Tonnage	Δ Distance	Real cost per ton-mile from table 5.2	Cost savings = (1) × (2) × (3)
U.S. intercontinental				
U.S. East–South America West	1,908,858	2,997	0.07¢	$3,783,945
U.S. East–Asia	1,641,950	5,275	0.07¢	$5,728,842
U.S. East–Australasia	768,305	2,189	0.07¢	$1,112,407
U.S. West (including Canada)–Europe	1,299,431	6,016	0.07¢	$5,170,654
Non-U.S. intercontinental				
Europe–Canada West	0	4,649	0.07¢	$0
Europe–South America West	1,219,665	4,649	0.07¢	$3,750,460
Mexico East –South America West	654,889	4,303	0.07¢	$1,863,904
Transcontinental using water counterfactual	1,372,388	7,131	0.15¢	$14,209,022
Transcontinental using rail counterfactual	1,372,388	na	na	$10,800,575
Subtotal (using rail counterfactual for trans-continental cargoes)	8,865,486			$32,210,788
Minus tolls				($6,216,739)
Plus profits remitted to U.S. Treasury				$1,074,427
Total				$27,068,476

Rail counterfactual calculations:	*Panama Canal*	*Cape Horn*	*Transcontinental railroad*	
Cost of transcontinental shipping, one ton	$12.93	$23.31	$20.80	
Cost of transcontinental shipping, 1,372,388 tons	$17,743,659	$31,992,532	$28,544,234	
Social savings from Canal, by alternate route	na	$14,248,873	$10,800,575	

TABLE 5.4B
Annual Social Savings from the Panama Canal, 1921–37
(1925 Dollars, Millions)

1921	1922	1923	1924	1925	1926	1927	1928	1929
27.1	27.9	86.5	137.9	97.6	113.7	117.4	116.2	121.0

1930	1931	1932	1933	1934	1935	1936	1937	
139.8	132.7	98.8	100.8	131.1	71.8	83.1	109.2	

the 1920s, however, 1921 was the year with the *lowest* transport cost savings generated by the Panama Canal. The social savings rapidly rose, and averaged 0.2% of GDP per year over the next two decades. Expressed another way, the social savings from the Panama Canal accounted for almost a tenth of U.S. economic growth over the late 1920s.

Could the railroad system have handled the traffic that passed through the Panama Canal? If not, then the previous social savings estimate is too small, because transferring intercoastal shipping to the railroads would have required investment in new rolling stock and new track, thus raising freight costs. If railroad freight rates went up in the absence of the Panama Canal, then the savings caused by the presence of the Panama Canal would *increase*. In point of fact, however, the capacity of the railroad system does not appear to have been a binding constraint. Between 1921 and 1929, ton-miles transported on U.S. railroads increased by 45 percent while the inflation-adjusted price of rail transport per ton-mile decreased by 13 percent.[28] This implies the United States could have further expanded its railroad freight capacity without significantly driving up the cost of rail transport per ton-mile.

In addition, this methodology ignores the possibility of additional social savings due to market expansion. By pushing transport costs below a key threshold, the Panama Canal could have potentially opened entirely new export markets. (This did in fact happen in the case of Chilean iron exports, which are discussed later.) Hutchinson and Ungo estimated a gravity model for U.S.

net exports in 1912, and used the resulting coefficients to predict American net exports in 1924. To the extent that their model underpredicted net exports, they attributed half of the difference to the Panama Canal.[29] Their estimates are likely too large: gravity models are a blunt instrument. The unexpected increases in net exports could have been due to policy changes in the importing countries or changes in the mix of American exports. That said, the new market effect of the Panama Canal is certainly real. The implication is that the prior methodology significantly underestimates the Panama Canal's actual social savings.

THE SOCIAL RATE OF RETURN

The direct social savings created by the Panama Canal were large, but were they large enough to justify the canal's high cost? In order to answer that question, we need to calculate a "social rate of return." The social rate of return is the ratio of the flow of social savings (including the profits and interest paid to the U.S. Treasury) to the full costs of the canal. These costs are not merely the construction costs of the canal. They include the additional cost of defense installations, the initial payment to Panama, the $25 million payment made to Colombia in 1921, and the interest costs accrued during the construction phase. If the resulting social rate of return is lower than the opportunity cost of capital, then the Panama Canal did not add value to the world economy. The opportunity cost of capital is measured as the rate of return on U.S. federal bonds—how much could be earned from the least risky alternative use of capital, paying down the national debt.

In 1921, the Panama Canal's first full year of operation, the estimated social rate of return was 2.9 percent, significantly less than the rate on U.S. federal ten-year bonds. The social rate of return on the Panama Canal did not remain low for long. By 1923, it exceeded 10 percent, and it remained above the 10 percent level until 1932. Even at its post-1923 nadir, in 1935, the social rate of return never fell below 7.7 percent. (All figures for the canal's construction

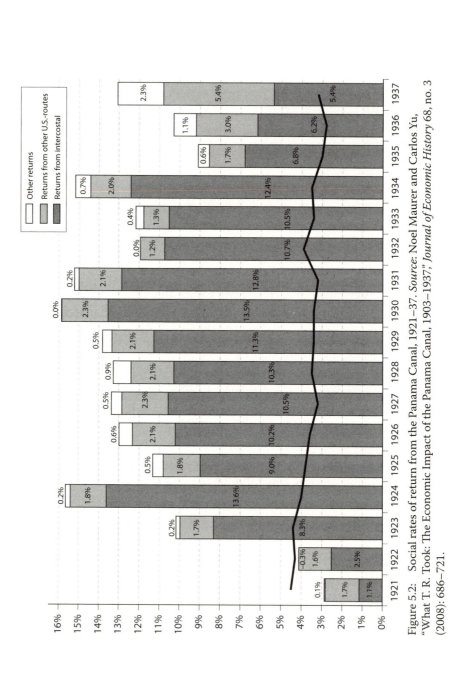

Figure 5.2:   Social rates of return from the Panama Canal, 1921–37. *Source:* Noel Maurer and Carlos Yu, "What T. R. Took: The Economic Impact of the Panama Canal, 1903–1937," *Journal of Economic History* 68, no. 3 (2008): 686–721.

cost and the cost savings generated every year are converted to 1925 dollars.) Not only were the social savings caused by the Panama Canal large, it was a remarkable return on investment. (See figure 5.2.) The lion's share of the social savings was generated by intercoastal traffic. International routes that began or ended in the United States generated less than 20 percent of social savings (until 1936), and purely international routes generated no more than 7 percent.

THE PRICE SENSITIVITY OF SHIPPERS

The previous calculation of the social rate of return assumes that the same amount of cargo would have been shipped to the same locations in the absence of the Panama Canal. This is clearly untrue. During the 1920s, the lion's share of the domestic cargo passing through the canal consisted of petroleum from Southern California and lumber from the Pacific Northwest. Both products had substitutes that did not need the canal: Venezuelan oil and southern pine lumber. The same can be said for many international cargoes which passed through the canal. For example, Philippine sugar or copra both had domestic substitutes. This implies shippers were sensitive to costs: had the shipping cost of the more distant good been too high, the cheaper substitute would have been used instead. Had the Panama Canal been suddenly shut down (or never built), consumers and producers would have found ways to adapt to the higher transport costs. In other words, the previous estimates of social savings are too large, because they assume that consumers had no options other than paying the higher transport costs in order to consume the same goods from the same places that they would have consumed with the Panama Canal in operation.

It is possible to calculate the social rate of return under various scenarios of the sensitivity of shippers to transport costs.[30] The price sensitivity of demand is usually measured by elasticity. Briefly, given a doubling of the transport cost per ton-mile, a price elasticity of demand of 1.0 implies that only half the amount of

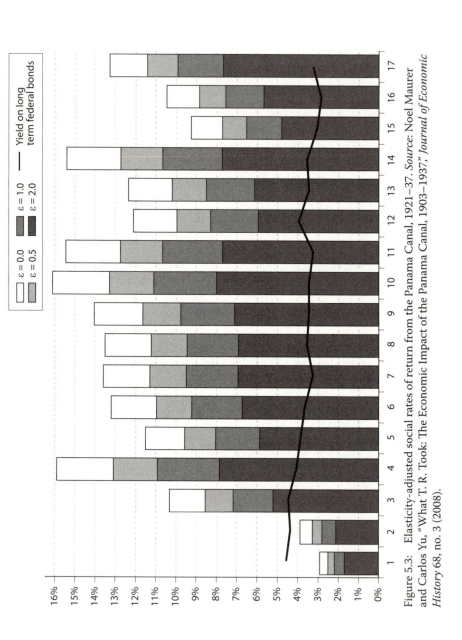

Figure 5.3: Elasticity-adjusted social rates of return from the Panama Canal, 1921–37. *Source:* Noel Maurer and Carlos Yu, "What T. R. Took: The Economic Impact of the Panama Canal, 1903–1937," *Journal of Economic History* 68, no. 3 (2008).

ton-miles would have been moved. A price elasticity of 2.0 implies that only a quarter of the original amount of ton-miles would have been shipped in the face of a price doubling. (A price elasticity of 0.0 implies perfectly inelastic demand: no change in price will affect the volume of shipping one way or the other.) Figure 5.3 presents estimates of the Panama Canal's social rates of return across a broad range of elasticities, comparing them against the initial assumption of perfectly inelastic demand.[31] Even with the extreme assumption of a demand elasticity for shipping of 2.0, the average social rate of return remains well in excess of the 4.2 percent real return on U.S. government bonds during the period. (See figure 5.3.)

An alternative way of looking at the social returns for the Panama Canal project is to calculate an "internal social rate of return" for the project. An internal rate of return is the discount rate at which the net present value of a series of cash flows is equal to zero. It can be used to compare the returns available from different projects with different patterns of outlays and revenues. The internal social rate of return adds social savings to the profits remitted to the U.S. Treasury in order to calculate the net cash flows generated by the Panama Canal. (See table 5.5.) Even at a high demand elasticity of 2.0, the internal rate of return for the Panama Canal is more than 50 percent higher than the internal rate of return generated by investing the same amount over the same period in government bonds.

TABLE 5.5
Inflation-Adjusted Internal Rate of Return, by Demand Elasticity

Base year = 1904	Panama Canal	Government bonds
$\varepsilon = 0.0$	9.4%	4.0%
$\varepsilon = 0.5$	8.7%	4.0%
$\varepsilon = 1.0$	7.8%	4.0%
$\varepsilon = 1.5$	7.1%	4.0%
$\varepsilon = 2.0$	6.4%	4.0%

Source: Noel Maurer and Carlos Yu, "What T. R. Took: The Economic Impact of the Panama Canal, 1903–1937," *Journal of Economic History* 68, no. 3 (2008), table 8.

The American politicians who backed the creation of the Panama Canal did not do so in order to benefit global commerce. The Taft administration tried to mandate that the canal would charge no tolls on intra-U.S. traffic, and the Wilson administration only backed down under intense pressure from the United Kingdom. The United States agreed to charge the same tolls and grant the same access to American and foreign-flagged vessels. The United States also agreed to refrain from discriminating between vessels bound to U.S. ports and vessels traveling purely international routes, although Washington prevented foreign warships from passing through the canal.[32] The goal of the politicians who backed the canal was the stimulation of *American* commerce and the capture of the canal's benefits by *American* producers and consumers.

Geography ensured that the United States would reap most of the benefits from the Panama Canal, despite the diplomatic need to grant its open access to ships of all nations on all routes. The fact that the United States possessed economic centers on both coasts meant that the Panama Canal would carry much of the U.S. East Coast's trade with Asia and the West Coast's trade with Europe, as well as a significant amount of intra-U.S. commerce. In fact, intra-U.S. transcontinental traffic averaged 41 percent of the cargo passing through the canal (by tonnage) in 1923–37. (Foreign-bound cargo originating in U.S. ports made up 19 percent, while foreign cargo terminating in U.S. ports made up an additional 15 percent over the same period. Only 25 percent of all cargo passing through the canal travelled entirely non-U.S. routes.) Figure 5.2 shows that the social rate of return on routes that originated or ended in the United States—or in the case of the intercoastal trade, both—was more than enough to justify the Panama Canal's high start-up costs. In fact, the returns presented in figure 5.2 are underestimates of the gains to the United States, since transit profits on all routes went to Washington but American shippers paid very few of the tolls on non-U.S. routes.

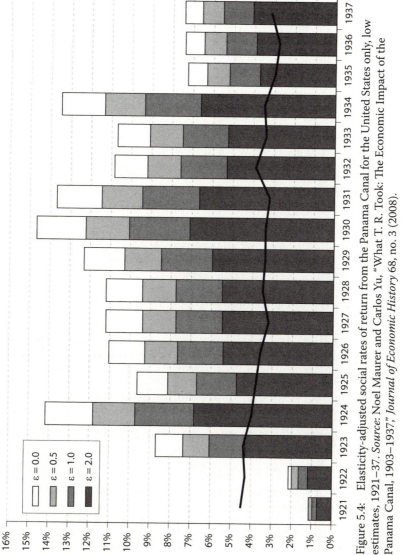

Figure 5.4: Elasticity-adjusted social rates of return from the Panama Canal for the United States only, low estimates, 1921–37. *Source:* Noel Maurer and Carlos Yu, "What T. R. Took: The Economic Impact of the Panama Canal, 1903–1937," *Journal of Economic History* 68, no. 3 (2008).

Americans could not have captured all of the social savings on international routes that started or ended in the United States. Consider the two extreme cases of perfect competition and monopoly. If markets were perfectly competitive, then foreign exporters to the United States would pass on all their cost savings to American consumers. The opening of the canal would cause the import prices including cost, insurance, and freight (CIF prices) faced by U.S. consumers to fall by an amount equal to the drop in transportation costs engendered by the canal. By symmetry, however, this same assumption implies that U.S. exporters would receive no benefits from the opening of the canal. Consumers in other countries would enjoy lower CIF prices for exports from the United States, while American exporters would receive the same free on board (FOB) prices as they had before the canal opened. Conversely, if import-export markets were monopolistic, American consumers would receive no benefit from the canal. Instead, foreign exporters would capture all the cost savings for themselves and not pass them along to consumers. Similarly, U.S. exporters would capture all the benefits from the Panama Canal, and pass none of the savings along to foreign shippers or consumers.

The United States exported more than it imported during the period in question. Thus, Americans would save more under the assumption of monopolistic import-export markets, and Americans would save less under the assumption of competitive import-export markets. In order to present the lowest possible estimates of the returns the Panama Canal generated for the United States, the social rates of return estimates in figure 5.4 assume perfectly competitive markets. (They also include the Panama Canal profits and interest payments historically remitted to the U.S. Treasury.) The lowest estimates are still well above the rate of return on U.S. government bonds.

Our internal social rate of return estimates through 1937 give similar results. (See table 5.6.) Even at a demand elasticity of 2.0, the social benefits received by American consumers and taxpayers from the Panama Canal more than justified the project's start-up costs. American taxpayers may have paid more than they expected

TABLE 5.6

Inflation-Adjusted Internal Rate of Return for the U.S. Only,
by Demand Elasticity

Base year = 1904	Panama Canal	Government bonds
ε = 0.0	9.1%	4.0%
ε = 0.5	8.4%	4.0%
ε = 1.0	7.5%	4.0%
ε = 1.5	6.7%	4.0%
ε = 2.0	6.0%	4.0%

Source: Noel Maurer and Carlos Yu, "What T. R. Took: The Economic Impact of the Panama Canal, 1903–1937," *Journal of Economic History* 68, no. 3 (2008), table 11.

for the Panama Canal, but they appear to have received a decent return on their investment. At a demand elasticity of 0.5, in line with other studies of transportation projects, Americans received a return on their investment of more than double the return on U.S. government bonds. Even at a high elasticity of 2.0, Americans received a return more than 50 percent above the risk-free rate.

How much of the returns to Americans were due to Theodore Roosevelt's strong-arming of the Panamanian government? Under all of the alternative agreements on the table (see chapter 3), significant portions of the social savings would have been transferred to the owners of the isthmus—either the Panamanian or Colombian government. (See tables 3.6 and 5.7.) Table 5.7 calculates the net present value of the Panama Canal project to the United States. It

TABLE 5.7

Loss to U.S. of Various Agreements Relative to Hay–Bunau-Varilla,
Percent of U.S. Social Savings (ε = 0.5), Net Present Value Terms

Hay-Herrán	19.6
Concha proposal	26.1
Menocal Contract	26.4
Wyse Concession	26.7
Senate offer	44.5
Frelinghuysen-Zavala	61.4

Source: See table 3.6.

treats construction, defense construction, and capitalized interest expenditures during the construction period as expenditures, and the net social savings—including payments to the U.S. Treasury and the small social savings generated by the limited number of transits between 1915 and 1920—as positive returns. Because of the higher net present value of the isthmus under the Hay-Herrán Treaty, the United States would have lost a fifth of the economic benefits that it in fact received. Under an agreement modeled after the Wyse Concession, the Colombian benchmark for a new agreement, the United States would have lost a quarter. The Colombian counteroffer in 1903 would have taken almost half the social returns, and an agreement modeled after the Frelinghuysen-Zavala Treaty signed between the United States and Nicaragua would have transferred almost *two-thirds* of the social savings to the local government.

THE CASE OF CHILE: IRON FOR WORLD INDUSTRY

Three countries gained particularly from the Panama Canal. One was the United States. The other two were Chile and Japan. Chile benefitted through increased exports of its natural resources to a larger market, while Japan benefitted from greater trade with the United States. Both Chile and Japan were distant from the economies of the North Atlantic, the global economic core of the early twentieth century. In both cases, by shortening the effective distance to market and decreasing the cost of ocean freight, the Panama Canal expanded trade at the margin and turned previously unprofitable assets into profitable ones.

Through most of the twentieth century, mineral and metal exports dominated the Chilean economy. As such, Chile immediately benefitted from the new canal. In the canal's first year of operation, Chilean nitrates were the largest commodity shipped through the canal, with over 650,000 gross tons sent to Atlantic ports. Chilean nitrates, however, faced increasing competition from American-produced substitutes, either as a by-product of coke manufacture or through the newly discovered Haber-Bosch process. World by-product nitrogen manufacture surpassed Chilean nitrate production in 1915, and production from the Haber-Bosch process exceeded it in 1921.[33] In short, Chilean nitrates were a declining industry. The savings provided by the Panama Canal gave it a new lease on life in the face of technological change, but they were not enough to resurrect the industry.

Nor did the canal have much of a direct effect on the Chilean copper industry. The Chilean copper boom following World War I can be traced to prewar American investment and technological improvements in mining techniques.[34] Copper was an absolutely necessary input for the construction of modern power transmission and communication lines. Demand for copper was therefore relatively inelastic. In addition, Chile was a low-cost producer relative to the United States and Mexico. The savings provided by the Panama Canal were useful but not necessary for the industry's development. During the 1920s, for example, transport costs per pound to New York averaged only 2.1 percent of the metal's market price and 4.9 percent of production costs, down only marginally from 2.6 percent of price and 6.9 percent of production cost in 1912–13.[35] A savings of 2 percent of production cost due to the Panama Canal is not nothing, but nor is it a huge change in the fortunes of the industry, which were far more dependent on price swings in the commodity markets than on the cost of transportation.

The Chilean export that did dramatically benefit from the Panama Canal was iron ore. Chile's unexploited El Tofo iron ore deposit astonished mining engineers. Its main mass consisted of an enormous reserve of forty million tons of high-grade iron ore, 20 percent richer than the declining Lake Superior ores, and its low phosphorus content made it eminently suitable for the Bessemer process of steelmaking. It was only seven and a half kilometers from the harbor at Cruz Grande, all downhill, and it was only ten kilometers from the mining town of La Higuera, which had water, mail service, and a telegraph.[36] Nevertheless, between 1910 and 1913, Altos Hornos de Chile mined only fifty thousand tons of iron ore from El Tofo, most of which was sold to France, travelling through the Straits of Magellan. The reason, quite simply, was that it could not be economically shipped to markets in the northeastern United States.[37]

The economics of El Tofo iron changed dramatically with the advent of the Panama Canal. Bethlehem Steel became very interested indeed in El Tofo. The FOB cost of El Tofo iron ore at the Sparrows Point industrial complex near Baltimore was $5.70 before the opening of the Panama Canal, compared to $4.70 per ton for Swedish or Spanish ore of a similar grade.[38] Three dollars of the cost of Chilean ore was due to shipping costs.[39] In 1913, with the canal's opening (mistakenly) believed imminent, Bethlehem signed a renewable thirty-year contract with Chile, leasing the mine for a rent of $250,000 per year plus a sliding royalty scale per ton of mineral extracted.[40] Bethlehem built a specialized dock near El Tofo, with exactly the seawater draft of the Panama Canal, and Bethlehem Shipyards built nine ore barges precisely fitted for the new dock and the canal.[41] (During the Second World War, German submarines sank five of them.)[42] Bethlehem's investment paid off even though the Panama Canal was not fully open to commercial traffic until 1920. After the canal opened, El Tofo ore cost only $4.10 per ton—a shipping reduction of 28 percent.[43] El Tofo became fully operational in 1924.

Bethlehem operated El Tofo and its associated mines until 1971, when they were expropriated by the Allende government.[44] El Tofo supplied between 5 to 10 percent of Bethlehem Steel's needed iron ore.[45] Between 1913 and 1955, the mine produced fifty-three million tons of mineral and paid $523 million (in constant 2009 dollars) in royalties to the Chilean government, providing 1.0 percent of Chilean government revenues.[46] Despite having no stake in the isthmus, Chile clearly benefitted from the Panama Canal.

THE CASE OF JAPAN: PREWAR TRADE AND THE PANAMA CANAL

The benefits of the Panama Canal for Japan were broad but difficult to quantify. Unfortunately, the canal administration in its early years did not collect the information that would make a detailed

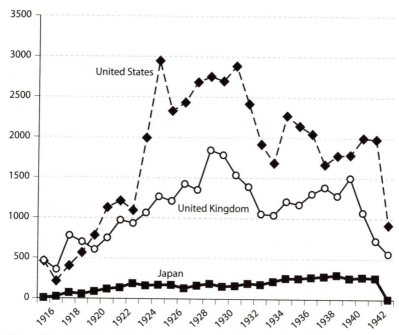

Figure 5.5:   Commercial Panama Canal transits, by nationality, 1915–42.
Source: *Annual Reports* (selected years).

social savings calculation for Japan possible. We can say, however, that the Panama Canal specifically benefitted one sector of the Japanese economy: the shipping industry. Japanese shipping was an "early adopter" of the Panama Canal. Japanese ships made six passages through the canal during its first year of operation, twice as many as France. With the expansion of Japanese overseas shipping during World War I, the country became one of the leading users of the canal. Japanese ships ranked third behind only the United States and Great Britain in terms of tons of cargo carried through the canal from 1920 through 1925, until surpassed by the Norwegian merchant marine in 1926.[47] (See figure 5.5.)

Most Japanese trade through the Panama Canal was carried by larger Japanese ships along scheduled lines, operated principally by the Osaka Shosen Kaisha (Osaka Mercantile Marine), Japan's "second" shipping company.[48] The OSK was a beneficiary of the expansion of Japanese international shipping during World War I, its international carriers growing from a single 5,000-ton ship in 1914 to forty-two ships totaling 333,000 tons by 1920.[49] As such, it was preadapted to take the bulk of the Japanese trade through the Panama Canal. The OSK specialized in long-distance routes, including an around-the-world line through the Panama Canal that doubled as a triangle trade. OSK ships would carry Japanese emigrants to Brazil via the Cape of Good Hope, coaling in Natal, then transport Brazilian coffee to New Orleans, and return American cotton back to Japan via the Panama Canal, for use in the Japanese textile and rayon industries.[50]

The OSK pioneered several new types of vessels specifically for the trade with the United States. For example, the fast diesel-powered "silk ship" the *Kinai Maru* brought raw silk from Yokohama to New York's garment district in twenty-six days. A typical New York run would carry raw materials like Japanese raw silk and Philippine sugar and coconut oil to the United States, as well as finished Japanese goods like lightbulbs, chinaware, and cotton cloth, and return to Japan with American raw cotton and scrap iron, but also American automobiles and machine tools.[51] Japanese shipping's prewar use of the canal peaked in 1938 with three hundred transits carrying 1.8 million tons of cargo.

Japanese trade through the Panama Canal was not confined to North American ports. The ocean liners the *Argentina Maru* and the *Brazil Maru* carried the last wave of prewar Japanese emigrants directly to South America via the Panama Canal. Even though Panama allowed free Japanese immigration—unlike the United States in this period—few emigrants stopped at Panama, although some Japanese served as barbers at the canal during the construction era. As of 1938, the Japanese Foreign Office recorded only 415 immigrants to Panama.[52] In any event, the outbreak of World War II would bring to a close this era of Japanese commerce through the Panama Canal.

DEFENSE BENEFITS OF THE PANAMA CANAL

The Panama Canal opened in a world at war, and the American builders of the Panama Canal did not conceive of it as a purely commercial enterprise. Did the Panama Canal generate defense-related savings for the United States? The Panama Canal was part of the American network of strategic military installations. Strategists, however, had to weigh its utility for shuttling American warships between the oceans against its ability to carry *enemy* warships between the oceans.

The Panama Canal, in other words, could not be allowed to fall into enemy hands. As the American naval theorist Alfred Thayer Mahan explained in 1890, considering the effect of an isthmian canal on a future war between the United States and a European power: "The danger . . . will be greater by so much as the way between it and Europe is shortened through a passage which the stronger maritime power can control. The danger will lie not merely in the greater facility for dispatching a hostile squadron from Europe, but also in the fact that a more powerful fleet than formerly can be maintained on that coast by a European power, because it can be called home so much more promptly in case of need."[53] Army theorists felt the same way. General Hains of the Army Corps of Engineers wrote in 1901, "An adequate defense of a fortified Isthmian canal can be made in no other way than by providing a navy of sufficient power to control the seas at either terminus."[54] In other words, the need to defend the Panama Canal meant that the canal could not be used to reduce the size of the navy. In fact, the logic implied that the United States would need an even *bigger* navy in order to defend it.

Given the strategic logic, it should be no surprise that attempts to use the Panama Canal to reduce naval spending failed.[55] In 1914, for example, Secretary of the Navy Josephus Daniels proposed to use the canal to partition U.S. battleships between the Atlantic and the Pacific. Mahan and former president Roosevelt blasted the idea for the cardinal sin of dividing the fleet.[56] Public criticism, a series of landslides in the canal, and the worsening international situation caused Daniels to change his mind.[57] In 1916, the United States committed itself to building a two-ocean navy regardless of the canal, "to make the United States secure in the Western Atlantic, the Caribbean, and the Pacific Oceans at the earliest possible moment."[58] Meanwhile, naval strategists continued to maintain that the United States needed to build up an even larger force in the Pacific against a possible Japanese threat to Hawaii and the Philippines.[59] Naval spending declined after World War I, but only to its pre-canal level. (See figure 5.6.) In other words, there was no sign of a "canal dividend" in terms of naval spending.

If the Panama Canal failed to reduce naval spending below its pre-canal level, might it have helped to keep spending *lower than what it would have been* in the absence of the canal? After the First World War, the U.S. Congress cancelled its commitment to a two-ocean navy. Instead of building up the navy, Congress committed the United States to the Washington Naval Conference, which aimed to negotiate binding limits on the navies of the United States, United Kingdom, France, Italy, and Japan. Congress ratified the resulting Five-Power Treaty of 1922, which obviated the need to build a two-ocean fleet—at least until Japan withdrew in 1934. The U.S. Navy met its commitments to the Caribbean by shifting resources from the North Atlantic and Pacific, rather than by expanding the fleet. Naval spending fell back to prewar levels by 1923. Spending rose somewhat in the early 1930s, as it became increasingly obvious that Japan intended to withdraw from the treaty, but the limits posed by the agreement allowed the United States to limit its naval spending for almost a decade.

Insofar as possession of the Panama Canal encouraged the United States to sign the Five-Power Treaty and thereby limit its naval expenses in 1922–30, the canal may have provided additional defense-related savings to the American economy. Whether such savings were prudent considering subsequent developments is, of course, an entirely different question.

Although American military planners viewed the Panama Canal mainly as a naval asset, the Panama Canal had significant land-

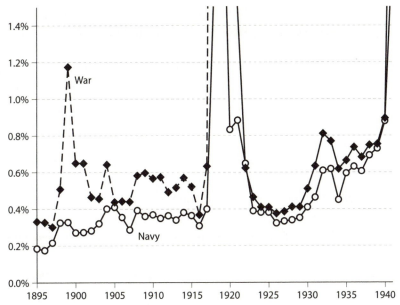

Figure 5.6: War and Navy Department spending as percentage of GDP, 1895–1939. *Source*: Calculated from data in U.S. Department of Commerce, Bureau of the Census, *Historical Statistics of the United States, Colonial Times to 1957* (Washington, DC: GPO, 1960), 718.

and air-based defenses as well. Might the Panama Canal have generated *non-naval* defense costs high enough to offset the social savings that it generated for the U.S. economy? Defense-related capital expenditures, including the installation of fixed weapons systems such as antiaircraft guns and antiship artillery, have already been included as part of the Panama Canal's capital cost, and thus are accounted for in the social savings estimates. The operating costs of canal defense, however, have *not* been accounted for.

How large were the operating costs of defense? There are two possible ways to estimate the operating costs of the Canal Zone garrison. The first assumes that the soldiers and materiel in the Canal Zone would be redeployed elsewhere in the absence of the canal. Under this assumption, canal-related defense costs would consist of only special noncapital expenditures for Canal Zone defense. According to the *Annual Reports of the Secretary of War* and the records of Senate hearings on War Department appropriations, special appropriations averaged only $350,000 (in 1925 dollars) in 1922–37—far too little to have any appreciable effect on the social savings produced by the Panama Canal.[60]

In the absence of the Panama Canal, however, it is plausible to believe that all soldiers stationed in and around the Zone would be demobilized and all specialized defense equipment decommissioned. We use this as our counterfactual scenario to estimate the non-naval defense costs of the canal. The 1923 Senate appropriations hearings provided estimates of the total cost of clothing, equipping, paying, provisioning, sheltering, and transporting an army with varying end-strengths of 122,000, 132,000, and 156,000 soldiers. The Senate figures make it possible to back-calculate the marginal costs of equipping, sustaining, and deploying an additional soldier.[61] In most categories, unsurprisingly, the marginal costs of equipping an American soldier were less than the average costs, but there were a few cases in which lumpy expenditures— notably for water and sewage provision and railroad transportation—led to significantly rising marginal costs.[62] Multiplying the resulting figure by the size of the Panama garrison and adding in all special appropriations for Zone defense provides a high estimate of the canal's defense cost—approximately $10.7 million per year in 1925 dollars. In 2007 dollars, that would be equivalent of $109 million, or $1.7 billion per year as an equivalent portion of GDP.

While the direct defense costs of the Panama Canal were considerable, even the high estimate of direct defense costs was not enough to offset the social savings the canal generated for the U.S. economy. Even under the double assumption of an extreme level of price sensitivity for shippers ($\varepsilon = 2.0$) and that all Panama Canal defense assets would be demobilized in the absence of the canal, defense costs are only enough to reduce the social rate of return below the opportunity cost of capital in the late 1930s. (See figure 5.7.)

Finally, is it possible that the Panama Canal raised *indirect* U.S. defense costs? In December 1904, President Theodore Roosevelt declared the following:

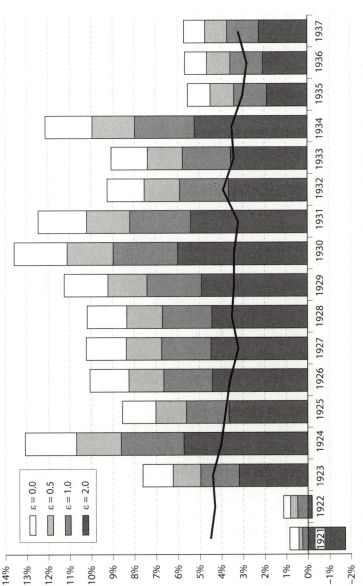

Figure 5.7: Elasticity-adjusted social rates of return from the Panama Canal for the United States only, low estimates, including defense costs, 1921–37. *Source:* Noel Maurer and Carlos Yu, "What T. R. Took: The Economic Impact of the Panama Canal, 1903–1937," *Journal of Economic History* 68, no. 3 (2008).

If a nation shows that it knows how to act with reasonable efficiency and decency in social and political matters, if it keeps order and pays its obligations, it need fear no interference from the United States. Chronic wrongdoing, or an impotence which results in a general loosening of the ties of civilized society, may in America, as elsewhere, ultimately require intervention by some civilized nation, and in the Western Hemisphere the adherence of the United States to the Monroe Doctrine may force the United States, however reluctantly, in flagrant cases of such wrongdoing or impotence, to the exercise of an international police power.

The Roosevelt Corollary to the Monroe Doctrine committed the United States to ensuring the political and financial stability of the entire circum-Caribbean region. It is historically unclear that the need to defend the Panama Canal drove Roosevelt's decision to commit the United States to Caribbean hegemony. Domestic political pressures from American overseas investors and the fear of European intervention in the hemisphere appear to have been the main drivers behind the decision.[63]

Nevertheless, even if one assumes that the Roosevelt Corollary was a direct result of the U.S. need to defend the Panama Canal, U.S. interventions did not impose a significant additional cost on the U.S. Treasury. Between 1903 and 1916, the United States intervened in Cuba (twice), Honduras, Mexico (twice), Nicaragua, the Dominican Republic (twice), and Panama itself (twice) outside the Canal Zone—but War Department spending did not rise appreciably.[64] (See figure 5.6.) War Department spending did not rise for two reasons. First, the marginal cost of brief interventions was small: stocks were not appreciably drawn down, and equipment was not destroyed in any great amount. Second, in its longer interventions, the United States required the nations that it occupied to pay most of the occupation costs, either out of current revenues or via bonds issued in the name of the occupied country. The sustained rise in War Department spending that took place after the Spanish-American War was due to the need to maintain a large military presence in the Philippines, not the circum-Caribbean—and while the American possession of the Philippines may have influenced the decision to build the Panama Canal, the Panama Canal did not affect the decision to annex the Philippines. The post-1930 rise in War Department spending, meanwhile, coincided with President Herbert Hoover's public disavowal of armed intervention in the Americas and the withdrawal of remaining U.S. troops from Haiti and Nicaragua.

DISTRIBUTIONAL EFFECTS OF THE PANAMA CANAL WITHIN THE UNITED STATES

The composition and scale of the intercoastal trade within the United States implies that the Panama Canal had significant regional and distributional effects on the United States. The railroads were one of the nation's largest enterprises. The Panama Canal competed for transcontinental cargoes, one of their most lucrative markets. How badly (if at all) were they hurt by the canal? Similarly, the lion's share of cargo passing through the Panama Canal during the interwar years was lumber from the Pacific Northwest and petroleum products from Southern California. How much did those regions gain from the Panama Canal? In the case of lumber, northwestern lumber directly competed with southern production. Did the Northwest gain at the South's expense? In the case of petroleum, how much of the gain flowed to consumers, and how much was captured by the oil oligopoly? Finally, considering the high levels of social savings specifically generated by the petroleum trade through the Panama Canal, might a transcontinental pipeline have been a better investment for the American taxpayer?

EFFECTS OF THE PANAMA CANAL ON THE U.S. RAILROAD INDUSTRY

The transcontinental railroads believed that the Panama Canal had a catastrophic effect on their business, and they complained bitterly to the Interstate Commerce Commission about it. ICC investigations and railroad company requests for rate relief provide valuable information of the scope of their complaints.[65] Beginning in 1923, transcontinental railroad carriers petitioned the ICC for rate relief for items including iron and steel manufactures, railroad materials, paper, and selected chemicals.[66] It is probably not a coincidence that these items represent well over half the cargo tonnage passing from the Atlantic to the Pacific through the canal in that year.[67] Western railroads earned only 3.75 percent their valuation in 1923, significantly below the 5.75 percent fair valuation fixed by the ICC.[68] The Chicago, Milwaukee, and St. Paul Railway fell into receivership in 1925, claiming that the Panama Canal had cut into their shipments of lumber and "Oriental" goods from the Pacific Northwest to the extent that their warehouses were "practically idle."[69] One vice president of a large transcontinental railroad anonymously wrote that "it seems to be the settled policy of our government that the railroads shall not compete with water carriers, or if they do compete they must make the same rates on other business not subject to water competition."[70] Elsewhere in the Midwest, the traffic director for the Chicago Association of Commerce stated that "we have largely withdrawn from the Pacific Coast markets account of the low water rates and frequent service via the intercoastal steamship lines. What little business remains is via the Gulf of Mexico in connection with the Mississippi River barge line and the ocean carriers beyond."[71] The traffic director for the largest steel producer in the Chicago area concurred. "Owing to the rate situation which has existed at the Pacific Coast in the last several years we have been unable to meet competition in that territory, and, therefore, have made no shipments."[72] In fact, between 1920 and 1923, iron and steel tonnage carried by rail from the Chicago area to the West Coast declined by 65 percent.[73] The anecdotes appeared compelling.

The aggregate data, however, do not support the argument that the opening of the Panama Canal adversely affected the railroad industry. If the Panama Canal had a significant negative effect on the railroads, then one would expect the data to show four patterns. First, the average length of cargo hauls carried on the railroads should fall, as the growth in long-distance cargoes failed to keep pace with those diverted to the Panama Canal. Second, the real price of transporting a ton-mile by rail should fall, as the railroads attempted to compete with the canal on price. Third, overall railroad profitability should fall. Finally, net fixed investment in railroad capital should fall.

Only one of these patterns holds. The growth in the average length of a cargo haul slowed briefly in the early 1920s, when the Panama Canal first opened to full commercial traffic, but there was no decline in the average length of a cargo hall. The real price per ton-mile fell *before* the Panama Canal fully opened, in 1914–17. The reason was that the wartime inflation reduced real rates, but a series of rate hikes returned freight rates to their prewar level by 1922. (See figure 5.8.) The total summer waterborne tonnage of iron and steel carried in the United States increased nearly fivefold between 1921 and 1923, but the total tonnage of iron and steel carried by rail—within the same summer series—remained steady.[74]

Railroad profitability did decline in the aftermath of World War I, but in the absence of a decline in the average length or average price of a cargo haul, it would be hard to argue that the Panama Canal caused the decline. In fact, railroad profit margins began to increase two years after the Panama Canal opened to commercial traffic, and continued to increase throughout the 1920s. Railroad executives, in turn, behaved as though they expected the increase in their profitability to be permanent: net investment (including depreciation) in railroad fixed capital continued to increase until the onset of the Great Depression. (See figure 5.9.) It is, of course, possible that railroad profits would have been even higher in the absence of the Panama Canal—that would depend on the counterfactual rate-setting policies of the ICC, which are beyond our purview—but that does not change the fact that the years when Panama Canal traffic saw its most rapid growth were good ones for the railroad industry in the United States.

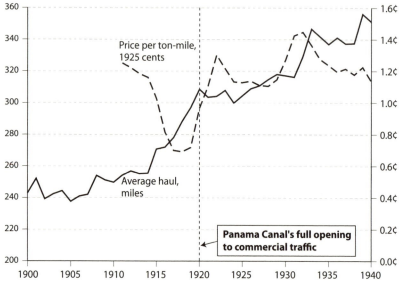

Figure 5.8: Average railroad freight hauls (miles) and average price per ton-mile (1925 cts.). *Source*: Louis P. Cain, "Railroad Freight Traffic and Revenue: 1890–1980." Table Df965-979 in *Historical Statistics of the United States, Earliest Times to the Present: Millennial Edition*, ed. Susan B. Carter, Scott Sigmund Gartner, Michael R. Haines, Alan L. Olmstead, Richard Sutch, and Gavin Wright (New York: Cambridge University Press, 2006).

A simple qualitative model can explain this paradox. Assuming a constant structure in railroad rates, goods produced nearer the Pacific coast had an absolute advantage in transport costs for sales on the West Coast before the opening of the Panama Canal. After the opening of the Panama Canal, not only were transport costs for goods produced near the Atlantic coast to the West Coast relatively cheaper—rates for Pittsburgh bar steel via a rail-water combination route to San Francisco were half as much as shipment purely by rail—but they were also absolutely cheaper than goods produced a range of distances further inland by West Coast producers.[75] The same reasoning applied to inland producers in the western United States, who used rail to carry their goods to the nearest port. The upshot was that the railroads benefitted from carrying more cargoes from inland areas to coastal areas.

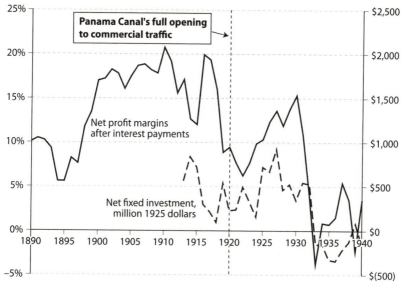

Figure 5.9: Railroad profits and fixed investment. *Source*: Louis P. Cain, "Railroad Property Investment, Capital, and Capital Expenditures: 1890–1980." Table Df980-990 in *Historical Statistics of the United States, Earliest Times to the Present: Millennial Edition*, ed. Susan B. Carter, Scott Sigmund Gartner, Michael R. Haines, Alan L. Olmstead, Richard Sutch, and Gavin Wright (New York: Cambridge University Press, 2006); and Louis P. Cain, "Railroad Income, Expenses, Interest, and Dividends: 1890–1979." Table Df991-1001 in *Historical Statistics of the United States, Earliest Times to the Present: Millennial Edition*.

EFFECTS OF THE PANAMA CANAL ON THE U.S. LUMBER INDUSTRY

The Panama Canal had a profound distributional effect on the American lumber industry. Although the industry used many types of trees, only a few were logged on a mass scale. Of these, Southern (yellow) pine from the American South was a close substitute for Douglas fir from the Pacific Northwest. Stumpage prices for both were significantly lower than for white pine, their major competitor.[76] Economies of scale made the production cost of Douglas fir substantially cheaper than Southern pine, but the high cost of transport from the Pacific Northwest put Southern pine on even terms with Douglas fir in most of the national market, in which both types of woods participated.[77] Figure 5.10 shows softwood production between Washington and Oregon on the one hand, and the Lower Mississippi region—Louisiana, Mississippi, Oklahoma, and Texas—on the other. Lower Mississippi hardwood production is included as a control; reported hardwood production in Washington and Oregon during this period was negligible.[78]

Pacific Northwest and Lower Mississippi softwood had very similar production trends for the first two decades of the twentieth century. After 1920, however, the woods diverge. Pacific Northwest softwood and Lower Mississippi hardwood continued to grow during the economic boom of the 1920s, while Lower Mississippi softwood production declined to below its 1910 levels. Lower Mississippi softwood was far from logged out—the region was still productive—but production declined nonetheless.

In effect, the two regions performed a natural experiment. The Pacific Northwest's Douglas fir and the Lower Mississippi's southern pine were close substitutes. Before the opening of the Panama Canal, regional softwood production tracked national demand, which in turn tracked general economic growth. The Lower Mississippi's hardwood production, serving as a control, did the same. After the opening of the Panama Canal, the Pacific Northwest and the Lower Mississippi found their softwoods competing in the national market, and the Lower Mississippi's softwood was found wanting. In comparison, Lower Mississippi hardwood was hardly affected. By 1922, the chief of the United States Forest Service prophesied that it was "doubtful if, within another decade, the pineries of the South will be an important factor in supplying the markets of the twenty-eight states which have become lumber importers."[79] Northwestern softwood rose from 27 percent of national production in 1919 to 47 percent by its peak in 1931, while the Southern industry declined from 27 percent to 16 percent over the same period.[80] The Pacific Northwest's timber boom was the Southern timber industry's bust.

The redistribution of the American lumber industry had one completely unforeseen side effect. The young president of the

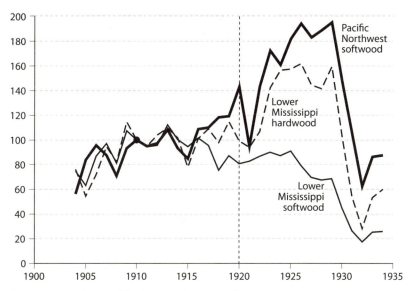

Figure 5.10: Regional lumber production indexes, 1904–34, 1910 = 100.
Source: Albert Halsey Pierson, *Lumber Production, 1869–1934* (Washington, DC: U.S. Department of Agriculture, 1936).

Greenwood Timber Company in Hoquiam, Washington, William Boeing, used his company's profits and aviation-grade timber to start a small airplane company during World War I, and to maintain it during the lean early years of commercial aviation.[81] By World War II, Boeing had dramatically changed the nature of the Seattle area's economy, with consequences strongly echoed today.[82]

EFFECTS OF THE PANAMA CANAL ON THE PETROLEUM INDUSTRY

The growth of the Southern Californian oil industry in the 1920s was one of the defining events of California history. Before the opening of the Panama Canal, the West Coast's petroleum market was independent of the rest of the United States. Local demand increased faster than local production, causing crude oil prices in

TABLE 5.8
California Oil Shipped through the Panama Canal, 1923–29

	Barrels	Percent of California production
1923	29,706,225	11.3
1924	68,412,723	29.9
1925	40,429,883	17.4
1926	38,230,766	17.0
1927	40,794,946	17.6
1928	31,326,412	13.5
1929	31,627,785	10.8
1930	36,424,685	14.2

Source: *Annual Report of the Governor of the Panama Canal* and U.S. Geological Survey, *Mineral Resources of the United States* (Washington, DC: GPO, selected years).

the region to double in 1920.[83] The subsequent burst of investment caused a production boom, and in the absence of a significant export market, would have caused a regional price collapse, since California generally enjoyed significantly lower oil prices than the rest of the United States.

California was saved from that eventuality in October 1922, when the first Californian oil tanker crossed the Panama Canal to the markets of the United States' East Coast. By February 1923, two tankers transited the canal every day; by April 1923, five tankers passed through the canal daily.[84] It was the beginning of a decade-long boom. Between October 1922 and June 1923, over 26 million barrels of California crude and refined petroleum products were shipped through the canal, at an overall rate of roughly 100,000 barrels a day. Through June of 1929, over 280 million barrels of Californian oil would be shipped through the canal to Atlantic ports.[85] This was the energy equivalent of transmitting seven thousand megawatts of electricity from coast to coast, about the output of several modern-day nuclear power plants.[86] At its peak in 1924, just under 30 percent of all Californian oil production passed through the canal. (See table 5.8.)

The opening of the Panama Canal prompted significant oil price convergence. Because California's oil prices were generally far lower than elsewhere in the United States, Californian manufacturers adopted oil-burning energy technologies significantly in advance of the rest of the country, and Californian manufacturing used rather more energy in production. In 1909, for example, 92 percent of the energy consumed by Californian manufacturers came from oil, at a time when the national figure was only 4 percent, with most of the remainder (92 percent) coming from coal. At the same time, Californian firms employed 304 horsepower of installed energy capacity per worker, far above the national average.[87] Wellhead oil prices, meanwhile, averaged between half and two-thirds of the national average.[88] Prices in California rose from an average of 61 percent of the national average before the Panama

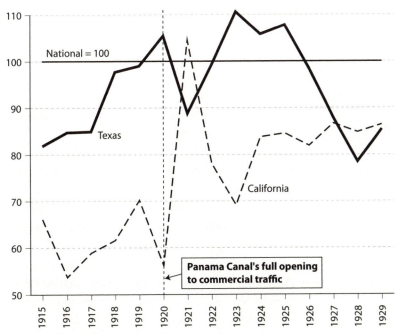

Figure 5.11: Crude oil price convergence, 1915–29. *Source:* U.S. Geological Survey, *Mineral Resources of the United States* (selected years).

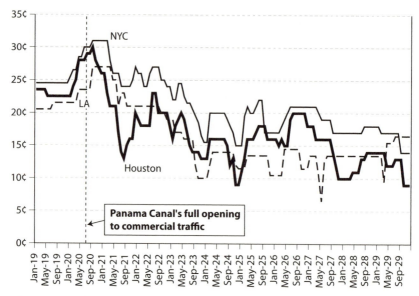

Figure 5.12: Regional gasoline prices, 1919–29. *Source: National Petroleum News*, first week of the month.

Canal to 85 percent by the second half of the 1920s. California's oil price also converged on Texas's: by 1927 there was little average difference between them, even though Texas crude continued to be of slightly higher quality. (See figure 5.11.)

Who benefitted from the oil price convergence prompted by the Panama Canal? It is not clear that "consumers" is the correct answer. The reason is the oligopolistic nature of the American market for *refined* petroleum products at the time. Refining, then as now, went on close to consumer markets, since crude oils are easier to transport than refined products (although this was less of a problem in the 1920s, when refined products were much less pure than they are today). The market for refined products, however, was far from competitive. Convergence in the wellhead price of crude oil did not translate into convergence in the market price of refined petroleum products. Figure 5.12 presents selected regional wholesale prices of the major refined product of the time, gasoline.

Unlike wellhead prices for crude, it shows no convergence after the opening of the Panama Canal, although national retail prices did enter a sustained decline within a few months of the canal's opening.[89]

A TRANSCONTINENTAL PIPELINE COUNTERFACTUAL

Oil tankers represented a known technology. Mexican and Venezuelan oil went to the United States via tanker, and the tight corporate connections between domestic and foreign oil producers ensured that tankers would be quickly adopted by Californian oil companies. While railroad tanker cars did exist, they did not represent a competitive alternative.[90] This suggests the following counterfactual: had the Panama Canal not been built, could a transcontinental oil pipeline have captured similar social savings for less cost?

Unlike the Panama Canal, a transcontinental pipeline would not have represented an effort on the frontier of engineering practice. Methods to prevent emulsions in Californian piped oil were patented in 1909 and 1914.[91] Welding technology had come of age during World War I. The need to heat the viscous California crude oil added to costs but was not technically difficult, nor was California crude significantly out of the range of the viscosity of other crudes that were routinely piped overland. A 104-mile pipeline opened from Coalinga to Monterey in 1904; other longer lines followed. The principal technological obstacle was the manufacturing of suitable high-pressure, large-diameter pipes by the steel companies. The problem, however, was not a technological bottleneck but a lack of demand for the product, which did not take off until the 1930s.[92]

How much would it have cost to construct a transcontinental pipeline? A 1952 study concluded that the optimal configuration for a pipeline with a throughput of 100,000 barrels per day would be a twenty-inch diameter, quarter-inch-thick line. The same study also estimated construction costs of $348,200 (in 2009 prices) per mile and annual operating costs of 2 percent of initial costs.[93] Historical cost data are somewhat higher than the study's calculations. During World War II, the U.S. Navy built an oil pipeline across Panama. The line consisted of forty-six miles of two twenty-inch fuel-oil lines, one twelve-inch gasoline line, and one ten-inch diesel line, with a capacity of more than 300,000 barrels a day. It cost $20 million in 1943 dollars, or $206 million in 2009 dollars—a cost of $4.5 million per mile. The line, however, consisted of heavily camouflaged tubes and was designed to carry refined products, not crude. Its high cost was probably not representative.[94]

A more representative example would be the Big Inch, also built during World War II, in response to U-boat attacks on American tanker traffic. The Big Inch connected Longview, Texas, to Phoenixville, Pennsylvania. From there it split to serve refineries in the Philadelphia and New York City areas. The main twenty-four-inch pipe ran a distance of 1,252 miles and cost $75 million in current dollars. It took only 350 days to build and pumped on average over 300,000 barrels of crude per day.[95] In addition, an oil pipeline connecting California across the continental divide was built in 1984–86. The thirty-inch All-American Pipeline connected Santa Barbara, California, to McCamey, Texas, a distance of 1,200 miles, at a cost of approximately a billion dollars. In real terms (using the GDP deflator) the All-American's per-mile cost ran 2.2 times the cost of the Big Inch pipeline. It also took a little over twice as long to build.[96]

Could a pipeline have generated social returns equivalent to the Panama Canal? Cost data from the previous four pipeline projects enables us to calculate the upper-bound costs for a counterfactual transcontinental pipeline. Cookenboo provided detailed fixed and variable cost estimates for pipeline construction. The counterfactual cost figures assume that material costs scale linearly with distance and geometrically with pipeline diameter, while other costs scale linearly with distance. Table 5.9 presents the counterfactual costs (in current and 2009 dollars) of a twenty-four-inch pipeline covering 1,750 miles based on the historical costs of various pipeline projects and Cookenboo's 1952 estimates. Unlike the

TABLE 5.9

Construction Cost Estimates of a Counterfactual Transcontinental
Pipeline, in Millions

	Current dollars	1925 dollars	2009 dollars
Secret USN	761	730	7,459
All-American	1,458	251	2,561
Big Inch	105	111	1,138
Cookenboo	144	96	978

Source: See text.

Panama Canal, a transcontinental pipeline would have incurred a much lower implicit interest cost, due to a maximum estimated construction time of only two years (versus sixteen for the canal), assuming no additional defense cost.

The start-up cost of the Panama Canal came to $9.2 billion in 2009 dollars. At the cost of the U.S. Navy's pipeline across Panama, a transcontinental pipeline covering the 1,750 miles from California to the Gulf Coast would have cost 81 percent as much. The U.S. Navy's construction costs, however, were unrepresentatively high—especially since the Panamanian pipeline required a great deal of protection against possible air raids. A transcontinental pipeline with similar costs to the All-American would have clocked in at 28 percent of the total cost of the Panama Canal; and a transcontinental pipeline with similar costs to the Big Inch would have cost only 12 percent as much as the Panama Canal.

Transcontinental pipeline transport from California to Houston (and then to the East Coast via tanker) would have cost roughly the same as the Panama Canal. Table 5.10 presents various estimates of the 1925 cost of transporting a barrel of oil from California to New York City using the Panama Canal, the transcontinental railroad, and a counterfactual pipeline using actual pipeline rates for a long-distance pipeline that ran from Tulsa to Cleveland in the 1920s. (The ICC fixed pipeline rates at this time.) The largest estimated cost differential between the Panama Canal and a hypothetical pipeline was 5¢ per barrel. This would not have been

TABLE 5.10

Cost in 1925 Dollars of Transporting Oil from the West Coast to New York City

Cost per barrel	
Via Panama Canal, high	1.32
Via Panama Canal, low	1.17
Via transcontinental railroad, high	2.46
Via transcontinental railroad, low	2.43
Via pipeline to Houston, and sea to NYC	1.27
Relative savings per barrel	
Pipeline versus railroad (pipeline, low RR)	1.16
Canal versus railroad (high Canal, low RR)	1.11
Difference	0.05

Source: High cost estimate of transporting oil through the canal calculated from data in Noel Maurer and Carlos Yu, "What T. R. Took: The Economic Impact of the Panama Canal, 1903–1937," *Journal of Economic History* 68, no. 3 (2008): table 4; and a conversion factor of 7.33 barrels per ton taken from the Energy Information Administration. Low estimate from *Senate Committee on Interoceanic Canals*, 63rd Cong., 2nd sess. (Washington, DC: GPO, 1914), 370, converted to 1925 dollars using the GDP deflator. High estimate of transporting oil by railroad from Maurer and Yu, What T.R. Took, table 2. Low estimate from *Senate Committee on Interoceanic Canals*, 63rd Cong., 2nd sess. (Washington, DC: GPO, 1914), 947. Observed pipeline rate (in effect from July 26, 1922, to April 23, 1926) for the 1,030-mile route between Tulsa, Oklahoma, and Cleveland, Ohio, taken from Standard Oil Company of Ohio, *Ajax Brief—Arguments for Reduction in Pipe Line and Other Transportation Rates on Crude Oil*, April 20, 1933. Transport cost from Houston to New York calculated from data in Maurer and Yu, What T.R. Took, table 4. For readers who prefer to think in 2007 dollars, the conversion factor from 1925 dollars using the GDP deflator happens to be exactly 10.0.

anywhere near enough to justify building a pipeline—*once the Panama Canal was already in operation.*

If the Panama Canal had never been built, on the other hand, a transcontinental pipeline most likely would have generated similar social savings at significantly lower cost. Even a transcontinental pipeline as costly per mile as the secret U.S. Navy line across Panama would have produced significant returns, albeit not as high as the Panama Canal itself. More realistic cost projections, however, would produce phenomenally higher rates of return. A pipeline that cost roughly the same as the All-American Pipeline would have generated an average social return of 15 percent; one that cost the same as the Big Inch would have generated an average social return of *40* percent. (See table 5.11.) Elasticity effects would not have altered these results. In addition, the rates charged by actual pipelines in the 1920s included a significant profit margin. The results in table 5.11 do not include profits and thus understate "true" social savings.

Additionally, a transcontinental pipeline could have been constructed at a far lower *human* cost than the Panama Canal. Few large-scale projects are without a death toll. But pipeline construction is much safer than digging a canal in a tropical disease environment. For example, the Trans-Alaska Pipeline employed seventy thousand workers during its construction, in rugged Arctic terrain, and suffered only 31 fatalities.[97] Almost certainly there would have been far fewer deaths during the construction of this hypothetical pipeline, in both absolute and proportional terms, than the 5,609 deaths officially reported during the American construction of the Panama Canal, or the 22,000 deaths that Colonel Gorgas estimated had occurred during the failed French effort.

TABLE 5.11
Social Rates of Return for Various Pipeline Costs, Zero Demand Elasticity

	Secret USN	All-American	Big Inch	Cookenboo
1921	1%	4%	10%	11%
1922	1%	3%	7%	8%
1923	5%	14%	31%	36%
1924	11%	32%	71%	83%
1925	6%	19%	42%	49%
1926	6%	18%	40%	46%
1927	6%	19%	43%	49%
1928	5%	15%	33%	38%
1929	5%	15%	33%	38%
Average	5%	15%	34%	40%

Source: The cost of each pipeline project from table 5.9. Savings per barrel from table 5.10. Total barrels transported through the Panama Canal from California in each year from *Annual Reports of the Governor of the Panama Canal*. 1921 and 1922 quantities of California oil transported through the canal estimated from California's average share of all eastbound oil shipments in 1923–29.

Finally, it seems likely that had there been existing pipeline infrastructure in place, the development of the massive West Texas oil fields, still under exploration in the 1920s, would have been accelerated. This would ultimately lessen the need for the transcontinental portion of the hypothetical pipeline—but here we hit the limits of counterfactual analysis.

SIX

PASSED BY THE DITCH

La República de Panamá existe por y para el Canal.

—*Panamanian president Belisario Porras, 1924*

BEFORE THE OPENING OF THE PANAMA CANAL, IT WAS WIDELY
believed that a canal across the Panamanian isthmus would trans-
form Panama into one of the great commercial centers of the world.
Bolívar compared Panama to Corinth, which owed its success in
the ancient world to its commanding position on the isthmus between the Ionian Sea and the Aegean Sea. Early twentieth-century
Panamanian politicians often used the wealthy Hanseatic cities of
medieval Europe which controlled the Baltic Sea trade as their
point of comparison.[1] Panama's ambassador to Washington waxed
enthusiastic about the canal in 1913, as he travelled the United
States to drum up investment: "Our country has the Canal within
its own territory, and therefore enjoys the greatest advantage. . . .
The market for the products consumed by ships passing from one
ocean to the other, or arriving at the Canal's terminal ports, is
a market that naturally belongs to Panama, and no other country can handle our competition."[2] So did the authors of the *Blue
Book of Panama*, declaring in 1917 that "[t]he Republic of Panama
should shortly become one of the business centers of the universe,"
claiming that "the administration and upkeep [of the Panama Ca-
nal] have brought large sums of money into the country."[3] A modern analyst might think of Singapore's relationship to the Straits of
Malacca.

A better analogy to Panama's situation in the early twentieth century might be Port Said, the Egyptian city founded by de Lesseps at the Mediterranean entrance to the Suez Canal, which developed into a squalid coaling station synonymous with vice.[4] The Panama Canal's direct benefits to Panama were small. A series of independent, piecemeal, but mutually supporting decisions made by American policy makers in Washington and in the Canal Zone combined to prevent Panama from enjoying the rents created by the Panama Canal. As an example, the canal administration deliberately avoided employing Panamanian workers, preferring instead to import low wage labor from elsewhere, mainly the Caribbean. Article 10 of the 1904 treaty prevented Panama from taxing any employee of the Panama Canal. The United States also explicitly prohibited Panamanian businesses from providing services to the canal, or to ships passing through the canal.

Not every denial of benefits to Panama was caused by deliberate American policy. In some cases, paternalistic behavior by the United States simply failed to have the expected positive effects. For example, the United States explicitly exercised a protectorate over Panama, including the installation of an American fiscal agent in Panama City to maintain Panama's finances. This imprimatur by the United States, however, did not translate into lowered borrowing costs for the Republic of Panama, nor did it result in Panamanian fiscal restraint. Panamanian officials found it too easy to circumvent American controls, and the United States refrained from imposing harsher sanctions or assuming greater direct control of Panama's administration for fear of inflaming Panama's chronic political unrest and destabilizing its government.

THE ESTABLISHMENT OF THE COMMISSARY

The largest barrier to Panamanian participation in the economy of the Panama Canal was an organization known simply as the Commissary. The Isthmian Canal Commission established the Commissary in order to provide food and housing at reasonable prices to canal workers during the Panama Canal's construction. The sudden arrival in 1904 of thousands of foreign workers caused shortages of food and retail goods, and Panamanian merchants took advantage of the situation to charge the often malnourished immigrant laborers exorbitant prices. Eggs and plantains sold at 10¢ each, the equivalent of an hour's wages for most Silver Roll workers. A pound of meat cost 25¢, and a quart of milk cost 40¢.[5] (To give more context, the roughly equivalent prices in 2009 dollars would be $29 for a dozen eggs, a quart of milk for $10, and a pound of meat for a mere $6—rural Panama having many ranches.[6]) Many canal workers chose to subsist on sugarcane. As a result, malnutrition greatly slowed their work effort.[7]

In response, in 1905 the United States government established a series of commissaries in the canal in order to feed and provision the workforce. "The silver men—that is, the common laborers—are being fed for 30¢ per day and the gold employees—that is, those of the higher class—at 90¢ per day, and they get good food in place of bad."[8] Within a few months, however, the Commissary expanded its purview into the sale of general goods, even selling imported luxury goods such as silks and lace to Gold Roll (and frugal Silver Roll) workers.[9] Unlike Panamanian merchants, the Commissary faced no taxes or tariffs, and its cargoes received preferential treatment and subsidized rates at the ports and the Panama Railroad.[10]

The Panamanian government unsuccessfully lobbied to stop the Commissary's mission creep. Governor Goethals verbally agreed to Panamanian requests stop the Commissary from selling luxuries, but he soon reneged. He explained that once Panamanian merchants "get their grip on us they will squeeze us dry."[11] In 1909, Panamanian negotiators signed an agreement with Secretary of State Elihu Root that was, in Root's words, "designed to restrict Commissary privileges."[12] The draft Root-Arosemena Treaty created an arbitration panel to decide U.S.-Panamanian disputes.[13] Goethals and the secretary of the Isthmian Canal Commission, Joseph Bishop, lobbied to have the treaty "killed or withdrawn."

Goethals and Bishop failed to kill the treaty, but the Senate removed the arbitration clause from the treaty before ratifying.[14] The resulting agreement proved toothless.

Governor Goethals turned the Commissary into a commercial juggernaut within the economy of the Canal Zone. By 1913, it included wholesale dry goods and grocery departments, a mail-order division, twenty-two general stores, seven cigar stores, a cold storage and ice-making facility, a tailor and cleaning shop, a bakery, a coffee-roasting plant, an ice cream factory, a laundry and packing department, seventeen hostels, two terminal hotels, and forty-eight mess halls, half for white workers and half for West Indians.[15] The mess halls served three meals a day to Silver Roll workers for 9¢ per meal. White workers on the Gold Roll ate better-quality food for the higher price of 40¢ ($8.64 in 2009 prices) for three meals.[16] The subsidized government-run retail stores in the Canal Zone sold goods imported from the United States and were open to all canal employees, contractors, and, once the Canal opened to commercial traffic, transiting passengers.[17] As Goethals told the *New York Times*, "Personally, I could never see why the canal should not be made a business proposition."[18] In 1913, the Commissary's turnover passed $7.5 million ($168 million at 2009 prices, using the CPI).[19]

In 1912, the Commissary moved into the business of supplying passing ships. The 1912 Panama Canal Act authorized the Commissary to supply "coal and other materials, labor, repairs, and supplies for vessels of the government of the United States and, incidentally, for supplying such at reasonable prices to passing vessels."[20] Governor Goethals then prevented Panamanian merchants from competing with the Commissary. Goethals justified the policy by saying, "Ships would be dependent upon a precarious local supply at prices that would probably be extortionate, and the conditions of such would make the canal route unattractive."[21]

In 1917, during World War I, the Panama Canal began implementing a plan of food self-sufficiency, "so that we would be able to support ourselves in case we should for any reason be cut off from all food supplies."[22] War worries prompted the development of this plan, but it took on a peacetime life of its own. By 1920, the Commissary operated thirteen "plantations" producing fruit and vegetables for local consumption, and imports of meat into the Zone had been curtailed.[23] (A few exemptions were made for specialty West Indian foods for canal laborers and brand-name goods regularly requested by foreign vessels.[24]) The Commissary operated all manner of food processing facilities, from abattoirs to ice cream plants.[25]

The deliberate isolation of the Panama Canal from the Panamanian economy went so far as the creation of cattle pastures inside the Canal Zone, despite Panama's extensive cattle ranches and status as a beef exporter. The Commissary purchased cattle from Colombia, Nicaragua, and Venezuela and fattened them on the extensive pastures planted within the newly depopulated Canal Zone. Public health was the original motive: Panama suffered from endemic anthrax and the cattle tick *Rhipicephalus annulatus*, an important vector for babesiosis (cattle fever).[26] Panama quickly got a handle on the health problems of its herds, but the Canal Zone imported no Panamanian cattle until the late 1920s, when imports of Venezuelan cattle caused an epidemic of botfly grub among the Canal Zone herds.[27] After this episode, the Canal Zone began importing Panamanian cattle, but its internal ranches were already up and running, and over 80 percent of the Commissary's isthmian cattle purchases remained internal to the canal. The remainder formed less than 5 percent of the Commissary's total purchases.[28] Even when the Commissary imported Panamanian cattle, it dressed them in its own abattoir—which shipped its by-products back to the United States for industrial use—and further processed the meat in a Commissary's sausage factory, to be served in Commissary restaurants and Commissary mess halls by Commissary employees.[29]

In order to promote the Commissary's business, the Canal Zone administration exempted it from all U.S. taxes (under the Hay–Bunau-Varilla Treaty, it was already exempt from Panamanian taxes or tariffs) and provided it subsidized rates on the Panama Railroad. Commissary cargoes paid a flat rate of $2.25 per ton, while Panamanian shipments over the same route paid between $6.80 and $10.00 per ton, depending on the class of service.[30] Panamanian merchants protested that the Panama Railroad had not been created "with the idea that it was to be utilized as a weapon to kill local business," and proposed it be run as a public utility. The United States did not respond. In 1933, Governor Julian Schley dismissed Panamanian complaints with the riposte that "the railroad rates charged are in the interest of the United States," not the Panamanian private sector.[31]

Panamanian merchants also lodged multiple protests that the Canal Zone administration locked them out of the business of providing supplies to passing ships. In December 1919, they complained directly to Goethals's successor, Chester Harding, about Commissary sales to passing ships. As a result of this protest, Harding granted sixteen local firms licenses for ship sales. Harding, however, simultaneously declared publicly that none of the firms to which he granted licenses were capable of fully provisioning passing ships. Meanwhile, the canal authorities continued to ban Panamanian companies from soliciting business on board passing vessels. Since no Panamanian firms were capable of arranging supply contracts at the ships' ports of embarkation, the end result was that nothing changed.[32]

Panamanian merchants continued to protest, by all accounts accurately, that the Commissary sold luxury items to passing vessels as well as basic supplies. In 1921, Governor Jay Morrow explained to the Panamanians that what they viewed as luxury items were in fact necessities to people with higher standards of living. In 1928, Governor Meriwether Walker refused to end the sales simply "in order to throw business to Panama merchants." In 1931, Walker's successor, Harry Burgess, also declined to end the subsidized sales of luxury items, although he did raise the prices the Commissary charged.[33]

The Panamanian government was angered by the fact that subsidized Commissary operations prevented its nationals from selling goods or services to the Canal Zone. In 1923, Panamanian foreign minister Ricardo Alfaro complained to Secretary of State

Charles Evans Hughes that the Zone ran "dairies, poultry farms, butcheries, packing and refrigeration plants, soap factories, laundries, plants for roasting and packing coffee, sausage and canned meat factories" with little benefit to Panama itself.[34] Further disputes broke out over the sale of 3.2 percent beer in the Canal Zone, which competed with Panamanian beers.[35]

Unfortunately for Panama's business community, Panamanian diplomatic negotiations with the United States over the Commissary issue failed. The American side granted only the most limited concessions, and the Panamanian legislature refused to ratify the resulting agreements. One anonymous Panamanian diplomat, most likely Ricardo Alfaro, made the analogy to a *New York Times* reporter, "When you hit a rock with an egg, the egg breaks. Or when you hit an egg with a rock, the egg breaks. The United States is the rock. Panama is the egg. In either case, the egg breaks."[36]

The upshot of the Commissary policy was to effectively isolate the Panamanian economy from the business provided by the Panama Canal. Between 1921 and 1936, an average of only 4.1 percent of Commissary purchases came from Panamanian sources. In fact, Panamanian purchases by the Commissary declined over time, from a high of 8.2 percent in 1921 to only 3.1 percent in 1929, the last year for which we have full data. (See table 6.1.)

Commissary sales were large enough to effectively insulate the Panamanian economy from the increased demand generated by the Panama Canal's workforce. Sales to Canal Zone workers averaged 62 percent of all Commissary sales between 1922 and 1936. With approximate average annual wages per employee of $500, and average annual Commissary sales per employee of $400, the typical Panama Canal worker had little need to source any of his or her basic needs from Panamanian merchants. (See table 6.2.)

In fact, the Commissary's principal benefit to Panama was through the black market. Goods, from staple items to luxuries, were resold to Panamanians at a price between what the Commissary charged to canal employees and the often significantly higher prices of Panamanian merchants. It was popularly believed that

TABLE 6.1

Commissary Purchases by Geographic Area, 1921–36

	From U.S.	From Eurasia	From Latin America	CZ cattle sales	Other CZ purchases	Cattle from Panama	Other from Panama
1921	$5,381,279	$526,412	$185,964	$1,221,230	$118,235	$268,202	$394,717
1922	$3,165,759	$101,217	$52,979	$751,968	$136,409	$140,228	$135,340
1923	$3,548,345	$142,827	$115,041	$318,990	$99,664	$74,586	$127,927
1924	$3,817,075	$389,494	$129,325	$416,345	$128,467	$68,089	$210,634
1925	$4,763,217	$555,603	$146,306	$482,211	$112,354	$39,583	$235,441
1926	$4,877,886	$551,756	$234,281	$565,011	$90,994	$31,961	$216,058
1927	$5,313,970	$1,030,280	$275,702	na	$112,613	na	$183,692
1928	$5,283,402	$947,319	$323,911	$391,322	$90,891	$77,202	$187,354
1929	$5,613,246	$1,109,003	$378,743	$546,685	$108,446	$74,152	$173,733
1930	$5,727,149	$965,917	$512,791	na	$110,471	na	$181,322
1931	$5,171,323	$777,967	$259,256	na	$90,872	na	$224,086
1932	$4,192,223	$621,423	$145,086	na	$69,947	na	$167,200
1933	$3,798,356	$482,590	$131,284	na	$70,558	na	$130,894
1934	$3,569,568	$472,386	$101,261	na	$67,445	na	$104,353
1935	$4,096,956	$440,435	$104,998	na	$64,305	na	$208,835
1936	$4,307,370	$614,907	$150,422	na	$72,374	na	$311,825

Source: Annual Reports (selected years).

TABLE 6.2

Commissary Sales, 1922–36

	(Thousands of dollars)						Dollars		
	U.S. government	Panama Canal Company	Steamships	Panama Railroad Company	Independent companies	Employees	Sales per employee	Average annual wage	Commissary sales as % of wages
1922	1,220	939	360	216	323	4,001	393	831	47
1923	1,084	696	344	170	602	3,797	345	811	43
1924	1,002	767	468	230	599	4,419	384	884	43
1925	1,063	744	605	192	732	4,409	359	868	41
1926	1,371	686	767	265	660	5,477	427	855	50
1927	1,322	697	794	265	698	5,751	429	870	49
1928	1,431	728	981	411	682	5,857	421	852	49
1929	1,515	852	1,135	287	713	6,431	409		
1930	1,435	811	1,099	373	653	6,870	454		
1931	1,455	701	789	300	685	6,546	471		
1932	1,070	627	237	528	459	5,768	470		
1933	964	563	294	180	493	5,107	405	901	45
1934	665	496	331	234	407	4,654	387		
1935	705	730	356	301	247	5,114	411		
1936	942	732	305	259	312	5,372	416		

Source: Thomas M. Leonard, "The Commissary Issue in American-Panamanian Relations, 1900–1936," *The Americas* 30, no. 1 (July 1973): table 2.

this smuggling greatly benefitted Panama. As one Panamanian congressman said, "Blessed be the commissaries of the Zone, for they are the salvation of our poor people."[37] President Harmodio Arias noted in 1933 that cigarette sales in the Zone were a staggering 4,400 packs per capita a year, the lost excise taxes *to the United States* representing three times the amount of the annuity paid to Panama.[38] Yet, insofar as the smuggling represented resale of Commissary items and not pilferage, the Panama Canal—and thus the United States—still took its cut. The Panamanian black marketeer simply had a cheaper and less licit wholesaler than the Panamanian merchant.

It might be argued that the Panama Canal provided a source of invisible exports for the Panamanian economy, despite the Commissary policy. The Canal Zone might have generated demand for sales of Panamanian services through several possible channels. Silver Roll workers, for example, often lived outside the Canal Zone, and spent some of their wages on housing and services purchased from Panamanians. (Most tenements in Colón where the Silver Roll workers lived, however, were owned by the Panama Railroad, which in turn was part of the canal administration.) In addition, Panamanian citizens worked within the Zone, primarily as domestic servants for Gold Roll employees. It is also possible that the increase in maritime traffic caused by the opening of the canal might have produced an increase in Panama's revenues from tourism and the reexport trade. Finally, American soldiers often purchased goods and services in Panama that were prohibited inside the Canal Zone.[39]

A crude indicator of the size of Panama's invisible earnings is the country's trade deficit minus its net financial inflows. Unfortunately, financial data on net inflows for Panama were not collected until 1945. On the other hand, it is possible to generate trade data for Panama from the Panama Canal and even from selected years before the building of the canal, despite the fact that Panama was a province of Colombia during that time. Since the Darien Gap prevented nearly all overland commerce with the rest of Colombia, imports from the rest of Colombia necessarily came through the

TABLE 6.3
Panama's Average Net Imports

	Current dollars	2009 dollars	Per capita, 2009 dollars
1856–58	1,647,600	32,935,442	209
1891–97	4,166,099	89,438,353	359
1921–29	10,864,015	108,565,918	238

Source: *Gaceta de Panamá* and *Estadística Panameña* (various).

Note: The Panama Railroad opened for business in 1855; 2009 dollars calculated using the U.S. GDP deflator.

ports, and Panamanian customs officials duly recorded their value along with the value of imports from outside Colombia. Table 6.3 presents those estimates.

Despite only having data on Panama's net imports during this period, we can still make claims about Panama's invisible earnings. In real terms, Panama's net imports had increased slightly from the 1890s to the 1920s. Panama's real net per capita imports, however, decreased from the levels of the 1890s to the 1920s. (In fact, Panama's real per capita trade deficit in the 1920s was barely above the level it had been during the heyday of the Panama Railroad in the 1850s.) For Panama's invisible earnings to *rise* after the opening of the canal, Panama's net financial inflows must have been significantly *lower* in the 1920s than during the 1890s. But the decade of the 1890s was a turbulent one for Panama, especially after the collapse of the French canal effort and during the run-up to Colombia's Thousand Days War. It seems unlikely in the extreme that foreign investment on the Isthmus of Panama during the 1890s was larger than foreign investment in the 1920s. We tentatively conclude that, because levels of foreign investment in the 1920s were likely at least at the levels of the 1890s, Panama's invisible earnings did not rise per capita after the opening of the Panama Canal.

The financial data on Panamanian foreign investment that exist before the opening of the Panama Canal support the hypothesis. Recorded foreign investment on the Isthmus of Panama in the years immediately before independence was decidedly penny-ante.

One American firm managed games of chance for the province, while another controlled the tobacco monopoly. The manganese deposits near Nombre de Dios on Panama's north coast were under development by an American firm, drawing the attention of the American press when it became a minor battlefield during Colombia's Thousand Days War.[40] The largest investor appears to have been the United Fruit Company, which by 1903 owned over twenty-three thousand acres in Panama, valued at slightly over $2 million, consisting mainly of bananas.[41]

Foreign investment in Panama increased markedly after Panamanian independence. Chase National and National City established bank branches in Panama outside the Canal Zone in 1910. United Fruit doubled its farm holdings and built small feeder railways to serve it.[42] A United Fruit subsidiary, the Tropical Telegraph and Telephone Company, received a monopoly concession to build the national telephone and telegraph network.[43] Pan-American Airlines began feeder and local air service in Panama in 1929. The Panamanian government, meanwhile, financed the construction of sixty-five miles of railway by 1920.[44] By 1929, foreigners, mostly Americans, had invested $29 million in Panama directly, and held a further $18 million in Panamanian government bonds.[45] This amount was the equivalent of $484 million in 2009 dollars. The implication is that Panama experienced a gross annual capital inflow of at least $59 per capita between 1910 and 1929. This corroborates our hypothesis that Panama experienced little benefit from invisible earnings from the Panama Canal.

AN EMPIRE EFFECT?

The inevitable effect of our building the Canal must
be to require us to police the surrounding premises.
In the nature of things, trade and control, and the
obligation to keep order which goes with them, must
come our way.

—*Secretary of War Elihu Root, 1905*

Although the Canal Zone generated little economic impact for the Panamanian economy, the presence of the Panama Canal on Panamanian territory might have influenced Panamanian economic development in other ways. The U.S. government exercised a high degree of political control over the Republic of Panama, through both formal and informal channels. If American control brought greater political stability and more secure property rights in Panama, then one would expect Panama's protected status to have reduced its government's cost of capital and to have created incentives for greater capital inflows from abroad.

In a study of the effects of imperialism on the borrowing costs of British dependencies at the turn of the twentieth century, Niall Ferguson and Moritz Schularick found that the governments of British colonies could borrow at significantly lower rates than the governments of similar jurisdictions outside the British Empire. They dubbed this finding "the empire effect."[46] Alfaro, Maurer, and Ahmed found that the informal American empire in the Caribbean basin produced an empire effect on the borrowing costs of many circum-Caribbean nations.[47]

Panama was a key part of that American empire, under explicit American protection; one might expect it to have enjoyed greater benefits than the other countries that fell under U.S. hegemony. After decades of using tortured readings of preexisting treaties to justify its interventions on the isthmus, in 1904 Secretary of State Hay communicated to the new United States minister to Panama, William Buchanan, that it would be "preferable that the Panama constitution should contain nothing in conflict with the widest liberty on our part." Buchanan in turn urged the Conservative Party in Panama to support the inclusion of Article 136 in the Panamanian constitution of 1904. Article 136 granted the government of the United States the right to "intervene in any part of Panama, to reestablish public peace and constitutional order."[48] As a result, Panama was more tightly integrated into the American orbit than any other Latin American jurisdictions save Cuba and Puerto Rico.

American intervention was not a legal abstraction for Panama. The United States exercised its right to intervene in Panama on multiple occasions. The first interventions abolished Panama's nascent army and effectively disarmed its police force. In November 1904, President Roosevelt deployed the Marine Corps to forestall an attempted military coup by a disgruntled former Colombian general. The coup leader soon resigned his commission, and Panama abolished its army soon thereafter.[49] The United States went further after anti-American riots broke out in the Panama City red-light district of Cocoa Grove in 1912 and again in 1915. The 1912 riots killed an American sailor; the 1915 riots spread to Colón. During the latter, Panamanian police assaulted sixteen soldiers in Panama City and shot another on patrol in Colón. After the 1915 riots, the U.S. government decided not to take over police responsibility in the port cities, but it did demand that Panama turn over all of its police force's high-powered rifles. When Panama protested and threatened to appeal to arbitration by other Latin American nations, the State Department responded that such proposals were "unworthy of serious consideration."[50]

The United States also intervened directly in Panama's chaotic politics. In 1912, the United States deployed two hundred soldiers in order to supervise a contested presidential election between the Conservative Pedro Díaz and the Liberal Belisario Porras. (After the Liberal victory, the Conservative Party accused the Americans of fraud.)[51] In 1918, President Ramón Valdés died unexpectedly, and factions within the Panamanian government declared the indefinite postponement of the legislative election due on July 7. An American died in the resulting riots. Washington deployed the U.S. Army outside the Zone in order to ensure that the election took place. Panama elected a new legislature under American supervision. The legislature proceeded to install Belisario Porras as president.[52] Three years later, in 1921, the U.S. Army had to rescue Porras from an angry mob in Panama City.[53] Later that year, the United States had cause to regret its decision to protect Porras, after Porras sent an armed Panamanian "expedition" to the contested Costa Rican village of Coto. President Warren Harding ordered the Panamanians to withdraw from Costa Rica, and deployed a battalion of U.S. Marines to back up his command.[54] In 1925, after local firemen failed to break up a Panama City rent riot by turning their hoses on the crowd, Porras called in the U.S. Army to restore order. Six hundred American soldiers moved into Panama City with fixed bayonets to quell the riots.[55]

The United States paid special attention to its privileges regarding transportation and communication in Panama. Under Article 5 of the Hay–Bunau-Varilla Treaty, the United States maintained a monopoly on railroad traffic across the isthmus. The U.S. government fiercely defended this right, vetoing railroad construction deemed a possible military hazard to the Panama Canal. In the words of the State Department in 1912, U.S. policy was "that no such concessions for railroads would be granted except under such safeguards as would enable the United States to control absolutely the railroads in case of war or other disturbance."[56] The U.S. Navy obtained a monopoly over radio communications on the isthmus in 1914.[57] In 1929, Pan-American received a monopoly over Panamanian air travel, under an official American policy "that the United States should, in so far as possible, control aviation in the Caribbean nations."[58]

The United States also supervised official Panamanian finances. Article 138 of the Panamanian constitution mandated that $6 million of the proceeds from the Hay–Bunau-Varilla Treaty remain invested in New York real estate. When the government attempted in 1911 to use the money to finance a railroad from Panama City to Chiriquí Province, the State Department announced that any diversion of the funds to other purposes would be a violation of the Panamanian constitution and activate the American obligation to intervene under Article 136. American officials later defended their supervision of Panamanian finances by insisting that it was "notorious that Latin American officials are apt to be anything but cautious in entering financial obligations."[59]

Stereotypes aside, American worries about Panamanian financial prudence proved to be well founded. In 1914, the United States approved a $3 million loan from National City Bank to finance the construction of a railroad from the town of David, in Chiriquí Province, to Panama City. The $250,000 annuity from the United States for the Panama Canal secured the loan.[60] The next year, however, the Panamanian National Assembly diverted one-third of the proceeds for an ill-defined series of "public works" projects. The United States protested the diversion but took no action, and in 1915 the Panamanian government issued a further $4.5 million in debt secured by the income on the $6 million invested in New York real estate.[61] Later that year, however, rumors surfaced that the Panamanian government under Belisario Porras had used $100,000 of the 1915 loan proceeds to meet the government's operating costs.[62] The next year, American officials learned that the country had borrowed $750,000 from United Fruit, secured by half the revenue from its banana export tax.[63] The government's operating budget, in rough balance from 1904, fell into a deficit of $2.2 million in 1916—fully 39 percent of the government's total expenditures.[64] In March 1917, the United States vetoed another Panamanian attempt to repatriate the New York fund.[65] Finally, in 1918 the U.S. government learned that that Panama had only "balanced" its operating budget by redirecting the remaining proceeds from the 1914 loan. (See table 6.4.)

As a result of the 1918 discovery, the State Department pressured Panama City into appointing an American "fiscal agent," who would have complete "control and charge of the national treasury." Addison Ruan, who had been the American financial advisor to Haiti and the disbursing officer for the American government in the Philippines, received the job.[66] Under American supervision, the Panamanian government ran generally balanced budgets— surpluses in 1919–20 covered deficits in 1921–22—and took out two more foreign loans for capital expenditures. In 1926, the government negotiated a $2.6 million loan for further work on the Chiriquí Railroad and the construction of a wharf at Armuelles. The government secured the loan with revenue from its export duties and the stamp tax.[67] In 1928 it refinanced its outstanding loan principal of $6.2 million, and took out an additional $10 million in new debt for public works.[68]

TABLE 6.4
Panamanian Government Finances, 1909–36

	Expenditures	Revenues	Surplus/deficit	% of revenues
1909	$2.8	$2.8	nil	nil
1910	$6.7	$5.9	($0.8)	−14
1911	$3.3	$3.3	nil	nil
1912	$3.3	$3.4	$0.1	3
1913	$3.3	$4.0	$0.7	18
1914	$4.4	$3.8	($0.6)	−16
1915	$3.1	$3.3	$0.2	6
1916	$5.7	$3.5	($2.2)	−63
1917	$3.6	$3.9	$0.3	8
1918	$3.4	$3.1	($0.3)	−10
1919	$4.3	$6.3	$2.0	32
1920	$4.4	$5.8	$1.4	24
1921	$7.3	$5.4	($1.9)	−35
1922	$6.1	$5.3	($0.8)	−15
1923	$8.0	$8.0	nil	nil
1924	$8.0	$8.0	nil	nil
1925	$6.0	$6.0	nil	nil
1926	$6.0	$6.0	nil	nil
1927	$8.5	$7.0	($1.5)	−21
1928	$8.5	$8.5	nil	nil
1929	$8.5	$8.5	nil	nil
1930	$8.5	$8.5	nil	nil
1931	$9.5	$9.5	nil	nil
1932	$9.5	$9.5	nil	nil
1933	$7.5	$8.0	$0.5	6
1934	$7.5	$8.0	$0.5	6
1935	$7.0	$7.0	nil	nil
1936	$7.0	$7.0	nil	nil

Source: Brian R. Mitchell, *International Historical Statistics: The Americas 1750–2000* (New York: Palgrave Macmillan, 2003), 699, 721.

Note: Panama switched to two-year budgeting in 1923. The 1927 revenue shortfall was unforeseen.

One might expect such close American supervision to have produced a significant empire effect for Panama. After all, the State Department closely watched Panamanian finances before 1918, under the threat of military intervention, and an American official directly signed off on budgets thereafter.

TABLE 6.5
Borrowing Costs, Adjusted for Maturity

	December 1914	May 1915	June 1926	May 1928
United States	3.6%	3.6%	3.6%	3.5%
Costa Rica	6.8%	na	4.1%	3.7%
Cuba	na	na	4.9%	4.6%
Colombia	6.0%	6.0%	6.5%	6.3%
Dominican Republic	na	na	5.6%	5.5%
Venezuela	5.5%	5.5%	3.6%	3.5%
Panama	5.2%	5.6%	6.3%	5.2%
Argentina	5.1%	5.1%	6.1%	6.0%
Brazil	5.0%	5.0%	6.6%	7.1%
Chile	5.0%	4.9%	6.9%	6.8%

Source: *Financial Times* and *Wall Street Journal* (various editions).

The data show little sign of an empire effect for Panama. American intervention did not lower the cost of capital faced by the Panamanian government. Panamanian bonds did not trade openly on the secondary markets, but it is possible to calculate the maturity-adjusted interest rate that lenders charged the Panamanian government on its four major debt issues, and compare that to the yield on bonds issued by other Latin American sovereign borrowers. (See table 6.5.) In 1914 and 1915, Panama's borrowing costs were slightly lower than Colombia's, but Panama's costs were higher than those of Argentina, Brazil, and Chile, none of which were paragons of fiscal responsibility. In the 1920s, Panama's borrowing costs were systematically higher than the costs of capital in other American protectorates, although still lower than Colombia's. By 1926, with an American fiscal agent in place, the Panamanian government could borrow from American lenders at lower rates than Brazil or Chile, but it still faced a significantly higher cost of capital than other American financial protectorates like Cuba or the Dominican Republic, or countries that faced American sanctions should they fail to repay their debts, such as Costa Rica and Venezuela.[69] Only in 1928, with the country having run a near-perfect streak of balanced budgets, was Panama able to borrow for less than the large South American countries and within the upper range of other American financial protectorates. The empire effect on the cost of capital for Panama was small.

Why did American protection fail to reduce borrowing costs in Panama as much as in other American protectorates? The reason was Panamanian evasion of American financial control. In 1919, President Belisario Porras obtained a loan of $150,000 from the United Fruit Company using Panama's banana export revenue as collateral. Porras then passed a bill allowing the Panamanian treasury to cash all drafts made by cabinet members, circumventing the fiscal agent entirely. When the American legation protested, Porras declared the fiscal agent's office unconstitutional, although Porras had signed it into law himself.[70] American pressure quickly forced Porras to reverse that decision, but Panamanian officials continued to circumvent American wishes.[71] In late 1922, a frustrated Addison Ruan—a man who had managed to organize *Haiti's* chaotic finances and maintain the budget of the Philippines—resigned his position.[72] His replacement as fiscal agent, Walter Warwick, in the words of the United States minister to Panama, "sat back and allowed the [Panamanian] government to do practically as it has seen fit, even to the extent of purchasing new, expensive automobiles for the use of the President and his cabinet, including one for the Fiscal Agent himself."[73] (One must wonder where Warwick drove his new, expensive automobile in a country with so few paved roads.)

The U.S. government ultimately admitted that its fiscal agent in Panama served as little more than an advisor. In early 1928, when the Panamanian government began planning a $16 million bond issue, Assistant Secretary of State Francis White publicly stated that while the United States had "certain treaty obligations of a financial character with Cuba, Haiti, and the Dominican Republic, and also a special relationship with Nicaragua . . . such a relationship does not exist with Panama."[74] As the data in table 6.5 illustrate, White's announcement appears to have come as little surprise to the markets.

On January 2, 1931, in a tactically brilliant operation, a small and poorly armed group of middle-class housing activists from Panama's Acción Comunal movement took over the Panamanian government.[75] In order to secure American support, Acción Comunal quickly appointed former foreign minister Ricardo Alfaro as interim president. The movement then fronted its own candidate, Harmodio Arias, for the presidency in 1932. Arias won the vote by 14 percent; American assistance in the election was limited to providing indelible red dye to stamp on voters' hands in order to prevent fraud.[76]

In contrast to Harmodio Arias's hectic path to the presidency, the election of Franklin Delano Roosevelt in 1932 to the presidency of the United States was a relatively sedate affair. Roosevelt's election, however, was as important as Arias's in terms of Panama's future. Roosevelt made this clear in his first inaugural address, stating the principles of what would be called the Good Neighbor policy: the United States would become "the neighbor who . . . respects the rights of others—the neighbor who respects his obligations and respects the sanctity of his agreements in and with a world of neighbors."[77]

Panama would be a proving ground for the new doctrine. Could the new American president reverse the policies that effectively insulated the Panamanian economy from the benefits generated by the canal? President Roosevelt's interest in Panama extended beyond the obvious family connection. In 1912, Roosevelt had visited the construction site shortly before becoming assistant secretary of the navy, where he enthused that the Panama Canal was a "wonder of the world, greater than the Tower of Babel or the Pyramids."[78] President Arias first met Roosevelt in Washington in October of 1933. At the meeting, Roosevelt personally pledged that he would curb some of the Commissary's excesses and maintain the value (in gold terms) of the Panama Canal annuity. The subsequent devaluation of the U.S. dollar in January 1934 deeply embarrassed the American president specifically with regard to Panama. Secretary of State Cordell Hull suggested that the need to renegotiate Panama's annuity could form the basis for a new treaty with Panama. Formal negotiations between Panama and the United States began in April 1934.[79] Roosevelt further met with President Arias during "informal" visits to Panama in July 1934 and October 1935.[80]

The toughest part of the talks often appeared to be between Washington and the Canal Zone, rather than between Washington and Panama City. The Panama Canal administration was a de facto third party to the treaty negotiations, one with a strong agenda of its own. The Canal Zone's governor, for example, insisted that the United States take over the town of New Cristóbal in the face of Panamanian protests. Washington supported Panama, and the provision died, despite protests that American women in New Cristóbal were "subjected to the grossest indecencies and physical handlings by hoodlums."[81] When it leaked that the treaty—which coincided with the end of Prohibition in the United States—would impose American excise taxes on beer sales, the local army commander had to warn that such taxes "might result in unfortunate incidents." The chief labor union in the Zone, meanwhile, protested that any agreement would require Americans "to contribute to the welfare of a foreign nation to whom they are not in any sense obligated." Roosevelt himself had to cram through a compromise that would leave low-alcohol beer and light wines untaxed, but require the Zone to purchase supplies of all stronger drink from Panama, paying Panamanian excises in the process. "Liquor is luxury," wrote the president, "and I see no reason for the government to supply it in the Zone as though it were a food necessity."[82]

The Canal Zone administration and Roosevelt's Good Neighbor diplomacy were in fact fundamentally opposed to each other. The Canal Zone's general counsel, Frank Wang, worried that official Washington believed that the United States did not have absolute sovereignty within the Zone. Canal governor Julian Schley confided that Roosevelt had "a big brotherly sympathetic feeling towards Panama" and resented the implication in the treaty drafts that there was "a partnership between the United States and Panama in the pecuniary profits from the Canal."[83] For his part, Schley succeeded in pressuring Washington to reject a Panamanian proposal to grant the Panamanian government a share of the canal's gross revenues in lieu of a fixed annuity. President Roosevelt, in response, tried to cut Schley out of the talks as much as possible: during the president's visit to Panama in October 1935, he instructed the American legation to keep all treaty amendments private and refused to communicate with Schley about the "informal" talks.[84]

The basic treaty was signed between Secretary of State Hull and Panamanian foreign minister Ricardo Alfaro on March 2, 1936. The nominal value of the Panama Canal annuity rose from $250,000 to $430,000, in order to compensate Panama for the dollar's lower gold value. The Commissary had to place a small surcharge on consumer goods intended for sales to passengers and crews, and Panamanian merchants gained the right to sell goods directly to passing ships and bid on other supply contracts within the Zone. The treaty did allow the Commissary to continue to operate bonded warehouses within the Zone, but specifically stated that bonded warehouses could be constructed in Panama under the same terms as the ones within the Canal Zone.[85] Roosevelt had decided, in the words of Sumner Welles, the chief U.S. spokesman for the negotiations, "that private business is to cease to exist in the Canal Zone except insofar as it relates to the operation and protection of the Canal."[86] It permitted the Panamanian government to begin construction on the Trans-Isthmian Highway between Panama City and Colón, which the canal administration had previously vetoed on military grounds. Finally, the treaty revoked the United States' right to intervene to preserve order in Panama City and Colón, although Article 136 remained in the Panamanian constitution.

The United States implemented the Hull-Alfaro Treaty only slowly and half-heartedly. In 1937 Congress finally agreed to let the Panama Railroad sell its properties in Colón to the Panamanian government, but only in return for the annexation of New

Cristóbal to the Canal Zone. Treaty ratification had to wait until 1939. When Panama asked for restrictions on Commissary and military post-exchange sales, the United States rejected offhand "the amazing proposition that the cost of living of all military and Canal Zone personnel be increased for the benefit of the Republic of Panama." In December 1939, the United States went further, and prohibited the importation of Panamanian meat, eggs, butter, cheese, and potatoes.[87] Finally, Roosevelt in late 1939 signed—under protest—a bill reserving high-paid canal jobs for American citizens.[88]

The Hull-Alfaro Treaty nevertheless established several important precedents for Panama. The United States had walked back from its absolutist position, that the Hay–Bunau-Varilla Treaty granted the United States *absolute* sovereignty over the Canal Zone. Panamanian arguments regarding commercial fairness had gained traction inside the United States. Most importantly, Panamanian diplomats learned, it was important to keep the Americans interested in a resolution.[89] The egg would start to chip away at the rock.

SEVEN
SLIDING INTO IRRELEVANCY

Panama is the one spot external to our shores which
nature has decreed to be most vital to our national
safety, not to mention our prosperity.

—*Secretary of War Henry Stimson, 1942*

Why, it's ours. We stole it fair and square.

—*Senator Samuel Hayakawa, 1977*

IN 1939, OWNERSHIP OVER THE PANAMA CANAL SEEMED TO BE A
cornerstone of national security and economic prosperity for the
United States. Six years later, by 1945, that characterization was
no longer as clear—in the aftermath of World War II, the canal appeared to have become more of a strategic liability than a military
asset. Twenty-five years later, by 1964, the same had happened to
the economic benefits of ownership over the Panama Canal as the
costs increasingly outweighed the benefits. The social savings of
the canal faded under the triple impact of the Interstate Highway
System, the dieselization of railroad freight, and the growth of the
Pacific coast as a market for its own raw materials. Moreover,
the benefits to American consumers and producers of American
control over transit rates dissipated as the domestic portion of canal traffic was replaced by goods carried between Asia and the
East Coast. Worse still, inflamed Panamanian national sentiment
forced the U.S. government to spend increasing amounts on aid to

the Panamanian government. These payments soon overwhelmed the small profits generated from the canal operation. While the *existence* of the Panama Canal remained important to the United States, the value of retaining ownership and control over its operation was rapidly disappearing.

Administrative inefficiency hastened the Panama Canal's relative decline. The canal's American managers lacked incentives to increase its efficiency, market its services, or adopt new technologies. The politics of the Canal Zone worsened the stagnation. The "Zonians"—the American inhabitants of the Zone, mostly canal employees and their dependents—thwarted reforms intended to make the canal operation run in a more businesslike fashion. The operation continued to be run for the benefit of the Zonians rather than the American consumer, the U.S. Treasury, or the Panamanian economy. By the time President Jimmy Carter began public negotiations to return the canal to Panama in 1977, the concrete benefits to the United States from ownership of the canal had essentially disappeared. The Panama Canal had become a bulwark of a defensive American nationalism, rather than of American national defense.

THE PANAMA CANAL IN THE SECOND WORLD WAR

How much was the Panama Canal worth during World War II? Consider the following scenario:

> The *Akashi Maru* was approximately midway in the [Culebra] Cut when a thunderous explosion was heard, and a gigantic column of water, smoke, and dust shot to the sky. Blending with the echoes of this terrible detonation was heard a roaring sound, of which the sinister import was but too well known to those familiar with the Canal. The shock of the explosion had dislodged millions of tons of earth from the steep sides of the Culebra ravine, causing a landslide of infinitely greater dimensions than any that had been previously experienced. . . . A thick pall of dust still hung over the Cut, both sides of which

had collapsed for nearly a thousand yards. Where a broad channel of water had existed half an hour before was now a rampart of earth twenty-five feet high. This, of course, was the bed of the Canal, which had been forced up by the overwhelming pressure of the adjoining hills. Of the Japanese steamer that had caused the havoc, not a vestige remained.[1]

Alternate history? Not quite. The idea that a Japanese suicide ship might explode in the center of the Culebra Cut and shut down the Panama Canal was first proposed in *1925*. American naval planners fretted over the canal's vulnerability, whether by suicide ship in the Culebra Cut or commandos at the Gatún Dam. While the Gatún Dam would be easy to repair, blowing up the dam would immediately drain Lake Gatún, and it would take at least a year for water levels to rise high enough for shipping to resume. Had the Panama Canal been shut down for the first year of World War II, what would have been the consequences?

There are two ways to analyze the impact that the closure of the Panama Canal would have had on the course of the American war effort during World War II. The first looks at the materiel that passed through the canal. Would it have been possible to move as much materiel as quickly by other means? If so, how much more would it have cost? The second examines the effect of forcing American warships stationed on the East Coast or in the North Atlantic to travel around Cape Horn on their way to the Pacific theater. Would the resulting delays have proven militarily decisive?

LOGISTIC EFFECTS

Over ten thousand American military vessels passed through the Panama Canal during the war, including support ships carrying nearly 20 million tons of materiel for the war effort. Unsurprisingly, most wartime cargo transits moved from the Atlantic to the Pacific. In the last full fiscal year of the war, 1945, the canal administration recorded that over 10.7 million tons of U.S. military

TABLE 7.1

Military Transits through the Panama Canal during World War II

	Military transits	Military cargo, tons	Military transits from the Atlantic to Pacific	Military cargo from the Atlantic to Pacific	Counterfactual increase in RR freight traffic
1940	602	198,893			0.2%
1941	955	222,927			0.1%
1942	1,516	566,637			0.3%
1943	2,373	419,080			0.2%
1944	3,333	4,572,034	75.0%		1.9%
1945	6,566	10,744,651	80.3%	99.9%	4.7%
1946	5,554	7,471,446	40.3%	92.9%	3.8%
1947	1,265	1,001,608	42.5%	83.0%	0.5%

Source: *Annual Report of the Governor of the Panama Canal* (1940–47).

cargo passed through the canal, mostly headed west.[2] A successful Japanese assault on the Panama Canal, however, was only likely in the opening days of the war. Once the fighting started, it would have been very difficult to get a suicide ship or sabotage team into place.

The railroad system could handle the cargo that was in fact moved by the Panama Canal during the war's first year. Had all canal cargo in 1942 been relegated to the railroads, total traffic would have increased only 0.3 percent. In fact, the railroads could have handled the traffic that went through the Panama Canal in 1945, its peak wartime year—transferring all cargo from the canal to the railroads in that year would have increased the amount of railroad freight ton-miles by only 4.7 percent.[3] A 4.7 percent increase might have posed a problem had the railroad system been at capacity in 1945, but that was not the case. Rather, the railroad system operated at only 93 percent of its peak capacity in 1945.[4] There would have been the possibility of local bottlenecks, of course, but in general the wartime Panama Canal served as a complement to rail transport, not a substitute.

While the United States had more than enough rail capacity to transport the Panama Canal's wartime tonnage, it might have been economically unfeasible. Would a shutdown of the Panama

Canal have driven up the cost of transporting goods by rail to unsupportable levels? Maritime transport, after all, cost less than railroad transport. It is possible to create a maximum estimate of how much it would have cost to transport the Panama Canal cargo via the railroads. Transcontinental freight rates were substantially less than average freight rates, which means that a maximum estimate of the cost of transporting canal cargo by rail can be derived under two assumptions. The first assumption is that the freight would have needed to travel the full distance from New York City to San Francisco. The second is that the freight would be charged the average rate per ton-mile rather than the long-distance freight rate. Under those assumptions, it would have cost $312 million, or 0.14 percent of America's GDP, to transport 1945's peak cargo by rail.[5]

Price controls froze nominal freight rates during the war, with the exception of a 5.3 percent rate hike in March 1942. A skeptical reader might argue that the price controls might have prompted the railway companies to defer maintenance expenses. The implication is that the actual economic cost of transporting freight by rail was higher than the posted cost. The problem with that argument, however, is that *real* annual spending on the maintenance and replacement of railroad way, structures, and equipment rose 87 percent between 1941 and 1945.[6]

The amount of $312 million represented the maximum cost of moving 1945's cargo by railroads—it is not the cost *difference* between using the railroads and using the Panama Canal. According to data in the 1944 report of the War Shipping Administration, the United States paid an average of 54¢ per ton-mile of waterborne shipping in 1942 and 60¢ in 1943.[7] Those numbers imply that the U.S. government spent *more* to transport goods via the Panama Canal than it would have cost to send them by railroad. This is highly unlikely. In fact, the War Shipping Administration constructed and operated its own vessels and port facilities, and its outlays included all "expenses for purchase, charter, and operations of vessels, reconditioning, outfitting, defense installations, operation of warehouses and terminals and other expenditures."[8]

TABLE 7.2

Cost of Transporting War Materiel via the Railroad versus the Panama Canal

	Counterfactual cost of transporting war materiel by railroad, in dollars	Estimated cost of transporting war materiel via canal, in dollars	Cost savings, current dollars	Cost savings, as % of U.S. GDP	2009 value of an equivalent % of GDP, in billion dollars
1940	4,232,415	2,891,904	1,340,511	0.00	0.19
1941	4,743,855	3,241,359	1,502,497	0.00	0.17
1942	12,692,585	8,238,902	4,453,683	0.00	0.39
1943	11,818,056	6,093,423	5,724,633	0.00	0.41
1944	131,263,096	66,477,374	64,785,722	0.03	4.20
1945	311,702,326	156,227,226	155,475,100	0.07	9.94
1946	221,005,373	108,634,825	112,370,548	0.05	7.21
1947	32,602,340	14,563,380	18,038,960	0.01	1.05

Source: Annual Report of the Governor of the Panama Canal (1940–47); War Shipping Administration, *The United States Merchant Marine at War* (Washington, DC: GPO, 1944); Arthur E. Rockwell, "The Lumber Trade and the Panama Canal, 1921–1940," *Economic History Review* 24, no. 3 (August 1971): 445–62.

A lower-bound estimate of the cost of using the Panama Canal can be derived from 1940 data on intercoastal water shipping rates. We subtract the tolls paid to use the Panama Canal, since the U.S. government did not pay tolls on military-related cargoes, and we add the canal's cost of operation, since the U.S. Treasury was responsible for those costs. This estimate is a lower bound, however, since it assumes that domestic shipping rates did not rise during the war. In fact, international tramp freight rates shot up fourfold, and although the War Shipping Administration imposed draconian price controls, it is unlikely that domestic water freight escaped all cost pressures.

The difference between the cost of using the railroads and the lower-bound cost of prewar canal transportation therefore provides an *upper-bound* estimate of the cost savings from using the Panama Canal. Closing the Panama Canal to war traffic would have raised war spending by 0.2 percent. (See table 7.2.) This still meant substantial savings to the United States. It is safe to say, however, that the United States would have had little difficulty financing the additional cost in the context of the already massive expenditures made on the war. In 1945, for example, war spending came to 37.5 percent of GDP.

THE PANAMA CANAL IN THE SECOND WORLD WAR: STRATEGY

If the economic benefits of the Panama Canal during World War II were minimal, what were its strategic benefits? To answer this question, we again look at the counterfactual: what would be the strategic costs of a yearlong shutdown at the beginning of the war? Seventeen battleships and twenty-nine aircraft carriers passed through the canal during World War II.[9] Without the Panama Canal, a *Yorktown*-class aircraft carrier or *New Mexico*–class battleship would have taken an additional seventeen days to travel from Norfolk to Pearl Harbor at a cruising speed of fifteen knots, including replenishment time at San Diego. Had a Japanese attack shut down the Panama Canal on December 7, 1941, the additional delay might have proven decisive in several of the war's early campaigns.

Seven battleships made the transit of the Panama Canal between December 7, 1941, and December 7, 1942. *Mississippi* and *Idaho*, older *New Mexico*–class battleships on duty near Iceland at the time of Pearl Harbor, passed through the canal in January 1942. *New Mexico* herself crossed to the Pacific later that year. In May 1943, all three vessels joined the Aleutians campaign, generally considered a sideshow by naval historians.[10] It is unlikely that a delay, or even a decision to keep these three ships in the Atlantic, would have had any material effect on the course of the war.

Of the four other battleships that passed through the canal in 1942, three —*North Carolina, Washington,* and *South Dakota*—did not see battle for at least two months after their passage through the Panama Canal. Historically, *North Carolina* and *Washington* were kept in the Atlantic in early 1942 at the personal request of Winston Churchill to Franklin Roosevelt to help secure the island of Madagascar—another sideshow—over the previous wishes of U.S. Admiral King, who had planned to use the battleships earlier in the Pacific.[11] Additionally, *South Dakota* was delayed five weeks in Pearl Harbor Navy Yard after striking a coral pinnacle in the Pacific.[12] Given the contingent nature of these delays, it is unlikely that days of additional transit time would have altered the planning for the campaigns in which they participated. Finally, *Indiana* participated in the Solomons campaign as part of the U.S. aircraft carrier screen, but its presence was not decisive.

The story is different for the three U.S. aircraft carriers that passed through the Panama Canal in the first year of the war. The *Hornet*, the *Wasp*, and the *Yorktown* had a direct impact on the conflict. The *Hornet* handled the Doolittle raid on Tokyo, a feat of naval aviation on the edge of the logistically impossible. The *Hornet* and the *Wasp* participated at Guadalcanal. Finally, the *Yorktown* fought in the Gilberts raid, the Battle of the Coral Sea, and most famously, the Battle of Midway.[13]

How would delaying the three carriers have affected the Pacific war in 1942? The primary effect would have been a two-week delay in the Doolittle Raid of April 18, 1942. The Doolittle Raid was the first American aerial attack on the Japanese Home Islands. The

TABLE 7.3

History of 1941–42 Warship Transits through the Panama Canal

Ship	Type	Hull no.	Comm.	Decomm. [or loss]	Location December 7, 1941	First wartime transit	First battle	Date of battle	Disposition
Yorktown	CV	5	9/30/37	6/7/42	Norfolk, VA	mid-December 1941	Gilberts raid	late Jan 1942	Sunk at Battle of Midway
Wasp	CV	7	4/25/40	9/15/42	Grassy Bay, BM	6/10/42	Guadalcanal	early Aug 1942	Sunk southeast of San Cristobal Island
Hornet	CV	8	10/20/41	10/26/42	Norfolk, VA	mid-March 1942	Doolittle raids	4/18/42	Sunk at Battle of Santa Cruz Islands
New Mexico	BB	40	5/20/18	7/19/46	Norfolk, VA?	prior to August 1942	Aleutians	5/17/43	Sold for scrap 10/13/47 to Lipsett, Inc., NY
Mississippi	BB	41	12/18/17	9/17/56	Iceland	January 1942	Aleutians	5/11/43	Sold for scrap 11/28/56 to Bethlehem Steel
Idaho	BB	42	3/24/19	7/3/46	Iceland	January 1942	Aleutians	5/11/43	Sold for scrap 11/24/47 to Lipsett, Inc., NY
North Carolina	BB	55	4/9/41	6/27/47	Caribbean	6/10/42	Eastern Solomons	8/7/42	Transferred to North Carolina 9/6/61; dedicated as memorial 4/29/62 at Wilmington, NC
Washington	BB	56	5/15/41	6/27/47	Gulf of Mexico	4/28/42	Guadalcanal	11/15/42	Sold for scrap 5/24/61 to Lipsett Div., Luria Bros. & Co.
South Dakota	BB	57	3/20/42	1/31/47	Camden, NJ (under construction)	8/21/42	Santa Cruz	10/25/42	Sold for scrap 10/25/62 to Lipsett Div., Luria Bros. & Co.
Indiana	BB	58	4/30/42	9/11/47	Casco, ME (under construction)	the year 1942	Solomons	late 1942	Sold for scrap 6/1/62

Source: See text notes.

Note: BB = battleship, CV = aircraft carrier.

U.S. Navy launched sixteen modified B-25 bombers from the *Hornet* on a one-way mission over Japan. After dropping their bombs, the plan was for the bombers to proceed to designated airfields in China. All bombers were in fact lost, but the Doolittle Raid had the strategic effect of prompting the Japanese to recall fighter units to the Home Islands. More intangibly, but possibly more importantly, the Doolittle Raid also boosted American morale.[14]

It is not clear, however, that the strategic and morale effects of the Doolittle Raid would have been significantly lessened had it occurred in early May instead of mid-April. That said, the rescheduled raid would have to occur on or before May 23, 1942, for the delay to have a minimal effect on the future course of the war. The reason is that *Hornet* required five days after the launch of the raid to replenish and refurbish, and if the ship were to engage attacking Japanese forces at the Battle of Midway (as it historically did), it would need to be ready to sail by May 28.

Closing the Panama Canal would have delayed the Battle of Guadalcanal for a week to ten days, but it would not have altered the battle's outcome in any predictable way. The *Wasp* played a key role in the Battle of Guadalcanal as one of three carriers providing air support for the initial U.S. Marine landings on August 7. It passed through the Panama Canal on June 10, 1942, and arrived in San Diego nine days later. Closing the canal would have delayed the vessel's arrival by seventeen days, pushing its arrival to July 6.

In theory, a seventeen-day delay could have adverse consequences on the American campaign. It is unlikely, however, that a delay in *Wasp*'s arrival would have affected the Battle of Guadalcanal in any predictable way. First, delays in the arrival of marine transports unrelated to *Wasp* had already pushed back the beginning of the battle by one week. A seventeen-day delay in *Wasp*'s arrival, therefore, would have meant only a ten-day delay in the American ability to launch the campaign. The effect of such a delay is unpredictable; one possible negative effect might be that the American forces would have had more difficulty remaining undetected by the Japanese had they arrived in better weather conditions.[15] On the other hand, since the Americans had the initiative, U.S.

commanders could have waited for the weather to inevitably worsen, as it in fact did about ten days later.

Finally, closing the Panama Canal would have caused the cancellation of the Gilberts raid. *Yorktown* played a key role in three battles: the Gilberts raid, the Battle of the Coral Sea, and the Battle of Midway. *Yorktown* arrived in San Diego from Norfolk on December 30, 1941; the counterfactual closing the Panama Canal would have pushed that date back to January 16, 1942. Since the Gilberts raid occurred on January 31, the delay almost certainly would have caused its cancellation unless military planners were willing to cut down *Yorktown*'s replenishment time. The Gilberts raid, however, was a marginal operation that had almost no impact on the course of the Pacific war. Hampered by thunderstorms, the Americans found no Japanese surface ships in the Gilberts, and did little to harm the Japanese strategic position. *Yorktown* returned to Pearl Harbor before departing to the Coral Sea on February 14. With the Panama Canal out of action, the *Yorktown* would have departed directly for the Coral Sea after several weeks in Hawaii and participated in its other battles as scheduled.

In short, the direct strategic effect of closing the Panama Canal at the beginning of World War II would have been minimal. The Guadalcanal campaign is the only operation where American commanders would have been forced to choose between delaying operations and starting the battle with less air cover than they planned—but, fortuitously, Guadalcanal was one of the few operations in the first year of the Pacific war in which the United States possessed the initiative and could choose when it wanted to fight.

In any event, American industrial capacity would soon render moot any Panama Canal–related delays. The United States launched seven *Essex*-class carriers and nine *Independence*-class light carriers in 1943. (The *Essex*-class could fit through the Panama Canal only by virtue of employing a removable starboard 40mm antiaircraft gun sponson.)[16] The *Essex* herself entered the Pacific in 1943, by which point the Panama Canal would likely have been back in operation.

Even if some combination of bad luck and sabotage had kept the canal inoperative for the rest of the war, a seventeen-day delay in the arrival of the new *Essex*-class carriers would have little effect. The reason is that by 1943 the United States had gained the initiative. American naval commanders could (within limits) choose the dates of their offensives. Overall, sixteen *Essex*-class and nine *Independence*-class carriers passed through the canal during World War II, as did the 1930s-vintage carrier *Ranger*, which was used for night training purposes. The naval might of imperial Japan would have been overwhelmed by American industry, with or without a Panama Canal.

THE CANAL AND THE COLD WAR

Why don't we get out of Panama gracefully, before we
are kicked out?

—Harry Truman, 1947

The strategic utility of the Panama Canal was rapidly declining by the end of World War II. A myth has emerged that the development of nuclear weapons rendered the Panama Canal strategically useless. Like most myths, it has some truth behind it. High-level American commanders—most notably, Harry Truman—did in fact conclude that the canal's military value had dropped precipitously, but the atomic bomb was not the reason. The Soviet Union had no atomic weapons until 1949, and the Soviets had no easy way of delivering a bomb to Panama until the 1960s. As late as 1961, U.S. planners estimated that the USSR Strategic Rocket Forces fielded only between ten and twenty-five missiles capable of hitting the Western Hemisphere.[17] (Those estimates were accurate: we now know that the Soviets had only ten operational ICBMs—intercontinental ballistic missiles—at the end of 1961.)[18] Russian submarine forces could have attacked the canal, but they were unreliable at best, and rarely at sea until the 1970s. Of course, Moscow could have tried to hide an atomic bomb inside a third-country vessel, but American defense planners had known since at least 1925 that conventional weapons hidden inside suicide ships were quite sufficient to disable the canal.

Rather, the Panama Canal's military value to the United States declined for two reasons. The first was that capital ships grew too large to fit through the locks. During World War II, the U.S. Navy retrofitted the aircraft carrier *Saratoga* and three battleships with antitorpedo blisters that made them too large to fit through the canal.[19] In 1952, the *Forrestal*-class aircraft carrier entered service, the first class deliberately designed too large for the canal. In 1961, the even larger *Kitty Hawk*–class of aircraft carrier succeeded *Forrestal*. In that same year, the U.S. Navy commissioned *Enterprise*, the first nuclear-powered aircraft carrier, also too big for the Panama Canal locks, as were the *Nimitz*-class carriers that succeeded *Enterprise*. With American naval strategy increasingly built around carrier groups, the inability of the centerpieces of those groups to transit the canal greatly reduced its utility.

The second reason for the decline in the canal's strategic value was that the American defensive perimeter became global after 1945. The United States no longer needed a two-ocean navy; it needed a five-ocean navy. American ships now patrolled the Mediterranean Sea, Persian Gulf, and Indian Ocean, as well as the Atlantic and the Pacific. President Franklin Roosevelt realized as early as 1942 that the need to maintain a global naval presence greatly reduced the strategic value of the Panama Canal, and he suspended work on a third set of locks designed to fit capital vessels too large for the existing locks.[20] Right after the war's end, Admiral Daniel Galley testified that there was no need for the Panama Canal at all, since modern ships could travel around Cape Horn with no difficulty and the U.S. Navy greatly outnumbered the Soviet fleet.[21]

After the war, the United States briefly explored the possibility of restarting the Panama Canal expansion project, in order to fit the larger military vessels being designed. Practicalities soon led to the plan's abandonment. There was no pressing commercial reason for expansion at the time, since the Panama Canal was far from capacity and commercial vessels had not yet grown too large for the existing locks. In addition, the cost of expansion was immense. In 1939, the Third Locks project had been estimated to cost $277 million; the United States spent $75.2 million before its cancellation in 1942. By 1947, however, those cost estimates had become outdated. First, the postwar inflation drove up the price level by 60 percent. Second, Defense Department planners concluded that the third locks would have to have dimensions of 1,500 × 200 × 50 feet in order to accommodate the projected size of future warships, rather larger than the 1,155 × 140 × 41 feet called for in the 1939 plan. The cost rose to $1.14 billion, or $9.0 billion in 2009 dollars.[22] (As a relative share of GDP, the cost would have been the 2009 equivalent of a $67 billion project.) Congress blanched.

In 1947, the U.S. government also explored the idea of removing the existing locks altogether, converting the Panama Canal into a sea-level waterway with a sixty-foot depth. The sea-level plan involved clearing out roughly 1.05 billion cubic yards of earth along the existing canal route, four times the amount excavated for the original canal. A single giant tidal lock would need to be constructed, measuring 200 by 1,500 feet. But the truly ambitious part of the scheme involved damming or rerouting *any* waterway that might lead into the deepened channel, including the Chagres River, which would be diverted into the Caribbean. The estimated cost of this plan came to $2.48 billion, or $19.6 billion in 2009 dollars.[23] Congress blanched even more. When a private engineering firm revisited the plans in 1955, they upped that estimate (in 2009 dollars) to $24.1 billion.[24] The fiscally prudent Eisenhower administration shelved the plans after only the most cursory consideration.

Parts of the U.S. military pressured the U.S. government to retain the extensive network of wartime bases that it had established in Panama. General Willis Crittenberger presented a canal defense plan that involved twenty-four-hour fighter patrols and enough aircraft to destroy any enemy fleet that got within striking distance of the canal. This part of Crittenberger's plan was slightly odd, considering that another part of the same plan stated that the only serious threats to the canal came from "suicidal attacks by submarine-based aircraft, or attacks by naval craft operating by stealth, or by aircraft operating from hidden bases in nearby jungles"—none of which required a massive series of bases to defend against.[25] In 1946, as now, it was hard for civilians to argue against military planners. Despite his better instincts, President Truman went ahead and asked Panama for an extension on most of its World War II–era bases, the largest of which was the thirty-square-mile Río Hato air base. The Americans initially (and somewhat inexplicably) asked for 999-year leases—under which the bases would have reverted to Panama in the year 2946—later backing down and requesting a 10-year lease with an option on another 10.

Fortunately for the United States, Panamanian resistance saved Washington from its own poor judgment. In December 1947, Panamanian president Enrique Jiménez submitted the prospective agreement to the National Assembly. On December 11, Panamanian students began rioting in protest. One student died and at least seventeen police officers were wounded. On December 16, the protests widened into mass demonstrations outside government buildings. "Amazing development is actual physical fear which had seized most deputies," wrote State Department observers. "President of Assembly spoke of '10,000 boys with knives' which might await them."[26] On December 22, 1947, the Panamanian National Assembly unanimously rejected the American defense plan.

American defense chiefs accepted the Panamanian decision with equanimity. The U.S. Army stated that it "felt no dissatisfaction about the evacuation." The Air Force relocated its Caribbean patrol flights to a base at Chaguaramas, Trinidad, which was in fact rather better located.[27] The next year, in 1948, the Defense Department finally dropped its plans to expand the Panama Canal, stating that they could not be justified. Admiral W.H.P. Blandy, the commander of the Atlantic Fleet, told the New York Times that the canal "is primarily of logistic rather than strategic importance."[28] The Times also reported that "the Canal Zone's small garrison is particularly concerned with sabotage or sneak attack—even more

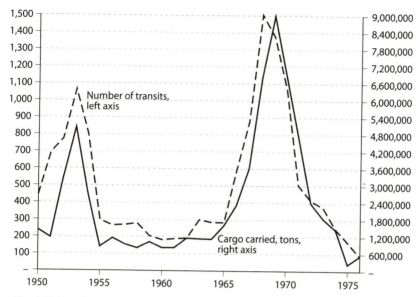

Figure 7.1: Military cargo transits through the Panama Canal, 1950–76. *Source: Annual Reports.*

so than with the atomic bomb."[29] By late 1949, even the U.S. Navy's strongest proponent of the Third Locks project, Captain Miles Duval, concluded that Panama was "no longer the strategic center of the Americas for war" and "the consolidation of potential land powers, the increasing destructiveness of modern weapons, and the relocation of the industrialization of the United States" to the West Coast had diminished the canal's strategic importance.[30]

Despite the vast increase in the volume of trade carried by the Panama Canal after World War II, the Panama Canal played a limited logistical role in the Korean and Vietnam wars. Neither conflict required significant movement of naval assets. Military cargoes passing through the canal spiked in both wars—during the Vietnam War the absolute amount of military-related cargo rivaled the peak years of the Second World War—but given the improvements that had been made to the nation's transportation infrastructure between 1945 and 1965, it is unlikely that the canal provided significant cost savings.

THE CANAL AND THE TREASURY

Ni millones ni limosnas, queremos justicia.
[Neither millions nor alms, we want justice.]

—*President José Antonio Remón, 1952*

In 1945, President Truman proposed to the Potsdam Conference that the United States should relinquish the Panama Canal to the United Nations. British and French opposition skewered that proposal, but two years later, Harry Truman was prepared to give back control of Panama's radio transmissions, telephone and telegraph network, and aviation system.[31] Why not also hand over the Panama Canal itself? The United States would have relieved itself of a strategic liability and improved its standing in the world—no small consideration as the nation embarked on what was to be a forty-year-long ideological struggle with Soviet Communism.

Truman and his immediate successors chose not to hand over the Panama Canal for two interrelated reasons. First, in terms of foreign policy, the United States did not trust Panamanian governments. If a future Panamanian government was likely to have malign intent—or be unable to operate the canal efficiently, which was very close to the same thing—thereby forcing the United States to intervene again, why leave in the first place and risk the collateral damage? The American presence was self-financing, and the Canal Zone literally drew a line around the canal operation inside which Panamanian governments could not interfere. Second, the Panama Canal had become a symbol of American nationalism, making any attempt to alter U.S. rule over the Canal Zone into a lightning rod that domestic political factions could use to mobilize opposition and garner support.

Dwight Eisenhower encountered both problems when he opened negotiations for a new Panama Canal treaty in 1953. Panama's recent political history was not one to inspire confidence in his Panamanian counterpart, José Antonio Remón. Remón's presidency followed ten years of revolving-door Panamanian governments.

The tumult started in 1941, when President Arnulfo Arias, who had previously expressed sympathies with Fascist regimes, suspended the Panamanian constitution and replaced it with a new one of his own design. On October 6, after German submarines sank several Panamanian flagged vessels, Arias declared that any armed merchant ship under the Panamanian flag would have its registry cancelled. The following day, he took a Pan-American flight to Havana for a weekday vacation with his mistress. On October 9, U.S. ambassador Wilson received a morning call from Panamanian cabinet members on the delicate subject of whether the United States would object to a coup. Later that day, the Supreme Court declared the presidency vacant—Arias was technically out of the country without the permission of the assembly—and the cabinet announced that Minister of Justice Ricardo de la Guardia would be Arias's successor. The following day, the Panamanian cabinet reversed Arias's cancellation order.[32] On October 16, Secretary of State Cordell Hull announced to the press that "the United States Government has had no connection, direct or indirect, with the recent governmental changes in Panama."[33] Arias spent the remainder of the war in Argentina.[34]

Four years later, the National Assembly forced President de la Guardia out of office, and Enrique Adolfo Jiménez assumed the presidency. Jiménez lacked his own base of support, and chose not to run in the 1948 election. Rather, the election saw the seventy-three-year-old Domingo Díaz Arosemena pitted against Arnulfo Arias, who had returned to the country from Argentina. Arias won the first count by 1,500 votes, at which point Díaz Arosemena supporters assaulted the Board of Elections, injuring two of the vote counters. José Antonio Remón, then chief of the national police, stepped in and conducted his own recount, which gave Díaz Arosemena the presidency. In turn, Díaz Arosemena gave Remón a monopoly over cattle slaughtering in partnership with Díaz Arosemena's son. Díaz Arosemena died in 1949, and his successor, Daniel Chanís, tried to break up the cattle monopoly. The National Guard responded by breaking up Chanís's presidency. Roberto Chiari, Remón's cousin, took power for a week before the National

Assembly condemned Chiari for orchestrating a coup. Chiari was about to step down and allow Chanís to return when Remón heard about his cousin's pusillanimity. Remón ousted his cousin but remained unwilling to assume power directly. Instead, Remón asked the Board of Elections to retroactively certify *Arias's* victory in the 1948 election. The board complied, and Arias returned from his second exile to don the presidential sash. Two years later, in 1951, Arias tried to suspend the constitution of 1946. Once again, Remón ejected him. Alcibíades Arosemena served as interim president until 1952, when Remón, tired of ruling from behind the scenes, ran for the presidency himself. It is no surprise that he won.[35]

Soon after his inauguration, "Chichi" Remón declared that he would travel to Washington to renegotiate the treaties between Panama and the United States. He rallied Panamanian public opinion behind the renegotiation with the slogan "Neither millions nor alms, we want justice."[36] Despite some reservations and Remón's relatively strong stance on the Panama Canal, the U.S. government generally welcomed his open accession to power. Remón had effectively controlled Panamanian politics since 1946, but his behind-the-scenes rule prompted sporadic outbreaks of unrest and agitation. The State Department hoped that Remón's decision to openly take the presidential seal would stabilize the country. It simultaneously feared, however, that Remón would be able to mobilize Panamanian public opinion against American interests. In any case, Washington's hopes and fears both pointed in the direction of the same policy: an increase in American financial support for Remón's new government, in the hope that such support would buy stability. Gross aid flows to the Panamanian government (excluding the rental payments from the Canal Zone) rose from $0.8 million in 1951 to $1.9 million the next year. (See table 7.4.)

Eisenhower met Remón at the White House in September of 1953, where the stocky police chief got along well with the retired general. Eisenhower ruefully admitted he was familiar with the problematic nature of Commissary operations from his years stationed in the Canal Zone in the early 1920s, and he was genuinely shocked to learn that Panama was forbidden by the 1903 treaty to tax Panamanian citizens who worked for the canal, even on Panamanian territory.[37] The meeting ended with a joint statement reading, "There should be an equitable benefitting of the two nations which made possible the construction of the canal as well as the enabling of Panama to take advantage of the market offered by the Canal Zone and the ships transiting the Canal."[38] Much as Harmodio Arias's face-to-face meetings with Franklin Roosevelt convinced Roosevelt to push the Hull-Alfaro Treaty forward, Eisenhower's personal meeting with Remón persuaded Eisenhower in favor of many of the Panamanian positions against the judgment of his White House advisors.

The Remón-Eisenhower Treaty was signed on January 25, 1955. Remón himself, however, did not live to see it, having been machine-gunned by unknown assassins while attending Juan Franco Racetrack in Panama City on January 2, 1955.[39] Ironically, his treaty provided Panama with far more alms and millions than justice. Panama's treaty annuity jumped from $430,000 to $1.93 million. The United States transferred property worth $4.4 million to Panama. Panama gained the ability to tax Panamanian employees of the canal, while the Commissary's exalted position in the Canal Zone was reduced to the level of a more typical Army Post Exchange store. The Commissary closed down several meat-processing plants, an industrial laboratory, and its ice-making enterprise.[40] Most influentially—and perhaps most justly—Panamanian employees of the Panama Canal now received equivalent pay to their American counterparts.[41] In exchange, Panama granted the United States the rent-free use of thirty square miles for fifteen years to reopen the Rio Hato Air Base.[42] The United States also abandoned its monopoly over the use of the Panama Railroad between Colón and Panama City, in exchange for which Panama gave up its right to transport its police for free on the railroad.[43]

The Congress of Industrial Organizations (which was to merge with the American Federation of Labor to form the AFL-CIO in 1956) supported the Remón-Eisenhower Treaty. The CIO first

TABLE 7.4

Official Transfers between the U.S. and Panama, Million 2009 US$, 1946–75

	U.S. official transfers to Panama						
	(a) Canal annuity	*(b)* Other transfers, net	*(a) + (b)* Total	*(c)* U.S. income from canal	*(a) + (b) − (c)* Net transfers from U.S. to Panama	Net transfers as % of Panama's tax revenue	Net transfers as % of Panama's GDP
1946	3.8	1.6	5.4	−6.3	−1.0	−0.4	0.0
1947	3.4	1.3	4.7	−6.5	−1.7	−0.6	−0.1
1948	3.2	1.1	4.3	−19.6	−15.3	−6.4	−0.8
1949	3.2	24.1	27.3	−$4.0	23.3	9.7	1.2
1950	3.2	1.1	4.3	−21.0	−16.7	−7.3	−0.9
1951	3.0	7.0	10.0	−14.1	−4.0	−1.8	−0.2
1952	2.9	21.1	24.1	−20.0	4.0	1.6	0.2
1953	2.9	6.8	9.7	−7.5	2.2	0.8	0.1
1954	2.9	7.2	10.0	−32.9	−22.9	−8.0	−1.1
1955	2.8	12.7	15.5	−51.2	−35.7	−12.1	−1.6
1956	12.2	40.2	52.4	−46.5	5.9	1.9	0.3
1957	11.8	150.4	162.2	−47.2	115.0	36.9	4.9
1958	11.5	19.9	31.4	−46.5	−15.1	−4.8	−0.7
1959	11.4	7.1	18.4	−53.0	−34.5	−11.5	−1.4

1960	11.2	7.2	18.4	-47.1	-28.7	-8.5	-1.2
1961	11.1	54.2	65.3	-44.7	20.6	5.7	0.8
1962	11.0	90.6	101.5	-47.2	54.3	14.1	1.9
1963	10.8	32.8	43.6	-48.4	-4.8	-1.2	-0.2
1964	10.7	101.3	112.0	-52.8	59.2	14.1	1.8
1965	10.5	83.8	94.3	-52.8	41.4	8.8	1.2
1966	10.2	42.6	52.8	-45.6	7.2	1.4	0.2
1967	9.9	99.2	109.0	-34.4	74.6	12.9	1.8
1968	9.5	52.1	61.6	-13.6	48.0	8.2	1.1
1969	9.0	40.0	49.0	-16.2	32.8	5.3	0.7
1970	8.6	39.7	48.3	-24.3	24.0	3.4	0.5
1971	8.2	44.1	52.2	-37.2	15.1	2.0	0.3
1972	7.8	160.2	168.1	-37.6	130.4	16.2	2.6
1973	7.4	164.9	172.3	-39.5	132.8	15.3	2.4
1974	6.8	45.2	52.1	-42.4	9.6	0.7	0.2
1975	7.5	89.2	$6.7	-43.3	53.4	3.7	0.9

Source: Panama Canal Company annual reports; Bureau for Legislative and Public Affairs, U.S. Agency for International Development, *U.S. Overseas Loans and Grants* [Greenbook] (Washington, DC: USAID, ongoing); Panama; Oxford Latin American Economic History Database (OxLAD).

Note: Amounts deflated using the U.S. GDP deflator.

waded into the thicket of Panama Canal politics in 1946, when it accepted a request by the Panama Canal West Indian Employees Association to organize a local. The CIO placed Local 713 under the rubric of the United Public Workers of America (UPWA); it issued its first wage demands in 1947. Unfortunately, the FBI began to investigate the UPWA as a Communist front organization. The CIO expelled the UPWA and sent Edward Welsh, a native New Yorker, to the Zone to organize a new local. Local 900 included approximately 5,500 workers.[44] The CIO recognized the local at its 1950 annual meeting in Chicago, after reciting a litany of Canal Zone injustices:

> In the face of our pledged word, the actual practices of the American government in the Canal Zone are, in truth, a travesty of those ideals which we in the United States regard as basic to a democracy. . . . Non-American citizens in the Zone— the same persons whose labor in large measure made possible the miracle of construction represented by the Canal—have long been the victims of inequities and discriminatory practices which can be neither justified nor explained away. For example, the average rate of pay for non-American citizens is 48¢ per hour, as against $2.06 per hour for the U.S. citizens employed in the Zone. For the non-citizen employee . . . we have no adequate pension system. We offer instead a cash relief of $25 per month. Housing provided in the Canal Zone to non-citizens employed as civilian workers is more humble than housing in the worst slums of our metropolitan cities. The worst that America has to offer in the way of race segregation has been transplanted in the Zone. It has affected the wages, the pensions, the housing, and even the education of Panama citizens.[45]

The Panamanian leader of Local 900, Ed Gaskin, came out in favor of the treaty. In fact, the State Department sponsored Gaskin to come to the United States and speak out in favor of the treaty and against America's own labor practices in the Canal Zone.

"The system of segregation and discrimination is a terrible blot on the conscience of America." Upon his return to the Canal Zone, Gaskin organized rallies of Zone workers to back Remón and the treaty.[46]

Despite union support at a time when unions greatly mattered in American politics, the treaty encountered vociferous opposition in the United States. The United States Citizens Association (USCA), a lobby group formed to defend Zonian interests, attacked the agreement. The USCA also attacked economy measures that the Canal Zone had implemented in 1951, reducing the rent and consumer goods subsidies granted to residents. The USCA also warned that the treaty eroded "the sovereignty of the United States over the Canal" and that it would allow inefficient Panamanians a role in "such a vital and complex institution as the Canal."[47] The Eisenhower administration persuaded the Senate to ratify the treaty by promising that the United States would retain absolute sovereignty over the Canal Zone. In the words of Secretary of State Henry Holland before the Senate: "The Panamanians advanced several small requests which, one by one, had considerable appeal, but all of which we refused, because we did not want to leave one grain of evidence that could a hundred years hence be interpreted as implying any admission by the United States that we possess and exercise anything less than 100 percent of the rights of sovereignty in this area."[48] Thus reassured, the U.S. Senate ratified the agreement 72–14.

The implementation of the Eisenhower-Remón Treaty left many in Panama unsatisfied. Panama's trade minister accused the United States in 1958 of importing Ecuadorean rice, Danish dairy products, German beer, and Australian meat in violation of the treaty.[49] The Eisenhower administration counterclaimed that it refused to enforce congressional demands that certain Canal Zone occupations be limited to Americans on the grounds that they violated the treaty.[50] Panamanian observers, however, stated that regardless of Washington's intentions, the Canal Zone administration continued to lock Panamanians out of most jobs. "The only difference of salary that we accept as fair and non-discriminatory," said

Panama's representative at the United Nations, "was that of the skill or experience of the worker."[51] Panamanian diplomats were careful to distinguish between the U.S. government and the Canal Zone administration, but the distinction was lost on the Panamanian public.

The American government was aware of the growing discontent in Panama. After Remón's assassination, foreign aid increased once more because the Eisenhower administration decided that the risk of instability in Panama *was even greater* than it had understood during the earlier negotiations. The Remón assassination triggered factional infighting among Panamanian elites. The first thing that Remón's successor did was arrest Arnulfo Arias, the right-wing former president, who had no apparent connection to Remón's death. The government then arrested and indicted Remón's successor, José Ramón Guizado, who was acquitted after serving some time in jail. The Panamanian police had to suppress rioting. The apparent involvement of American organized crime in the assassination further worried the U.S. government because it provided a lightning rod for Panamanian anti-Americanism. (See table 7.4 and figure 7.2.)

On November 3, 1959, Panamanian anger over the Canal Zone came to a head. Aquilino Boyd, the foreign minister and a member of one of the country's elite political families, led a preannounced march to the Canal Zone on Panama's independence day. The group intended to publicly hoist a Panamanian flag inside the Canal Zone. The Zonians called the march a publicity stunt, since the Canal Zone authorities always flew the Panamanian flag inside the Zone on November 3. Angry Zonians met the marchers, and violence broke out. After an American policeman allegedly trampled the Panamanian flag, the angry Panamanians retreated—but instead of returning to their homes, they marched on the U.S. Embassy and tore down the American flag. The Canal Zone governor closed the border and called out the U.S. Army to protect it. The demonstrators responded by setting cars on fire in front of the Zone.[52] More rioting broke out a few weeks later when demonstrators once again tried to hoist the Panamanian flag in the Zone.

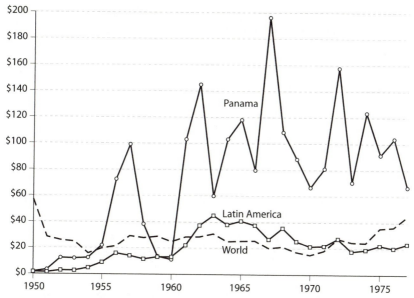

Figure 7.2: U.S. aid per capita, 2009 U.S. dollars. *Note*: The Latin American and world averages are unweighted by country. *Source*: Bureau for Legislative and Public Affairs, U.S. Agency for International Development, *U.S. Overseas Loans and Grants* [*Greenbook*] (Washington, DC: USAID, ongoing).

American soldiers and Panamanian police prevented the demonstrators from entering, but the angry protestors turned into a mob when they returned to Panama City and set off a wave of looting. Much of the violence was directed against symbols of American business, such as the Chase Manhattan Bank.[53]

In response to the crisis, the U.S. government raised its aid transfers to Panama. President Eisenhower wanted to compromise on the flag issue, but public and congressional opposition forced him to move very carefully. In December 1959, Eisenhower said at a press conference, "The question of the flag has never been specifically placed before me, but I do in some form believe that we should have visual evidence that Panama does have titular sovereignty over the region." In response, the U.S. House of Representatives passed a resolution insisting that the Panamanian flag *not* be flown in the Canal Zone, riots and Panamanian public opinion be damned. Eisenhower did not move until Congress recessed in September 1960, at which point he authorized both flags to be flown in one location along the border, across from Panama's legislature.[54] Letters to the White House ran sixty to one against Eisenhower's decision.[55]

A congressional committee dismissed Panamanian complaints. Its report claimed that the Canal Zone provided a sixth of Panamanian government revenue in 1958, including American aid and the income taxes paid by Canal Zone workers. It concluded that allowing the Panamanian flag would be "charged with dangers." The report, however, also dismissed most of the concerns of the Zonians. Requiring more purchases from Panama had neither decreased the quality nor increased the price of imports. Nor had Panamanians displaced Americans in large numbers: Panamanians occupied only 7 percent of skilled jobs.[56] The congressional report, unsurprisingly, failed to assuage Panamanian opinion. On November 16, 1961, the Panamanian National Assembly voted unanimously to revoke all existing canal treaties.[57] The Kennedy administration took no action on the flag issue, but it prudently continued Panama's high aid transfers. By the early 1960s, per capita aid to Panama easily outdistanced that given to any other Latin American country; only Bolivia came close for any sustained period. (See figure 7.2 and table 7.5.) In fact, outside the Middle East, only Iceland, Laos, and Cyprus received more aid per capita than Panama.

The decision to increase American aid to the Panamanian government had the unintended consequence of reducing the importance of the Panama Canal to the United States. The more that the United States had to compensate Panama for the Canal Zone's negative impact on Panamanian national pride, the less benefit the United States received from keeping formal control over the Canal Zone. Once the fiscal flows from Panama turned persistently negative in 1956, the only reasons to retain titular ownership over the Panama Canal were the fears that a future Panamanian government might raise tolls, fail to maintain the canal, or otherwise behave malevolently.

TABLE 7.5

Quinquennial Receipts of U.S. Aid per Capita, Panama = 1.00

	1950–54	1955–59	1960–64	1965–69	1970–76
Panama	1.00	1.00	1.00	1.00	1.00
World average	3.04	0.50	0.31	0.18	0.26
Latin average	0.32	0.27	0.34	0.26	0.20
Bolivia	1.19	1.35	1.10	0.37	0.49
Guyana	0.00	0.07	0.13	1.04	0.37
Costa Rica	1.30	0.78	0.66	0.48	0.33
Dominican Republic	0.07	0.01	0.46	0.98	0.33
Nicaragua	0.55	0.38	0.41	0.51	0.53
Chile	0.12	0.34	0.94	0.56	0.24
Guatemala	0.21	0.70	0.25	0.15	0.25
El Salvador	0.21	0.08	0.36	0.21	0.14
Brazil	0.08	0.08	0.18	0.16	0.04

Source: Bureau for Legislative and Public Affairs, U.S. Agency for International Development, *U.S. Overseas Loans and Grants* [*Greenbook*] (Washington, DC: USAID, ongoing).

Given the personalized nature of Panamanian politics, why didn't the United States make direct side-payments to influential Panamanian political actors? Bribing individuals would have been less expensive than trying to pay off an entire government. It might have even been more effective. The problem was threefold. First, the Panamanian government would view such payments as an attempt to undercut its authority. (This view would have the advantage of being true.) Second, direct interference in Panamanian politics would violate contemporary norms of sovereignty. If made public, such payments would cost the United States a great deal of international legitimacy. In the wake of the adverse world reaction to the U.S. interventions in Guatemala and Iran, President Eisenhower was reluctant to take such a chance. Finally, the United States would have found it difficult to judge whether it was paying enough to keep the various individuals satisfied, a political variant of Mises's famous economic calculation problem.

In effect, Panama and the United States became locked into a series of continual asymmetric renegotiations in which *Panama* had a better position. The Panamanian government could use a menu of carrots and sticks to negotiate with both internal interest groups and the United States. The U.S. government, on the other hand, could only offer a menu of carrots absent the use of military force against the Panamanians (or the Zonians). The Canal Riots of 1964 finally drove that lesson home. A group of five Canal Zone junior college students, led by a Junior Reserve Officer Training Corps cadet, managed to set off days of rioting when they insisted on hoisting the American flag in front of Balboa High School.[58]

The problem from the American side was that Panamanian-Zonian tensions had been increasing for some time. Under normal circumstances, a seventeen-year-old student and a high school flagpole do not precipitate deadly riots or an international incident. If it had not been the flag incident, some other event would likely have sparked a disturbance. The United States realized that putting down the riots with overwhelming force would unify Panama against its presence—and provide the Soviet bloc a golden propaganda victory—and therefore followed a policy of restraint. Even though three American soldiers died from Panamanian sniper fire, there were eyewitness reports of U.S. officers *striking* their soldiers in order to prevent them from firing back.[59]

DECLINING SOCIAL SAVINGS FOR THE PANAMA CANAL

The adjective most frequently applied to the Canal by Americans is "vital." In terms of U.S. trade, however, the numbers would justify more modest descriptions. Convenient. Useful.

—*Robert Cox, 1975*

Meanwhile, the Panama Canal's domestic importance for the United States economy was coming to an end. This was not due to any decrease in the volume of trade carried by the Panama Canal. After a wartime drop in civilian traffic, tonnage through the canal returned to its prewar levels by 1949, growing at an annualized rate of 6.5 percent between 1950 and 1975. Rather, the Panama Canal was losing its cost advantage for domestic cargoes compared to alternate methods of transportation. This is reflected in the canal's statistics: between 1950 and 1975, transcontinental shipments between U.S. ports carried by the Panama Canal *declined* at an annualized rate of 2.0 percent.

The cost of long-distance transport inside the United States dropped precipitously between 1950 and 1975. With the arrival of the Interstate Highway System, trucking eclipsed railroads in freight in terms of haulage. This was a rapid structural change in the nature of American transportation. The first transcontinental delivery by truck happened in 1912, but as late as 1946, the best that an economic study of the transportation industry could report was that "transcontinental truck lines are not unknown."[60] By 1969, however, transcontinental shipments of lumber had exploded to 7 million tons, *twenty-eight times* as much as was carried via the Panama Canal. Transcontinental shipments of lumber and iron-and-steel products together totaled 8.5 million tons—almost twice the 4.4 million tons of intercoastal traffic carried through Panama.[61] (By 1992, trucks would carry 28 million tons of freight on hauls exceeding two thousand miles.) Nor did railroad costs remain stagnant in the face of competition from trucking. Containerization and dieselization (among other innovations) drove down the cost of railroad transport.

By the mid-1970s, it had become *cheaper* to transport goods via the transcontinental railroad than through the Panama Canal. Additionally, containerization lowered the cost of unloading cargo from ships onto trucks and railroads, or vice versa. As a result, a 1976 congressional committee reported that West Coast ports enjoyed a cost advantage on "many container import shipments with destinations as far east as Cleveland."[62] Railroads also began to capture much of the export business. Grain exports to Asia had traditionally travelled from the Midwest to the Gulf Coast ports of New Orleans, Houston, and Galveston. Falling freight rates meant that it became viable to export midwestern wheat to Asia via the Pacific Coast: the cost of an additional seven hundred miles in railroad transit had become roughly equal to the cost savings

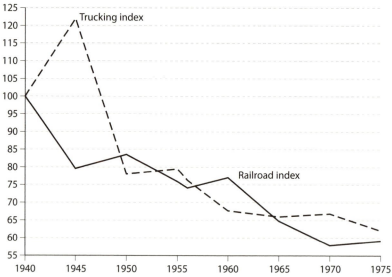

Figure 7.3: Real cost per ton-mile index, long-distance trucking and railroads, 1940 = 100. *Source*: Ton-mileage data from 1940 to 1945 from John W. Kendrick, assisted by Maude R. Pech, *Productivity Trends in the United States* (New York: National Bureau of Economic Research, 1961), app. G, 522; from 1945 to 1956, *Statistical Abstract of the United States* (Washington, DC: GPO, 1960); from 1960 onward, the Bureau of Transportation Statistics website on National Transportation Statistics, available at http://www.bts.gov/publications/national_transportation_statistics/, table 1-46a; revenue data up to 1960 from *Statistical Abstract of the United States* (selected years); after 1960, National Transportation Statistics, table 3.7; index from authors' calculations.

available from using vessels larger than the maximum that could fit through the canal locks and avoiding Panama Canal tolls. Nor were there any signs of capacity constraints: the Congressional Research Service reported in 1975 that "U.S. ports and waterways face no overall capacity restrictions . . . and existing physical plant of the railroads has much greater capacity than any foreseeable demand for rail freight service."[63]

The development of "post-Panamax" vessels too large for the Panama Canal also diminished the canal's economic importance. As late as 1974, petroleum imports accounted for 21.6 percent of all cargoes passing through the canal, but contemporary observers expected that number to fall with the introduction of supertankers. The limiting factor keeping supertankers from taking away most of the canal's petroleum traffic was the ability of Ecuadorian and American ports to accommodate them. "It is expected that once 200,000 ton tankers can be used," said a 1975 Congressional Research Service report, "shipments around the Horn would be more economical than transit in smaller vessels via the Canal." The same factor applied to ships carrying other commodities. "It is generally expected that once U.S. ports are capable of handling ships with drafts of 60 feet or so, practically all of the iron ore traffic [from Chile and Peru] will disappear from the Canal," the Congressional Research Service stated.[64]

Table 7.6 replicates the analysis undertaken in table 5.4 to generate a basic estimate of the social savings provided by the Panama Canal. The analysis assumes that the amount of cargo transported along each route would not change in the event that the canal closed down. For each aggregated route, representative distances were calculated with and without using the Panama Canal, selecting specific city pairs on the basis of anecdotal evidence from the official reports and congressional testimony. Traffic along the Europe-Asia and Europe-Oceania routes is included, because the 1967–75 closure of the Suez Canal meant that the Panama Canal provided a shorter route than travelling around the Cape of Good Hope. Shipping costs per ton-mile were derived from data in table 2 of Gibbs's contemporary study of Panama Canal costs.[65] The average cost for each route was calculated by assuming that iron and steel goods used container ships, whereas agricultural commodities travelled in dry bulk carriers, petroleum products in tankers, and other cargoes in general cargo vessels. Railroad costs were estimated by taking the costs of transcontinental railroad shipping from Rockwell, and assuming that they declined in real terms by the same amount as all long-distance railroad shipping provided by data from the National Bureau of Economic Research and Bureau of Transportation Statistics.[66] The estimates show that the

TABLE 7.6
1975 Social Savings from the Panama Canal

	1975 dollars			2009 dollars		
	Total cost for all cargo on route		Social savings	Total cost for all cargo on route		Social savings
	Via Panama Canal, including tolls	Cheapest alternative		Via Panama Canal, including tolls	Cheapest alternative	
U.S. intercostal	44	72	28	141	232	91
U.S. East–Asia	702	831	129	2,266	2,681	415
U.S. East–South America West	57	74	18	183	240	57
U.S. West–South America East	21	34	14	66	111	44
North America East–Oceania	46	51	4	149	164	14
North America West–Europe	127	206	79	411	665	254
Canada East–Asia	38	45	6	124	144	20
Europe–South America West	47	67	21	150	217	67
Europe–Australasia/Oceania	116	124	8	373	399	26
Europe–Asia	344	433	89	1,108	1,396	288
South American intercostal	22	42	20	71	134	63
Other	104	152	48	335	491	156
Subtotal			464			1,497
Plus toll revenues			143			462
Minus canal operating costs			(175)			(564)
Total			433			1,396

Source: Panama Canal annual reports; Stephen R. Gibbs, "The Economic Value of the Panama Canal," *Water Resources Research* 14, no. 2 (April 1978): 185–89; Leon Cole, "Economic Ramifications of Panama Canal Control and Use: A Survey," in 94th Cong, 1st sess., 1975, *Department of Transportation and Related Agencies Appropriations for 1976*, 65–79.

cheapest route for cargoes between the U.S. East Coast and Asia was not around Cape Horn, but via rail to Seattle and then ship, in agreement with 1976 congressional testimony.[67]

The numbers in table 7.6 are in fact an overestimate of the actual social savings generated by the Panama Canal in 1975. In contrast to our earlier social savings calculation for the canal, where we used pessimistic assumptions to show that, despite our underestimate, social savings in 1925 were large, table 7.6 uses optimistic assumptions to show that the social savings generated by the Panama Canal in 1975 were small. First, the shipping cost data assume that all vessels travelled at full capacity, when in fact most ships did not sail fully loaded. The actual freight rates paid by canal shipping were in fact higher than the rates used to estimate the canal's cost advantage over alternate transport routes. The estimates, therefore, overestimate the social savings from the Panama Canal. Second, the estimates assume zero elasticity of demand for transport. In other words, they assume that shippers are completely insensitive to cost, and will ship the same amount between the same destinations regardless of shipping cost changes. This assumption is clearly incorrect. A 1973 study by International Research Associates, a private consulting group, calculated that the average elasticity of demand for passage through the Panama Canal ranged between 1.19 and 1.52 for total shipping cost increases between 2 and 4 percent.[68] At an elasticity of 1.19, the global social savings would fall from $433 million to $310 million; at an elasticity of 1.52, global social savings would fall to $249 million. Considering the huge improvements in alternative and intermodal technologies—containerization, trucking, railroads, post-Panamax freighters—it should be no surprise that the elasticity of demand for canal cargo rose substantially between the 1930s and the 1970s.

In absolute terms, the Panama Canal generated *less* social savings in 1975 than it had before the Depression. In its peak year, 1930, the Panama Canal generated global social savings of $1.5 billion in 2009 dollars (assuming zero demand elasticity), 1.5 percent more than it did in 1975. The volume of cargo travelling the canal outpaced U.S. economic growth, but the social savings generated by moving that cargo via the canal significantly lagged it. The Panama Canal's social savings for the United States fell even more than they did for the world as a whole. In 1937, for example, intercoastal tonnage made up 28 percent of all cargoes carried through the canal, by tonnage. By 1975, that number had fallen to 3 percent. In terms of the canal's social savings, intercoastal routes generated 46 percent of the canal's social savings in 1937. By 1975, intercoastal routes generated only 6 percent of the canal's social savings. Routes bypassing the United States altogether rose from 29 percent of all canal traffic in 1937 (by tonnage) to 39 percent by 1975. The percentage of total social savings generated by non-U.S. routes rose even faster, from 26 percent in 1937 to 45 percent by 1975.[69] In short, the economic importance of the Panama Canal dropped after World War II for the same reason that the Panama *trajín* declined after 1613 and the Panama Railroad faded after 1869: competition. As land transport costs fell, the social savings that the Panama Canal generated for the United States dropped.

THE TOLLS CONTROVERSY REDUX

One of the strongest arguments against the United States transferring control of the Panama Canal to the Panamanian government was the fear that Panama would significantly raise rates on passing ships. Many observers feared that the Panamanian government would use its monopoly position to raise tolls sufficiently high to affect American businesses, driving up the costs paid by American importers and driving down the prices received by American exporters.

How realistic were these fears? The era when the owner of an isthmian canal could theoretically extract spectacular monopoly rents had long vanished. The canal enjoyed much less of a monopoly over transport routes in 1975 than it had enjoyed when it opened in 1921. Even if canal owners adopted a more rational pricing system than the flat rate per ton charged by the Americans, they would still have to face this new era of competition. In 1973,

International Research Associates (IRA) prepared a traffic sensitivity study for the Panama Canal Company to determine how high of a toll increase was too high. IRA reported with real toll hikes at or above 150 percent, "with the possible exception of one commodity group, the data indicate that total revenues decline when the increase is that high."[70] IRA estimated that a toll increase of 100 percent would produce a 26 percent fall in traffic, netting the Panama Canal's owners 48 percent more total revenue.[71] In fact, between 1999 and 2008 the canal's new Panamanian owners would raise base reference tolls by 23 percent over their 1975 levels in real terms.[72]

How much of the social savings would be lost to the world outside Panama if the new owners doubled tolls? Theoretically, the loss could be quite significant. If Panama acted as a price discriminator, choosing how much to increase tolls based on the demand elasticity for access to the canal route for the products passing through, Panama could potentially capture 25 percent of the world social savings. This policy would impose on the world an additional deadweight cost of 4 percent of the social savings, for a total reduction of 29 percent in the canal's economic benefit for the world outside Panama, in 2009 dollar terms, $403 million.[73] Of that, the United States would have lost a maximum of $222 million, under the somewhat improbable assumption that Americans captured all the social savings on all the routes that began or ended at American ports. A more reasonable estimate, in line with the contemporary conclusions of Gibbs and IRA, would assign the United States a potential loss of slightly more than a quarter of the social savings, or $106 million.[74]

Despite this loss, however, handing over the canal to the Panamanian government would *still* produce economic benefits for the United States. (See table 7.6.) First, the United States would no longer need to pay Panama an annuity for the use of the Canal Zone, which had risen to $2.3 million by 1975 ($7.4 million in 2009 dollars). Second, by 1975 the United States spent $23.5 million ($75.9 million in 2009 dollars) to run courts, police, and schools in the Zone, rather more than the $14.8 million ($47.8 million in

2009 dollars) that the Panama Canal Company remitted to the U.S. Treasury. Finally, handing over the Panama Canal to Panama City would allow the United States to cut the extraordinary amount of economic aid that it provided the Panamanian government. In 1975, the U.S. government provided Panama with $15.5 million in grants ($49.9 million in 2009 dollars). The $181 million (in 2009 dollars) cost savings from returning the Panama Canal to Panama—ditching the Big Ditch—would more than offset the amount that a future Panamanian canal management could extract from American users of Panama Canal services.

BAD MANAGEMENT

As the idea of transferring the Panama Canal back to Panama gained currency, many Americans grew increasingly worried that the Panamanians would be unable to manage the canal. In retrospect, these worries seem doubly ironic. Not only did the post-1999 Panamanian management of the canal turn out to be first-rate, but there is significant evidence that the United States managed the canal particularly poorly during the postwar period.

Despite multiple reorganizations and continual reforms, the Americans never succeeded in creating an incentive structure for the upper management of the Panama Canal Company that placed economic efficiency in the forefront. In 1950, the Panama Canal Act reorganized the commercial side of canal management into the Panama Canal Company. The chief executives of the Panama Canal Company, however, were neither drawn from private industry, nor ambitious younger members of the civil service, nor political appointees anxious to perform well. Rather, they were military bureaucrats at the end of their careers, given a plum job as a reward before retirement. (See table 7.7.) Canal management failed to increase the prime performance indicator of any self-sufficient enterprise: profitability. The Panama Canal's net profits declined over time. (See figure 7.4.)[75] During the 1950s, margins rose along with the volume of commercial traffic, which exploded from 6,524 transits in 1952 to 10,795 in 1960. After 1960, however, growth in

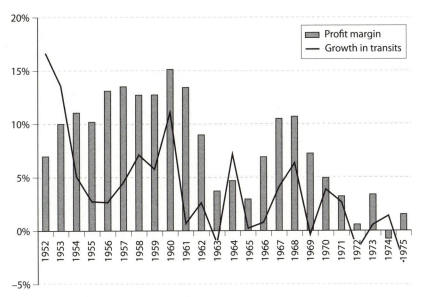

Figure 7.4: Panama Canal Company profit margins and growth in transits, 1952–76. *Source*: Panama Canal Company, *Annual Reports*. *Note*: In 1976, transits fell 11 percent.

canal traffic slowed dramatically, and the administration proved incapable of maintaining profitability in the face of slower growth.

Making matters worse, the United States never managed to make it clear that the Panama Canal existed to generate value for its "shareholders": the people of the United States. This allowed canal employees—that is to say, the Zonians—to capture control of the operation. The peculiar place of the Panama Canal in America's national mythology made this accomplishment much easier than it would have been for employees of such other public enterprises as, say, the Tennessee Valley Authority, the New Jersey Turnpike, or the National Aeronautics and Space Administration. Conservatives who would otherwise have been absolutely appalled at employee capture of domestic agencies not only tolerated but even applauded the same phenomenon in the Panama Canal.

The problem was productivity. During the high growth years of the 1950s, productivity grew faster than the number of transits. In fact, the Panama Canal Company managed to reduce the number of employees from 15,552 in 1952 to a low of 10,398 in 1959. After 1960, however, productivity growth slowed dramatically. (See figure 7.5.) In the mid-1970s, as transits began to decline, the Panama Canal succeeded in cutting its workforce—but most of the downsizing occurred among the company's lower-paid Panamanian workers. Between 1966 and 1976, the number of "employees paid at non-U.S. rates" declined from 9,192 to 6,665, while the number of employees paid at U.S. rates *rose* from 2,472 to 3,455. Average annual wages (in 2009 dollars) rose from $29,816 in 1965 to $38,581 by 1975, roughly paralleling the growth of nominal income in the United States. As a result, however, labor costs skyrocketed compared to revenue. During the expansion of the 1950s, payroll as a fraction of Panama Canal Company total revenue rose

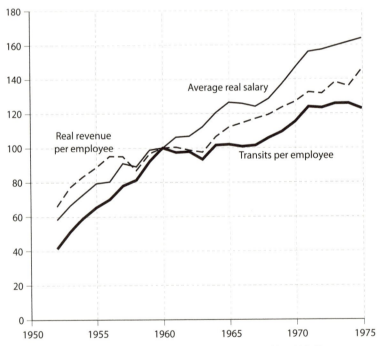

Figure 7.5: Productivity, cost, and revenue measures, 1960 = 100. *Source:* Panama Canal Company, *Annual Reports.*

from 41 percent to 47 percent. It rose again to 53 percent by 1965, before peaking at 56 percent in 1972. Making matters still worse, the costs of the Canal Zone government, entirely financed from Panama Canal Company revenues, rose from 13 percent of total revenues in 1952 to 16 percent twenty years later.[76]

The Panama Canal Company tried several measures to control labor costs. The Secretary of the Army (who appointed the Panama Canal Company's Board of Directors) ordered that the "tropical differential" paid to American employees be reduced from 25 percent of the base wage to 15 percent. He also ordered that married women would lose their differential. Unsurprisingly, employees sued. The Army won the case in 1967, but cutting the differential failed to put a cap on escalating personnel costs.[77] Further attempts to control costs culminated in an August 1973 "sick-out" by the Panama Canal Pilots Association. A 1974 report on labor relations on the canal concluded that the Panama Canal Company "tended to make every labor problem a crisis, because union leaders knew that that was the only way problems were solved."[78]

As labor relations deteriorated, accident rates ballooned. The number of accidents, as measured by the numbers of investigations requested by shipowners, rose by nearly 50 percent between the late 1960s and 1975. The seriousness of each accident rose even more. The Panama Canal Company recorded the value of all accident liabilities that had been accrued but not yet paid on its balance sheet. Since it usually took more than a year for the canal to pay out, changes in the value of accrued accident liabilities provide a rough indicator of the seriousness of canal accidents. (See figure 7.6.)

The reluctance of the Panama Canal Company to raise per-ton transit tolls was *not* the primary reason for the decline in the canal's profitability. It is true that the Panama Canal Company refused to raise nominal tolls until 1974, when it hiked them by 19.7 percent, even though the Panama Canal Act of 1950 granted its board the power to do so.[79] (The company raised tolls again by 19.5 percent in 1976.)[80] It is also true that the real value of per-ton canal tolls fell by half from the early 1950s until the mid-1970s, under the

Figure 7.6:   Transit accidents on the Panama Canal. *Source*: Panama Canal
Company/Commission, *Annual Reports*; Jeff Levon, "Alternative Dispute
Resolution at the Panama Canal: Negotiating a Collective Bargaining
Agreement," in *Portraits of Business Practices in Emerging Markets: Cases for
Management Education*, ed. Richard G. Linowes, 83–92 (Washington, DC: U.S.
Agency for International Development, 1999).

impact of inflation. (See figure 7.7.) Nevertheless, the increasing
size of cargo ships meant that nominal *per transit* tolls rose consistently between 1952 and 1975. Real per transit tolls remained
roughly constant. The Panama Canal Company probably should
have raised tolls, in light of its rising costs, but its reluctance to do
so did not cause its falling profitability.

Panama Canal management had few incentives to improve canal
efficiency or profitability. They did have incentives to maintain the
canal, but that did not lead to sustained innovation or improvement. Governors had short tenures and high turnover. Serving as
governor was not much of a career stepping-stone. Rather, it was
a cushy position given at the end of a long career in the U.S. Army
Corps of Engineers.

Only one Panama Canal Company governor remained in government service after running the Panama Canal, and his last job was far from a step upward. Walter Leber served as canal governor between 1967 and 1971. After his service at the Panama Canal, Leber moved to the Safeguard antiballistic missile program.[81] Leber, however, was not assigned to run Safeguard so much as he was to wrap it up. The Safeguard program aimed to defend American ICBM sites in the northern Great Plains against incoming Soviet warheads using nuclear-tipped missiles. After all, atomic bombs did not have to be particularly accurate. The Nixon administration, however, did not want to build the full system. Rather, it intended Safeguard as a feint in order to convince the Soviet Union to sign an arms limitation treaty, which the United States first proposed in 1967. The feint succeeded—the Soviets came to the table, and the Strategic Arms Limitation Treaty of May 1971 limited the United States to two Safeguard sites, just as Leber took over the program. The subsequent Anti-Ballistic Missile Treaty of 1972 reduced the

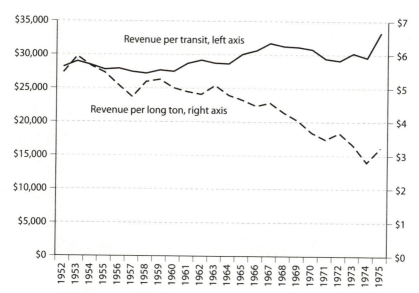

Figure 7.7: Panama Canal tolls, 2009 dollars. *Source*: Panama Canal Company, *Annual Reports*.

TABLE 7.7
Biographies of Postwar Panama Canal Governors

Name	DOB	Term	Background	Rank	Age at end of term	Post-canal career
Joseph Mehaffey	11/20/89	1944–48	USACE	Brigadier General	59	Consulting engineer for the World Bank in Turkey
Francis Newcomber	9/4/89	1948–52	USACE	Brigadier General	63	Retired
John Seybold	7/2/97	1952–56	USACE	Major General	59	Retired
William Potter	7/17/05	1956–60	USACE	Major General	55	Executive VP for the 1963 World's Fair, under Robert Moses. Later helped design Disney World's water and power systems.
William Carter	6/27/07	1960–62	USACE	Major General	55	Senior engineering advisor for the IDB
Robert Fleming	1/13/07	1962–67	USACE	unknown	60	Executive vice president of Anderson Nichols Co.
Walter Leber	9/12/18	1967–71	USACE	Major General	53	Safeguard ABM program
David Stuart Parker	3/22/19	1971–75	USACE	Major General	56	Retired
Harold Parfitt	8/6/21	1975–79	USACE	Major General	58	Retired
Dennis McAuliffe	4/8/22	1979–89	JCS/SHAPE/DoD	Lt. General	67	Retired

Source: Panama Canal Authority, "Governors and Administrators," http://www.pancanal.com/eng/history/biographies/index.html.
Note: USACE = U.S. Army Corps of Engineers; JCS/SHAPE/DoD = Joint Chiefs of Staff/Supreme Headquarters Allied Powers, Europe/Department of Defense.

number of Safeguard sites to one. Construction halted in 1972, and the system shut down in 1975.

Why did the American attempt to run the canal more commercially fail? In 1950, the Panama Canal Act theoretically reorganized canal management. Given that the visible benefits from the canal were dropping fast, however, no U.S. administration wanted to take the effort that a serious reorganization of canal corporate governance would require. Reorganization in the face of organized and increasingly militant opposition from the Zone employees, their dependents, and their union would have required a great deal of political capital. No administration was going to spend much political capital on reorganizing the enterprise—especially when every U.S. administration from Lyndon Johnson onward hoped to be able to get the United States out of the business of running the Panama Canal altogether.

DITCHING THE DITCH

I don't want to go into history; I want to go into the
Canal Zone.

—*Omar Torrijos, 1973*

Various U.S. governments tried and failed to find politically palatable ways to extricate themselves from the Canal Zone in the two decades following the end of World War II. President Truman proposed the internationalization of Panama Canal at the Potsdam Conference in 1945, but the proposal went nowhere.[82] Eisenhower signed the Eisenhower-Remón Treaty and increased aid to the country, but domestic pressure prevented going any further. Toward the end of the Eisenhower administration and under President Kennedy, several trial balloons were floated regarding the canal's potential internationalization under the aegis of the Organization of American States—but they were rejected by the Panamanian government.[83]

In the wake of the 1964 riots, the Johnson administration finally put some muscle into negotiating the handover of the canal. Johnson was an excellent politician and well aware of the canal's hot-button status. He therefore cleared his decision with ex-president Eisenhower before proceeding.[84] The resulting draft Panama Canal Treaty, unveiled in 1967, proposed to place the canal under a joint administration of five Americans and four Panamanians. All jobs would be immediately opened to Panamanians, and within five years the Joint Authority would get out of the business of running department stores, groceries, cafeterias, hotels, laundries, and gas stations. Panamanian law would apply within the renamed "Canal Area," but its schools and police would remain separate. Panamanians could only reside in the Area with the permission of the Joint Authority, and an eight-person court of four Americans and four Panamanians would be the highest appellate authority. The annuity would be replaced with a payment to the Panamanian government of 17¢ per ton, which would rise to 22¢ after five years. (Under that arrangement, Panama would have received $20.5 million in 1967, more than ten times the value of the annuity, but less than a fifth of the amount transferred to it in aid.) The Panama Canal would fully revert to Panama in 1999, but a parallel treaty would give the United States indefinite responsibility for Panamanian defense and control over several "defense areas."[85]

The draft treaty gained support from prominent conservatives like Dwight Eisenhower, but Congress balked. By 1967, Vietnam had almost destroyed the Johnson presidency. Facing strong primary challenges with the Democratic Party, and losing his influence over Congress, Johnson decided to postpone ratification. In October 1968, Colonel Omar Torrijos made the point moot when he seized control of the Panamanian government. Torrijos wanted a greater share of the revenues, and the end of the Canal Zone, not its replacement with a nebulous "Canal Area." The incoming Nixon administration did not agree with the general's point of view, and the proposed treaty died a quiet death.

Torrijos chose not to threaten violence or unleash mobs against the Americans, which might have invited a backlash from the

United States. Rather, he skillfully used the United Nations to internationalize the Panama Canal issue. Torrijos invited the U.N. Security Council to meet in Panama, where he maneuvered the United States into vetoing a resolution in favor of a "just and fair" new treaty. Embarrassed and aware that the United States now received few military or economic benefits from its control of the canal, Richard Nixon called for a "fresh look" at the issue. In May 1973, a somewhat chastised Henry Kissinger met with Panama's foreign minister, Juan Antonio Tack, to hammer out a list of principles for a new canal treaty.[86] Torrijos's accomplishment should not be exaggerated: the eight Kissinger-Tack principles essentially repeated the provisions of Johnson's draft treaty:

(1) The treaty of 1903 and its amendments will be abrogated by the conclusion of an entirely new interoceanic canal treaty;

(2) The concept of perpetuity will be eliminated. The new treaty concerning the lock canal shall have a fixed termination date;

(3) Termination of United States jurisdiction over Panamanian territory shall take place promptly in accordance with terms specified in the treaty;

(4) The Republic of Panama shall be the sovereign over the Panama Canal Zone;

(5) During the life of the treaty, Panama shall grant to the United States the right to use the lands, water and airspace necessary for operation, maintenance and defense of the Canal and the transit of ships;

(6) Panama will have a "just and equitable share" of the benefits derived from the operation of the Canal in its territory;

(7) Panama shall participate in the administration of the Canal and will have total responsibility for the operation of the Canal upon the termination of the treaty;

(8) Panama shall grant to the United States the rights necessary to regulate, operate, maintain and protect the Canal,

and to take specific steps related to those ends as agreed upon in the treaty.[87]

Nixon's presidency soon passed into history, but his successor, Gerald Ford, took up the negotiations, even more strongly favoring a treaty than Nixon. President Ford faced opposition to a new treaty from Congress, but also from the Defense Department, in particular the U.S. Army. The president believed that these two opposing factions were linked; Secretary of State Kissinger had told him that elements within the Defense Department were lobbying Congress against negotiating with Panama. President Ford, in turn, believed that the opposition within the Department of Defense was not due to strategic reasoning, but rather the Zonians' deep influence within the military:

> [In 1951] I was a member of the House Appropriations Subcommittee that had jurisdiction over the Panama Canal. At that time I had the temerity to look at the sinecures that some of the civilian employees of the canal had acquired, such as rents, which I think were $15 a month [$104 in 2009 dollars], and a raft of other gratuities that few other people working for the Federal government received. I objected and sought to decrease these benefits. I was met with an onslaught from a highly organized group which I hadn't anticipated.... [They] have a sinecure down there which they don't want to give up.... That is the most highly organized group of American employees I know. They have a vested interest in the status quo. This is a group that gives the public the impression of what we should be doing down there. We are not going to decide this issue on these grounds. They ought to know it. The Army gets its information from them and they infect it with their views. But they're not going to decide this.[88]

Ford was wrong: Pentagon opposition wrecked his attempt to negotiate a treaty. The Defense Department demanded that the treaty include fifty-year leases on Panamanian bases, at which point the talks with Panama reached a deadlock. In response, on June 26,

1975, the House voted 264–146 to defund the negotiations. Congressional opposition to a new Panama Canal treaty faded over the rest of the year—by June 1976 opposition was down to a hard core of 121 representatives—but Ronald Reagan took up the Panama Canal issue as a means to mobilize support for his Republican primary challenge to President Ford. Negotiations were on hold until the 1976 election.[89]

James Earl Carter won those elections. President Carter approached the canal issue "with no great enthusiasm," but decided to use his political capital to conclude a treaty. He chose to do so for three mutually reinforcing reasons. First, the Panama Canal was a constant sore spot in the United States' relations with Latin America. A treaty would not diminish the United States economically or militarily, and it would improve U.S. diplomatic relations generally within the hemisphere. Second, in the words of Secretary of State Cyrus Vance, "[I]f [Torrijos] were rebuffed on the canal issue, a successor government might be too weak or too radical to make a deal."[90] Torrijos represented the best opportunity for the United States to return the canal and walk away safely. Finally, there was worry about what would happen should a repeat of the 1964 riots break out in the chastened geopolitical climate of the 1970s. One U.S. Army spokesperson stated that so soon after Vietnam, "the last thing in the world we want now is to be ordered to start shooting into a crowd of Panamanians."[91] The United States would have to choose between using violence against foreign civilians or appearing to retreat from the canal in the face of mob violence.[92] That was a choice that no American president would find palatable, especially so soon after the American withdrawal from Vietnam. The Carter administration reopened talks on February 15, 1977, and completed the Panama Canal and Neutrality Treaties by August 10. They were signed in Washington to great fanfare on September 7.

Both Panama and the United States got most of what they wanted from the negotiations. The two treaties themselves bore a close resemblance to the 1967 draft put forth by Johnson: in fact, in many ways they were *more* advantageous to the United States than the earlier proposal. The Panama Canal Treaty stipulated that until the 1999 handover, the United States would appoint five members of the board of the new Panama Canal Commission. The United States would select the remaining four members from a list provided by the Panamanian government. Zonians who worked for the Panama Canal itself would keep their jobs until they retired. (This did not apply to Commissary employees.) The Panama Canal Commission would continue to bank its cash reserves with the U.S. Treasury at no interest. Better still for the United States, the commission would continue to *make* interest payments (at a rate determined by the Treasury) to the United States for its investment in the canal until 1999. The United States and Panama would retain their rights to have their government ships jump any queue to use the canal. Panama would take over the functions of the former Canal Zone government, a service for which the new Panama Canal Commission would pay $10 million per year, a sizeable amount, but less than half of what it had cost the Panama Canal Company to carry out the same functions. Panama would also receive 30¢ per ton for each long ton transiting the canal—a vast increase from the zero cents per ton it had previously received—and it would have a claim on all canal profits up to $10 million, the remainder of which would go the United States. Panama would also receive $50 million in military assistance from the United States over ten years. In addition, most of the lands of the Canal Zone (except for those needed for the operation of the Panama Canal) would revert to Panamanian control in October 1, 1979. (The provision abolishing the Canal Zone was the most significant way in which the 1977 treaties were more favorable to Panama than the 1967 proposal.) Finally, the Neutrality Treaty granted the United States the permanent unilateral right to use military force to keep the Panama Canal open. When Congress asked Carter's national security advisor what would happen if the Panamanian government closed down the canal "for repairs," Zbigniew Brzezinski replied, "In that case, according to the provisions of the Neutrality Treaty, we will move in and close down the Panamanian government for repairs."[93]

President Carter engaged in an energetic campaign to shepherd the Panama Canal Treaty through Congress. He wooed individual members. He invited civic groups from across the country to the White House. He spoke by telephone to six "town meetings" and addressed the nation about the Panama Canal on television. He flew senators to Panama, where they met with the extremely charismatic Omar Torrijos. Finally, he traded votes. Bob Beckel, the president's point man on the treaties, later recalled: "By the end they were coming in with lists of demands, four or five senators. We had to put an informal task force on it. It was mostly appointments, weather stations, small projects, loose ends mostly, but it kept us busy." The press became convinced that the president agreed to add to the nation's strategic copper stockpile and pass an emergency farm bill in order to get votes from Arizona and Georgia, while Carter himself later admitted that he approved a desalination plant to get a vote from Oklahoma.[94] The treaties passed the Senate, 68–32, a margin of only 2 votes.

TABLE 7.8

Official Transfers between the U.S. and Panama, Million 2009 US$, 1970–80

	Canal rent	Other transfers	Total	Canal payments to U.S. Treasury	Net transfers from U.S. to Panama	% of Panama's GDP
1970	8.6	39.7	48.3	−24.3	24.0	1
1971	8.2	44.1	52.2	−37.2	15.1	0
1972	7.8	160.2	168.1	−37.6	130.4	3
1973	7.4	164.9	172.3	−39.5	132.8	2
1974	6.8	45.2	52.1	−42.4	9.6	0
1975	7.5	89.2	96.7	−43.3	53.4	1
1976	7.1	45.7	52.8	−48.5	4.2	0
1977	6.7	6.0	12.7	−49.6	−36.9	−1
1978	6.2	15.2	21.4	−49.4	−28.0	−0
1979	5.8	16.0	21.8	−48.7	−26.9	−0
1980	0.0	12.0	12.0	−27.0	−15.0	−0

Source: Panama Canal Company *Annual Reports*; Bureau for Legislative and Public Affairs, U.S. Agency for International Development, *U.S. Overseas Loans and Grants* [*Greenbook*] (Washington, DC: USAID, ongoing); Panama; Oxford Latin American Economic History Database (OxLAD).

Note: Amounts deflated using the U.S. GDP deflator.

If the American case for ditching the Ditch was so clear, why was there so much domestic opposition to the transfer? The answer is that American possession of the Panama Canal unexpectedly became a symbol of American nationalism. In the 1970s, many Americans felt that the country was in decline. The defeat in Vietnam was part of that, as were the oil shock, race riots, and social changes at home. "People sense in this issue some way, after Vietnam, and Watergate, and Angola, of reasserting the glory of the country," explained a strategist for the 1976 Reagan primary campaign. "People once more see a chance for Americans to stand up as Americans." For the Republican Party, "drawing the line at the Big Ditch" was a *relatively* low-cost way to indulge Americans' growing defensive nationalism and to gain some electoral support on the margin. The Democrats lost three Senate seats in 1978. The Panama Canal treaties played a decisive role in two of those losses: Dick Clark's defeat in Iowa and Tom McIntyre's rout in New Hampshire. McIntyre, in fact, invited his wife to "come on and watch me lose my seat" when he voted in favor of ratification.[95]

AFTER THE DITCH

When the U.S. Senate ratified the Panama Canal treaties, it put an end to seventy-five years of American possession of the Panama Canal Zone. The Panamanian flag now flew across the national territory, the Panamanian government received a far larger share of the revenues, and Panamanian citizens gained a role in the management of the operations. Aid payments from the United States dropped—incidentally confirming the relationship between aid payments and American attempts to appease Panamanian national sentiment—and America's involvement in Panama changed from a net fiscal negative to a positive. (See table 7.8.) Annual aid flows to Panama averaged $59 million during the Kennedy administration (in 2008 dollars), $76 million under Johnson, $90 million under Nixon, and $60 million under Ford, before falling to only $12 million under Carter.

At the same time, the Panamanian government began receiving payments from the Panama Canal Commission. In 1980, the first full year of treaty implementation, the Republic of Panama received $170 million (in 1980 dollars) in payments from the canal, more than twice what it had previously received from the canal annuity and aid transfers combined. (The annuity came directly from the U.S. Treasury, not the Panama Canal Company.) Some of the Panamanian receipts went to defray the costs of replacing the Canal Zone government, but the Panama Canal Treaty nevertheless appears to have been a financial win-win for both parties.

Three questions remained about the future. First, would the Panama Canal generate enough revenue for Panama to make its payments on the remaining canal debt still owed to the U.S. government? Although the U.S. Treasury possessed the power to abolish those payments, there was no will to do so before the final handover in 1999. Second, would Panama be able to run the canal operation itself, free of political interference and patronage? Finally, would the Panamanian economy be able to take advantage of the opportunities presented by the abolition of the Canal Zone and the Commissary, and the removal of the artificial barriers between the Panamanian economy and the operation of the Panama Canal?

EIGHT

DITCHING THE DITCH

Fully functioning democratic institutions in Panama
are the best guarantee to Americans and Panamanians
alike for success in the turnover of the Canal
to Panama.

—Ambassador Arthur Davis, 1986

THE YEAR 1978 WAS A WATERSHED YEAR FOR THE PANAMA CA-
nal. On March 16, the U.S. Senate ratified the Neutrality Treaty.
A month later, on April 18, it ratified the parallel Panama Canal
Treaty. Under the terms of the treaties, the Canal Zone would disappear in 1979, Panamanians would slowly take over the duties
of the new Panama Canal Commission, and finally, in 1999, the
United States would hand the canal over to Panama.

The American public greeted the Panama Canal agreements
with a mixture of apathy and disappointment. The handover's supporters had little reason to celebrate. The economic and strategic
effects of the agreements were very slightly positive, but not overwhelmingly so. On the other hand, opponents of the handover
based their opposition on nationalist symbolism. Once the handover was accomplished, opponents turned to other symbolic issues. As a public enterprise, the Panama Canal carried on much as
before. The treaties installed a new framework for correcting de-
ficiencies in administration and increasing Panamanian participation in the management of the canal, but the changes took a long
time to be felt, and the canal's decline continued. In the 1980s, in

fact, the Panama Canal suffered its first major decline in volume since the end of World War II as the result of competition with a *Panamanian* enterprise, the Transisthmian Pipeline.

The Panamanian reaction to the two treaties was the polar opposite of the American one. The treaties were immensely popular, winning two-thirds of the vote in a national plebiscite on October 23, 1977.[1] Nevertheless, the immediate benefit for Panama was purely symbolic. The Canal Zone would formally disappear in 1979, but the Panamanian government would not gain full control over it until 1982. The increased payments to the Panamanian government would not begin until 1980. Moreover, for Panama to enjoy any long-term benefit from the Panama Canal—and for the United States to follow through with its promises—Panama needed to meet two preconditions: it needed a government with strong incentives to refrain from using the Panama Canal as patronage, and it needed managers to have strong incentives to be as professional as their American predecessors. For Panama to *maximize* its benefits from the Panama Canal, it needed to meet a further condition: the Panamanian administration of the canal needed to *exceed* the efficiency of the Americans. Unlike its past management, the canal's new Panamanian managers would need to run the operation with an eye toward profitability, rather than in the interest of a select group of privileged employees.

Manuel Noriega's consolidation of power in Panama in the wake of Omar Torrijos's death in 1981 made these preconditions moot as long as he controlled the country. Under Noriega, the condition of the Canal Zone properties turned over to the Panamanian government declined precipitously. The Panama Railroad ceased functioning, while buildings turned over to Panama were stripped of their furnishings and abandoned, and the ports stagnated. This stagnation was in fact benign neglect compared to Noriega's efforts to criminalize other parts of official Panama for his own profit, but it did not bode well for the future of the Panama Canal.

Panamanian electoral politics traditionally revolved around personalized patronage networks based on ethnic and class self-identification. Ironically, Panama's dictators set the stage for electoral democracy by destroying the parties' traditional patronage networks. Torrijos did so in order create a broadly based populist movement that would sustain his regime, while Noriega did so in order to create a new patronage network centered on himself. By 1990 a critical mass of the Panamanian electorate no longer responded to identity-based appeals. While its previous attempts to guarantee Panamanian electoral democracy had failed, the United States now had Panamanian voters convinced that electoral democracy was in their best interest. Once the United States removed Noriega through the brute application of American military force, a large bloc of Panamanian swing voters emerged to participate in Panama's elections. Panamanian parties had to compete for their votes, rather than appealing to symbolic issues or ethnic identity. This enabled the creation of a Panamanian democracy in which a winning electoral coalition could not rely simply on transferring wealth from the losers to the winners. In this political environment, Panama's government passed a constitutional amendment that made it difficult (although not impossible) for any future Panamanian government to interfere with canal management or use it for patronage. As a result, any elected Panamanian government had strong incentives to make and to keep canal management as efficient as possible, to benefit the Panamanian electorate in general.

Once the United States removed Noriega, Panama met the preconditions needed to maximize its benefits from the Panama Canal. Panamanian management of the canal surpassed American standards by the end of the lengthy twenty-year transition mandated by the Panama Canal treaties. The end result was a well-trained and professional Panamanian workforce across the skill spectrum—and, ultimately, an end to the Panama Canal's long stagnation.

PANAMANIAN ECONOMIC DEVELOPMENT BEFORE 1977

Panama, effectively isolated from the Canal Zone, developed into a fairly typical Latin American autocracy. This occurred despite the occasional attempts of the United States to reinforce the rule of law and the norms of electoral democracy. A relatively small rent-seeking coalition controlled the state. Governments coaxed the wealthy elite into investing their capital in Panama by granting them special privileges. In turn, these special privileges raised the returns earned by the elite sufficiently high to compensate the elite for the risk of expropriation in an environment where the rule of law meant relatively little. Until the 1970s, Panama did not generate much tax revenue—by design. The Panamanian economy bifurcated into a relatively fast-growing sector that received special privileges and paid few taxes, and a slow-growing sector whose property rights were precarious and subject to (at least on paper) heavy tax rates.

The irony of the situation was obvious: the part of the Panamanian economy that produced most of the output paid few taxes, whereas the other part of the economy produced so little that there was almost nothing to tax. The Panamanian government, denied substantial public revenues, in turn provided few public goods for the benefit of the population as a whole. The density of roads suitable for motor vehicles remained low, even by Central American standards. Similarly, public spending on primary schools failed to exceed the (low) norms of the country's neighbors. (See table 8.1.) Spending focused on the terminal cities of Panama and Colón, while the countryside continued to be occupied by peasants who generally lacked formal title to their land and lacked access to capital or modern agricultural technology. Panamanian governments distributed benefits to two privileged constituencies: the select group of wealthy elites who controlled investment capital and the organized patronage networks whose support the Panamanian government of the moment needed to remain in power.

Panama's governments relied heavily on trade taxes for revenue until the 1950s. Trade taxes provided several advantages over internal taxes. First, they required relatively little administrative capacity to collect, as long as the United States cooperated in policing smuggling via the Canal Zone. Second, a dependence on tariff revenues allowed other taxes to remain at low levels, especially taxes that might affect powerful elite constituencies. Between 1946 and

Table 8.1
Public Good Provision in Selected Latin American Countries, 1940–90

	Panama	Costa Rica	El Salvador	Guatemala	Honduras	Nicaragua	Mexico	Colombia
Permanent roads suitable for motor vehicles, km per sq. km								
1940	0.02	0.06	0.24	0.06	0.01	0.02	0.01	0.02
1950	0.03	0.16				0.03	0.01	
1960	0.04			0.11	0.03	0.04	0.02	0.02
1970	0.09	0.41	0.43		0.04	0.12	0.04	0.04
1980	0.15	0.57	0.57	0.24	0.08	0.15	0.11	0.04
1990	0.15	0.70	0.62		0.12		0.12	0.05
Primary school spending as % of GDP								
1960	1.9	1.9		0.9	1.4	1.1	0.7	0.9
1965	1.9	2.6	1.6	1.0	2.0	1.1	0.7	0.8
1970	1.9	2.3	1.6	0.9	1.9	1.4	0.7	0.4
1975	2.0	2.2	1.9	0.8	1.9	1.1	1.0	0.8
1980	2.0	1.7	2.3	0.6	1.7	1.2	0.8	0.7
1985	1.8	1.3			2.1	2.2	0.6	1.0
1990	1.8	1.5			2.0	3.5	0.6	0.8

Source: Calculated from Robert J. Barro and Jong-Wha Lee, "International Data on Educational Attainment: Updates and Implications" (Working Paper No. 42, Center for International Development, April 2000), data set and Oxford Latin American Economic History Database (OxLAD).

1968, Panama collected less than 10 percent of GDP from nontrade taxes.[2] Third, tariffs could be used to increase the profits available in domestic industries that competed with imports. Protective tariffs could be deployed to reward particular interest groups or political supporters. Starting in 1952, Panamanian governments became more creative in their attempts to use trade policy to reward favored factions, and began to impose import quotas in addition to tariffs. By 1980, quotas covered no less than 470 different products, imposed at the request of specific political clients.[3] Of course, the quotas (unlike tariffs) did not produce any government revenue. As they proliferated, Panama City's primary revenue source declined. The resulting combination of high protectionism and low levels of public investment in a small economy caused economic growth to slow. Of course, Panama was not alone in Latin America pursuing this particular model of political economy. Many other countries embraced the same combination of distorted trade policies and low public investment. Compared with the rest of Latin America, therefore, Panama's economic performance was not bad. In fact, Panamanian GDP per worker grew from roughly the Latin American average in 1950 to 36 percent above the Latin American average by 1981. On the other hand, Panama performed far worse than other poor and undereducated countries that adopted a different policy mix, such as Portugal and Greece in the European southern periphery, or much of the English-speaking Caribbean (sans Jamaica).

Panama's economic growth was almost entirely a result of the country's specialized high-growth sectors, which were intimately tied to the presence of the Panama Canal. Panamanian governments promoted three specific sectors designed to capitalize on the Panama Canal as best as the country could without having control over the canal itself. These sectors were the flag of convenience, the Colón Free Zone, and the International Banking Center. These sectors generated economic growth for Panama, but little employment or tax revenue. As a general development strategy for Panama, they must be reckoned a failure.

Panama at independence had no shipbuilding industry. Panamanian consuls abroad, however, could provisionally register vessels for use by Panamanian citizens and companies. This law, like similar laws in Guatemala, Honduras, and Nicaragua, was intended to encourage the development of a local fleet. Two 1916 reforms made the Panamanian registry attractive to American shipowners. The first allowed foreign-owned Panamanian corporations to register their ships under the Panamanian flag. The second was a law requiring the recognition of English language contracts. When added to the fact that Panama used the American dollar as legal tender, the attraction of the Panamanian ship registry became obvious.[4]

Strong institutional barriers, however, made it difficult to transfer an American ship's flag to another country. After the Civil War, the U.S. government operated on the principle that American ships must remain American—in flag, construction, and crew. In 1866, Congress passed a law preventing ships that had transferred their flag during the Civil War from returning to United States registry.[5] In 1916, Congress established the United States Shipping Board with the power to deny the transfer of ships from U.S. registry, as well as to veto the sale, transfer, mortgage, or rental of a ship to a non-American.[6] The Shipping Board generally denied transfer of American-owned vessels. It feared that American shipowners might attempt to evade U.S. maritime labor legislation by registering their ships with another country. In 1923, the chairman of the Shipping Board, Admiral William Benson, wrote, "These financial handicaps may in a measure be eliminated by the citizen in his individual business relations with shipping, for he can invest in foreign built ships and operate them under foreign flags. But this solution of the problem of the individual would not contribute to the development of the American merchant marine."[7]

Given these institutional barriers, it should be no surprise that the first transfers to the Panamanian flag were marginal and somewhat shady. The very first ship to transfer its flag to Panamanian registry was the *Belen Quezada* in 1919, a Canadian-flagged vessel under partial U.S. ownership. The Panamanian consul in Vancouver reflagged the ship. Originally a supply and dispatch vessel for Admiral Dewey's fleet in the Philippines, the *Belen Quezada* was repurposed as a rumrunner for liquor smuggling to the United States—a fairly good reason to reflag. Unfortunately, the strategy backfired for its owners. Docked in Puntarenas, Costa Rica, in February of 1921, the Costa Rican government seized the nominally Panamanian ship during the brief border conflict between Panama and Costa Rica.[8]

Later American ships transferred to the Panamanian registry under circumstances only slightly less dubious. In August 1922, the Shipping Board auctioned off six confiscated Central Powers merchant freighters under the stipulation that the ships would be transferred to a foreign flag. The Shipping Board stated this was to prevent the vessels from competing on routes with significant American shipping. Pacific Freighters of San Francisco, a subsidiary of Admiral-Orient Lines, bought the ships. In order to use them for the Seattle-Shanghai trans-Pacific trade, Pacific Freighters needed a foreign flag of convenience: it chose the new Panamanian one. The ships' officers were the same German merchant officers who had commanded them before the war, now paid at Japanese rates.[9]

The Panamanian registry grew in size, despite the opposition of the Shipping Board. California shipbuilder W. Leslie Comyn, a corporate officer of Pacific Freighters, popularized Panama's advantages to the *New York Herald*. "The chief advantage of Panamanian registry is that the owner is relieved of the continual but irregular boiler and hull inspections and the regulations as to crew's quarters and subsistence. We are under absolutely no restrictions, so long as we pay the $1 a net ton registry fee and 10¢ yearly a net ton tax."[10] In short, Pacific Freighters used the Panamanian flag for exactly the reasons the United States Shipping Board feared.

The United States changed its policy against flags of convenience due to a combination of pressure from domestic shipping companies and a desire to find an inexpensive way to aid its

Panamanian client state. By 1922, enough U.S. shipping companies had expressed interest in the Panamanian registry that the Department of Commerce requested that the U.S. consul in Panama, George Orr, compile Panama's registry laws for their benefit. At that time Panama's laws were scattered among its commercial codes, but Panamanian legislators, spotting an opportunity, composed a more streamlined version of its maritime code and presented it to the National Assembly in 1923.[11] It passed in 1925. By 1928, Panama had a network of consuls who, as part of their duties, could register ships under the Panamanian flag. As a favor to its Panamanian client state, the United States agreed that if no Panamanian consul were available, U.S. consuls could make the transfer.[12]

In the 1930s even more ships sought the Panamanian flag. As a small neutral nation under the broad hegemonic umbrella of the United States, Panama suited shippers of all persuasions: oil tankers from the Free City of Danzig anticipating hostilities with Poland;[13] Norwegian whalers avoiding double taxation;[14] Greeks smuggling weapons to Republican Spain or Jewish refugees to Palestine.[15] Panama's flag even attracted an American pirate radio station operating in international waters outside Los Angeles.[16]

The Panamanian flag of convenience was not, as has often been claimed, an attempt by the Roosevelt administration to avoid the restrictions the Neutrality Act placed on delivering goods to Great Britain before full American entry in World War II. By 1939 it was entirely possible to transfer an American ship to the British registry. Rather, for a brief period many ships tried to take Panamanian registry to continue trading with Axis belligerents in the face of the Roosevelt administration's opposition. The Panamanian government, however, discouraged such transfers, insisting that the newly transferred ships maintain true neutrality. President Juan Demóstenes Arosemena summed up the reasons when he said that he did not believe that "for the sake of a little additional revenue, that the Panamanian flag figure as an object in prize lists of captured vessels." Of the 267 transfers from United States registry to foreign flags between September 1939 and July 1941, 126 went to Britain, while a further 63 transferred to Panama, mainly Esso oil tankers.[17] After the simultaneous entry of the United States and Panama into World War II, however, questions about the neutrality of Panamanian shipping became moot.

World War II brought Panama's registry system to the attention of a much wider audience. After 1945, American shippers looking for tax breaks used it to quickly build up new fleets.[18] Ships under Panamanian registry shot up from 174 in 1946 to 573 in 1950.[19] Panama soon faced competition from Liberia and the Bahamas. Liberia adopted shipping legislation in 1948 explicitly as an improvement on the Panamanian model.[20] In 1956, Liberia surpassed Panama in registries and tonnage; Panama's merchant flag stagnated for another two decades.[21] Panama faced additional competition when the Commonwealth of the Bahamas entered the registry business in 1976. Nevertheless, a combination of competitive fees, a wide network of consuls, easy access to banking and factoring services in Panama, and deliberate marketing by the Panamanian government allowed the Panamanian registry industry to recover during the late 1970s and 1980s. By 1985, the ship registry generated 5 percent of the government's total revenues: $44 million in fees ($78 million in 2009 dollars, using the GDP deflator) and an additional $20 million from sale of mandatory Panamanian identity cards to the sailors on Panamanian-flagged vessels.[22]

BARRIERS TO GROWTH

Despite the Hull-Alfaro Treaty, the wall between the Canal Zone and the rest of the Panamanian economy remained high. That is not to say that there were no attempts by Panamanian entrepreneurs to break through the barriers; it is to say that those attempts generally ran into insuperable institutional obstacles. One of the few successful attempts was the 1948 establishment of the Terminales Panama trucking company by Oswaldo Heilbron and Alberto Motta—and the tale of Terminales Panama's putative success shows just how difficult it was for Panamanian entrepreneurs to crack the wall of the Canal Zone.

Oswaldo Heilbron worked as a boarding officer in Cristóbal during World War II. The boarding officer's job was to ensure that waiting ships received the repairs and provisions that they had contracted for. It was a busy job: at any given moment, more than one hundred ships (mostly Liberty ships and T-2 tankers) queued up awaiting repairs and provisions. Heilbron had earlier worked in the Canal Zone, where he had been surprised to find himself consigned to the Silver Roll and denied entry into "white" areas; by 1943 he was further surprised to discover that the Panama Canal Company had a complete monopoly over all cargoes entering Panama. The American government owned the docks at Cristóbal and Balboa, from which they shunted all freight onto the Panama Railroad. The Americans classified any freight intended for Panama City as "through-freight" and charged a 33 percent premium over the freight-rate from the port of origin to deliver the cargo.[23] Panamanian trucks were not allowed to enter the port area to pick up cargo.

The 1936 Hull-Alfaro conventions contained provisions for the United States to build a highway between Panama City and Colón. That highway opened during the war. The opening of the highway gave Heilbron the idea that the trucking company could compete with the Panama Railroad in taking cargoes from Cristóbal to Panama City—if they could get access to the docks. In 1950, Heilbron managed to get a $25,000 loan from the Banco Nacional's Colón branch (roughly $224,000 in 2009 dollars), which he used to buy two modern tractor-trailers. The Canal Zone, however, still denied him access to the docks. Heilbron went to see President Arias—"A very grouchy man, the type who would arrive at his office with crowds waiting and yell at them, 'Don't you have work?'"—who fobbed him off to Vice President José Ramón Guizado. "He [Arias] talked to Guizado very roughly," recounted Heilbron. "I was incredibly embarrassed." Guizado told the Panamanian ambassador to make representations in Washington, but nothing came of it. Months turned into years.[24]

"It is better to be lucky than smart." What came next can only be described as a stroke of good fortune. His wife received a phone call from an old school friend, who had married a Brooklynite and moved back to New York. She was visiting from New York and wanted to have dinner. It turned out that her husband happened to know Francis Dorn, who had just been elected to Congress from Brooklyn's Twelfth Congressional District in November 1952. Dorn also happened to have been assigned to the Merchant Marine and Fisheries Subcommittee that oversaw Zone legislation. A few months later, Heilbron got a call to appear before the subcommittee. Two months after his testimony, an official from the Government Accountability Office (GAO) visited the Canal Zone to order Governor Seybold to open the docks to Panamanian trucks. "I later heard that they gave the Governor a thrashing," said Heilbron. He finally got the trucking business started, charging 25 percent over shipping costs for door-to-door delivery from the docks. "We were thieves, too," recounted Heilbron, "but rather less than the Americans."[25]

THE COLÓN FREE ZONE

Without economic access to the Panama Canal, Panamanian leaders sought ways to expand the Panamanian economy around the edges of the Zone. In 1946, President Enrique Adolfo Jiménez invited Thomas Lyons, the executive secretary of the Foreign-Trade Zones Board of the United States Department of Commerce, to visit Panama with an eye to developing a free trade zone on the isthmus. After surveying a number of potential locations, Lyons chose the terminal city of Colón as the best possible site in Panama because of its large vacant lots near an excellent port.[26]

The Panamanian National Assembly legislated the Colón Free Zone (CFZ) into existence on June 17, 1948. For its first two years, the Zone remained purely conceptual. On December 21, 1950, the Assembly passed legislation to allow *zonitas* within the buildings of participating firms in the city of Colón itself. Each *zonita*, "little zone," acted as a bonded warehouse for the firm. The Gillette Safety Razor Corporation became the first company to create a *zonita*.[27] Within two years, these scattered facilities imported

$11 million.[28] North American pharmaceutical companies like Pfizer and Parke-Davis used the CFZ to repackage and transship drugs for the greater Latin American market, and it was said that the CFZ contained Latin America's largest supply of antibiotics.[29] In 1953, the CFZ finally moved to a centralized location outside the city limits. Covering only thirty-nine acres, the new CFZ was constrained in all directions—by the city of Colón, the waters of Manzanillo Bay, and the Canal Zone.[30]

In 1956, the Colón Free Zone hired Thomas Lyons to publicize its services to an American corporate audience.[31] Lyons emphasized air freight. The CFZ used Tocumen Airport on the Pacific side of the isthmus, near Panama City. Since the airport was fifty miles away from Colón along the newly built Trans-Isthmian Highway, the focus on air transport meant that the CFZ transshipped mostly high-value, low-weight cargoes like pharmaceuticals, spare parts, and women's clothing.[32] In 1956, the Colón Free Zone moved $12 million of goods by air ($95 million in 2009 dollars)—one-third of its total reexports.[33]

The Tocumen Airport–Colón Free Zone combination became an air transport hub, shipping duty-free goods from the United States—and later Asia—to locations throughout Latin America. By 1968, the CFZ share of reexports transported by air had increased to 79 percent of the CFZ's total exports of $163 million.[34] The CFZ's area slowly increased through landfills in Manzanillo Bay and negotiations with the Canal Zone. Between 1960 and 1981, nominal exports from the CFZ increased at an annualized rate of 20 percent.[35] The Colón Free Zone's phenomenal growth only began to stall in the early 1980s, with the onset of the Latin American debt crisis.

Panamanians were aware of the limitations of basing economic development on transshipment. Companies in the Colón Free Zone hired relatively skilled workers and paid them high wages. That increased the demand for skilled labor, but did little for the unskilled urban workers who formed the bulk of Colón's population. In 1961, CFZ firms employed only 1,400 workers, with an average salary of $1,500 (approximately $10,900 in 2009 dollars), more than three times Panama's GDP per capita at the time.[36] In 1958, Manuel Everardo Duque, the CFZ's general manager, announced a plan to spur manufacturing. Not only would profits on exports manufactured within the CFZ receive a twenty-year tax exemption, but all plant machinery would be exempt from import duties, and the CFZ administration itself would build assembly plants to user specifications.[37] Nevertheless, it took six years for the CFZ to announce its first factory, a textile mill capitalized by French investors and the Chiari family, part of Panama's politically connected elite.[38] The mill was not a success, and it remained Panama's only textile factory for over a decade. The Panamanian government soon instituted textile quotas to protect the Chiari family's investment. The implementation of textile quotas spurred the development of three other mills in Panama, none of which were internationally competitive.

Two factors combined to prevent Panama from using the Colón Free Zone to encourage export manufacturing. The first factor was the economic effect of the Remón-Eisenhower Treaty. The treaty stipulated that "the basic wage for any given grade level will be the same for any employee [of the Panama Canal] eligible for appointment to the position without regard to whether he is a citizen of the United States or of the Republic of Panama." In 1952, before the treaty, median Panama City wages were $50 a month, and median wages in the provincial capitals averaged $30.[39] After the treaty, relatively unskilled Panamanian workers in the Canal Zone received wages commensurate with their American counterparts: minimum wages in the Zone in 1956 came to $40 *per week*. As the second largest employer in Panama after the Panamanian government itself, the Panama Canal's new policy led to rapid wage inflation within Panama City and Colón; real wages jumped 40 percent by 1960, and another 40 percent by 1968.[40] Rising wages were not a bad thing for the people of Panama, of course, but they made it hard for the country's fledgling manufacturers to compete with emerging Asian exporters.

The second problem was that the Colón Free Zone was simply too small for large-scale manufacturing. At ninety-nine acres in 1964, the entire CFZ was only the size of a minor industrial park.[41] Whatever success the CFZ had as a mercantile center was not expandable in the Panamanian context. In 1952, for example, Panama's Chamber of Commerce advocated that the entire country of Panama become duty-free, eliminating the need for a geographically constrained CFZ.[42] This was politically impossible, as in the 1950s over half of Panama's tax revenue came from import duties and associated consular fees.[43] The next largest source of government revenue came from the income tax, which was prone to widespread and systematic evasion, falling on a narrow base even after the Remón-Eisenhower Treaty allowed canal employees to be taxed by Panama.[44] Another mercantile republic, Singapore, was able to follow a strategy of turning the entire country into a giant Free Zone due to the simple fact that its government was able to extract high levels of public revenue through the expedient of direct taxes on wages and property. Due to its patronage-based political system, Panama lacked that ability, and the obvious source of revenue to substitute for lost import duties, the Panama Canal itself, was unavailable. In 1957, looking for a way to distribute political favors to supporters, the Panamanian government finally abandoned any attempt to keep trade taxes low and adopted a comprehensive schedule of high tariffs.[45]

THE PANAMANIAN INTERNATIONAL BANKING SECTOR

The origin of Panama's international banking sector can be traced to one man: Nicolás Ardito Barletta, Omar Torrijos's minister of Planning and Economic Policy. Barletta, a University of Chicago–trained economist, worked behind the scenes to turn Torrijos's populist political improvisations into a coherent economic policy. Barletta recognized that Panama's economy had developed an array of services complementary to but independent of the Panama Canal, in the form of the ship registry, the Colón Free Zone, and the country's dollarized banks. Barletta's goal was to seize this Panamanian comparative advantage in services and leverage it into a national economy centered on finance. Numbered bank accounts, generous corporate tax policies, a major reexporting hub, and the use of the dollar—Barletta believed all these in combination would make Panama an attractive site for international business.[46]

Panama's first banks entered the market to provide financial services to Panama Canal workers, one of the few commercial functions not under the canal administration's purview. The International Bank Corporation—later part of First National City Bank of New York, today's Citibank—established itself in Panama on August 17, 1904. Two months later, the domestically owned Banco Nacional de Panama opened.[47] Branches were set up in Panama, Colón, and the town of Empire near the Culebra Cut.[48] Once the canal opened, the banks began to provide financial services to passing ships. (The Commissary monopolized the provisioning of passing ships, but it did not extend credit.) The banks also extended financial services to tourists and sailors. By 1928, National City's operations had increased to the extent that it built a new $250,000 headquarters in Panama City.[49] World War II served as a further windfall for Panama's banking industry. Bank deposits swelled 550 percent to $60 million between 1939 and 1946, over half of which were private deposits.[50] In fact, deposits soared so high during the war that some banks stopped paying interest.[51]

In 1959 the Panamanian National Assembly passed Law 18, which allowed Panamanian banks to offer coded bank accounts that provided secrecy as to the amount and possessor of the account. The law's backers claimed that the need to maintain a good reputation would lead to effective self-policing against questionable accounts. As one specialist in Latin American law said, "*Nous verrons*" (we will see).[52] The new bank secrecy laws, the growing overseas dollar market, and the general increase in international trade allowed the Panamanian banking sector to expand. From six banks employing 889 people in 1960, by 1969 the country had twenty-two banks, eighteen of them foreign, employing 2,518 people. The Panamanian financial sector grew 10 percent annually between 1960 and 1968, and 24 percent in 1969 and 1970.[53]

In 1970, Barletta proceeded to reorganize Panama's banking system, using a mixture of regulation and incentive. Under Cabinet

Decree 238 of 1970, he abolished "paper" banks that took no outside deposits, previously allowed under Panama's incorporation laws, and raised reserve requirements for domestic banks. He repealed Panama's 9 percent cap on interest rates. He then freed offshore banks from income taxes.[54] The plan was to channel volatile overseas capital flows into a few well-capitalized and conservative banks, thus hopefully preventing adverse monetary shocks to Panama's dollarized economy.[55] Barletta engineered two other reforms to grow the banking sector. First, he enhanced bank secrecy by limiting the audit power of the National Banking Commission. Audits could only be published in the form of aggregate statistics, and should a bank refuse to report, the maximum fine would be only $1,000. The commission was also forbidden to investigate the private affairs of bank clients, and no specific information about a client could be released without judicial approval. The law mandated fines for any employee convicted of leaking private financial information.[56] Second, he increased the links between the banking sector and the Colón Free Zone. More credit to buyers through Panamanian banks spurred an expansion of the volume of trade passing through the Free Zone.[57]

As a result of Barletta's regulatory changes, the total assets of Panama's International Banking Center increased from $854 million in 1970 to $49 *billion* in 1982. Even after accounting for the high inflation of the period, this represented a twenty-five-fold expansion. Employment increased from 2,881 in 1970 to 8,726 in 1982. (Unlike later offshore financial centers in places like Dubai and Abu Dhabi, 97 percent of the sector's employees were Panamanian.) Foreign deposits reached nearly $37 billion.[58] One-third of foreign deposits came from Latin America.[59] Panama benefitted from capital flight from other Latin American countries and the flow of petrodollars seeking a convenient tax-free haven. The country also benefitted from a relative abundance of bilingual financial workers, and from the more prosaic fact that it was in the same time zone as Wall Street.[60] In addition, the rise of the Panamanian banking sector had the side effect of revitalizing the ship registry. The Panamanian government directly marketed to foreign shippers the benefits of the integration of its ship registry with its banking system. The number of Panamanian registries, basically stagnant since the end of World War II, jumped from 886 in 1970 to 5,032 in 1982. In addition, the integration of the ship registry and the banking system promoted the growth of Panamanian legal services.[61]

For all its explosive growth, however, the Panamanian banking cluster provided relatively few jobs and generated little tax revenue. In 1982, the Panamanian international banking cluster directly employed only 3 percent of Panama's nonagricultural labor force. A 1988 study estimated that the cluster generated four indirect jobs—in construction, hotels, professional services, reinsurance, and the Colón Free Zone—for every direct one, upping the combined impact of the banking cluster and the CFZ to 13 percent of Panama's labor force and 14 percent of GDP at its peak in the early 1980s.[62] This was significant, but it was not broadly distributed economic growth.

THE TRANSISTHMIAN PIPELINE

Panamanian governments attempted to capture the rents generated by Panama's favorable geographical location in other ways. In early 1968, the Atlantic Richfield Company made public its discovery of oil near Prudhoe Bay, Alaska.[63] On July 18, 1968, a Dallas consulting firm estimated reserves between five billion to ten billion barrels.[64] On this announcement, the New York Stock Exchange banned orders in Atlantic Richfield stock; when the stock was allowed to trade the following Monday, it opened nearly 30 percent higher at $182 a share.[65] The North Slope discoveries were a potential windfall for the Atlantic Richfield Company, its partners, and the United States.

The problem was how to transport the oil.[66] Maritime conditions north of the Arctic Circle at the time were not suitable for regular tanker traffic. The solution was to build a pipeline across Alaska, from north to south, and use tankers to ship the oil from there. Unfortunately, West Coast refineries could only process two-thirds of Alaska's production, meaning that the rest needed to be transported east via the Panama Canal. The construction of the Trans-Alaska Pipeline delayed the first shipment of North Slope oil from Valdez, Alaska, until August 1, 1977. The first tanker carrying North Slope oil through the Panama Canal, the *Washington Trader*, made its transit thirty days later.[67] North Slope oil quickly dominated Canal traffic, reaching 17 percent of total tonnage shipped through the canal in 1982. The number of transits across the Panama Canal increased by 17 percent.

The Panama Canal had trouble handling the traffic increase caused by the additional tanker traffic. The average time spent in Canal Zone waters by a ship making a transit of the canal more than doubled from 1977 to 1981. In addition, the size of the canal locks meant that the largest supertankers could not be used to transport Alaskan oil. The solution was obvious: a short interoceanic pipeline to move crude oil shipped from the North Slope to the Pacific coast to tankers on the Atlantic coast ready to deliver it to East Coast markets. Several countries were rumored to be in the running: Guatemala, Nicaragua, Costa Rica, and Panama.[68]

Panamanian leader Omar Torrijos successfully negotiated with the American construction firm of Morris-Knudsen to build a pipeline from Charco Azul, a deepwater port on the Pacific, to Chiriquí Grande on the Atlantic.[69] The Transisthmian Pipeline was built in eighteen months, employing 1,200 workers at a total cost of $363 million. The new pipeline company, Petroterminal de Panamá S.A., was 40 percent owned by the Panamanian government; the two American partners were to hand over their share to Panama in 1999.[70] The pipeline opened in October 1982 and paid for itself in three years.[71] By 1983, the terminals and their associated oil tanker marine services produced about 3.8 percent of Panama's government revenue and 3.5 percent of the country's GDP.[72]

The Transisthmian Pipeline competed directly with the Panama Canal. Early forecasts projected the drop in canal transits caused by tankers unloading their cargo at Charco Azul instead of transiting through the canal at three ships per day.[73] In fact, the drop in transits was closer to seven.[74] The Panama Canal's loss was Chiriquí's

TABLE 8.2

Petroleum Transits through the Panama Canal and Wait Times, 1976–84

	Cargo, million long-tons			Petroleum cargos, million long-tons			Share of all cargo			Average time in CZ waters (hours)
	Commercial	Government	Total	Total petroleum	North Slope crude	Other petroleum	Total petroleum	North Slope crude	Other petroleum	
1976	117.2	0.2	117.4	21.9	—	21.9	18.7%	0.0%	18.7%	21.2
1977	123.0	0.2	123.2	22.7	—	22.7	18.4%	0.0%	18.4%	20.0
1978	142.5	0.3	142.8	40.5	16.1	24.4	28.4%	11.3%	17.1%	29.0
1979	154.1	0.4	154.5	42.9	15.8	27.1	27.8%	10.3%	17.5%	24.0
1980	167.2	0.4	167.6	47.4	22.1	25.3	28.3%	13.2%	15.1%	34.9
1981	171.2	0.3	171.5	49.4	24.6	24.8	28.9%	14.4%	14.5%	40.7
1982	185.5	0.3	185.7	59.0	32.4	26.6	31.8%	17.5%	14.3%	33.0
1983	145.6	0.4	145.9	33.9	4.4	29.5	23.3%	3.0%	20.2%	20.1
1984	140.5	0.3	140.8	30.7	—	30.7	21.8%	0.0%	21.8%	23.3

Source: Panama Canal Company/Commission *Annual Reports*. Note that the "average time in Canal Zone waters" is not comparable to the current definition. The PCC definition did not include wait times outside the Canal Zone's official maritime boundary, while the current definition does.

gain—doubly so, since the Canal Zone itself was the obvious place for a pipeline across the isthmus, as with the Suez Canal and the Sumed Pipeline. The collapse in oil traffic and subsequent loss of tolls revenue caused the Panama Canal Commission to increase its rates 9.8 percent on March 12, 1983, the first increase in rates since the commission's reorganization in 1979. Despite the additional $14 million of earnings gained by the rate increase, the Panama Canal's operating revenue fell sharply into the red.

THE RISE OF MANUEL NORIEGA

In 1978, after successfully resolving the most important policy question in Panamanian history—the status of the Panama Canal—General Omar Torrijos "returned to the barracks." Torrijos relinquished the autocratic powers granted to him by the constitution of 1972, which had proclaimed him "Maximum Leader of the Revolution" for a six-year period, while maintaining control from behind the scenes through his position as head of the National Guard. In his characteristic style, Torrijos planned to reintroduce partisan democracy to Panama in phases, with direct presidential elections to return in 1984. Torrijos distrusted the country's existing political parties, viewing them (correctly) as patronage machines for the elite, so he quite logically created his own. The Partido Revolucionario Democrático (PRD) represented Torrijos's somewhat odd political coalition of organized labor, government employees, women, students, peasants, and small businessmen.[75]

It is impossible to know how Torrijos's plan for the democratization of Panama would have turned out. On July 31, 1981, his DeHavilland Twin Otter airplane mysteriously crashed, killing everyone on board. Panama's move toward democracy subsequently encountered a small problem in the form of Manuel Antonio "La Piña" Noriega. Manuel Noriega was Torrijos's de facto intelligence chief. As such, his was a large talent in a small country. Noriega's biggest intelligence coup during the Torrijos era was the acquisition of the complete list of communication links intercepted in Latin America by the U.S. National Security Agency, which he allegedly sold to Cuba. Noriega had also been involved with drug smuggling and money laundering since the 1970s, when he was actively linked to the Central Intelligence Agency (CIA).[76] Noriega quickly moved to consolidate power in Panama after Torrijos's death.[77]

The illegal drug trade was nothing new to Panama.[78] Nor was Panamanian governmental involvement in the trade. As early as 1950, Tocumen Airport had been used as a transshipment point for narcotics from South America with the active connivance of the Panamanian commissioner of civil aviation—who also happened to be President Arias's nephew. Narcotics were openly sold in Panamanian bordellos, which were under the control of the Panamanian police, where they could be purchased for use or resale elsewhere: the Panama price was $8 per gram, compared to a New York price of $25 per gram. The U.S. Navy delayed at least one payday until after shore leave in Panama to prevent American sailors from taking advantage of this price differential.[79] The 1955 assassination of President Remón was believed by many to have resulted from his alleged involvement in the narcotics trade.[80]

Under Noriega, however, Panama shifted from being a bit player in the illegal drug trade to a leading actor. The growth in the United States demand for cocaine during the 1970s caused a large expansion in the global narcotics traffic. Circa 1970, the cocaine trade was a small-scale business run out of laboratories in northern Chile, near the coca plant's ethnobotanical homeland. Typical shipments amounted to kilograms. In 1974, a more entrepreneurial group based out of Medellín, Colombia, began exporting cocaine in far larger quantities. By the early 1980s, cocaine shipments of a metric ton were common, usually packaged in container shipments of other goods.[81]

Noriega spotted an opportunity: just as Panama served as a convenient transshipment point for Asian manufactures, it could serve as a convenient transshipment point for South American narcotics. Better still, from Noriega's entrepreneurial point of view, the country's professionally secretive financial center would be perfect for money laundering. Panama—or at least Manuel

Noriega—could gain both as goods flowed north and as money returned south. By 1987, the Treasury Department estimated that Panamanian banks laundered $600 million of drug-related money annually.[82] Ramon Milian Rodriguez, an American accountant connected to Noriega, testified to the U.S. Senate in 1988 that he laundered $2.8 billion per year for the Medellín cartel in Panama.[83] The Colombian cocaine industry was estimated to have generated only $3 billion per year in profit annually during the 1980s—the implication being that most of that money was laundered through Panama.[84]

Noriega himself acted as guarantor for the laundered assets. Paper money flew into Panama as freight; uniformed soldiers picked it up at the airport in armored cars. The cash went into numbered accounts in the name of dummy corporations created under Panama's liberal incorporation laws. The money was then split up into multiple numbered accounts within the same bank, leaving no paper trail, transferred to different banks, and finally placed in legitimate investments outside of Panama.[85] Noriega allegedly received a commission between 1 and 10 percent for providing this service.[86] When asked by the U.S. Senate which Panamanian banks were involved in money laundering, Rodriguez replied, "I think it's fair to say we used just about every bank in Panama."[87]

Despite these considerable shortcomings, Noriega remained in good standing with the United States. The reason was that Noriega aided the American campaign against what Washington viewed as a Soviet-backed regime in Nicaragua. Noriega allowed the United States to run spy missions out of Howard Air Force Base in contravention of the Neutrality Treaty. He allowed U.S. Colonel Oliver North to establish dummy corporations to funnel financial aid to the "contras" fighting Nicaragua's Sandinista government. He also allowed contras to be trained in Panama. In addition, Noriega's agents directly ran an ongoing covert operation in Nicaragua. In 1985, Noriega's men managed to explode several bombs in Nicaragua's military headquarters in Managua.[88]

As a direct result of Noriega's relationship with the United States, American aid to Panama increased markedly during the 1980s.

This negated one of the benefits with which the Carter administration persuaded the Senate to ratify the Panama Canal Treaty,
that the United States cut aid flows to Panama. When Republican
senator Jesse Helms of North Carolina—no political ally of Jimmy
Carter—moved to cut off aid to Panama during the Reagan administration, CIA director William Casey insisted that "Noriega was
doing things for the U.S. that Helms didn't know about."[89]

THE FALL OF MANUEL NORIEGA

Why did the United States ultimately turn against Noriega? By attacking the Sandinista regime, Noriega served the Reagan administration's foreign policy. In addition, while Noriega might have allowed the former Canal Zone's assets to decay, he refrained from
directly interfering with Panama Canal operations. Noriega may
have been a bad actor, but he was *America's* bad actor from the
perspective of the Reagan administration.

The problem was that Noriega overestimated his value to the
United States. On May 6, 1984, Panama held its first elections
since the 1968 coup. Once again, Panama's extraordinary political survivor, Arnulfo Arias, now eighty-two years old, declared
his candidacy. His opponent, Nicolás Ardito Barletta, had been
Torrijos's minister of economic planning and, afterward, vice president of the World Bank. Barletta's superb technocratic credentials,
however, had been tainted by his association with Noriega and
the Panamanian Defense Forces (PDF). Arias, whose fascist ties
during World War II were revisited during the campaign, ran as
a populist antimilitary candidate. Even before the election, there
were fears of violence.[90]

The fears of violence proved justified: the presidential election
devolved into a tumultuous fiasco. The final opinion poll before
the election gave Barletta an 8-point margin, but with only 20 percent of the vote counted, the *La Prensa* newspaper reported that
Arias already enjoyed an 8-point lead.[91] The government then
suspended the count.[92] Demonstrations by Arias's supporters followed, which members of one of Noriega's paramilitary groups

broke up with gunfire. At least one person died.[93] Tallies changed in transit from regional voting places to the National Vote Counting Board. Election judges nullified other vote counts went they went against Barletta. Eventually, a final count came out favoring Barletta by 1,713 votes out of more than 600,000 cast.[94]

On May 16, 1984, Barletta became Panama's official president-elect.[95] The U.S. government showed relief—no one in Washington particularly wanted an octogenarian fascist sympathizer to head the Panamanian government. Most Panamanians, however, suspected they knew the score, and Barletta quickly received the nickname "Fraudito" by *La Prensa*.[96] Arnulfo Arias left Panama for Miami. President Barletta inherited a position with little real power. Noriega headed the Panamanian Defense Forces. More importantly, Noriega had created other sources of personal power in Panama, through licit and illicit political patronage, the creation of extra-governmental paramilitary groups, and his connections to international narcotics traffickers. Barletta was essentially a figurehead.

Despite Barletta's victory, Noriega thought it necessary to remove all potential sources of political opposition. Ironically, this decision proved to be the cause of his downfall. Noriega's first target was Hugo Spadafora, one of Noriega's most vocal opponents. Spadafora in many ways was emblematic of Torrijos's previous populist coalition. A committed leftist, Spadafora served as a combat medic in Africa during Guinea-Bissau's revolution. Omar Torrijos had arrested him in 1969, for antigovernment subversion. Torrijos then brought Spadafora to his office. "We had a strange conversation," Spadafora recounted. "It began stiffly, but slowly warmed up. He gave his point of view, I gave mine and eventually I was persuaded that his Government would evolve in accordance with my revolutionary ideals."[97] Torrijos ordered Spadafora to expand government medical services in the boondocks of Panama's Darien Province, and Spadafora became Torrijos's deputy minister of health in 1976.[98]

Noriega decided to kill Spadafora. On September 13, 1985, members of the Panamanian Defense Forces detained Spadafora.

Within hours of his arrest, after extensive torture, a PDF cook killed Spadafora by slowly severing his head while he was still breathing.[99] The PDF then dumped the body across the Costa Rican border in a United States mailbag.[100] The murder proved to be Noriega's first miscalculation. Instead of looking the other way, a shocked President Barletta personally pledged to investigate the murder.[101]

Barletta quickly discovered the limitations of his power. Thirteen days after his pledge, right after addressing the U.N. General Assembly in New York, Barletta received a message from his foreign minister to quickly return to Panama. He left New York that evening, cutting short his official reception. Returning to Panama, he was called into Noriega's office and asked to call off the Spadafora investigation. Barletta refused. This was not an appropriate answer. Noriega's second-in-command accused Barletta of treason and threatened his family.[102] While trapped in Noriega's office, with the threat of personal political violence at hand, Barletta called U.S assistant secretary of state Elliott Abrams to apprise him of the situation. Abrams's sage advice to Barletta was to "hang tough."[103] This advice, of course, helped neither Barletta nor Panama at all. By midnight, an exhausted Barletta had signed a statement of "leave of absence" from the presidency. At three o'clock that morning, Barletta was videotaped announcing his "separation from power." The videotape played on national television, after which Noriega called the legislature into late-night session, where it unanimously accepted Barletta's resignation. Debate was prohibited. By four o'clock that morning, Vice President Eric Arturo Delvalle had been sworn in.[104]

Removing Barletta turned out to be Noriega's second miscalculation. Noriega had not consulted the United States before acting, and Washington neither approved nor condoned Noriega's actions. In fact, the Reagan administration strongly wanted Barletta to remain in office. Nonetheless, the administration took little action, limiting itself to an ambassadorial speech about the need for civilian authority in a democracy and the diversion of $14 million in aid money from Panama to Guatemala. The Drug Enforcement

Agency continued to send thank-you notes to Noriega. When CIA director William Casey (a Queens native) summoned Noriega to Washington on November 1, 1985, he said nothing about Spadafora or Barletta.[105]

The problem for Noriega was that the combination of Spadafora's brutal death and Barletta's undemocratic ejection from the presidency catalyzed American opposition to the Reagan administration's tacit support of Noriega's regime. In January 1986, Spadafora's brother showed Senator Jesse Helms photographs of the doctor's decapitated body. Helms froze. "I'm going to do something, right away," he said. "We will hold hearings on Panama. I promise you I will make this a presidential issue."[106] With his impeccably far-right Republican credentials, Senator Helms was able to confront the Reagan administration about Noriega, attacking his role as Panama's unelected strongman. In Senate hearings in the spring of 1986, Elliott Abrams sought to defend Noriega against Helms's attack by redefining Noriega's role in Panama's government. "I think conceptually, it is not that the military makes all these decisions and is in control of the Government, as would be the case in a military dictatorship or a full military government. Rather, it is a civilian government with military interference in areas of interest to the military." Helms riposted, "I think I could save both of us time by asking you to identify those activities that the defense forces do not operate and control," drawing laughter at Abrams's expense from those attending the hearings.[107] The Senate hearings made Noriega radioactive in Washington. A year later, in July 1987, the U.S. Senate voted in favor of Noriega's resignation.

Noriega found himself increasingly radioactive at home as well. His new figurehead president, Eric Delvalle, found himself isolated. Partygoers threw ice cubes at him at his country club. Perhaps more painfully, Delvalle's own synagogue ostracized him during the high holidays. On Yom Kippur, congregation members turned their backs to Delvalle as they prayed for Hugo Spadafora.[108] Noriega's actions cost him the favor of the Panamanian elites.

Most problematically, Noriega's actions cost him the support of his second-in-command, Roberto Díaz Herrera, a cousin of Omar

Torrijos. Díaz openly supported the Sandinistas in Nicaragua, and he provided Noriega with left-wing political cover and credibility. Díaz called reporters into his office and told them over a meal of McDonald's hamburgers that Noriega had assassinated Torrijos, fixed the 1984 presidential elections, trafficked in narcotics, and tortured Spadafora to death. The reporters asked Díaz why he was speaking up. He told them that he had received psychic instructions from an Indian mystic named Satya Sai Baba.[109] While it is possible that psychic messages were in fact Díaz's motivation—he had a mystical streak—it is more likely that Díaz was angered that Noriega had reneged on a promise to step down as head of the Panamanian Defense Forces in 1987. Regardless of his motives, Díaz's comments set off a wave of middle-class street demonstrations—the largest, on June 8, 1987, drew almost 100,000 people.[110] In response, Noriega organized a counterdemonstration of five thousand people, which attacked the U.S. Embassy and knocked over a statue of Theodore Roosevelt. Noriega then arrested Díaz, along with six hundred others, and raided opposition headquarters.

Arresting Díaz proved to be Noriega's third error. Once Díaz was out of the picture, the U.S. government no longer needed to fear that Noriega might be succeeded by a Sandinista sympathizer. In short, Washington no longer had any reasons to continue supporting La Piña's control over the Panamanian government. On June 26, the U.S. Senate voted 84–2 to call for Noriega to resign. In response, Noriega organized a demonstration near the U.S. Embassy, which rapidly devolved into a riot which overturned embassy employees' cars parked outside.[111] Noriega's violent counterreaction to the demonstrations that followed Díaz's comments provoked the U.S. Congress into suspending all aid, and prompted a wave of capital flight from Panama. In response, Noriega piled another error onto all the miscalculations he had already made: he tried to sell docking rights to the Soviet fishing fleet and asked the rogue state of Libya for aid.

On February 4, 1988, American patience ran out. The Justice Department indicted Noriega in courts in Miami and Tampa on twelve separate counts of racketeering, money laundering, and involvement in cocaine and marijuana smuggling.[112] It was only the second time the U.S. government had indicted a foreign leader, the previous case being the hapless Norman Saunders, chief minister of the Turks and Caicos Islands, who had been caught in a bribery and drug trafficking sting in a Miami hotel in 1985.[113]

President Delvalle saw the chaos as an opening through which he could broker a deal for Noriega to step down. In a meeting with Elliott Abrams while in the United States for a medical checkup, Delvalle got Abrams to agree that the charges against Noriega could be dropped if Noriega left politics and went into exile.[114] When Delvalle presented the deal to Noriega, however, he refused it. Noriega suspected—quite rightly—that the Department of Justice had no intention of following through.

On February 25, Delvalle dismissed Noriega as head of the Panamanian Defense Forces.[115] Nonplussed, Noriega had the National Assembly dismiss Delvalle the next day. Minister of Education Manuel Solís became president.[116] In the morning of February 27, 1988, Delvalle received word that Noriega intended to have him arrested. Delvalle climbed over the fence in his backyard and fled in a waiting car to a hideout near an American military base.[117] That same day, a Panamanian ambassador-at-large hired a Washington lawyer named William Rogers. Rogers, a Latin American specialist, had been special counsel for John F. Kennedy's Alliance for Progress, resigning after Lyndon Johnson's invasion of the Dominican Republic in 1965.[118] As Gerald Ford's assistant secretary of state for inter-American affairs, he helped negotiate the transfer of the Panama Canal on the American side, and then, during the Carter administration, on the Panamanian side.[119] In Rogers, Delvalle had found himself a ringer.

From Washington, Rogers developed an ingenious legal strategy against the Noriega regime, based on the fact that Panama essentially used the U.S. dollar as its currency. (Balboa notes had been issued by Panama only once, by President Arnulfo Arias in a bizarre episode a week before his overthrow in 1941.)[120] On March 1, 1988, Rogers's firm filed suits to freeze Panamanian assets in the United States, beginning with the banks.[121] On March 3, the courts froze the U.S. accounts of the Banco Nacional de Panama (BNP).[122] The BNP could no longer access the deposit accounts it held in American banks. Nor could it clear checks through American institutions. The BNP had to close its doors, and other Panamanian banks soon followed. Rogers then went after other Panamanian assets within the United States, including Air Panama, the state-owned airline. American courts even placed the monthly payment the United States sent to Panama into escrow.[123] In effect, Rogers engineered a depression specific to Panama. As one Panamanian put it, "Panama is the only country that can be subjected to an economic blockade from its interior."[124]

Within days, Panama's economy started to weaken. Since the Banco Nacional de Panama was also the Panamanian clearing-house for cashing domestic checks, the subsequent payday, March 14, 1988, became problematic for the Panamanian economy. How would Panamanian firms make payroll? Over 145,000 people, 20 percent of Panama's labor force, had no access to $30 million in wage payments. A general strike quickly ensued, beginning with the dockworkers.[125] As Rogers stated, "It was a conscious plan to tighten the financial noose around the neck of the Noriega regime. The consequences were seen with precision: Starve the banking system of cash, force the banks to close, and thus cause—not to put too fine a point on it—considerable financial, economic distress in Panama. The economy doesn't function now."[126]

By the end of March, Panama's economy was in disarray, and the country defaulted on its foreign debts.[127] Rogers was quietly pleased with himself. "I don't know of anyone else who—I mean on the assumption that it works, and Noriega is out—I don't know of any effort to overturn another government by litigation which really was based on, and derived from, litigation in the United States. Or that worked as fast as this, or that had the consequences this one has."[128] A week later, on April 8, the executive branch of the United States added its muscle to Rogers's judicial blockade of Panama: Executive Order 12635 blocked further American transactions with Panama as "an unusual and extraordinary threat to the national security, foreign policy, and economy of the United

States."[129] Elliott Abrams gloated to the press about Panama's financial catastrophe, quipping that Noriega was hanging to power "by his fingertips."[130]

Unfortunately, Abrams had overstated the case. The Panamanian economy shrank by 20 percent in 1988. Electricity consumption fell by 21 percent, and industrial production plunged 23 percent.[131] These were the most powerful economic sanctions imposed on another country to that date. In comparison, sanctions on Iran in 1951 and Rhodesia in 1965 caused their GDP to fall only by 13 to 14 percent.[132] The Panamanian financial system, however, proved to be remarkably resilient. As Rogers (if not necessarily Abrams) was no doubt aware, Panamanian bankers were not unsophisticated rubes fresh from the banana plantation. Generations of Panamanians had been trained at American universities and companies.[133]

Commerce Minister Mario Rognoni, a Georgia Tech graduate, engineered the Panamanian government's response. At first Rognoni toyed with a scheme to pay the workers in commemorative coins. Panamanian workers rejected this plan.[134] Soon the government began issuing fractional paychecks which circulated like bills of exchange. It issued paychecks in denominations of $1, $10, and $100, and declared these fractional checks acceptable at all government agencies, utilities, and businesses which catered to the Panamanian Defense Forces. Soon, other stores and businesses began to accept the checks at a discount. In fact, Noriega's opponents began to purchase the checks and use them to pay their utility bills, reasoning that they were paying Noriega's government using worthless government checks.[135] Unfortunately, their logic was backward: they were in fact investing in Noriega's government by buying its checks with hard money. Noriega himself personally set up Eurodollar accounts—allegedly using laundered drug money—in order to allow the Banco Nacional de Panama to reopen and restart clearing checks and credit card bills. Panamanian banks resumed operations on April 18, 1988, issuing negotiable certificates of deposit based on savings accounts, which the government agreed to accept and were used for large purchases of consumer goods.[136] In addition, Texaco, Eastern Airlines, and United Brands (the successor company to United Fruit) undercut the American sanctions by sending $3 million to Panama in the form of early tax payments, in order to keep their local operations liquid.[137]

Despite Rogers's efforts, the Panamanian economy contracted but did not collapse, and Noriega held on to power. A minor coup attempt by a handful of Panamanian air force officers was put down by Noriega's security guards. If anything, the sanctions weakened the middle-class opposition to his regime.[138] Ultimately, the sanctions emboldened Noriega. As the *New York Times* reported later in 1988: "When asked if he and other Administration officials had been cautioned to bite their tongues before barking about the Panamanian leader, Elliott Abrams . . . replied: 'I have no comment. I have no comment. I have no comment.'"[139]

Noriega still might have survived, had he not made his final miscalculation: he decided to retaliate directly against American interests in Panama. Noriega escalated the intimidation of American military personnel and their dependents in Panama. He also began targeting Panamanian employees of the Panama Canal. The Panama Canal Commission's Office of the Ombudsman's hotline began to receive fifty calls an hour from worried employees, their dependents, and canal retirees concerned about their safety.[140] One method of harassment was particularly ingenious. The Panama Canal Commission withheld Panamanian payroll taxes from its workers' checks. As a result of the U.S. sanctions, however, those taxes were held in escrow in the United States. Noriega, therefore, passed a law requiring proof that applicants for annual license plates paid their taxes. Drivers without new plates were subject to legal harassment, up to and including the confiscation of their car.[141] By March of 1989, the American chairman of the Panama Canal Commission, William Gianelli, stated, "If Noriega continues his campaign against our work force—which is 85 percent Panamanian—the efficiency of the Canal will so deteriorate that international shipping will have to consider other forms of moving cargo."[142] Gianelli himself resigned in April. "They've been giving me hell for years. That doesn't bother me any. But what does bother me, is that we haven't been able to do anything about the Noriega situation under either the Reagan or Bush Administrations."[143]

The Panamanian presidential elections of May 5, 1989, were widely expected to be fraudulent, and Manuel Noriega did not disappoint. Polls conducted before the election by American, Mexican, and Venezuelan firms showed opposition candidate Guillermo Endara winning the election by a 2-to-1 margin, while exit surveys conducted by an organization representing Panama's twelve Roman Catholic bishops indicated that Endara won the election by a *3-to-1* margin.[144] When Noriega's chosen candidate, Carlos Duque, claimed a 6-point victory, former U.S. president Jimmy Carter called for Noriega to abide by the legitimate results of the election and step down.[145] Noriega's response was immediate and intemperate. During a peaceful demonstration protesting election fraud on May 10, members of the Panamanian Defense Forces and Noriega's Dignity Battalions beat Endara's entourage with metal pipes, clubs, and tire irons, shooting a bodyguard dead while knocking the 250-pound presidential candidate unconscious. Official trucks painted with pictures of blue Smurfs—children's cartoon characters—then sprayed the crowds with water and tear gas. On Panamanian national television that night, an official spokeswoman for the election tribunal declared the election results nullified "in their totality."[146]

Noriega then tried to disrupt the Panama Canal by having Panama's representatives boycott Panama Canal Commission meetings. On July 26, 1989, in response to the canal's deteriorating fiscal situation, the Panama Canal Commission approved a 9.8 percent increase in toll rates, citing a growing deficit caused by the costs of doing business under an increasingly hostile regime. It was only the second toll increase after the commission's reorganization in 1979, and only the fifth increase in rates in the history of the canal. The commission's five American members approved the increase. The commission's four Panamanian members were not present.[147] A Panamanian was slated to take over as administrator of the Panama Canal Commission on January 1, 1990. Noriega announced that the job would go to Tomás Altamirano Duque, a Noriega loyalist.[148] It was impossible for the United States to contemplate giving that position to a Noriega crony, and the incoming George H. W. Bush administration announced that it would not accept anyone nominated by Noriega's regime.

Noriega's decision to boycott the Panama Canal Commission turned out to be the edge of the abyss for his regime. The election results demonstrated that Noriega had lost the support of the Panamanian electorate. Americans living in Panama were threatened by Noriega's thugs, and American service people stationed in Panama and their dependents were increasingly subject to attacks. American courts had indicted Noriega of criminal activities on a vast scale. Finally, Noriega's interference with the operations of the Panama Canal threatened to affect global commerce. Even for the famously prudent George H. W. Bush, there was no longer any upside to leaving Noriega in power. The U.S. military finished the Blue Spoon operational plan on October 30, 1989. It called for U.S. forces already stationed within Panama to secure the Madden Dam and former Canal Zone residential areas within two hours. Twenty-seven thousand additional troops would arrive by air within five days.[149] All that remained for President Bush to implement this war plan was what the plan called a "trigger event."

Noriega pulled that trigger on December 15, 1989. That day, the Panamanian National Assembly declared war on the United States. Manuel Noriega—following, it must be said, in Omar Torrijos's footsteps—then named himself Maximum Leader of Panama. Panamanian Defense Force members began to attack American troops and their dependents, killing one, wounding three, and sexually assaulting a fifth. On December 17, President Bush made his decision, with the words: "Okay, let's do it. The hell with it!"[150] Military operations against the Noriega regime—renamed Operation Just Cause for public relations purposes—began at forty-five minutes past midnight on December 20, 1989.[151] Within four days, Noriega was in hiding at the embassy of the papal nuncio in Panama City.[152] On January 3, 1990, after less than two weeks of diplomatic and psychological pressure, Noriega surrendered to American troops, who handcuffed him outside the embassy gate. Less than an hour later, the United States airlifted the Maximum Leader of Panama to Homestead Air Force Base in Florida.[153]

The U.S. Southern Command tallied 314 Panamanian military dead, and 23 Americans. The Endara government estimated that an additional 203 Panamanian civilians died in the fighting.[154] The Roman Catholic Church in Panama calculated that 673 Panamanians were killed.[155] (Higher estimates made in the immediate aftermath of the invasion have become less credible as the missing have been accounted for.) The director of Panama's Chamber of Commerce estimated economic losses at $2.2 billion.[156] The only organization in Panama left relatively unscathed was the Panama Canal itself, which shut down for thirty hours at the beginning of the invasion on December 20, and resumed its twenty-four-hour schedule on Christmas Day, 1989.[157]

A NEW NORMALCY

It is unlikely that either Jimmy Carter or Omar Torrijos envisioned that the first Panamanian national to be appointed administrator of the Panama Canal Commission would take office in the immediate aftermath of a full-scale invasion. Nevertheless, that is exactly what happened. The commission's deputy administrator, Fernando Manfredo, moved into the top spot on a temporary basis.[158] Manfredo had been personally nominated by Torrijos in 1979 and worked closely with his American counterpart, Dennis McAuliffe, to "Panamanianize" the canal's workforce, resisting pressure from Noriega to parcel out positions as patronage.[159] A few months later, in September 1990, Gilberto Guardia Fabrega succeeded Manfredo as permanent Panamanian head of the Panama Canal.[160]

Guardia's work as the new chief administrator of the Panama Canal Commission was cut out for him. Guardia needed to put the canal's finances on a sound basis, finish the Panamanization process, and rehabilitate the ports near Panama City and Colón, which had fallen into disrepair under Noriega.[161] This is not to say that *no* progress had been made during the 1980s. The Panama Canal Commission installed high-mast lighting to improve nighttime visibility for small vessels and extend the hours during which large vessels could cross. It also added more towing locomotives to pull ships through the locks, widened dangerous parts of the canal passage, and for the first time brought its buoys and beacons up to accepted international standards.[162] As a result, accident rates came down from their 1970s peak—although they remained a full third above the rate in the 1950 and 1960s.

Despite good headline numbers, only partial progress had been made toward Panamanizing the Panama Canal's workforce.[163] Panamanians moved into higher-level occupations, but they filled only the lower ranks of management. For the high-status position of canal pilot, which required years of on-the-job training, the number of Panamanians increased from only 4 out of 228 in 1979 to 61 out of 228 in 1989.[164] Meanwhile, the U.S.-Panamanian wage gap increased from 7 to 1 in 1980 to an astonishing 11 to 1 by 1993. (See table 8.3.)

No further progress would be possible unless the Panama Canal could be protected from political interference. In the aftermath of the invasion, the Endara administration took a number of steps to ensure that the canal would remain independent from the government. The first step was to repair Panama's broken political institutions. The Endara administration abolished the Panamanian Defense Forces, Noriega's old power base. This provoked a brief rebellion by disaffected former officers in December 1990, which the U.S. Army quickly suppressed. Additionally, in 1993 the Endara administration revised the electoral code to give the electoral courts much greater autonomy, in order to ensure fairer electoral counts than had occurred in the recent past. The revisions to the electoral code also placed the Panamanian national police under the control of the electoral court for a six-day period before the election until the announcement of the official results.

The second step was to institutionalize the Panama Canal management's independence from the Panamanian government. The Endara administration proposed legislation that would establish

TABLE 8.3

Panamanian Participation in the Panama Canal Workforce

	October 1979		September 1989		July 1999	
	Number	Percent	Number	Percent	Number	Percent
Skilled crafts	568	58.7	860	84.9		93.0
Professional and managerial	44	13.8	143	42.6		
Floating equipment	39	20.0	187	70.6		82.0
Power group	9	23.0	30	68.2		
Canal pilots	4	1.7	61	26.8		72.0
TOTAL	664	38.1	1,281	67.9		

Source: Panama Canal Commission, *A Decade of Progress in Canal Operation and Treaty Implementation* (Panama City: PCC, 1989), 28; and Charles Gillespie, Brandon Grove, David McGiffert, and C. Richard Nelson, "Panama Canal Transition: The Final Implementation" (policy paper, Atlantic Council, July 1999), 4.

	Permanent workforce	% U.S.	% non-U.S.	% of non-U.S. paid at U.S. rates	2009 dollars	
					Average annual U.S. wage	Average annual non-U.S. wage
1979	12,139	31	69			
1980	7,599	25	75	24	78,497	11,518
1981	7,846	24	76	27	77,059	11,450
1982	7,559	22	78	27	85,578	12,316
1983	7,745	21	79	31	80,488	11,160
1984	7,475	20	80	33	83,808	11,484
1985	7,521	18	82	32	83,965	10,387
1986	7,521	16	84		87,333	10,045
1987	7,561	15	85		90,537	9,766
1988	7,538	14	86		90,014	9,299
1989	7,584	13	87		90,509	8,609
1990	7,281	13	87		87,122	8,514
1991	7,206	12	88		93,901	8,823
1992	7,301	11	89		89,655	8,122
1993	7,420	11	89		86,734	7,934

Source: Panama Canal Commission reports. Salaries deflated by the Panamanian CPI.

a "Panama Canal Authority" as an autonomous agency, free from day-to-day government supervision.[165] Starting in 1999, the Authority's administrator would serve a seven-year term (with the possibility of reappointment) under the supervision of a board of eleven directors, nine of whom would be appointed by the Panamanian president with the consent of the legislature. Members of the board would serve overlapping terms, to minimize political interference. On the fiscal side, the Panama Canal Authority would have control over its own budget, which it would set on a three-year cycle separate from the Panamanian government's one-year cycle. The Authority would also have the ability to choose the level of its dividend payments to the national government, as long as they remained higher in nominal terms than the last payment made by the Panama Canal Commission in fiscal 1999. The National Assembly passed the Panama Canal Authority law as a constitutional amendment in December 1993, but according to the Panamanian constitution it would have to be approved again by the incoming Assembly after the May 1994 elections.[166]

In the new political environment of post-Noriega Panama, politicians soon discovered that they had to be able to refute charges that they would interfere with canal operations if they were to retain popular support. This shift away from pure partisan interest group politics was a new thing in Panama. The Panameñista Party, traditionally the "hispano" party in Panamanian politics, gained traction in the 1940s through Arias's Social Security program, which deliberately excluded Panama's West Indian–descended population and provided benefits only to formal sector urban workers.[167] In the same way, Torrijos gave a variety of benefits to the diverse groups within his populist coalition: higher pay to teachers, land redistribution to peasants and small farmers, and patronage to the National Guard.[168] Noriega co-opted both the Panamanian Defense Forces and the urban poor, via his Dignity Battalions, and systematically eroded other sources of power within Panama. Political parties after Noriega, however, had been stripped of their traditional control over patronage, and a large body of swing voters had emerged.

Panama's first election after Noriega's ouster was a complicated affair. Instead of the "typical" Panamanian pattern of incumbency versus opposition, seven candidates fronting coalitions composed of sixteen different parties campaigned against each other. The two principal alliances were the Alianza Pueblo Unido, led by Ernesto Pérez Balladares, who had managed Carlos Duque's ill-fated 1989 presidential campaign for Manuel Noriega, and the Alianza Democrática, headed by Mireya Moscoso, the widow of Arnulfo Arias. (Arias himself, who had been involved in Panamanian national politics since the 1930s, had died in 1988 in his Coconut Grove bungalow while watching CNN.)[169] Pérez claimed the mantle of Torrijos's Partido Revolucionario Democrático, but many people considered him tainted by his association to Noriega. On the other hand, Moscoso, dynastic heiress to the Panameñista Party—now officially called the Arnulfistas—entered the election with limited popularity, but grew stronger as the campaign continued.[170] The wild card was the Movimiento Papa Egoró, headed by the intellectual Panamanian salsa star Ruben Blades, which in early polling showed a substantial lead.[171] Gilberto Guardia, with the support of the American chairman of the Panama Canal Commission, Robert McMillan, banned canal employees from running for office in order to cement a precedent that the canal would be apolitical.[172]

Pérez won the presidential election narrowly, with only 32 percent of the vote, a margin of only 2½ points over Moscoso. His administration shepherded Endara's canal reform through a second Assembly vote, and enshrined it as Title 14 of the Panamanian constitution. Pérez also privatized the ports of Balboa and Cristóbal, which the government had taken over from the Canal Zone. To the dismay of many American politicians, the company Hutchison Whampoa Limited of Hong Kong received a fifty-year concession to rehabilitate and operate the ports. Panama's choice of a non-American foreign firm was no accident. Panamanian politicians believed that a Chinese company, with little regional political influence, would be easier to hold accountable than a local or an American firm, while simultaneously avoiding the patronage problems that would plague a government-run attempt to reverse the ports' drastic decline under Noriega.[173]

Unfortunately, while Pérez's policies were good for Panama's attempts to free its flagship business from political interference, his policies were bad for his own political future. Pérez managed to alienate both the United States and the Panamanian population, which suspected him of seeking other methods to use the Panama Canal for political patronage. A 1998 referendum to amend the constitution to allow him to seek a second term failed by nearly a 2 to 1 margin, on fears that Pérez planned to reward his associates with privatized canal property.[174]

Mireya Moscoso would preside over the historic turnover of the Panama Canal to Panama. Voter dissatisfaction with the Panamanian economy would lead to her victory in the 1999 election. Heading the Panameñista coalition, the Unión por Panama, Moscoso ran against Omar Torrijos's American-educated son, Martín Torrijos, the head of the PRD's coalition. Some Panamanians did not see either of the two dynastic candidates as especially new, quipping that it was an election between "two corpses." Despite the population's reflexive cynicism about domestic politics, Moscoso won in an election marked by high turnout, defeating Martín Torrijos by 7 points.[175] But her party failed to win the legislature: the PRD captured 47 percent of the seats in the Assembly, and its allies took an additional 4 percent, giving the PRD an effective legislative majority. Even had Moscoso wanted to pack the Panama Canal Authority with her supporters, she would have been unable to.

The official transfer of the Panama Canal to Panama at the end of 1999 was not enough to maintain Moscoso's popularity. Plagued by high unemployment and low growth, the Panameñistas collapsed in 2004. The party came in third in the presidential vote and barely managed to hang onto 22 percent of Assembly seats. Running on a platform of expanding the Panama Canal, Martín Torrijos captured 47 percent of the vote (on 76 percent turnout), defeating former president Endara by 16 points and the Panameñista candidate, José Miguel Alemán, by an astounding 31 points.[176]

Moreover, Torrijos's referendum on expanding the Panama Canal to include a third lock system passed with 78 percent of the vote.

THE LONG-TERM PROFITABILITY OF THE PANAMA CANAL

The overthrow of Noriega and the establishment of strong democratic norms in Panama were necessary conditions for Panama to enjoy the economic benefits from its ownership of the Panama Canal. They resulted in a new constitutional amendment in 1994, separating the Panama Canal from direct Panamanian governmental authority. Interference in the operation of the Panama Canal became the "third rail" of Panamanian politics. Panamanian voters treated politicians who they believed interfered in canal operations poorly at the polls. But these conditions were not sufficient for the Panama Canal to remain profitable. The Panama Canal Commission and its successor, the Panama Canal Authority, had to figure out how to put the canal on a sound financial footing.

When the Panama Canal Commission took over in 1979, the Panama Canal was barely a money-making operation. The commission faced the challenge of not only making the Panama Canal profitable, but also making it profitable enough to make the payments stipulated by the Panama Canal Treaty. The immediate answer was to raise tolls. The year 1980 saw a 29.3 percent toll rise. The opening of the Transisthmian Pipeline resulted in the loss of approximately $50 million in toll revenue, forcing the commission to hike rates by 9.8 percent in 1983.[177] Tolls jumped by another 9.8 percent in 1990.The commission ultimately raised nominal rates 56 percent during the 1980s, but that failed to keep pace with prices, which rose 66 percent during the same period.

In addition to the rate hikes, the Panama Canal Commission undertook a series of drastic cost-cutting measures. In 1980, the commission's new administrator, Dennis McAuliffe, used his authority under the Panama Canal Treaty to slash the workforce by a full 34 percent. Of these job reductions, 31 percent fell on Americans, almost entirely through voluntary retirements. These cuts

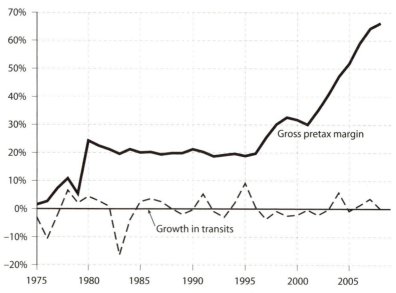

Figure 8.1: Panama Canal margins and annual growth in interoceanic transits. *Source*: Panama Canal Company/Commission, *Annual Reports*; Autoridad del Canal de Panamá, *Annual Reports*.

saved $40 million. An addition $15.4 million of cuts came from passing the cost of the Canal Zone government to the Republic of Panama. These cuts plus the 1980 rate hike proved enough to make the $65 million in payments to the Panamanian government (not including $10 million to carry out governmental functions in the former Canal Zone) mandated by the Panama Canal Treaty.[178] The Panama Canal's profit margin before interest and taxes rose from around 5 percent in the late 1970s to 20 percent during the 1980s.[179] (See figure 8.1.)

The commission's better financial footing during the 1980s allowed it to make essential improvements in safety measures for the Panama Canal, which had lapsed during the previous administration of the Panama Canal Company. The commission installed better lighting and buoys, widened bottlenecks, and acquired better guidance locomotives along the canal, all of which reduced accident rates. The commission also deepened the ship channel between the Miraflores and Gatún locks. In previous years, periods of low rainfall meant that there were periods during which the Panama Canal had to limit the depth of transiting vessels below the maximum that could fit through the locks; after the completion of the ship channel project in May 1984, this was no longer necessary. Finally, the commission introduced a managerial innovation to allow shipping companies to reserve a specific transit slot in advance. If a ship with a reservation arrived on the scheduled day, it would be allowed to jump to the front of any canal queues. The resulting additional revenues went to capital improvements.[180]

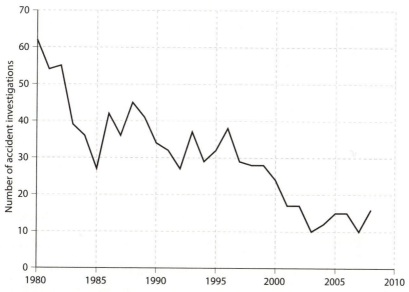

Figure 8.2: Accident investigations on the Panama Canal. *Source*: Jeff Levon, "Alternative Dispute Resolution at the Panama Canal: Negotiating a Collective Bargaining Agreement," in *Portraits of Business Practices in Emerging Markets: Cases for Management Education*, ed. Richard G. Linowes (Washington, DC: U.S. Agency for International Development, 1999); 1997–2000 from Rodolfo Sabonge, "The Panama Canal: Modernization and Expansion," Autoridad del Canal de Panamá report, June 26, 2001, 19; 2001–2 from ACP report, "Advisory to Shipping No. A-36-2002," October 14, 2002, 2; 2003–4 from ACP report, "Panama Canal Authority Announces Fiscal Year 2005 Metrics," October 21, 2005; 2005–6 from ACP report, "Panama Canal Authority Announces Fiscal Year 2006 Second Quarter Metrics," June 6, 2006; 2007–8 from ACP report, "Panama Canal Authority Announces Fiscal Year 2008 Metrics," October 24, 2008.

In the 1990s, the Panama Canal administration adopted a new strategy to deal with the increasing size of ships passing through the canal. Panamax ships, specifically designed to be the largest ships that could transit through the Panama Canal, were forming a greater fraction of canal traffic. In theory, Panamax-size ships could fit through the Panama Canal locks, but they had difficulty safely navigating the narrower parts of the canal passage itself. When water levels in Lake Gatún fell, as they tended to during El Niño climate events, Panamax ships could not transit at all. Due to their size, Panamax vessels took two hours rather than one to transit the locks, required six to eight locomotives to assist their transit instead of four, used the services of seven to ten tugboats instead of four, and their increased transit time—as well as the difficulty of piloting large ships through the canal—meant that they required the services of two or three pilots instead of one.

The Panama Canal Commission and its successor organization, the Panama Canal Authority (ACP, for its initials in Spanish),

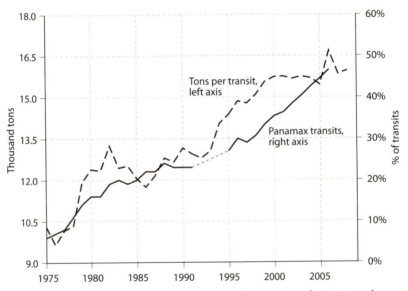

Figure 8.3:   Panama Canal tons-per-transit and percentage of transits made by Panamax vessels. *Source*: Panama Canal Company/Commission, *Annual Reports*; Autoridad del Canal de Panamá, *Annual Reports*.

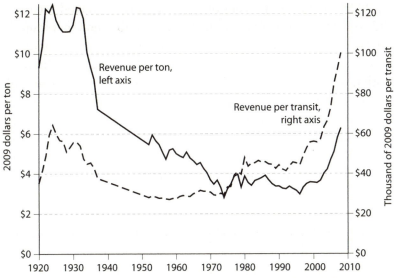

Figure 8.4: Panama Canal revenue per-ton and per-transit, 2009 dollars. *Source*: Panama Canal Company/Commission, *Annual Reports*; Autoridad del Canal de Panamá, *Annual Reports*.

spent $2 billion on capital improvements intended to deal with the needs of larger ships between 1992 and 2001. In 1992, the commission began widening the Culebra Cut, so that, in the words of the administrator Gilberto Guardia, "then the bottleneck will be at the lock."[181] (See figure 8.3.) In 1997, a second round of widening the Culebra Cut began. Three years later, the ACP again set itself to deepening Lake Gatún by an additional three feet.[182] The ACP also replaced electric lock mechanisms with hydraulic mechanisms, purchased more locomotives to pull the ships through the locks, and increased the maintenance of the locks themselves. Finally, in 2001, it ended the practice of allowing two-way transits of the canal. Instead, all traffic between noon and midnight would move from the Pacific to the Atlantic, and traffic between midnight and noon would go the other direction, a tactic designed to streamline canal operations and prevent accidents. (See figure 8.2.)

In addition, the ACP expanded and revamped the reservation system that the commission had initially put in place back in 1984.

By 2000, roughly 40 percent of all vessels that traversed the canal did so with a reservation. By 2006, that number had increased to 59.7 percent. An additional 31 percent had requested a reservation and were unable to get one. Reservations did much to increase both the speed of transit and canal revenues. In 2000, a vessel with a reservation spent 17.2 hours in Panama Canal waters, whereas a vessel without one spent 40.0 hours. By 2006, those numbers had decreased slightly, to 16.0 and 37.9, but the increase in the number of vessels using reserved slots meant that overall average canal waters time fell from 30.8 to 24.8 hours.[183] (Due to a definitional change, these numbers are not directly comparable to the numbers in table 8.2.)

With these improvements to Panama Canal operations in place, the last item the ACP needed to accomplish in order to maximize its revenues from the canal was to overhaul the canal's toll structure. Unlike the previous operators of the Panama Canal, the ACP would become a price discriminator. Different types of canal traffic would be charged different tolls. In 2000, the ACP divided traffic into seven categories: general cargo, refrigerated cargo, dry bulk carriers, tankers, vehicle carriers, passenger vessels, and other. The canal administration then developed different rates for each class. In addition, the canal began to charge larger vessels disproportionately more, in recognition of both the higher costs that they imposed and their operators' greater willingness to pay. The new tolls also included a separate charge for using the locomotives that hold ships steady in the locks. The ACP administrator, Alberto Alemán Zubieta, called the new pricing system "a change of philosophy."[184]

The revival of the Panama Canal prompted the creation of ancillary enterprises. In 1998, the Kansas City Southern Railroad and Mi-Jack Products, an American intermodal terminal operator, gained a fifty-year concession to rebuild and operate the Panama Railroad. The railroad went into operation in 2002, using entirely new cars running along brand-new concrete-tie tracks. The railroad moved relatively little freight compared to the Panama Canal—in 2007, the Panama Railroad moved 537,998 twenty-foot containers (TEU, for twenty-foot equivalent unit), compared to 13.8 *million* TEU on the Panama Canal.[185] In terms of volume alone, it might be thought that the Panama Railroad was simply a sideshow to Panama Canal operations.

Such a conclusion would not be correct: the new Panama Railroad formed an effective complement to the Panama Canal's operation. First, the Panama Railroad allowed for improved "carrier asset utilization." Ships could arrive at the Panama Canal carrying too much cargo for the canal to handle, unload some of it for the Panama Railroad to transport to the other side of the isthmus, and then either pick up the cargo there or transfer it to another vessel.[186] The ability to transfer 4 percent of the canal's container traffic to the railroad reduced the cost of using the canal, some of which the ACP recaptured in higher tolls. In addition, the Panamanian government considered the Panama Railroad to be part of Panama's larger duty-free zone. The Panama Railroad therefore allowed ships to disembark cargoes in Balboa, and ship them directly to the Colón Free Zone, rather than having to rely on Cristóbal or Tocumen Airport. Ships carrying cargoes for the Colón Free Zone could arrive on the Pacific side and unload their cargo without needing to cross the Panama Canal.

In short, the Panama Canal underwent a management revolution after 1990. Once the political conditions were met to prevent the canal from becoming a source of elite patronage—first with the ouster of Noriega, then with the 1994 amendment to the Panamanian constitution, and finally with the emergence of a voter-enforced norm of keeping a "hands-off" attitude to the canal—the Panama Canal could operate as a commercial enterprise free of adverse political interference. Under the Panama Canal Commission, and later, the Panama Canal Authority, the canal professionalized its management and began making long-term investments with an eye to the commercial potential of the canal for the first time since the 1920s.

Perhaps most importantly, the Panama Canal became a revenue-maximizing enterprise. (See figure 8.4.) For the first time in its history, the Panama Canal was no longer run as a public utility.

Rather, the canal was run as a profit-making enterprise for the benefit of its shareholder: the Republic of Panama. Not only was the Panama Canal able to meet the added payments to the Panamanian government specified in the Panama Canal Treaty, it was able to exceed that profitability and turn itself into one of the most profitable transportation enterprises on the planet—despite continuing steep competition from trucks, railroads, and intermodal transportation within the United States. In 2000, the Panama Canal operation's total contribution to the Panamanian treasury was only $167 million. By 2008, that figure had risen to $701 million: $357 million in tonnage and public service fees and an additional $344 million in dividends, making up 7.2 percent of all government revenues.

NINE

CONCLUDING THE DITCH

On May 3, 2009, Panamanian supermarket magnate and New York Yankees fan Ricardo Martinelli defeated former Panamanian housing minister Balbina Herrera of the incumbent Partido Revolucionario Democrático by 22 points. By Latin American standards, the candidates were strongly pro-business; for example, both the conservative Martinelli and the left-wing Herrera supported the U.S.-Panama Free Trade Agreement. Nonetheless, Martinelli's reputation as a successful businessman was more than enough to counter the PRD's faltering cachet as a provider of public goods and services in the wake of the continuing Great Recession. Clearly, the majority of Panamanians in 2009 thought that the proper business of Panama was business. And in 2009, business in Panama still centered on the Panama Canal.

The contemporary importance of the Panama Canal to world trade and to Panamanian economic development is impossible to dispute. But the Panama Canal has a broader relevance to social scientists. Panama's unique geographical location and historical position show how various economic and political themes replay themselves over and over again through time. From an analytic viewpoint, the story of the Panama Canal illuminates aspects of large infrastructure projects, imperialism, and decolonization.

SOCIAL SAVINGS AND THE PANAMA CANAL

The social savings generated by the Panama Canal were large. The canal generated a minimum global social rate of return of 6.4 percent for the first seventeen years of its operation, assuming an extremely competitive elasticity of demand for transport costs. Using estimates of the elasticity in line with studies of other transportation projects, we calculate the Panama Canal had a global social rate of return of 8.7 percent. These, in turn, are underestimates of the "true" value of the social savings, due to the downward biases in the calculations. Most of these social savings were captured by American producers, consumers, and taxpayers: at minimum, the Panama Canal "repaid" the United States its total start-up costs within eight to twelve years of starting operation.

While the social savings caused by the Panama Canal were large, however, they were not transformative for the American or the global economy. The railroads, for example, generated social savings on the order of 4.7 percent of GDP in the United States, and they utterly transformed the economies of Brazil and Mexico, where they accounted for as much as 20 percent and 32 percent of GDP, respectively. Measured this way, the Panama Canal generated on average a far more modest 0.2 percent of GDP for the United States in the two decades before World War II.[1] The Panama Canal's social savings elsewhere around the world were an order of magnitude smaller still. Hutchinson and Ungo used a rather optimistic gravity model of world trade to estimate the Panama Canal increased American net exports sufficiently to increase the canal's contribution to social savings to 1.0 percent of GDP.[2] Their model assumed that all the "excess" net exports were due to the Panama Canal; this strikes us as unlikely, since most American exports in 1924 were manufactured goods sold to Europe, few of which travelled through the canal. The trade flows through the Panama Canal were highly heterogeneous over time and very contingent. Subtracting this contribution brings Hutchinson and Ungo's estimate more in line with our own calculations.

That said, the price reduction caused by the Panama Canal catalyzed new industries in California, the Pacific Northwest, and Chile, where it produced economic benefits well in excess of our minimum estimate, if not as high as Hutchinson and Ungo's. Inside the United States, the Panama Canal enabled the great Californian petroleum boom—the gains from which, at least in terms of retail gasoline sales, were mostly captured by the oil companies. It also may have retarded California's industrialization, at least on the margin: early industry in California was largely based on the availability of cheap diesel fuel. The Panama Canal brought the price of crude in California into line with the rest of the country, removing one source of Californian competitive advantage in manufacturing, but benefitting the United States as a whole. In addition, the Panama Canal catalyzed the growth of the Pacific Northwest's lumber industry at the expense of the South. Unexpectedly, the Panama Canal also turned out to be responsible for Boeing's location in Seattle. It also single-handedly catalyzed the Chilean iron industry.

Was the Panama Canal "the best investment the United States government has ever made based on the social benefit relative to the cost"?[3] The question should be posed within a narrower scope, to exclude such things as public health improvements, the TIROS series of weather satellites, and the Immigration and Nationality Act of 1965, whose social rates of return we suspect were astronomical. Within the realm of U.S. transportation infrastructure, however, the Panama Canal is clearly behind the Interstate Highway System, which Nadiri and Mamuneas found produced a social rate of return of 35 percent over its first twenty years of operation, before declining to 10 percent.[4] The Panama Canal, on the other hand, generated a social rate of return of 9 percent during its first two decades of operation under plausible assumptions. This percentage represents a lower bound for the canal and includes both the capital and operating expenses of the defense installations that served to protect it, but it nonetheless appears clear that the interstates generated a significantly higher social rate of return for the United States than the Panama Canal. The Interstate Highway System was transformative for the United States; the Panama Canal was merely very useful.

Changes in the distribution of social savings explain specifically why ownership of the Panama Canal declined in value for the United States, despite the vast increase in trade through the canal over time. The most important factor was competition caused by technological change. This worked through two channels. First, improved freight transport on the railroads and over the postwar Interstate Highway System lowered transcontinental shipping costs relative to shipping through the Panama Canal. This directly decreased the social savings to the United States. Second, as alternative methods of transportation became more competitive relative to the Panama Canal, the price sensitivity of shippers rose, increasing the elasticity of demand for transport through the canal, and thus indirectly decreasing the social savings. By the 1970s, the volume of U.S. transcontinental trade through the Panama Canal had declined even in *absolute* terms compared to the volume of trade before World War II. Agricultural exports to Asia expanded, but the cost savings provided by the Panama Canal over westbound railroads were small. In short, by the 1970s the social savings generated by the Panama Canal accrued more and more to Japanese exporters rather than to American consumers—and therefore the burden of any higher rates charged by a non-American owner of the Panama Canal would fall on them.

All else being equal, a later canal would have generated fewer social savings, while an earlier canal would have caused greater social savings. The earliest point at which a Panama Canal was technologically feasible, however, was de Lesseps's failed effort in the 1880s. Roughly twenty-two thousand people died in that effort, imposing a vast human cost, but with better planning and even higher casualties it could have succeeded. De Lesseps's company as a private enterprise would have tried to capture the lion's share of the social savings generated by the Panama Canal. Given the importance of the U.S. transcontinental trade to early commerce through the canal, a Panama Canal operated by the Compagnie Universelle under the terms of the Wyse Concession would have represented a large-scale net transfer from American consumers to the French small investor class and the government of Colombia. We suspect the United States, as guarantor of the neutrality of the French-operated canal, would find its role increasingly awkward. But here, however, we reach the limits of safe counterfactual analysis.

THE PANAMA CANAL AND THE ECONOMICS OF IMPERIALISM

American imperialism created the Panama Canal, and the Panama Canal strongly benefitted the United States. Thus, in the case of the Panama Canal, imperialism paid. As the monetary costs of neutralizing Panamanian national sentiment grew, however, the United States received less and less benefit from its ownership of the canal. It is not a coincidence that the United States negotiated a formal agreement to hand over the canal to Panama just as the balance sheet of "imperial accountancy" for the canal fell into the red.

The classical economic theory of imperialism, promoted in the early twentieth century by Hobson and expanded more influentially by Lenin, made three major assertions about the economic effects of imperialism and set the terms for most subsequent discussions.[5] First, it asserted that imperialist nations profit from imperialism via greater returns on investment in subordinate regions. Second, it argued that by its very nature imperialism is exploitative: all else being equal, a region subordinate to an outside power will have more unfavorable outcomes than a similar region outside imperial control. Finally, the political institutions of the imperial power have little role in the development of the subordinate region. As Lenin put it shortly after the Panama Canal's initial opening, a comparison of "the republican American bourgeoisie with the monarchist Japanese or German bourgeoisie shows that the most pronounced political distinction diminishes to an extreme degree in the epoch of imperialism."[6] Did America's somewhat incoherent empire in Panama meet with the predictions of the Hobson-Lenin thesis?

The United States clearly benefitted from its actions in Panama. Considered as an investment, the Panama Canal produced a significantly higher rate of return than U.S. government bonds, or Panamanian loans for that matter. These benefits, however, arrived through the indirect channel of lowered transport costs; the mechanism was *not* financial instruments or toll collection on the Panama Canal. Nor did the returns pass to an investor class. Rather, they travelled more diffusely to a wide range of exporters, importers, and consumers across the United States and the globe. The Panama Canal yielded dividends, but they were not paid in coupons.

In terms of Panama, U.S. "exploitation" occurred in two steps at the very beginning: first when it strong-armed a better agreement than it could have obtained through voluntary negotiations, and then when it effectively separated the Canal Zone from the Panamanian economy. The United States did fairly brazenly exploit its non-American labor force for decades, through its discriminatory wage differentials and hiring policies, its use of antiunion violence, and its proprietorship of tenement housing. Jim Crow was an American import to the Panama Canal. The labor force, however, was not Panamanian—rather the majority consisted of Barbadians especially recruited for the project. Once the Canal Zone was in place, the United States does not seem to have especially exploited Panama. This formulation is awkward, but the creation of the independent Panamanian state is impossible to disentangle from the construction of the American-controlled Panama Canal.

The flip side of a lack of ongoing exploitation was a lack of ongoing institution building: the United States did not transfer its political institutions to Panama or to the Panama Canal in any significant way. Panamanian political institutions developed from Colombian models, provincial Panama having enjoyed considerable autonomy during Colombia's federal period. The United States' early active interventions in Panamanian politics soon faded—perhaps for the best, given America's inability to keep its own peculiar racial attitudes out of its foreign policy. Passive acquiescence in Panamanian authoritarianism became the norm. Although the United States initially attempted to suppress the formation of a Panamanian military, one developed anyway out of the country's national police force. In addition, American political institutions (other than courts) were not imported into the Canal Zone, which the United States military ran as a "paternalistic socialism" where "the State does everything."[7] Private property rights were so vague in the Canal Zone at the time of the handover that the new Panamanian administrators had to use lawn care records to establish the boundaries of residential plots.[8]

It should not be surprising that the Panama Canal appears to fit Hobson and Lenin's schematic theory of imperialism, albeit with some squints and reservations. In their way, Hobson and Lenin were trying to create a descriptive and analytic economic narrative of contemporary events. For decades, Hobson and Lenin's stylized facts were part of economic conventional wisdom, forming an "international *communis opinio*" on the subject.[9] Lebergott, in his hasty dismissal of the returns to American imperialism caused by the Panama Canal, used the Leninist formulation quite explicitly.[10]

As with all bold hypotheses, Hobson and Lenin's points came under sustained questioning by later scholars. These new lines of research fell under three broad categories. The first line of research investigated the true costs of empire, re-asking whether imperialism really paid for the metropoles. The second line attempted to quantify the benefits imperialism brought its subject peoples. Finally, the third line asked whether and why different empires brought about different distributions of gains and losses for the metropole and for the subject peoples.

Hobson and Lenin did not hold up very well in terms of the profitability of imperialism. Rather, in the case of the European colonial empires of the late nineteenth and early twentieth centuries, the economic benefits to the mother country appeared in general to be somewhere between small and negative. The new "imperial accountancy," as Offer derisively called it, explicitly used counterfactual analysis in its methodology.[11] As Thomas pointed out in 1968, "[T]he contribution of a colony or of any economic activity to the economic growth of the overall economy is precisely the difference (positive or negative) earned by the resources employed there relative to what they would have earned in their next best alternative."[12] Fieldhouse made the same point more explicitly: "It is impossible to draw up a reliable calculus of the benefits and disadvantages of Empire to an imperial state such as Britain without setting up a counter-factual: how might the British economy have performed had Britain possessed no colonies?"[13] In other words, to determine the economic value of imperialism, one must determine the economic value of its absence.

The canonical example of the era of high imperialism, the British Empire circa 1870–1913, was the main proving ground for these studies. The conclusions were fairly clear. Davis and Huttenback found that, while individual British industries benefitted from imperialism, "the British as a whole certainly did not benefit economically from the Empire." Rather, the empire was instead a complicated "mechanism for transferring wealth from the [British] middle to the upper classes."[14] Fieldhouse largely concurred. "Before 1914, the Empire was not in any way essential to the British economy but provided some tangible benefits," largely in the form of exports for "certain key British manufactures which faced increasing competition in foreign markets."[15] Edelstein calculated a net gain from the British Empire between 0.4 percent and 1.5 percent of GDP in 1913 (depending on assumptions about imperial defense costs).[16] It should be noted that half of the imperial benefits that Edelstein found derived from trade with the dominions of Canada, Australia, New Zealand, and South Africa—three of which were largely populated by British and Irish settlers and voluntarily associated with Great Britain.[17] In comparison, the Panama Canal saved the United States 0.2 percent of its GDP before 1937. In other words, the minor imperial venture of the United States in Panama was *alone* proportionately equivalent in terms of benefit to the mother country somewhere between *all and one-quarter* of the most generous estimates of what the non-self-governing portions of the British Empire generated for Great Britain.[18]

Why did the Panama Canal pay so well in comparison to other imperial ventures? In the British case, defense costs were the largest component to reduce the potential returns to empire. In the American case, the benefits from the Panama Canal did not accrue because of particularly low defense costs. The Panama Canal was a linchpin of the American defensive perimeter before World War II. Despite being essentially indefensible—or because of it—the Panama Canal used a relatively high proportion of military resources. Neither the Theodore Roosevelt administration nor the Taft administration had any desire to stint on defense spending for the sake of the overall profitability of the Panama Canal. Rather, the returns to empire from the Panama Canal were so high because the zone of imperial control was so limited. In his brasher moments, Theodore Roosevelt might have wanted to purchase or conquer Panama, but the U.S. Congress would have rejected overt colonialism, with the costly example of the Philippine Insurrection still fresh in legislative minds. After the Canal Zone was acquired, George Washington Goethals had no interest in ruling the Zone's Panamanian population, and so he actively expelled it—nearly 10 percent of Panama's total population. The Canal Zone became in effect an extremely small (and at the time, white supremacist) settler colony of the United States. Like other settler colonies, it was essentially self-governing and self-financing. Most importantly, however, it was just large enough to exploit Panama's privileged geographical position without having to bear the additional costs of administering the affairs of Panama and its population.

What benefits did imperialism bring to Panama? It must be remembered that the first time empire reached Panama's shores, under the reigns of Carlos V and Felipe II, the imperial power depopulated large portions of Central America for its construction projects in Panama, introducing in the process chattel slavery and new endemic diseases to the isthmus. Obviously, the bare condition of empire alone is not necessarily benevolent for its subject peoples. The United States of the Progressive Era, despite its philanthropic reputation, was not particularly interested in improving the lives of Panamanian citizens or non-American canal workers. From Washington's point of view, these people were not even imperial subjects—U.S. nationals without U.S. citizenship—in the way that Filipinos were before 1935 or Puerto Ricans were before 1917 (or the people of American Samoa still are today).

U.S. policy went out of its way to deny Panamanians the benefits of having the canal on their soil. The Commissary system, in which the Canal Zone administration monopolized almost all of the Panama Canal's support services, made it impossible for Panamanian businesses to compete. Their firms were practically banned from selling services to the Canal Zone or passing ship traffic; their citizens were treated as second-class within the Zone. It wasn't until 1936 that the wall around the Canal Zone lifted even a little; as late as the 1950s, Panamanian firms needed to call in fortuitous congressional contacts to be able to compete with the Commissary. Panamanian politicians and businesses did eventually find three ways to benefit from their links with the United States—the flag of convenience, the Colón Free Zone, and the financial cluster—but all three were second-best adaptations. American policy, it should be noted, was not deliberately directed from Washington. Rather, the Commissary system started as a way to cheaply supply the canal construction effort. Once in place, the Commissary's administration engaged in empire-building, expanding into more and more fields. It became another illustration of the Zonians' capture of the canal administration. Washington occasionally reigned in the Commissary (via the Hull-Alfaro Treaty of 1936 and the Remón-Eisenhower agreement of 1955), but such interventions were few and far between.

It cannot be denied that the United States brought significant and long-lasting health benefits to the people of the isthmus. Its physicians and epidemiologists, working in the best tradition of their professions, were clearly people of goodwill. That said, disease eradication and control in Panama was intended for the benefit of the construction workforce on the Panama Canal. The biology of yellow fever and malaria meant that, to minimize the adverse effects of disease on the canal workforce, they had to be controlled over a geographically wide area, including among the Panamanian urban population, which would otherwise harbor the diseases. The general tendency for the United States to choose policies to reduce or remove positive externalities of the canal for Panama leads us to suspect that had a cost-effective way existed to protect only the canal workforce from malaria and yellow fever, the United States would have chosen to employ it. After all, while the United States did build sanitary works for Panama, bringing clean water to Panama's urban population—it did so at Panama's expense.

Similarly, while the United States' labor policies on the Panama Canal proved an undoubted boon for the economy and people of Barbados, they were not intended to be humanitarian. For the canal administration, Barbadians were simply the least bad choice after the canal's Spanish workforce turned out to be easily radicalized and highly strike-prone. Few Americans initially treated the canal's Barbadian workers with respect. They were discriminated against in pay, rank, and custom. They were well fed only because it enabled them to perform more demanding physical labor more efficiently. It is frankly unclear, surveying the historical record, whether living conditions for most Silver Roll workers met the United Nations Standard Minimum Rules for the Treatment of Prisoners of 1955. That the Barbadians and other West Indians employed by the canal could not only survive but thrive under these conditions is testament to their inner human qualities, not to the benevolence of the American administration. In this, the proper counterfactual is not Barbadian outcomes in the absence of the Panama Canal, but Barbadian outcomes in the presence of labor standards equivalent to those prevailing in the continental United States.

Was there a specifically American imperialism in Panama? In other words, did the United States transmit to Panama distinctively American institutions via the Panama Canal that altered Panama's developmental path, for better or for worse? This line of thought follows Engerman and Sokoloff's hypothesis that founding economic and political institutions determined the long-term path of economic development in the Americas.[19] The hypothesis was generalized most notably in Acemoglu, Johnson, and Robinson's classic 2001 paper on the colonial origins of comparative development, which postulated a causal chain between settler mortality, the development of local institutions, and long-term growth.[20] It is a compelling argument, especially for the Panama Canal, since disease reduction and the concurrent decrease in mortality made the American construction of the canal and its long-term presence in the Canal Zone possible. This argument, however, is very close to saying that "history only matters once" in economic development—that long-term growth or its lack is caused by a single defining historical event. Looking at the institutional details of Panamanian development, the linkages between the American canal and later Panamanian growth are much more causally complex than a simple transfer of institutions. In fact, very few American institutions were transferred to Panama, other than the Panama Canal itself.

The United States created Panama as an American protectorate, with the U.S. dollar as its unit of currency and the right to intervene enshrined in its constitution. There are reasons to believe that the protectorate might have generated significant benefits for Panama. Ferguson and Schularick, for example, found a substantial "empire effect" within the British Empire, which decreased the cost of capital for British colonies by 100 to 175 basis points in the years before World War I.[21] Mitchener and Weidenmier found an even larger effect in the Caribbean and Central America following Theodore Roosevelt's 1904 declaration of a U.S. policy of intervention in regional financial affairs.[22] Alfaro, Maurer, and Ahmed found that the effect was persistent.[23] Panama's costs of capital, however, did *not* decrease substantially under its formal American protectorate: its borrowing rates, while slightly lower than Colombia's, were significantly higher than those of the informal U.S. protectorates in the region. In other words, private investors did not believe that the United States would take any greater action to protect their investments in Panama than it would elsewhere in the circum-Caribbean region. Conversely, Mitchener and Weidenmier found that the American announcement of construction of the Panama Canal caused little change in bond prices throughout the American sphere of influence. In other words, private investors of the time believed—correctly—that the Panama Canal would contribute little to regional development. Nor did they believe that the Panama Canal made the United States more likely to intervene to protect property rights within its sphere. In short, there is little evidence for a positive "empire effect" caused by the United States from the Panama Canal.

THE PANAMA CANAL AND THE POLITICAL ECONOMY
OF DECOLONIZATION

The United States government was never hands-off with respect to Panama. U.S. Marines intervened on the isthmus as far back as 1856, to protect the American-owned Panama Railroad and its American passengers. Decades before the Panama Canal was built, American diplomats hammered out agreements to ensure that any canal built across the isthmus would not discriminate against American commerce.

After World War II, however, the benefits of American ownership of the Panama Canal faded. The canal was indefensible, militarily obsolete, and provided fewer and fewer economic returns to the United States. Its existence was still relatively important to American agricultural export, but the cost-benefit balance of *ownership* was rapidly sinking deeper into the red. At the same time Panama grew increasingly nationalist. Two generations of Panamanians had been born since independence from Colombia. As a client state within a larger power's sphere of influence, two factors determined its freedom of action—the relative ability of Panama to resist American power and, as importantly, the relative willingness of Panama to legitimize that power. As a small and militarily weak nation, Panama could hardly resist the United States by force of arms. On the other hand, in the diplomatic climate of the Cold War, Panama could bargain with the United States over the price of legitimizing American power on the isthmus. Growing Panamanian national sentiment required the United States to channel compensating aid flows to Panama. In per capita terms, postwar Panama received more aid than any other country in Latin America. Fiscal transfers to Panama soon dwarfed the interest payments the Panama Canal made to the U.S. Treasury.

The red balance on America's possession of the Panama Canal meant that its retrocession to Panama was in the national interest—but it did not mean that retrocession would occur. There is no simple mechanistic model of decolonization. After all, a world in which empires immediately cast off regions as they produced more loss than gain would look very different from our own. Under normal circumstances, a negotiation between Panama and the United States regarding control over the Panama Canal would have been straightforward. The rub was that there was a third party involved, unrepresented at the negotiating table, but with significant influence in American domestic politics: the Zonians.

The Panama Canal administration's early policies had the unintended effect of producing a numerically small but highly influential class of what were essentially American colonial settlers. The Zonians—mainly American canal employees, ex-military personnel, and their dependents—lived American lifestyles in the Canal Zone literally hundreds of feet away from the relative poverty of Panama. They thwarted attempts to put the operation of the canal on a more businesslike footing and essentially captured the Panama Canal administration. The canal was eventually run on behalf of its primary stakeholders—that is to say, the Zonians. Ironically, Zonian administrative inefficiency exacerbated the Panama Canal's decline. Costs rose and safety fell. The incentives for the American managers of the Panama Canal became simply to avoid doing harm to the canal. The U.S. government was too large and too far away to be particularly vested in the Panama Canal's operation, absent some sort of disaster. By letting the Panama Canal become a comfortable sinecure, the Zonians made it even less valuable to the United States.

By the time President Jimmy Carter began public negotiations to return the canal to Panama in 1977, the concrete benefits to the United States from ownership of the canal had essentially disappeared. Despite this, it was still politically problematic for Carter to proceed with the treaty negotiations. The Zonians found allies in American politics. In a mirror image of Panamanian nationalism, American national sentiment for some voters required the United States to maintain its control over the entire Canal Zone. For the politicians who supported the status quo—such as the 1976 conservative Republican primary candidate, Ronald Reagan—the symbolic benefits of American national greatness outweighed the extremely small per capita economic loss caused by ownership of the Panama Canal.

Carter's decision was an act of political bravery. A different president, even if in favor of a canal handover, might not have had the same priorities. (Omar Torrijos, as military dictator of Panama, had no such problems; and in fact the treaties were wildly popular in Panama.) After a contentious battle, in 1978 the U.S. Senate ratified the two treaties that set the terms of the handover of the Panama Canal to the Panamanian government. The American public greeted the Panama Canal treaties with a notable lack of enthusiasm. The treaties had small positive effects on the economic and strategic interests of the United States—had it been otherwise, no president would have signed them—but those positive effects were small enough to be negligible per person for a country the size of the United States. It was hard for the American supporters of the treaties to generate much enthusiasm for an agreement with small concrete benefits but large symbolic costs. The domestic political cost of passing the treaties contributed to Carter's defeat by Ronald Reagan in 1980, albeit in a small way.

The Big Ditch marked the end of America's formal imperial control over Panamanian territory. The canal itself, however, would not be handed over until 1999, and the Neutrality Treaty provided the United States with a pretext to call off the handover should anything go seriously wrong during the transition. Panama needed to meet two additional preconditions for the United States to realize its promise to hand over control of the canal. First, Panama needed to have a government that would refrain from using the Panama Canal as a source of political patronage. Second, the Panamanian managers of the Panama Canal needed to be *at least* as efficient as their American predecessors. (Admittedly, by 1980 this bar was not terribly high.) Additionally, Panama needed to meet a third precondition if it was to make the most of the treaties' new opportunities. Instead of merely operating the Panama Canal at the same levels of efficiency as its previous American managers, Panamanian management of the canal needed to *exceed* the standards of their predecessors.

Many American opponents of the handover doubted Panamanian ability to manage the canal at all, let alone manage it more efficiently than its American administration. There was little in mid-century Panama to reassure outsiders that a Panamanian-controlled canal would be more than another source of patronage for Panamanian political elites. Corruption in Panama ran rampant. Panamanian elections meant little; few contests escaped charges of fraud, and governments regularly changed hands by extra-constitutional means. Panamanian political parties existed essentially as patronage devices. As military dictator, Omar Torrijos disrupted Panama's existing patronage networks in order to build his own counterintuitive coalition of the rural poor, students, teachers, soldiers, and bankers. It is possible, had Torrijos transferred power to a functioning Panamanian democracy, that the Panama Canal would have stayed reasonably inviolate and managerially competent. The example of the abrupt nationalization of the Suez Canal under Nasser showed that Egypt—a state not less corrupt than Panama under Torrijos—could run the Suez Canal as well as its former European owners.[24] (That said, the Suez Canal, being broad and lockless, was a far less technically complicated operation than the Panama Canal.) But Omar Torrijos's small plane crashed in 1981, killing the general three years before the scheduled transfer of power. Manuel Noriega took over in his stead. Panama would never be able to meet any positive precondition as long as Manuel Antonio "La Piña" Noriega controlled the government.

Ultimately, the United States removed Noriega from Panama by military force. This was not a spur-of-the-moment decision. Noriega had been useful for Washington's foreign policy in Central America, and he had personal allies in the Reagan administration. These facts led Noriega to miscalculate his worth to the United States. When his excesses became apparent, the United States pursued personal, diplomatic, political, judicial, and economic methods to cause Noriega to relinquish power. They all failed. In fact, the United States applied the largest set of economic sanctions ever used in the postwar period, engineering the equivalent of a major economic depression. But Noriega was a dictator: by definition, he was unresponsive to the popular will. He very well might have survived had he not made it clear that he intended to use the Panama Canal for political purposes. Once this happened, however, the remaining political lifetime of Noriega as "Maximum Leader" of Panama was measured in weeks.

The American invasion of 1989 could by itself no more create democracy in Panama than had U.S. military interventions in 1904, 1912, 1918, 1921, and 1925. Fortunately, after the fall of Noriega, a critical mass of the Panamanian electorate no longer felt obliged to follow traditional Panamanian politics. Manuel Noriega transformed Panamanian politics in spite of himself, breaking Panama's traditional patronage networks and party affiliations in order to advance his own personal power. In the process, a broad-based coalition of Panamanians mobilized against the dictator. After American troops captured the self-proclaimed "jefe máximo" in 1989, Panama's new democratic candidates needed to gain the support of a suspicious electorate not obliged to any party machine. A large bloc of swing voters emerged, enabling the creation of a democracy in which a winning electoral coalition could not simply rely on transferring wealth from the losers to the winners. The regime change of 1989 succeeded because there were now enough Panamanians convinced that a vigorous electoral democracy was in their best interest. The U.S. Army was the catalyst, not the cause.

In Panama's new political environment, the three preconditions for a successful handover of the Panama Canal were unmistakable to the Panamanian electorate. Panamanian democracy worked as a direct feedback against political interference in the operation of the Panama Canal. The transition to full Panamanian administration and modernization of the canal accelerated after 1989. In 1994, Panama easily passed new constitutional articles to ensure the political independence of the canal administration. Credible accusations of corrupting, politicizing, or even failing to invest sufficiently in the Panama Canal became an electoral kiss of death. In 2006 Panamanians evinced enough faith in their government

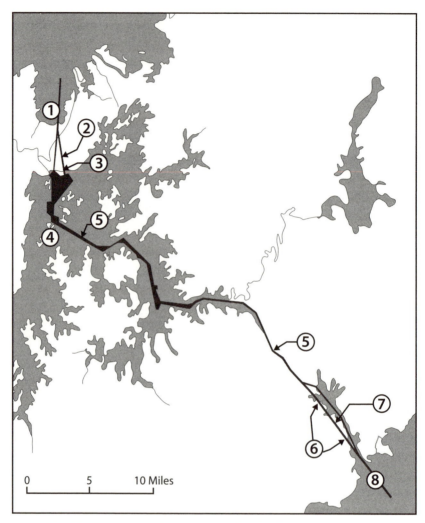

Map 9.1: The Panama Canal expansion project, 2007—
1. Deepening and widening of the Atlantic entrance channel.
2. New approach channel for the Atlantic Post-Panamax locks.
3. Atlantic Post-Panamax locks with three water savings basins per lock
   chamber.
4. Raising the maximum Gatun Lake operating water level.
5. Widening and deepening of the navigational channel of Gatun Lake and the
   Culebra Cut.
6. New approach channel for the Pacific Post-Panamax locks.
7. Pacific Post-Panamax locks with three water savings basins per lock chamber.
8. Deepening and widening of the Pacific entrance channel.

to vote overwhelmingly in favor of expanding the Panama Canal. A century after its construction, the fate of the Panama Canal was now firmly in the hands of Panamanians. (See map 9.1.)

THE FUTURE OF THE PANAMA CANAL

The final transfer of the Panama Canal from the United States to Panama—the Big Ditch of the Big Ditch—ensured that the Panama Canal entered the twenty-first century better managed than ever before in its history. Simultaneously, the country of Panama was more strongly positioned to capitalize on the presence of the Panama Canal than ever before. While Panama still suffered from a relatively high level of corruption, the nation was better educated and more democratically governed than at any other time in its history. Its relatively well-educated population, long use of the dollar, and the revenues generated by the Panama Canal gave Panama a fighting chance to make it into the First World.

There are still many ways Panama might fail. The Panamanian economy has historically lived and died by trade. The global economic downturn that began in 2008 caused global trade to contract at a rate more quickly than during the Great Depression. By early 2010 the downturn in trade appeared to have ended, but a risk remained that global trade would fail to recover. In the short run, nevertheless, the canal infrastructure projects approved before the crisis ensure that Panama enjoyed a buffer from the Great Recession, with the construction projects acting as an accidental Keynesian stimulus. In addition, Panamanians have reasons for optimism going ahead. The continuing growth of the Chinese economy stimulated a wave of new eastbound exports through the canal, from Brazilian soya to (astonishingly) American coal. If the Panama Canal declines in the future, it will be because of shifts in the global economy or (more likely) shifts in global geography— e.g., the opening of the Northwest Passage as a result of climate change—not because of a Panamanian inability to run the Panama Canal.

The Big Ditch also crystallized a shift in the United States' role in Latin America. America's imperialism in Panama was not particularly successful in terms of benefitting the Panamanians. Its political protectorate failed to create democracy. Its economic protectorate failed to create prosperity. Its Canal Zone enclave created a powerful colonial interest group that made it very hard for Washington to change its policies even when they were no longer in the national interest. The modern, negotiated "empire by invitation" that replaced the old system after 1989 appears to have been far more successful than the older version ever was. Rather than act as an imperial power, the United States now implicitly guarantees Panamanian security through the Neutrality Treaty and economic prosperity through Panama's use of the dollar and the recently negotiated U.S.-Panama Free Trade Agreement. In return, Panama adheres to the norms of democratic rule and professional management of the canal—which also happen to be in the country's own best interest.

There are pitfalls in this new role for the United States. Legal relationships between two elected democracies based on treaties are far less flexible than a patron-client relationship with an authoritarian satrapy. The danger, of course, is that with less power will come less responsibility. Nonetheless, the United States did not act as a particularly responsible patron when it had more power, and the Panamanian electorate seems to be doing a rather good job thus far of keeping Panama's own politicians in check. In all likelihood, the new relationship between Panama and the United States, centered as ever around the Panama Canal, will be healthier and more stable for both nations in the decades ahead and may provide an example for other countries with important interests in their own *vecinos extranjeros*.

NOTES

ONE Introduction to the Ditch

1. Under this definition, empires end in three ways. First, the stronger political community loses interest in using sanctions to impose its preferred policies on the weaker community. Second, the threat of sanctions (or the sanctions themselves) at the disposal of the stronger community lose their ability to compel the weaker. Third, the two political communities merge in some sense that is perceived as legitimate by the vast majority of both populations. Although we will use John Gaddis's felicitous phrase "empire by invitation" later on in this volume, a voluntary relinquishment of some amount of sovereign authority by one government to another is not truly imperialism by this definition if enforcement by sanctions is off the table.

2. Niall Ferguson and Moritz Schularick, "The Empire Effect: The Determinants of Country Risk in the First Age of Globalization, 1880–1913," *Journal of Economic History* 66, no. 2 (June 2006): 283–312; Kris James Mitchener and Marc Weidenmier, "Empire, Public Goods, and the Roosevelt Corollary," *Journal of Economic History* 65, no. 3 (September 2005): 658–92; Peter Svedberg, "Colonial Enforcement of Foreign Direct Investment," *Manchester School of Economic and Social Studies* 49, no. 1 (March 1981): 21–38; Michael Edelstein, "Realized Rates of Return on U.K. Home and Overseas Portfolio Investment in the Age of High Imperialism," *Explorations in Economic History* 13, no. 3 (July 1976): 283–329; Lance Edwin Davis and Robert A. Huttenback, *Mammon and the Pursuit of Empire: The Political Economy of British Imperialism, 1860–1912* (Cambridge: Cambridge University Press, 1986).

3. David Landes, "Some Thoughts on the Nature of Economic Imperialism," *Journal of Economic History* 21, no. 4 (December 1961): 496–512, 505.

4. Robert H. Bates, Avner Greif, Margaret Levi, Jean-Laurent Rosenthal, and Barry R. Weingast, *Analytic Narratives* (Princeton, NJ: Princeton University Press, 1998).

5. Robert William Fogel, *Railroads and American Economic Growth: Essays in Econometric History* (Baltimore: Johns Hopkins Press, 1964).

6. Stanley Lebergott, "The Returns to U.S. Imperialism, 1890–1929," *Journal of Economic History* 40, no. 2 (1980): 229–52.

7. William K. Hutchinson and Ricardo Ungo, "Social Saving of the Panama Canal" (working paper 04-W23, Vanderbilt University, 2004).

8. Colombia, *Libro azul: Documentos diplomáticos sobre el canal y la rebelión del Istmo de Panama* (Bogotá [Colombia]: Imprenta nacional, 1904).

9. Adam Clymer, *Drawing the Line at the Big Ditch: The Panama Canal Treaties and the Rise of the Right* (Lawrence: University Press of Kansas, 2008); Julie Greene, *The Canal Builders: Making America's Empire at the Panama Canal* (New York: Penguin Press, 2009).

TWO   Before the Ditch

1. Samuel Eliot Morison, *The European Discovery of America: The Southern Voyages, A.D. 1492–1616* (New York: Oxford University Press, 1974), 596–616; Hans Kraus, *Sir Francis Drake: A Pictorial Biography* (Amsterdam: N. Israel, 1970), available at http://www.loc.gov/rr/rarebook/catalog/drake/drake-5-spanishdef.html.

2. Mary W. Helms, *Ancient Panama: Chiefs in Search of Power* (Austin: University of Texas Press, 1979), 35.

3. Eugenia Ibarra, "Gold in the Everyday Lives of Indigenous Peoples of Sixteenth-Century Southern Central America," in *Gold and Power in Ancient Costa Rica, Panama, and Colombia*, ed.

Jeffrey Quilter and John W. Hoopes, 383–413 (Washington, DC: Dumbarton Oaks Research Library and Collection, 2003).

4. Helms, *Ancient Panama*, 55.

5. Pascual de Andagoya, *Narrative of the proceedings of Pedrarias Davila*, trans. Clements R. Markham, 23 (London: Hakluyt Society, 1865). Spanish text: "En este Nombre de Dios había cierta gente que se decían los Chuchurs, gente de lengua extraña de los otros: vinieron a poblar allí en canoas, por la mar, de hacia Honduras; y como la tierra era montuosa y enferma, antes se disminuyeron los que allí vinieron que se multiplicaron, y así había pocos; y destos pocos no quedó ninguno con el tratamiento que se les hizo después de poblado el Nombre de Dios." Pascual de Andagoya, *Relación y documentos*, edición de Adrián Blázquez, 97.

6. Izumi Shimada, "Evolution of Andean Diversity: Regional Formations (500 B.C.E.–C.E. 600)," in *The Cambridge History of the Native Peoples of the Americas*, vol. 3, part 1, ed. Frank Salomon and Stuart B. Schwartz, 350–517 (Cambridge: Cambridge University Press, 1999), especially "Meso-American-Northwest South American Connections," 430–34.

7. Linda A. Ramírez, "Exchange and Markets in the Sixteenth Century: A View from the North," in *Ethnicity, Markets, and Migration in the Andes: At the Crossroads of History and Anthropology*, ed. Brooke Larson, Olivia Harris, and Enrique Tandeter, 135–64 Durham, NC: Duke University Press, 1995).

8. Joanne Pillsbury, "The Thorny Oyster and the Origins of Empire: Implications of Recently Uncovered Spondylus Imagery from Chan Chan, Peru," *Latin American Antiquity* 7, no. 4 (December 1996): 313–40.

9. Richard Cooke, Ilean Isaza, John Griggs, Benoit Desjardins, and Luís Alberto Sánchez, "Who Crafted, Exchanged, and Displayed Gold in Pre-Columbian Panama?" in Quilter and Hoopes, *Gold and Power*, 91–158.

10. António Galvão, and Richard Hakluyt, *The Discoveries of the World from Their First Original Unto the Year of Our Lord 1555* (New York: Burt Franklin, 1963), 180. Portuguese text: "que

mandasse abrir esta terra de Castella do ouro & noua Espanha de mar, a mar, porque se podia fazer por quarto lugares, que he do Golfam de sam Miguel a Vraba, em que ha vinte & cinco legoas de trauesa, ou de Penama ao nombre de Dios, que ha dezasete, ou pello Sangra douro de Nicaraga, que começa em hua alagoa tres ou quarto legoas da parte do sul, & vay sair a agoa della ao norte, por onde nauegam barcas, & nauios pequenos. Há outro passo Tagante pera o rio da Vera Cruz, que tambem se podia abrir estreito, & se se fizesse, nauegar se hia das Canarias a Maluco por baixo do zodiaco clima temperada, & em menos tempo & com menos perigo, que pello cabo de Boa esperança nem estreito do Magalhães."

11. Galvão and Hakluyt, *Discoveries of the World*, 174–79. The Spaniards did not accomplish this goal until Andrés de Urdaneta's voyage from Cebu to Acapulco in 1565.

12. Galvão and Hakluyt, *Discoveries of the World*, 180.

13. Ibid.

14. Gerstle Mack, *The Land Divided* (New York: Alfred Knopf, 1944), 41.

15. Mack, *Land Divided*, 41.

16. Ibid.

17. Pascual de Andagoya to Charles V, letter, October 22, 1534, *Relación y documentos*, edición de Adrián Blázquez, 219–20. Spanish text: "Por otra manda V.M. que se vea por dónde se podía juntar esta mar con la otra; también fue éste aviso de hombre de muy leve ingenio, y que habrá de haber paseado y entendido poco la tierra. Yo haré lo que V.M. manda en este verano que entrará ahora por Navidad, porque sin quemarse las sabanas, ni se puede andar, ni ver. Certifico a V.M. que no creo que hay príncipe en el mundo que con todo su poder saliese con ello, cuanto más poderse hacer con ayuda de los vecinos destas partes."

18. Mack, *Land Divided*, 46–47.

19. José de Acosta, *Natural and Moral History of the Indies*, bk. 3, chap. 10, ed. Jane E. Mangan, trans. Frances Lopez-Morillas, 123–24. The Spanish text of this passage: "Han platicado algunos de romper este camino de siete leguas, y juntar el un mar con el otro, para hacer cómodo el pasaje al Pirú, en el cual dan más costa

y trabajo diez y ocho leguas de tierra que hay entre Nombre de Dios y Panamá, que dos mil y trescientas que hay de mar. Mas para mí tengo por cosa vana tal pretensión . . . pero eslo para mí que ningún poder humano bastará a derribar el monte fortísimo e impenetrable que Dios puso entre lo dos mares, de montes y peñas durísmas que bastan a sustenar la furia de ambos mares. Y cuando fuese a hombres posible, sería a mi parecer muy justo temer del castigo del cielo, querer enmendar las obras que el Hacedor, con sumo acuerdo y providencia, ordenó en la fábrica de este Universo." From José de Acosta, *Historia natural y moral de las Indias*, edición de José Alcina Franch, 178.

20. Christopher Ward, *Imperial Panama: Commerce and Conflict in Isthmian America, 1550–1800* (Albuquerque: University of New Mexico Press, 1993), 56.

21. Peter Martyr D'Anghera, *De Orbe Novo*, vol. 2, trans. Francis Augustus McNutt (New York: Putnam's, 1912), 214.

22. Linda Newson, "The Depopulation of Nicaragua in the Sixteenth Century," *Journal of Latin American Studies* 14, no. 2 (1982): 278.

23. Ward, *Imperial Panama*, 35.

24. Linda Newson, "The Demographic Impact of Colonization," in the *Cambridge Economic History of Latin America*, vol. 1, ed. Victor Bulmer-Thomas, John Coatsworth and Roberto Cortes Conde, 143–184 (Cambridge: Cambridge University Press, 2006), 154.

25. *Encyclopædia Britannica Online*, s.v. "Central America," http://www.britannica.com/EBchecked/topic/102196/Central-America (accessed September 15, 2008).

26. William Sherman, *Forced Native Labor in Sixteenth-Century Central America* (Lincoln: University of Nebraska Press, 1979), 16–17.

27. David Radell, "Exploration and Commerce on Lake Nicaragua and Río San Juan, 1524–1800," *Journal of Interamerican Studies and World Affairs* 12, no. 1 (January 1970): 107–25, 113.

28. Hubert Howe Bancroft, *History of Central America*, vol. 1, *1501–1530* (San Francisco: A. L. Bancroft, 1883), 577–94.

29. "Carta con documentos del Licenciado Francisco de Castañeda a S.M.," León, March 30, 1529, in *Colección Somoza: Documentos para la historia de Nicaragua*, ed. Andrés Vega Bolaños (Madrid: Imprenta Viuda de Galo Sáez, 1954–57), 1:479–508.

30. Sherman, *Forced Native Labor*, 68.

31. Ibid.

32. "Carta con documentos del Licenciado Francisco de Castañeda a S.M.," León, March 30, 1529, in *Colección Somoza*, 1: 479–508.

33. "Información que hace a S.M. el Escribano Francisco Sánchez," Granada, August 2, 1535, in *Colección Somoza*, 3:406–12.

34. Newson, "Depopulation of Nicaragua," 253–86, 273; David Radell and James Parsons, "Realejo: A Forgotten Colonial Port and Shipbuilding Center in Nicaragua," *Hispanic-American Historical Review* 51 (1971): 295–312, 300–301.

35. "Carta con documentos del Licenciado Francisco de Castañeda a S.M.," León, March 30, 1529, in *Colección Somoza*, 1: 479–508.

36. "Registro del navio Santiago," León, April 26, 1543, and July 17, 1543, in *Colección Somoza*, 10:485, 9:39; "Registro del galeón San Esteban de la Cruz," Xagueyes, July 12, 1542, in *Colección Somoza*, 10:516–18.

37. Sherman, *Forced Native Labor*, 75.

38. "Información que hace a S.M. el Escribano Francisco Sánchez," Granada, August 2, 1535, in *Colección Somoza*, 3:406–12; and "Petición que Diego Núñez de Mercado, Alcalde de la Fortaleza de la Ciudad de León, presentó al Consejo de las Indias," Madrid, November 16, 1541, in *Colección Somoza*, 7:151–224.

39. Sherman, *Forced Native Labor*, 75–76.

40. "Información que hace a S.M. el Escribano Francisco Sánchez," Granada, August 2, 1535, in *Colección Somoza*, 3:406–12.

41. David Radell, "The Indian Slave Trade and Population of Nicaragua during the Sixteenth Century," in *The Native Population of the Americas in 1492*, ed. William Denevan (Madison: University of Wisconsin Press, 1976), 67–76.

42. Newson, "Depopulation," 264.

43. Murdo J. MacLeod, *Spanish Central America: A Socio-economic History, 1520–1720* (Austin: University of Texas Press, 2008), 50–52.

44. MacLeod, *Spanish Central America*, 98.

45. Portobelo replaced Nombre de Díos after Sir Francis Drake sacked the Nombre de Díos in 1595.

46. Ward, *Imperial Panama*, 19–21.

47. eWard, *Imperial Panama*, 67–77. In 1721–39, textiles accounted for 87 percent of all imports.

48. Georges Schelle, *Histoire Politique de la traite negriie aux Indes de Castille, contrats et traités d'Asiento* (Paris: 1906), 1:502–3.

49. Omar Jaén Suárez, *La población del Istmo de Panamá* (Madrid: Agencia Española de Cooperación Internacional, 1998), 248.

50. Ward, *Imperial Panama*, 34–36.

51. Jaén Suárez, *La población*, 256.

52. The town mayor controlled the warehouses, making it a lucrative office.

53. Ward, *Imperial Panama*, 56–57.

54. Ibid.

55. The quote, found in Ward, *Imperial Panama*, comes from W. D. Weatherhead, *Account of the Late Expedition Across the Isthmus* (London: 1821), 70–80.

56. Ward, *Imperial Panama*, 62–63.

57. Jaén Suárez, *La población*, 130; and Alfredo Castillero Calvo, *Economía terciaria y sociedad, Panamá siglos XVI y XVII* (Panamá: Instituto Nacional de Cultura de Panamá, 1980), 30–31.

58. Kris Lane, "Captivity and Redemption: Aspects of Slave Life in Early Colonial Quito and Popayán," *The Americas* 57, no. 2 (October 2000): 225–46, 235.

59. Charles Haring, *Trade and Navigation between Spain and the Indies* (Cambridge, MA: Harvard University Press, 1918), 183.

60. Jaén Suárez, *La población*, 130.

61. Ward, *Imperial Panama*, 55–58.

62. MacLeod, *Spanish Central America*, 274; Ward, *Imperial Panama*, 60–61.

63. Ward, *Imperial Panama*, 61.

64. Jaén Suárez, *La población*, 257.

65. Ward, *Imperial Panama*, 63–65, 231 note 67.

66. Enrique Tandeter, "The Mining Industry," in *The Cambridge Economic History of Latin America*, ed. Victor Bulmer-Thomas, John Coatsworth, and Roberto Cortés Conde (Cambridge: Cambridge University Press, 2006), 1:330.

67. Ward, *Imperial Panama*, 130.

68. Ward, *Imperial Panama*, 151.

69. Ward, *Imperial Panama*, 155–57.

70. Ward, *Imperial Panama*, 157.

71. Raymond Rydell, *Cape Horn to the Pacific: The Rise and Decline of an Ocean Highway* (Berkeley: University of California Press, 1952), 23–43.

72. Raymond A. Rydell, *Cape Horn to the Pacific; the rise and decline of an ocean highway*, University of California Press, 1952, 44–57.

73. J. Ignacio Mendez, "Azul y Rojo: Panama's Independence in 1840," *Hispanic American Historical Review* 60, no. 2 (May 1980): 269–93.

74. Alexander von Humboldt, *Political Essay on the Kingdom of New Spain* (London, 1811), 1:18–43.

75. Ibid., 36.

76. Ibid.

77. Ibid., 45.

78. Ibid., 35–36.

79. Ibid., 45.

80. Ibid., 37.

81. "¡Qué bello sería que el Istmo de Panamá fuese para nosotros lo que el de Corinto para los griegos!" Translation from *El Libertador: Writings of Simón Bolívar*, ed. David Bushnell, trans. Fred Fornoff (New York: Oxford University Press, 2003), 28.

82. Diego Uribe Vargas, *Los últimos derechos de Colombia en el Canal de Panama: el Tratado Uribe Vargas-Ozores* ([Bogotá]: Facultad de Derecho, Ciencias Políticas y Sociales y Empresa Editorial, Universidad Nacional de Colombia, 2003), 19–23.

83. *Minutes of Proceedings of the Institution of Civil Engineers* (London: 1849–50), 9:68–69.

84. *Minutes of Proceedings of the Institution of Civil Engineers* (London: 1849–50), 9:59.

85. John Augustus Lloyd, "Account of Levellings Carried across the Isthmus of Panama, to Ascertain the Relative Height of the Pacific Ocean at Panama and of the Atlantic at the Mouth of the River Chagres; Accompanied by Geographical and Topographical Notices of the Isthmus," *Philosophical Transactions of the Royal Society of London* (1830), 120:59–68.

86. Johann Wolfgang von Goethe, *Conversations with Eckermann*, trans. John Oxenford (New York: M. Walter Dunne, 1901), 180.

87. William Duane, *A visit to Colombia, in the years 1822 & 1823, by Laguayra and Caracas, over the Cordillera to Bogota, and thence by the Magdalena to Cartagena* (Philadelphia: T. H. Palmer, 1826), iv.

88. Mack, *Land Divided*, 123. Colombia was called New Granada at the time.

89. E. Taylor Parks, *Colombia and the United States, 1765–1934* (Durham, NC: Duke University Press, 1935), 185.

90. Iris Guiver Wilkinson, [Robin Hyde], *Check to Your King: The Life History of Charles, Baron de Thierry, King of Nukahiva, Sovereign Chief of New Zealand* (Wellington: A. H. & A. W. Reed, 1960), 50–54.

91. Wilkinson, *Check to Your King*, 74.

92. Marion Mills Miller, ed., *Great Debates in American History* (New York: Little and Ives, 1913), 3:326.

93. Parks, *Colombia*, 184–85.

94. Ibid., 185–86.

95. Parks, *Colombia*, 186–87; John Steuart, *Bogotá in 1836–7* (New York: Harper and Brothers, 1838), 246, 250.

96. Steuart, *Bogotá*, 247–48.

97. Ibid., 249–50.

98. Parks, *Colombia*, 187–88; Steuart, *Bogotá*, 251–53.

99. Mack, *Land Divided*, 126.

100. Parks, *Colombia*, 188.

101. Steuart, *Bogotá*, 254.

102. John Haskell Kemble, "The Gold Rush by Panama, 1848–1851," *Pacific Historical Review* 18, no. 1 (February 1949): 45–56.

103. Parks, *Colombia*, 200–207; Stephen J. Randall, *Colombia and the United States: Hegemony and Interdependence* (Athens: University of Georgia Press, 1992), 26–30; Michael L. Conniff, *Panama and the United States: The Forced Alliance* (Athens: University of Georgia Press, 1992), 18–20.

104. Parks, *Colombia*, 208. It should be noted that Bidlack wrote this to Buchanan after signing the treaty, which he did not have the authority to make.

105. George Minot, ed., *Statutes at Large and Treaties of the United States of America from December 1, 1845, to March 3, 1851* (Boston: Little, Brown, 1862), 9:897–98.

106. Parks, *Colombia*, 207–10.

107. Uribe Vargas, *Los últimos derechos*, 54.

108. John Haskell Kemble, *The Panama Route: 1848–1869* (Berkeley: University of California Press, 1943), 12–23.

109. Kemble, "Gold Rush," 45–56.

110. Mack, *Land Divided*, 141.

111. Calculated from *Historical Statistics of the United States, Millennial Edition*, ed. Susan B. Carter, Scott Sigmund Gartner, Michael R. Haines, Alan L. Olmstead, Richard Sutch, and Gavin Wright (Cambridge: Cambridge University Press, 2006), 1:193.

112. Kemble, *Panama Route*, 31–35.

113. Ibid., 39.

114. David I. Folkman, *The Nicaragua Route* (Salt Lake City: University of Utah Press, 1972), 18.

115. William Scroggs, "William Walker and the Steamship Corporation in Nicaragua," *American Historical Review* 10, no. 4 (July 1905): 793.

116. Orville Childs, *Report of the Survey and Estimates of the Cost of Constructing the Interoceanic Ship Canal* (New York:

W.M.C. Bryant, 1852), 138. Current dollars converted to 2009 prices using the GDP deflator.

117. Folkman, *Nicaragua Route*, 27–33.

118. Lawrence Clayton, "The Nicaragua Canal in the Nineteenth Century: Prelude to American Empire in the Caribbean," *Journal of Latin American Studies* 19, no. 2 (November 1987): 326. It should be noted that $31 million was no small investment for Britain in 1852. As a share of GDP, it would be the equivalent of a £16 *billion* project in 2009.

119. Folkman, *Nicaragua Route*, 163.

120. T. J. Stiles, *The First Tycoon: The Epic Life of Cornelius Vanderbilt* (New York: Random House, 2009), 204.

121. Ibid., 205.

122. Ibid., 197.

123. Scroggs, "William Walker," 793.

124. Tim Merrill, ed. *Nicaragua: A Country Study* (Washington, DC: GPO, 1993).

125. Stiles, *First Tycoon*, 203.

126. Ibid., 211.

127. *Treaties between Turkey and Foreign Powers, 1535–1855* (Turkey: Foreign Office, 1855), 276–82.

128. Lawrence O. Ealy, *Yanqui Politics and the Isthmian Canal* (University Park: Pennsylvania State University Press, 1971), 19–24. British Honduras (now Belize) was not considered part of Central America for the purposes of the treaty. See Charles Huberich, *The Trans-Isthmian Canal: A Study in American Diplomatic History (1825–1904)* (Austin: University of Texas, 1904), 10–11.

129. Stiles, *First Tycoon*, 211–12.

130. Ealy, *Yanqui Politics*, 25.

131. Kemble, *Panama Route*, 179.

132. Kemble, *Panama Route*, 178; Parks, *Colombia*, 324.

133. Henry Poor, *History of the Railroads and Canals of the United States* (New York: John Schultz, 1860), 300.

134. Mack, *Land Divided*, p. 150.

135. Francis L. Hawks, "The Late John L. Stephens," *Putnam's Monthly Magazine of American Literature, Science and Art* 1, no. 1 (January 1853): 64–68.

136. Kemble, *Panama Route*, 181–82.

137. Mack, *Land Divided*, p. 157.

138. Kemble, *Panama Route*, 181–82.

139. Kemble, *Panama Route*, 185–86.

140. Fessenden N. Otis, *Illustrated History of the Panama Railroad*, 2nd ed. (New York: Harper, 1862), 22.

141. Wage rates from Kemble, *Panama Route*, 190. Steerage tickets from Panama City to California calculated as half the value of a $225 steerage fare from New York to San Francisco. Mack, *Land Divided*, 144.

142. *Historical Statistics of the United States, Millennial Edition*, 2:262–63.

143. Lucy M. Cohen, "The Chinese of the Panama Railroad: Preliminary Notes on the Migrants of 1854 Who 'Failed,'" *Ethnohistory* 18, no. 4 (Autumn 1971): 309–20; and Fessenden Otis, *A History of the Panama Railroad* (New York: Harper and Brothers, 1867), 35–36.

144. Michael Conniff, *Black Labor on a White Canal*, 17; and Kemble, *Panama Route*, 191–93.

145. For an example of the extremely diverse origins of labor working on the Panama Railroad, see Moustafa Bayoumi, "Moving Beliefs: The Panama Manuscript of Sheikh Sana See and African Diasporic Islam," *Interventions* 5, no. 1 (2003): 58–81.

146. According to Kemble, the Panama Railroad Company had spent $6,564,552.95 on construction by the time it completed the route across the isthmus. Kemble, *Panama Route*, 195.

147. Poor, *History of the Railroads*, 300.

148. Poor, *History of the Railroads*, 302. For comparison, the overruns on the Panama Railroad are in the same ballpark as contemporary cost overruns on urban heavy rail projects in the United States. Atlanta's MARTA, for example, ran over by 58 percent in inflation-adjusted terms. Baltimore's Metro Subway ran over by 60 percent, Los Angeles's Red Line by 47 percent, Miami's Metro-

rail by 33 percent, San Francisco's BART by 60 percent, and Washington's Metro by 83 percent. All estimates save San Francisco from Nasiru Dantata, Ali Touran, and Donald Schneck, "Trends in U.S. Rail Transit Project Cost Overrun" (paper presented at the eighty-fifth annual meeting of the Transportation Research Board, January 22–26, 2006, Washington, DC).

149. Mack, *Land Divided*, 153.

150. Kemble, *Panama Route*, 186; Joseph L. Schott, *Rails Across Panama* (Indianapolis: Bobbs-Merrill, 1967), 192.

151. Kemble, *Panama Route*, 196.

152. For comparison, $28.5 billion is twice the cost of Boston's Big Dig, including that project's astounding overruns. All calculations made using data from Samuel Williamson, "Six Ways to Compute the Relative Value of a U.S. Dollar Amount, 1790 to Present," MeasuringWorth, 2009, and Louis Johnston and Samuel Williamson, "What Was the U.S. GDP Then?" MeasuringWorth, 2009, available at http://www.measuringworth.com.

153. The Golden Gate Bridge's final construction cost came to $33.66 million. As a constant fraction of GDP, $33.66 million in 1932–37 was the equivalent of $8.3 billion in 2009.

154. Mack, *Land Divided*, 158.

155. Matthew Fontaine Maury, "Maury's estimate of the resources of the Gulf of Mexico and of the Caribbean sea, and of the importance of interoceanic communication," in John T. Sullivan, *Report of Historical and Technical Information Relating to the Problem of Interoceanic Communication by Way of the American Isthmus* (Washington, DC: GPO, 1883), 149–58.

156. Calculated from data in William Goetzmann, Roger Ibbotson, and Liang Peng, "A New Historical Database for the NYSE, 1815 to 1925" (working paper 00-13, Yale International Center for Finance, March 5, 2001), 24. The total return includes both dividends and capital gains.

157. Mack, *Land Divided*, 286.

158. W. Rodney Long, *Railways of Central America and the West Indies* (Washington, DC: GPO, 1925), 124.

159. Ibid.

160. Henry Petroski, *Engineers of Dreams: Great Bridge Builders and the Spanning of America* (New York: Knopf, 1995), 22–29.

161. Ibid., 37–59.

162. "The Interoceanic Ship Railway," *Scientific American* 51, no. 26 (December 27, 1884): 428–31; John A. Dillon, "Tehuantepec and the Eads Ship Railway," *Harper's New Monthly Magazine* 63, no. 378 (November 1881): 905–11. The Ship Railway was that week's cover story for *Scientific American*.

163. Tehuantepec Railway Company, *The Tehuantepec Ship Railway: Its Practicability and Commercial Features* (New York: Bowne, 1884), frontispiece.

164. *Scientific American*, "Interoceanic Ship Railway," 429.

165. James Buchanan Eads, "Address Before The House Select Committee On Inter-Oceanic Canals, 9th Of March, 1880, In Reply To Count De Lesseps," in *Addresses and Papers of James B. Eads* (St. Louis: Slawson, 1884), 418. Also see Tehuantepec Railway Company, *The Tehuantepec Ship Railway: Its Practicability and Commercial Features* (New York: Bowne, 1884), 42. In 1880, $75 million is the equivalent of $1.5 billion, using the GDP deflator. It was also the equivalent of 0.7 percent of U.S. GDP, or $105 billion in 2009.

166. Tehuantepec Railway Company, *Tehuantepec Ship Railway*, 38.

167. Mack, *Land Divided*, 234.

168. Petroski, *Engineers of Dreams*, 64.

169. Armando Rojas Rosales, "Transporte ferroviario en el Istmo de Tehuantepec, 1896–1913" (paper presented at the Second Congress of Economic History [Segundo Congreso de Historia Económica] held by the Mexican Association of Economic History [Asociación Mexicana De Historia Económica], October 27–29, 2004, Mexico City).

170. Edward B. Glick, "The Tehuantepec Railroad: Mexico's White Elephant," *Pacific Historical Review* 22 (1953): 373–82, 373.

171. Cited in Paul Garner, "The Politics of National Development in Late Porfirian Mexico: The Reconstruction of the Tehuan-

tepec National Railway, 1896–1907," *Bulletin of Latin American Research* 14, no. 3 (September 1995): 339–56, 348. Authors' own translation from the Spanish.

172. Petroski, *Engineers of Dreams*, 60–62.

173. *The Mexican Year Book: A Statistical, Financial, and Economic Annual, Compiled from Official and Other Returns* (London: McCorquodale, 1912), 87–88.

174. International Bureau of the American Republics, *Bulletin of the Pan American Union* (Washington, DC: GPO, 1910), 630.

175. "Tehuantepec Railroad Opened by Gen. Diaz," *New York Times*, January 24, 1907, 3.

176. The total cumulative peso cost to the Mexican government of 45.7 million from International Bureau of the American Republics, *Mexico*, 58th Cong., 3rd sess., doc. 145, pt. 5 (Washington, DC: GPO, 1904), 331–32. Subsidy expenditures in particular years were identified from data in "El Canal de Panamá y el Ferrocarril Nacional de Tehuantepec," *Economista Mexicano*, August 20, 1904. We subtracted those from the total and assumed the remainder was spent evenly in 1883–87 and 1900–1904. We converted peso expenditures to dollars at the current exchange rate.

177. International Bureau of the American Republics, *Bulletin of the Pan American Union*, 87.

178. Pearson's stake in the railroad from *Mexican Year Book*, 87–88. The cost of the ports from International Bureau of the American Republics, *Bulletin of the Pan American Union*, 608. A similar estimate can be found in Phillip Lee Phillips, *Mexico: A Geographical Sketch, with Special Reference to Economic Conditions and Prospects of Future Development* (Washington, DC: GPO, 1900), 282.

179. *Mexican Year Book*, 87–88. The first loan was for £2,000,000 at 5 percent, amortized for forty years starting in 1914. The second loan was authorized for £1,500,000 at 4.5 percent, but the company only issued £400,000.

180. "El Canal de Panamá y el Ferrocarril Nacional de Tehuantepec," *Economista Mexicano*, August 20, 1904.

181. The difference is less stark as a percentage of U.S. GDP, although it isn't clear whether that is a relevant measure. As a percentage of U.S. GDP, the Tehuantepec National Railroad and ancillary construction was the equivalent of a $46.3 billion project in 2007, compared to $27.2 billion for a project the relative size of the Panama Railroad. We deflated expenditures using the index for the year in which they were made, as best as could be estimated given the available data. Samuel Williamson, "Six Ways to Compute the Relative Value of a U.S. Dollar Amount, 1790 to Present," MeasuringWorth, 2009; and Louis Johnston and Samuel Williamson, "What Was the U.S. GDP Then?" MeasuringWorth, 2009, available at http://www.measuringworth.com.

182. Glick, "White Elephant," 375, 377–378; John S. Kendall, *Seven Mexican Cities* (New Orleans: Picayune Job Print, 1906), 64.

183. Humboldt, *Political Essay*, 26.

184. W. J. Steenburgh, D. M. Schultz, and B. A. Colle, "The Structure and Evolution of Gap Outflow over the Gulf of Tehuantepec, Mexico," *Monthly Weather Review* 126 (1998): 2673–91.

THREE   Preparing the Ditch

1. Werner Baer, "The Promoting and Financing of the Suez Canal," *Business History Review* 30, no. 4 (December 1956): 361–81, 365.

2. Baer, "Promoting," 369.

3. Twenty-four percent of the shares were owned by the Egyptian government as a dependency of the Ottoman Empire, while another 21 percent were personally owned by the Khedive. *1911 Encyclopedia Britannica*, vol. V26, s.v. "Suez Canal," 25.

4. In fact, the company did not receive its subscribed capital all at once. French law fixed the actual purchase price of the shares at the nominal declared value of 500 francs, but let purchasers pay in over time. A share initially cost 50 francs, or US$9.72 at the time. Shareholders needed to pay in an additional 50 francs in 1859, 100 francs in 1860, and 50 francs in 1862, 1864, and 1866. Baer, "Promoting," 376. Conversions from francs to dollars made using

annual exchange rate data from the Global Financial Database, http://www.globalfinancialdata.com/ (accessed March 2009).

5. This amounted to 84 million francs. Forty-five percent of the indemnity was due to the abolition of corvée labor. *1911 Encyclopedia Britannica*, vol. V26, s.v. "Suez Canal," 25.

6. *A handbook for travellers in Egypt: including descriptions of the course of the Nile through Egypt and Nubia, Alexandria, Cairo, the pyramids and Thebes, the Suez Canal, the peninsula of Mount Sinai, the oases, the fyoom, etc*, (London: John Murray, 1875), 233.

7. Baer, "Promoting," 378.

8. *1911 Encyclopedia Britannica*, vol. V26, s.v. "Suez Canal," 25.

9. *A handbook for travellers in Egypt*, 233.

10. Calculated from figures in *1911 Encyclopedia Britannica*, vol. V26, s.v. "Suez Canal."

11. In 2007 dollars (using the U.S. GDP deflator), the Suez Canal cost $1.2 billion. Calculated using the indices from Johnston and Williamson, "What Was the U.S. GDP Then?" Measuring-Worth, 2008.

12. David G. McCullough, *The Path Between the Seas: The Creation of the Panama Canal, 1870–1914* (New York: Simon and Schuster, 1977), 45–59.

13. "Piercing the American Isthmus," *Scribner's*, June 1879, 268–80; McCullough, *Path Between Seas*, 62–65.

14. Senate Ex. Doc. 112, 46th Cong., 2nd sess., 84. The staggered profit sharing timetable was modified from the original terms of the contract, which specified a flat rate of 5 percent, to terms more favorable to the Colombians.

15. *New York World*, January 29, 1880; Tracy Robinson, *Panama: A Personal Record of Forty-six Years, 1861–1907* (New York: Star and Herald, 1907), 161.

16. A. G. Menocal, "Intrigues at the Panama Canal Congress," *North American Review* 129, no. 274 [Boston] (September 1879): 288–93.

17. McCullough, *Path Between Seas*, 73.

18. Mack, *Land Divided*, 296.

19. Mack, *Land Divided*, 301.

20. José Carlos Rodrigues, *The Panama Canal: Its History, Its Political Aspects, and Financial Difficulties* (New York: Charles Scribner's Sons, 1885), 76.

21. Mack, *Land Divided*, 308.

22. Mack, *Land Divided*, 310–13. Mack gives a breakdown of shareholder distribution on page 313.

23. Long, *Railways*, 124.

24. As anticipated, De Lesseps's company assumed the Panama Railroad's debts of $7 million. *Report of the Isthmian Canal Commission, 1899–1901* (Washington, DC: GPO, 1902), 204; Robinson, *Panama*, 159–60.

25. Carlos Rodrigues, *Panama Canal*, 111–13.

26. Donald F. MacDonald, "Outline of Canal Zone Geology," in *The Panama Canal, an Engineering Treatise*, ed. George W. Goethals (New York: McGraw-Hill, 1916), 1:79–83.

27. Philippe Bunau-Varilla, *Panama, The Creation, Destruction, and Resurrection* (New York: McBride, 1914), 68–70.

28. William Gorgas, "Mortality in Panama," *Journal of the American Medical Association* 58 (1912): 907–9. Gorgas's exact figure is 22,189, "from the best information I can get, and which I consider accurate."

29. Bunau-Varilla, *Panama*, 44.

30. "The Panama Canal. III. Disease and the Weapons with Which It Is Fought," *New York Tribune*, August 22, 1886, 9.

31. McCullough, *Path Between Seas*, 171–72.

32. Conniff, *Black Labor on a White Canal*, 17.

33. Peso revenues from Suarez, *La población*, 308. Exchange rates from Marco Palacios, *Coffee in Colombia, 1850–1970* (Cambridge: Cambridge University Press, 2002), 262–63.

34. Suarez, *La población*, 525.

35. *Report of the Isthmian Canal Commission, 1899–1901*, 207–8; "The Plans of De Lesseps," *New York Times*, January 20, 1888; "Locks in the Panama Canal," *New York Times*, June 7, 1888.

36. Mack, *Land Divided*, 358.

37. Chambre des Députés, "Rapport fait au nom de la Commission d'enquête chargée de faire la lumière sur les allégations

portées à la tribune à l'occasion des Affaires de Panama," *5e législature, session de 1893,* no. 2921, vol. 1.

38. "De Lesseps Is Despondent," *New York Times,* February 6, 1889.

39. Mack, *Land Divided,* 361–63.

40. *Report of the Isthmian Canal Commission, 1899–1901,* 209; "The Panama Canal," *New York Times,* February 10, 1889.

41. "Leaving the Isthmus," *New York Times,* March 14, 1889; "Work At Panama Stopped," *New York Times,* March 28, 1889.

42. Chambre des Députés, "Rapport fait au nom de la Commission," 120.

43. Ovidio Díaz Espino, *How Wall Street Created a Nation* (New York: Four Walls Eight Windows, 2001), 11–12.

44. Conniff, *Panama and the United States,* 53.

45. Ralph Avery, *America's Triumph at Panama* (Chicago: L.W. Walter, 1913).

46. Maron J. Simon, *The Panama Affair* (New York: Scribner, 1971).

47. "La Chesnaye in Sorrow," *New York Times,* December 8, 1894.

48. "Piercing the American Isthmus," *Scribner's* (June 1879): 268–80. Kelley had previously sponsored a mission to the Atrato River for a possible canal route on the basis of Humboldt's accounts, in fact meeting with Humboldt in 1856, when Humboldt was eighty-eight years old. Kelley later favored a tunnel route through the isthmus.

49. Senate Doc. 112, 46th Cong., 2nd sess., 1; *New York Times,* "The Great Canal Project," March 9, 1880, 2.

50. Nicaragua Canal Construction Company, *The Interoceanic Canal of Nicaragua,* app. 5; "The Nicaraguan Treaty," *New York Times,* December 15, 1884.

51. Huberich, *Trans-Isthmian Canal,* 21.

52. The actual title used by elected provincial chief executives in Colombia at the time was "presidente." Núñez used the word "gobernador" to describe the appointed officials that would replace the *presidentes.* For clarity, however, the text in this chapter uses the word "governor" to describe the provincial *presidentes.*

53. Daniel Wicks, "Dress Rehearsal: United States Intervention on the Isthmus of Panama, 1885," *Pacific Historical Review* 49, no. 4 (November 1980): 587.

54. Section 2 of the Neutrality Act of 1838 reads: "The several officers mentioned in the foregoing section shall be, and they are hereby respectively authorized and required to seize any vessel or vehicle, and all arms or munitions of war, about to pass the frontier of the United States for any place within any foreign state, or colony, conterminous with the United States, where the character of the vessel or vehicle, and the quantity of arms and munitions, or other circumstances shall furnish probable cause to believe that the said vessel or vehicle, arms or munitions of war are intended to be employed by the owner or owners thereof, or any other person or persons, with his or their privity, in carrying on any military expedition or operations within the territory or dominions of any foreign prince or state, or any colony, district, or people conterminous with the United States, and with whom the United States are at peace."

55. Mack, *Land Divided*, 352–53.

56. "Aspinwall Laid Waste," *New York Times*, April 1, 1885; "Swept Away by the Flames," *New York Times*, April 2, 1885.

57. "The Burned City," *New York Times*, September 24, 1890.

58. Mack, *Land Divided*, pp 352.

59. Wicks, "Dress Rehearsal," 581–605, 595–96.

60. U.S. Department of State, *Foreign Relations of the United States: Index to the Executive Documents of the House of Representatives for the First Session of the Forty-ninth Congress, 1885–86*, IV–V.

61. Mack, *Land Divided*, 354.

62. Nicaragua Canal Construction Company, *Interoceanic Canal*, app. 2.

63. Roscoe Hill, "The Nicaraguan Canal Idea to 1913," *Hispanic American Historical Review* 28, no. 2 (1948): 197–211, 203.

64. Ibid., 197–211, 207.

65. *Report of the Isthmian Canal Commission*, 79–80.

66. Archibald Ross Colquhoun, *The Key of the Pacific* (New York: Longmans, Greene, 1898), 403, 408. The agreement gave Costa Rica

a 1.5 percent interest in the canal, unless the MCC issued less than the $100 million in capital that its U.S. charter authorized, in which case Costa Rica would receive at least $1.5 million in shares.

67. *Report of the Isthmian Canal Commission*, 110.

68. Mack, *Land Divided*, 220–21.

69. Lawrence Clayton, "The Nicaragua Canal in the Nineteenth Century: Prelude to American Empire in the Caribbean," *Journal of Latin American Studies* 19, no. 2 (1987): 323–52, 328.

70. *Report of the Isthmian Canal Commission, 1899–1901*, 409–10.

71. "The Oregon Sails For Callao," *New York Times*, March 20, 1898; "Destination of the Oregon," *New York Times*, March 27, 1898; "The Oregon in No Danger," *New York Times*, April 4, 1898; "No News of the Oregon," *New York Times*, April 22, 1898; "The Oregon in Danger," *New York Times*, April 23, 1898; "The Oregon Heard From," *New York Times*, April 24, 1898; "No Anxiety about the Oregon," *New York Times*, May 17, 1898; "Oregon in Home Waters," *New York Times*, May 26, 1898; "The Oregon at Key West, No News Since She Left Rio," *New York Times*, May 27, 1898.

72. Charles E. Clark, *My Fifty Years in the Navy* (Boston: Little, Brown, 1917), 263–64.

73. "Nicaragua Canal Needed," *New York Times*, May 22, 1898.

74. Dwight Miner, *The Fight for the Panama Route* (New York: Columbia University Press, 1940), 93–95.

75. Díaz Espino, *Wall Street*, 14.

76. Adam Hochschild, *King Leopold's Ghost: A Story of Greed, Terror, and Heroism in Colonial Africa* (Boston: Houghton Mifflin, 1999), 79–80.

77. Díaz Espino, *Wall Street*, 15.

78. Sarah Vowell, *Assassination Vacation* (New York: Simon and Schuster, 2005), 196.

79. "Dedication of the Buffalo Exposition," *New York Times*, May 21, 1901,

80. "President at Buffalo," *New York Times*, September 5, 1901.

81. "President Shot at Buffalo Fair," *New York Times*, September 7, 1901.

82. "Hunt over Mountains for Mr. Roosevelt," *New York Times*, September 14, 1901.

83. *Report of the Isthmian Canal Commission, 1899–1901*, 174–75. The amount of $109 million in 1903 dollars is the equivalent of $2.3 billion in 2007 dollars, or *$67.6 billion* when adjusted for relative share of GDP.

84. Díaz Espino, *Wall Street*, 20.

85. Bunau-Varilla, *Panama*, 187–88.

86. Miner, *Fight for Panama Route*, 207–8.

87. Ibid., 209–12.

88. Miner, *Fight for Panama Route*, 120–21; Senate Doc. 123, 57th Cong., 1st sess., 10.

89. Miner, *Fight for Panama Route*, 123–25.

90. Ibid., 55–62.

91. Uribe Vargas, *Los últimos derechos*, 202–4.

92. Miner, *Fight for Panama Route*, 200–201.

93. Frank Otto Gatell, "The Canal in Retrospect: Some Panamanian and Colombian Views," *The Americas* 15, no. 1 (July 1958): 23–36, 30.

94. Miner, *Fight for Panama Route*, 143–45.

95. Ibid., 202–4.

96. Milton Offutt, *The Protection of Citizens Abroad by the Armed Forces of the United States* (Baltimore: Johns Hopkins Press, 1928), 89–92.

97. Miner, *Fight for Panama Route*, 128–29.

98. Martínez Silva died from pneumonia shortly after his return to Colombia. See *New York Times*, April 2, 1902.

99. Miner, *Fight for Panama Route*, 130.

100. Uribe Vargas, *Los últimos derechos*, 216–17.

101. Bunau-Varilla, *Panama*, 221.

102. Miner, *Fight for Panama Route*, 138–39; *Libro Azul*, 116–17.

103. Miner, *Fight for Panama Route*, 137; *Libro Azul*, 85–86.

104. Miner, *Fight for Panama Route*, 139.

105. Miner, *Fight for Panama Route*, 139; *Libro Azul*, 86–89.

106. Bunau-Varilla, *Panama*, 221.

107. Miner, *Fight for Panama Route*, 138.

108. Miner, *Fight for Panama Route*, 143; *Libro Azul*, 175–76.

109. "Volcano Destroys West Indian Town," *New York Times*, May 9, 1902.

110. Bunau-Varilla, *Panama*, 246–47 and illustration.

111. Miner, *Fight for Panama Route*, 151–55.

112. Ibid., 160, note 6.

113. Uribe Vargas, *Los últimos derechos*, 237; *Libro Azul*, 270ff.

114. Miner, *Fight for Panama Route*, 182.

115. Ibid., 184–88.

116. Alfred L. P. Dennis, *Adventures in American Diplomacy* (New York: E. P. Dutton, 1928), 314, citing Cromwell to Hay, telegram, December 30, 1902, Hay Papers.

117. Gatell, "Canal in Retrospect," 23–36, 30.

118. Miner, *Fight for Panama Route*, 189.

119. Ibid., 194–95.

120. Ibid., 247.

121. Ibid., 266.

122. Ibid., 283.

123. Henry F. Pringle, *Theodore Roosevelt: A Biography* (New York: Harcourt, Brace, 1928), 313.

124. Pringle, *Roosevelt*, 311.

125. Miner, *Fight for Panama Route*, 323–26.

126. Pringle, *Roosevelt*, 311.

127. McCullough, *Path Between Seas*, 326–27.

128. Miner, *Fight for Panama Route*, 327–28.

129. Pringle, *Roosevelt*, 311.

130. Miner, *Fight for Panama Route*, 341–45.

131. Bunau-Varilla, *Panama*, 310–12.

132. Bunau-Varilla, *Panama*, 316–18; Miner, *Fight for Panama Route*, 357–58.

133. Bunau-Varilla, *Panama*, 320–22.

134. Miner, *Fight for Panama Route*, 361–62.

135. Díaz Espino, *Wall Street*, 101.

136. While the story of the lone Chinese man killed during the Panamanian revolution has acquired a life of its own, the *Panama*

Star and Herald claimed "two Chinamen" had been killed by the *Bogotá*. Senate Doc. 51, 58th Cong., 2nd sess., 131.

137. McCullough, *Path Between Seas*, 361–79.

138. Roosevelt, *Theodore Roosevelt: An Autobiography* (New York: Macmillan, 1913), 564.

139. Miner, *Fight for Panama Route*, 369–70.

140. Ernesto Castillero Pimentel, *Panamá y los Estados Unidos, 1903–1953* (Panamá: Republica de Panamá, 1953), 43–45.

141. For comparison purposes, $10 million was roughly equal to three years of Panamanian government revenues. In per capita terms, it came to $36 per person ($642 in 2004 dollars).

142. "Panama Gold for New York: $6,000,000 of Canal Payment for Investment in Mortgages," *New York Times*, May 22, 1904.

143. "Panama Agrees to Sell $10,500,000 of Refunding Bonds to Lehman Bros," *Wall Street Journal*, August 19, 1950.

144. Castillero Pimentel, *Panamá y los Estados Unidos*, 46–54; McCullough, *Path between Seas*, 394–97; "Colombian Generals' Offer" and "Gen. Reyes to Confer with other Envoys," *New York Times*, November 29, 1903.

145. *New York Tribune*, December 18, 1884.

146. Huberich, *Trans-Isthmian Canal*, 21.

147. Nicaragua Canal Construction Company, *Interoceanic Canal*, app. 2.

148. *Report of the Isthmian Canal Commission, 1899–1901*, 403–12.

149. Roosevelt to William Roscoe Thayer, letter, July 2, 1915, in W. R. Thayer, *The Life and Letters of John Hay* (Boston: Houghton Mifflin, 1915), 327–28.

150. Letter to William Roscoe Thayer, July 2, 1915, in Thayer, *Life and Letters*, 328.

FOUR   Digging the Ditch

1. *Report of the Isthmian Canal Commission, 1899–1901*, 174.

2. Mack, *Land Divided*, 518.

3. *Annual Report* (Washington, DC: GPO, 1920).

4. Data on cost overruns on the Erie Canal, Hoover Dam, and Big Dig from Stanley Engerman and Kenneth Sokoloff, "Digging the Dirt at Public Expense: Governance in the Building of the Erie Canal and Other Public Works" (working paper 10965, National Bureau of Economic Research, Cambridge, MA, December 2004), 38. BART overruns from San Francisco Cityscape, http://www.sfcityscape.com/transit/BART.html. BQE overruns calculated from data found at NYCRoads.com, http://www.nycroads.com/roads/brooklyn-queens. MassPike costs calculated from data at Bostonroads.com, http://www.bostonroads.com/roads/mass-pike. Miami and Washington metro system data from Dantata, Touran, and Schneck, "Trends in U.S. Rail Transit Project Cost Overruns."

5. Mack, *Land Divided*, 485–86.

6. Ibid., 491.

7. "Hot Time in Prospect for Canal Commission," *New York Times*, November 22, 1905.

8. John Stevens, "An Engineer's Recollections," *Engineering News-Record* 115 (September 5, 1935): 332.

9. *Annual Report* (1905), 117.

10. *Annual Report* (1905), 121.

11. Mack, *Land Divided*, 497.

12. James Richardson, *A Compilation of the Messages and Papers of the Presidents* (Washington, DC: Bureau of National Literature and Art, 1910), 10:7707.

13. Mack, *Land Divided*, 507.

14. Ibid., 500–501.

15. Ibid.

16. John Major, *Prize Possession: The United States and the Panama Canal, 1903–1979* (Cambridge: Cambridge University Press, 1993), 86. McCullough, *Path between Seas*, 509–10.

17. Mack, *Land Divided*, 506–7.

18. Goethals to Judson, June 21, 1912. Goethals Papers, Library of Congress Manuscript Collection.

19. Executive order of November 15, 1904, available at The American Presidency Project, "Theodore Roosevelt," http://www.presidency.ucsb.edu/ws/index.php?pid=69503.

20. "Says T.R. Defied Law to Dig Canal," *New York Times*, January 14, 1917.

21. Thatcher to Interstate Commerce Commission, 80-A-3, memorandum, July 20, 1911; and *Hearings before the Committee on Interoceanic Canals*, 62nd Cong., 2nd sess., Doc. 191, October 26–28, 1911 (Washington, DC: GPO, 1912), 204–9, 224–26.

22. Major, *Prize Possession*, 71–73.

23. Mack, *Land Divided*, 509.

24. Smithsonian Institution Libraries, "Make the Dirt Fly!" http://www.sil.si.edu/Exhibitions/Make-the-Dirt-Fly.

25. Mack, *Land Divided*, 516.

26. Calculated from the *Annual Reports* (1905–14, 1915, and 1922).

27. Mack, *Land Divided*, 511.

28. The amount of $3.6 billion as an equivalent share of GDP. Nominal costs from *Annual Report* (1915), 297.

29. Peter C. Hains, "An Isthmian Canal from a Military Point of View," *Annals of the American Academy of Political and Social Science* 17 (May 1901): 1–12, 4; and the *Report of the Isthmian Canal Commission, 1899–1901*, 167–68.

30. Major, *Prize Possession*, 158.

31. Avery, *America's Triumph at Panama*.

32. Memorandum, JB senior member to the Secretaries of War and the Navy, November 14, 1916, JB Panama Canal File, serial 47, roll 12, M 1421; Paolo E. Colletta and K. Jack Bauer, eds., *United States Navy and Marine Corps Bases, Overseas* (Westport, CT: Greenwood Press, 1985), 80.

33. U.S. Congress, Committee on Naval Affairs, *Hearings Before Committee on Naval Affairs of the House of Representatives on Sundry Legislation Affecting the Naval Establishment, 1920–1921*, 66th Cong., 3rd sess. (Washington, DC: GPO, 1921), 413–14.

34. This was $618.8 million in 2007 dollars, using the GDP deflator. As a percentage of GDP, the cumulative expenditure was the equivalent of $121.9 billion in 2007.

35. *Panama Canal Act of 1912*, § 3. The text of the Panama Canal Act can be found in 37 Stat. 390.

36. Vaughan Cornish, "The Flooding of the Panama Canal," *Geographical Journal* 42, no. 5 (November 1913): 469–70.

37. 1921 *Report of the Governor*, 87.

38. Stanley Heckadon-Moreno, "Impact of Development on the Panama Canal Environment," *Journal of Interamerican Studies and World Affairs* 35, no. 3 (Autumn 1993): 129–49, 133. For a fictionalized treatment, see Gil Blas Tejeira's novel, *Pueblos Perdidos* (Panamá: Editorial Universitaria, 1995).

39. *Annual Report* (1913), 53.

40. Brigadier-General Peter C. Hains, "The Labor Problem on the Panama Canal," *North American Review* 179 (July 1904): 42–54, 50.

41. *Annual Report* (1914), 294.

42. Major, *Prize Possession*, 84–85.

43. *Annual Report* (1914), 294.

44. *Annual Report* (1906), 5.

45. Julie Greene, "Spaniards on the Silver Roll: Labor Troubles and Liminality in the Panama Canal Zone, 1904–1914," *International Labor and Working-Class History* 66 (Fall 2004): 80.

46. "Shonts Broke Pledge on Chinese—Gompers," *New York Times*, August 12, 1906.

47. Major, *Prize Possession*, 83.

48. "No Coolie Labor for Canal," *New York Times*, March 8, 1907.

49. Greene, "Spaniards on the Silver Roll," 78–98, 82–83.

50. Jackson Smith, "European Labor on the Isthmian Canal," March 25, 1907, U.S. National Archives, Record Group 185, 2-E-3-(I).

51. Unsigned letter (assistant chief engineer) to Acting Division Engineer D.W. Bolich, August 4, 1906, U.S. National Archives, Record Group 185 [Records of the Panama Canal], 2-F-14 (General Force)

52. The French used the possibility of a transfer to the better-paying roll as a reward for exceptional service. *ICC Report, 1914*, 294.

53. *Annual Report* (1904), 98.

54. *Annual Report* (1909), 253–55.

55. *Annual Report* (1912), 453.

56. *Annual Report* (1918), 23.

57. *Annual Report* (1914), 294.

58. Conniff, *Black Labor on a White Canal*, 32. Some managers defended their "colored" American Gold Roll workers more strongly than others, most notably Division Engineer J. G. Holcombe. See Holcombe memos, November–December 1906, U.S. National Archives, Record Group 185 [Records of the Panama Canal], 2-F-14 (General Force).

59. United States, Theodore Roosevelt, Calvin Coolidge, Woodrow Wilson, and J. J. McGuigan, *Executive Orders Relating to the Panama Canal (March 8, 1904 to December 31, 1921), Annotated 1921* (Mount Hope, CZ: Panama Canal Press, 1922), 78.

60. Conniff, *Black Labor on a White Canal*, 32.

61. *Executive Orders Relating to the Panama Canal*, 84.

62. Conniff, *Black Labor on a White Canal*, 33–34.

63. Ibid., 31.

64. *Annual Report* (1906), 115.

65. Matthew Parker, *Panama Fever: The Epic Story of the Building of the Panama Canal* (New York: Doubleday, 2007), 316.

66. Senate Committee on Interoceanic Canals, 62nd Cong., 1908, 90; and Velma Newton, *The Silver Men: West Indian Migration to Panama, 1850–1914* (Kingston: University of the West Indies, 1984), 125.

67. Vaughan Cornish, *The Panama Canal and Its Makers* (Cambridge, MA: Harvard University Press, 1909), 103–4.

68. Greene, "Spaniards on the Silver Roll," 89.

69. Ibid., 87.

70. Ibid., 90–94.

71. Conniff, *Black Labor on a White Canal*, 50.

72. Major, *Prize Possession*, 88.

73. Chester Harding to Secretary of War, telegram, February 26, 1920, USNA Record Group 185, 2-P-59/20.

74. Conniff, *Black Labor on a White Canal*, 59.

75. Major, *Prize Possession*, 95–96.

76. Conniff, *Black Labor on a White Canal*, 17–18.

77. Ibid., 20.

78. Goethals, *Government of the Canal Zone* (Princeton, NJ: Princeton University Press, 1915), 64.

79. Canal Zone statistics included all employees as part of the permanent population until 1920, regardless of their actual residential status.

80. Conniff, *Black Labor on a White Canal*, 69.

81. Ibid., 69.

82. Ibid., 35.

83. Conniff, *Black Labor on a White Canal*, 34. In 1909, 35 percent southern; in 1932, 28 percent. For his 1909 figure, Conniff uses the place of origin of American schoolchildren in the Canal Zone as a proxy for employee origin.

84. *Annual Reports* (selected years).

85. James Howe, *A People Who Would Not Kneel: Panama, the United States and the San Blas Kuna* (Washington, DC: Smithsonian Institution Press, 1998), 71.

86. State Department, 1906–10, 847/230, George T. Weitzel to Secretary of State Knox, March 3, 1910.

87. State Department 1906–10, 847/236, Reynolds Hitt to Knox, June 11, 1910. Hitt would later become better known for scandals in his personal life. See "Flask Causes Arrest of Reynolds Hitt and Woman in Washington Dining Room," *New York Times*, October 2, 1920; "Katherine Elkins Divorced from Hitt," *New York Times*, January 12, 1922.

88. State Department 1906–10, 847/240, Richard Marsh to Knox, July 28, 1910.

89. State Department 1906–10, 847/240, Marsh to Knox, August 10, 1910.

90. State Department 1906–10, 847/253, Marsh to Knox, August 15, 1910.

91. State Department 847/248, Marsh to Knox, August 17, 1910.

92. State Department 847/244, De la Guardia to Knox, August 4, 1910; Conniff, *Black Labor on a White Canal*, 42.

93. "May Intervene in Panama," *New York Times*, August 23, 1910.

94. "Mendoza Drops Contest," *New York Times*, August 28, 1910.

95. State Department 819.00/265, Marsh to Knox, September 2, 1910. Marsh's State Department correspondence is almost unbelievable from a modern perspective. See also Howe, *A People Who Would Not Kneel*, which covers Marsh's later championing of Panama's indigenous Kuna people and his assistance in their abortive 1925 rebellion against the Panamanian government. Marsh had several unusual racial theories based on the Kunas' propensity toward albinism.

96. "grossly misrepresented": State Department 819.00/285, William Howard Taft to Acting Secretary of State Wilson, September 9, 1910; "fresh and insubordinate": State Department 819.00/281, William Howard Taft to Acting Secretary of State Wilson, September 2, 1910.

97. "Carlos Mendoza Dead," *New York Times*, February 14, 1916.

98. Jaén Suárez, *La población*, 506.

99. Gorgas, "Mortality in Panama," *Journal of the American Medical Association* 58 (1912): 907–9; William Crawford Gorgas, *Sanitation in Panama* (New York: Appleton, 1915), 149.

100. Enrique Chaves-Carballo, "Carlos Finlay and Yellow Fever: Triumph over Adversity," *Military Medicine* 170, no. 10 (2005): 881–85; *Yellow Fever: A Compilation of Various Publications* (Washington, DC: GPO, 1911), 17–31; Gorgas, *Sanitation in Panama*, 18–39.

101. Gorgas, *Sanitation in Panama*, 51–76.

102. Ibid., 150–51.

103. *Annual Report* (1905), 6–7.

104. Gorgas, "Mortality in Panama," 908; *Annual Report* (1906), 2.

105. *Annual Report* (1905), 7.

106. Gorgas, *Sanitation in Panama*, 275.

107. Ibid., 191–93.

108. Ibid., 182–91.

109. Ira Bennett, *History of the Panama Canal* (Washington, DC: Historical Publishing, 1915), 124.

110. Gorgas, *Sanitation in Panama*, 275.

111. Department of Health and Human Services, Centers for Disease Control and Prevention, "Malaria," www.cdc.gov/malaria/history/panama_canal.htm.

112. Fred L. Soper, "The Newer Epidemiology of Yellow Fever," *American Journal of Public Health* 27, no.1 (January 1937): 1–14, 3.

113. Hoyt Bleakley, "Malaria Eradication in the Americas: A Retrospective Analysis of Childhood Exposure" (working paper, University of Chicago, August 17, 2007).

114. David Cutler and Grant Miller, "The Role of Public Health Improvements in Health Advances: The Twentieth-Century United States," *Demography* 42, no. 1 (February 2005): 1–22.

115. *Annual Report* (1905), 127; also see "Canal Ends Half Century's Association with Municipal Services in Panama, Colon," *Panama Canal Review*, July 3, 1953.

116. *Annual Report* (1906), 8–9.

117. *Annual Report* (1907), 8.

118. *Annual Report* (1914), 41.

119. *Annual Report* (1915), 81.

120. *Annual Report* (1907), 59–60.

121. *Annual Report* (1946), 100.

122. Acueducto, Agua y Alcantarillado de Bogotá, Reseña histórica, available at http://www.acueducto.com.co/wpsv5/wps/portal (accessed January 19, 2010).

123. "Historia Cronológica de Aguas EPM," found at the Biblioteca EPM (Empresas Públicas de Medellín), Medellín, Colombia.

124. Ángela Agudelo González, "'Entre los Gallinazos y el sol': Los problemas de salubridad pública y delincuencia en Barranquilla, 1900–1940," *Historia Caribe* 14 (2009): 211–25, 215.

125. Bonham Richardson, *Economy and Environment in the Caribbean: Barbados and the Windwards in the Late 1800s* (Gainesville: University Press of Florida, 1997), table 2.1, 33.

126. Bonham Richardson, *Panama Money in Barbados, 1900–1920* (Knoxville: University of Tennessee Press, 1985), 17–18.

127. Richardson, *Economy and Environment*, 24–25.

128. Jean Besson, "Freedom and Community in the West Indies," in *The Meaning of Freedom: Economics, Politics, and Culture After Slavery*, ed. Frank McGlynn and Seymour Drescher, 183–220 (Pittsburgh: University of Pittsburgh Press, 1992), 197.

129. Richardson, *Economy and Environment*, 36, citing Colonial Office 321/74, "Depressed Condition of the Sugar Industry," July 26, 1884.

130. South Atlantic day wages in 1899 assuming a six-day workweek calculated from *Historical Statistics of the United States, Millennial Edition*, 2:260.

131. Richardson, *Panama Money*, 67.

132. Richardson, *Economy and Environment*, 37.

133. Richardson, *Panama Money*, 54–55.

134. Ibid., 77–78.

135. Richardson, *Economy and Environment*, 56.

136. Ibid., 228.

137. For the stipulations of the Barbadian reciprocity agreement, see Josephus Larned, Charles Seymour, Donald Smith, Augustus Shearer, and Daniel Knowlton, *The New Larned History for Ready Reference, Reading and Research* (New York: C. A. Nichols, 1922), 873. For the base rate on sugar imports, see Alan Dye, "Cuba and the Origins of the U.S. Sugar Quota," *Revista de Indias* 65, no. 233 (2005): 193–218, 204.

138. Michael Conniff, *Black Labor on a White Canal, 1904–1981*, 28.

139. *ICC report, 1914*, 294.

140. Arthur Bullard, *Panama: The Canal, the Country, and the People* (New York: Macmillan, 1909), 27–29.

141. Newton, *Silver Men*, 79.

142. Hilary Beckles, *A History of Barbados* (Cambridge: Cambridge University Press, 2006).

143. Parker, *Panama Fever*, 310.

144. Beckles, *History of Barbados*.

145. Richardson, *Panama Money*, 125.

146. Parker, *Panama Fever*, 312.

147. Newton, *Silver Men*, 85.

148. Ibid., 62.

149. Ibid., 62–63.

150. Ibid., 92.

151. Ibid., app. 1, 198–99.

152. Natural growth rates from Newton, *Silver Men*, 93.

153. John Turner, "Commercial Conditions in Barbados," *Daily Consular and Trade Reports* 13, no. 77 (October 3, 1910): 18.

154. Richardson, *Panama Money*, 132.

155. John Turner, "Commercial Conditions," 18.

156. Richardson, *Economy and Environment*, 230.

157. Newton, *Silver Men*, 98.

158. Richardson, *Panama Money*, 144, 157.

159. Richardson, *Panama Money*, 189.

160. Beckles, *History of Barbados*.

161. Richardson, *Panama Money*, 165.

162. In fact, this is likely an underestimate, since these figures do not include deposits at the Barbados branches of the Colonial Bank (which Barclays purchased in 1921), the Canadian Bank of Commerce, or the Royal Bank of Canada. Spanish and Italian dollar-equivalent deposits per person are calculated from Brian Redman Mitchell, *International Historical Statistics: Europe 1750–2000* (New York: Palgrave Macmillan, 2003), 885–86 and 900–901.

163. Beckles, *History of Barbados*.

FIVE   Crossing the Ditch

1. Senate Doc. 51, 58th Cong., 2nd sess., 41.

2. Senate Doc. 51, 58th Cong., 2nd sess., 43. Vice-Consul Dickson reasoned that the west coast of the Americas was productively "a small strip of territory, very narrow and comparatively sterile," whereas most of the transoceanic trade in the Americas would go from the developed east coasts to Europe.

3. G. G. Huebner, "Economic Aspects of the Panama Canal," *American Economic Review* 5, no. 4 (1915): 816–29, 819. Sending cargoes by the isthmian railroads cut shipping costs, but at an

additional cost of $3.00 per ton at Panama and $3.50 per ton at Tehuantepec. The additional cost obviated most of the cost savings from the shorter route.

4. These estimates assume that the Panama Canal had no effect on insurance and other costs, and include the $1 toll paid by transiting vessels.

5. We estimated this fixed cost of shipping by solving the following pair of equations with two unknowns: *(fixed cost) + (distance before canal) × (per-mile cost) = (total cost per ton before canal)* and *(fixed cost) + (distance after canal) × (per-mile cost) = (total cost per ton after canal).* The fixed cost per ton came to $3.18 the year the canal opened, including an average Panama Canal toll of $1. See Noel Maurer and Carlos Yu, "What T. R. Took: The Economic Impact of the Panama Canal, 1903–1937," *Journal of Economic History* 68, no. 3 (September 2008): 686–721.

6. E. S. Gregg, "Transportation: Part 2—Shipping," in *Recent Economic Changes in the United States*, vol. 1 and 2 (New York: McGraw-Hill, 1929), 313.

7. Gregg, "Transportation," 314.

8. Huebner, "Economic Aspects of the Panama Canal," 828.

9. Gregg, "Transportation," 315, 317.

10. These estimates assume that the Panama Canal had no effect on insurance and other costs, and include the $1 toll paid by transiting vessels.

11. U.S. Department of State, *Foreign Relations of the United States: Papers Relating to the Foreign Relations of the United States with the Annual Message of the President Transmitted to Congress December 3, 1912*, 469–70.

12. Ibid., 477.

13. "Tariff Chokes U.S., Wilson Declares," *New York Times*, August 16, 1912.

14. "Senate, by 47 to 15, Passes Canal Bill," *New York Times*, August 10, 1912, 1.

15. Arthur Link, *Wilson: The New Freedom* (Princeton, NJ: Princeton University Press, 1956), 306.

16. Link, *Wilson*, 306–7.

17. William Jennings Bryan, "The Tolls Question," *Commoner* 14, no. 4 (April 1914).

18. Link, *Wilson*, 313–14.

19. George Talley, *The Panama Canal* (Wilmington, DE: Star Publishing, 1916), 56.

20. Talley, *Panama Canal*, 66.

21. Robert William Fogel, *Railroads and American Economic Growth: Essays in Econometric History* (Baltimore, MD: Johns Hopkins Press, 1964).

22. Paul David expressed this idea on multiple occasions, most vividly on page 508 of Paul A. David, "Transport Innovation and Economic Growth: Professor Fogel on and off the Rails," *Economic History Review* 22, no. 3 (December 1969): 506–25.

23. Lincoln Hutchinson, "Voyage Costs via Panama and Other Routes," *American Economic Review* 4, no. 3 (1914): 575–87, 577.

24. *Annual Report* (various years). Other potential choices, e.g., using Manila instead of Shanghai, or Baltimore instead of New York, did not affect distances by more than 10 percent.

25. The per-mile cost of transporting goods around Cape Horn dropped after the opening of the canal. The reason is that the opening of the canal prompted more firms to enter the market, which was limited to American-owned and American-staffed vessels by the Jones Act of 1920. Nevertheless, the calculated cost of transporting goods via Cape Horn never fell consistently below the cost of transporting goods via the transcontinental railroad, although there was some year-to-year variation.

26. Eliot Grinnell Mears, *Maritime Trade of Western United States* (Stanford: Stanford University Press, 1935), 240–41; Emory R. Johnson, *Panama Canal Traffic and Tolls* (Washington, DC: GPO, 1912), 39.

27. Arthur Rockwell, "The Lumber Trade and the Panama Canal, 1921–1940," *Economic History Review* 24, no. 3 (1971): 445–62.

28. U.S. Department of Commerce, Bureau of the Census, *Historical Statistics of the United States, Colonial Times to 1957* (Washington, DC: GPO, 1960), 431.

29. William Hutchinson and Ricardo Ungo, "Social Saving of the Panama Canal" (working paper 04-W2, Department of Economics, Vanderbilt University, December 2004).

30. We calculated the ratio between the social savings at a given price elasticity and the social savings with the price elasticity of zero using the following two equations, where ϕ is the ratio between the cost of ocean transport without the use of the Panama Canal and the cost of ocean transport using the Panama Canal and ε is equal to the price elasticity of demand:

$$\frac{S_\varepsilon}{S_0} = \frac{\phi^{1-\varepsilon}-1}{(1-\varepsilon)(\phi-1)} \text{ for } \varepsilon \neq 1 \text{ and } \frac{S_\varepsilon}{S_0} = \frac{\ln\phi}{\phi-1} \text{ for } \varepsilon = 1.$$

See Robert William Fogel, "Notes on the Social Saving Controversy," *Journal of Economic History* 39 (1979): 1–54.

31. Since the proportional cost savings of the canal were different for every route, we calculated the change in the cost savings for various demand elasticities separately for every route and then aggregated upward.

32. Link, *Wilson*, 304, 306; *New York Times*, July 3, 1912; and *Commoner*, April 1914.

33. Thomas F. O'Brien, "'Rich beyond the Dreams of Avarice': The Guggenheims in Chile," *Business History Review* 63, no. 1 (Spring 1989): 122–59, 137–39.

34. Ibid., 129–31.

35. Copper prices from K. E. Porter and D. L. Edelstein, *Copper Statistics*, U.S. Geological Survey, January 14, 2008. Production costs from Joanne Fox Przeworski, *The Decline of the Copper Industry in Chile and the Entrance of North American Capital, 1870–1916* (New York: Arno Press, 1980), 286.

36. Augusto Millán Urzúa, *Historia de la minería del hierro en Chile*, 69–70.

37. Ibid., 70.

38. Assuming no fixed cost in shipping, and a linear relationship between cost and distance. Charles Schwab, Bethlehem Steel's CEO, considered $6 per ton acceptable, given the high grade of the ore, stating that "the ore advantage of the Eastern seaboard plant

is such that pig iron can be made more cheaply at Sparrows Point than at any point in the Middle West." Mark Reutter, *Sparrows Point: Making Steel: The Rise and Ruin of American Might* (New York: Summit Books, 1988), 161–62.

39. Urzúa, *Historia de la minería*, 68.

40. Urzúa, *Historia de la minería*, 63; Reutter, *Sparrows Point*, 161–62.

41. Urzúa, *Historia de la minería*, 71.

42. Ibid., 74.

43. Ibid., 68.

44. Ibid., 87–89.

45. Ibid., 67.

46. Urzúa, *Historia de la minería*, 64. Government revenues from Oxford Latin American Economic History Database (Ox-LAD), available at http://oxlad.qeh.ox.ac.uk/.

47. *Annual Report* (selected years).

48. Tomohei Chida and Peter N. Davies, *The Japanese Shipping and Shipbuilding Industries* (London: Athlone Press, 1990), 9–10.

49. Chida and Davies, *Japanese Shipping and Shipbuilding*, 30.

50. Keiichiro Nakagawa, "Japanese Shipping in the 19th and 20th Centuries: Strategy and Organization," in *Business History of Shipping*, ed. Tsunehiko Yui and Keiichiro Nakagawa (Tokyo: University of Tokyo Press, 1985), 9–10.

51. Nakagawa, "Japanese Shipping," 13–14; Seizo Motora, "A Hundred Years of Shipbuilding in Japan," *Journal of Marine Science and Technology* 2 (1997): 197–212; E. Mowbray Tate, *Transpacific Steam: The Story of Steam Navigation from the Pacific Coast of North America to the Far East and the Antipodes, 1867–1941* (New York: Cornwall Press, 1986), 99–100; Chida and Davies, *Japanese Shipping and Shipbuilding*, 38.

52. Daniel M. Masterson and Sayaka Funada-Classen, *The Japanese in Latin America* (Urbana: University of Illinois Press, 2004), 108.

53. Alfred Thayer Mahan, "The United States Looking Outward," *Atlantic Monthly*, December 1890, 816–824.

54. Hains, "Isthmian Canal," 1–12, 10.

55. Naval expenditures (in 1925 dollars) rose steadily from $81 million in 1897 to $223 million in 1905, as part of the naval buildup initiated by President McKinley and continued by President Roosevelt. Figures from *Historical Statistics*, 718.

56. Alfred Thayer Mahan, "The Panama Canal and the Distribution of the Fleet," *North American Review* 200 (September 1914): 406–17; Theodore Roosevelt, "The Foreign Policy of the United States," *Outlook*, August 22, 1914, 1011–15.

57. William Braisted, *The United States Navy in the Pacific, 1909–1922* (Austin: University of Texas Press, 1977), 174.

58. Ibid., 189–90.

59. Gerald Wheeler, "The United States Navy and the Japanese 'Enemy,' 1919–1931," *Military Affairs* 21, no. 2 (1957): 61–74, 63.

60. Data from *Annual Reports of the Secretary of War* and *War Department Appropriations Bill*, 173–75, 179, 226, 258, and 603. The distribution of costs roughly broke down into 41 percent for maintenance and planning, 40 percent for ordnance (mines, ammunition stocks, and the like), and 19 percent for extraordinary medical expenses.

61. Since the marginal cost is the cost of "one more" unit at the margin, the Senate estimates quickly allow one to calculate the marginal cost of equipping 10,000 (132,000 minus 122,000) and 24,000 (156,000 minus 132,000) more soldiers, and from that to calculate their costs on a per-unit basis.

62. Data from *Annual Reports of the Secretary of War* and *War Department Appropriations Bill*, 706–63.

63. For more detail on American interventions in the circum-Caribbean during the period, see Laura Alfaro, Noel Maurer, and Faisal Ahmed, "Gunboats and Vultures: Market Reaction to the 'Enforcement' of Sovereign Debt" (working paper, Harvard Business School, 2008). See also Mitchener and Weidenmier, "Empire."

64. Nominal figures on American defense spending come from *Historical Statistics*, 718. We converted nominal figures to real ones using the U.S. GDP deflator.

65. Arnold Kahle Henry, "The Panama Canal and the Intercoastal Trade" (Ph.D. thesis, University of Pennsylvania, 1929), 41.

66. Ibid., 42.

67. *Annual Report* (1923).

68. Calvin Crumbaker, "The Panama Canal and the West," *Journal of Business of the University of Chicago* 2, no. 2 (April 1929): 151–76, 157.

69. "I.C.C. Begins Its St. Paul Inquiry," *Wall Street Journal*, December 1, 1925, 4.

70. Henry, "Panama Canal and Intercoastal Trade" (in response to an anonymous survey).

71. Henry, "Panama Canal and Intercoastal Trade," 72.

72. Ibid.

73. Henry, "Panama Canal and Intercoastal Trade," 43. The comparison is made during the summer months due to the closing of important North American internal waterways during the winter months.

74. Henry, "Panama Canal and Intercoastal Trade," 43. The comparison is made during the summer months due to the closing of important North American internal waterways during the winter months.

75. The amount was $1.15 per one hundred pounds, all rail to San Francisco, $0.61, rail-water to San Francisco, of which $0.31 was the cost of rail to an Atlantic port. Henry, "Panama Canal and Intercoastal Trade," table XVII, 66.

76. In 1907, the United States Forest Service recorded an average stumpage price of $8.09 per M feet for white pine, $3.16 for yellow pine, and $1.44 for Douglas fir. Nevertheless, direct comparison of stumpage prices is problematic. See Wilson Compton, *The Organization of the Lumber Industry* (Chicago: American Lumberman, 1916), 69.

77. Paul Willard Garrett, *Government Control Over Prices* (Washington, DC: GPO, 1920), 329.

78. Data from Albert Halsey Pierson, *Lumber Production, 1869–1934* (Washington, DC: U.S. Department of Agriculture, 1936).

79. W. B. Greeley, "Economic Aspects of Our Timber Supply," *Journal of Forestry* 20, no. 8 (1922): 837–47, 838.

80. Pierson, *Lumber Production*.

81. Boeing, "Commercial Airplanes," http://www.boeing.com/commercial/boeing_bio/chapter4.html.

82. Mia Gray, Elyse Golob, and Ann Markusen, "Big Firms, Long Arms, Wide Shoulders: The 'Hub-and-Spoke' Industrial District in the Seattle Region," *Regional Studies* 30, no. 7 (1996): 651–66, 656–58.

83. Alan L. Olmstead and Paul Rhode, "Rationing without Government: The West Coast Gas Famine of 1920," *American Economic Review* 75, no. 5 (December 1985): 1044–55.

84. *Annual Report* (1923), 3–4.

85. Petroleum data are taken from the *Annual Report*. As with other cargo data from this period, due to the nature of official canal record-keeping, these represent minimum numbers for the amount of Californian petroleum shipped through the canal.

86. Using the calculated conversion factor 1 bbl ~ 1700 kW-hr.

87. Paul Rhode, *The Evolution of California Manufacturing* (San Francisco: Public Policy Institute of California, 2001), 47–48.

88. U.S. Geological Survey, *Mineral Resources of the United States* (Washington, DC: GPO, selected years).

89. Statistical tests confirm the results of the eyeball regression.

90. Crumbaker, "Panama Canal and the West," 153–54.

91. Francis Manning and Richard Thompson, *Oilfield Processing*, vol. 2, *Crude Oil* (Tulsa, OK: PennWell Books, 1995), 113.

92. *The Big Inch and Little Big Inch Pipelines* (Houston: Texas Eastern Transmission Corporation, 2000), 12–13.

93. Leslie Cookenboo Jr., *Costs of Operating Crude Oil Pipelines* (1953; repr., New York: Arno Press, 1979). Cookenboo's estimated initial cost is most sensitive to the cost of steel (150 tons per mile), while his operating costs are most sensitive to the price of power (1 cent per kilowatt-hour). In light of this latter point, we assume that diesel pumps would have been used where electrical power was too costly.

94. *Building the Navy's Bases in World War II: History of the Bureau of Yards and Docks and the Civil Engineer Corps, 1940–1946* (Washington, DC: GPO, 1947), 2:19; "Pipeline Across Panama

Revealed by Navy; $20,000,000 Artery of Great Value," *New York Times*, September 7, 1945, 3.

95. *Big Inch and Little Big Inch Pipelines.*

96. Originally operated by a subsidiary of Goodyear, it functioned in its intended capacity for less than a decade. At present, much of it has been repurposed for natural gas delivery in the Southwest. Gregory Stricharchuk, "Goodyear Is Becoming Force in Oil Industry," *Wall Street Journal*, January 14, 1986, 6; All American Pipeline System, project document, Willbros Group, available at http://www.willbros.com/fw/main/Selected_Projects_List-155.html (accessed September 30, 2007); "Company News: Goodyear to Sell Its Oil Pipeline," *New York Times*, August 20, 1988; "Company News: El Paso Energy Plans to Buy Part of Southwest Pipeline," *New York Times*, February 4, 2000.

97. Melissa Campbell, "25th Anniversary of the Alyeska Pipeline Service Co.," *Alaska Business Monthly*, June 2002.

SIX Passed by the Ditch

1. Peter A. Szok, *La última gaviota: Liberalism and Nostalgia in Early Twentieth-Century Panamá* (Westport, CT.: Greenwood Press, 2001).

2. Eusebio Morales, *Ensayos, Documentos, y Discursos* (Panama City: Autoridad del Canal de Panamá, 1999), 119.

3. William Scoullar, *The Blue Book of Panama* (Panamá, Imprenta nacional, 1917), preface and 62.

4. Derek Hopwood, *Sexual Encounters in the Middle East: The British, the French and the Arabs* (Reading, UK: Ithaca Press, 1999), 128.

5. "Pay Klondike Prices for Food in Panama; Native Laborers Suffer," *New York Times*, September 25, 1905.

6. The average retail price for a pound of USDA-certified beef in 2007 was $4.16. Blair Fannin, "Higher Retail Beef Prices Caused by Rising Production, Transportation Costs," *AgNews*, Texas A&M AgriLife Extension Service, March 17, 2008. Whole milk cost 98¢

per quart in 2007. "Retail Food Prices Decline Slightly at End of 2007," *High Plains Journal*, January 15, 2008.

7. Major, *Prize Possession*, 102.

8. *Annual Report* (1905), 8.

9. Major, *Prize Possession*, 102.

10. Thomas M. Leonard, "The Commissary Issue in American-Panamanian Relations, 1900–1936," *The Americas* 30, no. 1 (July 1973): 95.

11. Major, *Prize Possession*, 102.

12. Ibid., 103.

13. Bennett, *History of the Panama Canal*, 505.

14. Major, *Prize Possession*, 103. The Root-Arosemena Treaty was part of a pair of entwined pacts that the United States signed with the governments of Panama and Colombia. When the Colombian government failed to ratify its agreement with the United States, it also rendered void the pact with Panama.

15. Major, *Prize Possession*, 102; and Thomas Russell, *The Panama Canal* (Chicago: Hamming, 1913), 22.

16. Russell, *Panama Canal*, 22.

17. "Goethals as Canal Critic," *New York Times*, September 9, 1915.

18. Ibid.

19. Russell, *Panama Canal*, 22.

20. *Panama Canal Act of 1912*, § 6. The text of the Panama Canal Act can be found in 37 Stat. 390.

21. Leonard, "Commissary Issue," 83–109, 92.

22. *Annual Report* (1917), 161.

23. Robert M. Brown, "Five Years of the Panama Canal: An Evaluation," *Geographical Review* 9, no. 3 (March 1920): 191–98, 198.

24. *Annual Report* (1929), 47.

25. William D. McCain, *The United States and the Republic of Panama* (Durham, NC: Duke University Press, 1937), 230, citing Alfaro to Hughes, January 3, 1923.

26. *Annual Report* (1917), 167.

27. *Annual Report* (1928), 47; (1929), 54.

28. *Annual Report* (various years).

29. *Annual Report* (various years).

30. Leonard, "Commissary Issue," 95.

31. Ibid., 96.

32. Ibid., 92–93.

33. Ibid.,97.

34. McCain, *United States and Republic of Panama*, 230, citing Alfaro to Hughes, January 3, 1923.

35. Sandra Meditz and Dennis Hanratty, eds., *Panama: A Country Study* (Washington, DC: GPO for the Library of Congress, 1987).

36. Drew Pearson, "Panama Agitated by Zone Trading," *New York Times*, October 27, 1927.

37. John Biesanz, "The Economy of Panama," *Inter-American Economic Affairs* 6 (Summer 1962): 13.

38. U.S. Department of State, *Foreign Relations of the United States: Diplomatic Papers, 1933*, vol. 5, *The American Republic* (Washington, DC: GPO, 1933), 855.

39. On January 16, 1919, the United States banned the importation of liquor, opium, cocaine, and prostitutes into the Canal Zone. See *The Panama Canal Record* 12, no. 24 (January 29, 1919): 274.

40. "Fights in Colombia," *New York Times*, December 17, 1901, 8. The engineer who first described the Nombre de Dios manganese deposits, Eduardo Justo Chibás Guerra, was the father of the Cuban presidential candidate Eduardo René Chibás Rivas, whose suicide attempt was broadcast on Cuban radio in 1951.

41. McCain, *United States and Republic of Panama*, 97–98.

42. Walter LaFeber, *The Panama Canal: The Crisis in Historical Perspective* (New York: Oxford University Press, 1989), p. 61.

43. Marcelo Bucheli, "Good Dictator, Bad Dictator: United Fruit Company and Economic Nationalism in Central America in the Twentieth Century" (working paper 06-0115, University of Illinois at Urbana–Champaign, College of Business, 2006).

44. Calculated from data in *Statistical Yearbook of the League of Nations* (Geneva, Switzerland: League of Nations, Economic and Financial Section).

45. LaFeber, *Panama Canal*, 62.

46. Ferguson and Schularick, "Empire Effect."

47. Mitchener and Weidenmier, "Empire"; Alfaro, Maurer, and Ahmed, "Gunboats and Vultures."

48. Harold F. Peterson, *Diplomat of the Americas* (Albany: State University of New York Press, 1977), pp. 246–248.

49. McCain, *United States and Republic of Panama*, 54–60.

50. *Foreign Relations of the United States 1915*, 1236.

51. McCain, *United States and Republic of Panama*, 72–73.

52. Major, *Prize Possession*, 138; *Annual Reports of the Secretary of War, 1916*, 3:27.

53. McCain, *United States and Republic of Panama*, 207–8.

54. McCain, *United States and Republic of Panama*, 219–20. Ironically, the anti-Porras mob rioted because they believed Porras was too conciliatory to Costa Rica.

55. McCain, *United States and Republic of Panama*, 89; and Biesanz, "Economy of Panama," 20.

56. U.S. Department of State, *Foreign Relations of the United States: Papers Relating to the Foreign Relations of the United States with the Annual Message of the President Transmitted to Congress December 3, 1912*, 1178–79.

57. George Baker, "The Wilson Administration and Panama, 1913–1931," *Journal of Inter-American Studies* 8 (April 1966): 279–93, 281.

58. U.S. Department of State, *Foreign Relations of the United States, 1929*, 1:542–45.

59. Major, *Prize Possession*, 129–30.

60. Calculated from data in "Newspaper Specials," *Wall Street Journal*, December 3, 1914.

61. Ibid.

62. Major, *Prize Possession*, 132.

63. Ibid., 133.

64. Calculated from data in *International Historical Statistics*, 3:699, 721.

65. Major, *Prize Possession*, 137.

66. Ibid., 139–40.

67. Calculated from data in "Republic of Panama Loan," *Wall Street Journal*, June 15, 1926.

68. Calculated from data in *Wall Street Journal*, May 25, 1928.

69. See Alfaro, Maurer, and Ahmed, "Gunboats and Vultures," for the details of American debt enforcement during this period.

70. Major, *Prize Possession*, 144–45.

71. "Panama Reappoints American as Agent; Choice of Fiscal Officer Thought Significant," *New York Times*, April 1, 1921.

72. USNA State Department, 1910–45, 819.51A/24, Addison Ruan to Secretary of State Hughes, December 18, 1922.

73. USNA State Department, 1910–49, 819.154/115, U.S. Minister John South to Secretary of State Hughes, April 11, 1924.

74. USNA State Department, 819.51/615, Assistant Secretary of State White to Lawrence Bennett of Murray, Aldrich, and Roberts, May 28, 1929.

75. Thomas L. Pearcy, *We Answer Only to God: Politics and the Military in Panama, 1903–1947* (Albuquerque: University of New Mexico Press, 1998), 64–66.

76. Ibid., 68.

77. First inaugural address of Franklin Delano Roosevelt. Accessed at the Avalon Project, http://www.yale.edu/lawweb/avalon/presiden/inaug/froos1.htm.

78. Rexford Tugwell, *The Democratic Roosevelt: A Biography of Franklin D. Roosevelt* (Garden City, NY: Doubleday, 1957), 90.

79. John Major, "F.D.R. and Panama," *Historical Journal* 28, no. 2 (June 1985): 357–77, 359–60.

80. *Annual Report* (1935), 114; (1936), 110.

81. Major, *Prize Possession*, 232.

82. Ibid., 234.

83. Ibid., 235–36.

84. Ibid., 236–37.

85. The bonded warehouses stored goods for which no duties had been paid. Their presence allowed shippers to transfer goods inside the Zone, or engage in additional work to prepare goods for their final destination.

86. Major, *Prize Possession*, 238.

87. Ibid.

88. LaFeber, *Panama Canal*, 70.

89. Major, "F.D.R. and Panama," 357–77, 366–67.

SEVEN   Sliding into Irrelevancy

1. Hector C. Bywater, *The Great Pacific War: A History of the American-Japanese Campaign of 1931–1933* (Bedford, MA: Applewood Books, 2000), 22–23.

2. Compiled from *Annual Reports.*

3. This calculation assumes that all Panama Canal cargoes would have travelled three thousand additional miles on the railroad. Since many of the cargoes shipped from East Coast ports originated inland and moved to the coast, this assumption provides an upper bound.

4. Harold Barger, *The Transportation Industries, 1889–1946: A Study of Output, Employment, and Productivity* (New York: National Bureau of Economic Research, 1951), Table B-1, 183–84. Freight ton-miles in the United States for 1943 were 730 billion; 1944, 741 billion; 1945, 684 billion.

5. Railroad data from *Historical Statistics of the United States, Millennial Edition*, table Df965-979, 4-932, "Railroad Freight Traffic and Revenue."

6. Calculated from figures in *Historical Statistics of the United States, Millennial Edition*, Table Df991-1001, 4-938.

7. The 1944 report provided the total outlays "for purchase, charter, and operations of vessels, reconditioning, outfitting, defense installations, operation of warehouses and terminals and other expenditures" on page 32. It also provided data on page 6 for the total number of tons carried and, for cargoes originating in U.S. ports, their region of destination. The latter data allowed us to calculate the average length of a cargo haul in 1942 and 1943. We then assumed that inbound cargoes (34 percent of the total), for which we did not have exact data on their origin, travelled the same average distance.

8. *1944 report of the War Shipping Administration*, 32.

9. Compiled from James L. Mooney, *Dictionary of American Naval Fighting Ships* (Washington, DC: Naval Historical Center, Department of the Navy, 1991).

10. Samuel Eliot Morison, *History of United States Naval Operations in World War II*, vol. 7, *Aleutians, Gilberts and Marshalls, June 1942–April 1944* (Boston: Little, Brown, 1947–62), 55–56.

11. Morison, *History of United States Naval Operations*, vol. 1, *The Battle of the Atlantic: September 1939–May 1943*, 167–68.

12. Robert Leckie, *Challenge for the Pacific: The Bloody Six-Month Battle of Guadalcanal* (New York: Da Capo Press, 1999), 286.

13. Morison, *History of United States Naval Operations*, vol. 4, *Coral Sea, Midway and Submarine Actions, May 1942–August 1942*, 21–56, 127–37, 153–156; Morison, *History of United States Naval Operations*, vol. 5, *The Struggle for Guadalcanal, August 1942–February 1943*, 130–38, 209–22; and Morison, *History of United States Naval Operations*, vol. 3, *The Rising Sun in the Pacific, 1931–April 1942*, 389–98.

14. Carroll Glines, *The Doolittle Raid: America's Daring First Strike Against Japan* (New York: Orion Books, 1988), 60–62, 219.

15. William McGee, *The Solomons Campaigns, 1942–1943: From Guadalcanal to Bougainville—Pacific War Turning Point*, vol. 2, *Amphibious Operations in the South Pacific in WWII* (Santa Barbara, CA: BMC Publications, 2002), 21.

16. Sidney Shalett, "The 'Big Ditch' Reveals Its Secrets," *New York Times*, November 18, 1945, 82; Norman Polmar, "Improving the Breed," *Naval History* 21, no. 5 (October 2007).

17. Central Intelligence Agency, TS#142423-c, "Intelligence Assumptions for Planning: Soviet ICBM Sites, 1961–1967," November 9, 1961. Declassified November 13, 1990 under the Freedom of Information Act.

18. Data from the Natural Resources Defense Council, Archive of Nuclear Data, "Table of USSR/Russian ICBM Forces," http://www.nrdc.org/nuclear/nudb/datab4.asp (accessed March 8, 2009).

19. Major, *Prize Possession*, 306.

20. Major, *Prize Possession*, 306; and Rigoberto Delgado, "Comparison of One 3-Lift Lock with One 1-Lift plus One 2-Lift Lock at the Pacific Side," *Canal Capacity Projects Division*, ACP-IPCE, May 16, 2003, 3.

21. Major, *Prize Possession*, 315.

22. Delgado, "Comparison of One 3-Lift Lock," 3.

23. "Isthmian Canal Studies—1947," in the *Report of the Governor of the Panama Canal*, 79th Cong., 1st sess., app. 2. See also "Isthmian Canal Studies—1947: Sea-Level Model—Panama Canal," Department of Operation and Maintenance, Special Engineering Division, Canal Zone, 1946.

24. "Sea Level or a Lock Type Canal? Battle of the Levels Is Not New," *Panama Canal Review*, June 7, 1957.

25. U.S. National Archives, Washington, DC. Record Group 407, Adjutant General's Office, Registered Documents, 381. *Panama Canal Department Basic War Plan*, edition of October 2, 1946.

26. *Foreign Relations of the United States 1947*, 7:943–46.

27. Major, *Prize Possession*, 322.

28. Hanson Baldwin, "Canal Defense Role Cut," *New York Times*, March 5, 1949, 6.

29. Hanson Baldwin, "Caribbean Chiefs Work in Harmony," *New York Times*, March 6, 1949, 12.

30. Memorandum, June 6, 1949. Miles Duval Papers, Operational Archives Branch, Naval Historical Center, Washington, DC.

31. Mercer Tate, "The Panama Canal and Political Partnership," *Journal of Politics* 25, no. 1 (February 1963): 119–38, 138.

32. Rodney Carlisle, *Sovereignty for Sale: The Origins and Evolution of the Panamanian and Liberian Flags of Convenience* (Annapolis, MD.: Naval Institute Press, 1981), 94–95; Robert Harding, *The History of Panama* (Westport, CT: Greenwood Press, 2006), 42.

33. Cordell Hull, "Statement by the Secretary of State Regarding Recent Events in Panama," *Department of State Bulletin*, October 18, 1941, 293–95.

34. Pearcy, *We Answer Only to God*, 94.

35. LaFeber, *Panama Canal*, 85.

36. Larry Pippin, *The Remón Era* (Stanford: Stanford University Press, 1964), 108.

37. U.S. Department of State, *Foreign Relations of the United States, 1952–1954*, vol. 4, *The American Republics (1952–1954)*, 1420–21.

38. John Woolley and Gerhard Peters, "Joint Statement by the President and President Remon Cantera of Panama, October 1, 1953," in *The American Presidency Project* (Santa Barbara: University of California, 1999–), http://www.presidency.ucsb.edu/ws/?pid=9713.

39. Pippin, *Remón Era*, 121–22.

40. Mercer Tate, "Panama Canal and Political Partnership," *Journal of Politics* 25 (February 1963): 126–27.

41. Technically, this was part of an annex to the treaty, not the treaty itself.

42. No. 3454. *Tratado de Mutuo Entendimiento y Cooperacion entre los Estados Unidos de America y la Republica de Panamá. Firmado en Panamá, el 25 de Enero de 1955*, Nations Unies—Recueil des Traités (1956), 242.

43. *1950 Proceedings of the Twelfth Constitutional Convention of the Congress of Industrial Organizations*, November 20–24, 1950, Chicago, IL.

44. Robert Alexander and Eldon Parker, *A History of Organized Labor in Panama and Central America* (Westport, CT: Praeger Publishers, 2008), 27.

45. *1950 Proceedings of the Twelfth Constitutional Convention of the Congress of Industrial Organizations*, November 20–24, 1950, Chicago, IL, 318–19.

46. "The Role of Leadership and Unionism," *Rainbow City High Newsletter* 4, no. 22 (September 2006): 2.

47. U.S. Senate, Committee on Foreign Relations, *Hearings on the Panama Treaty* (Washington, DC: GPO, 1955), 78–79.

48. Ibid., 164.

49. Ministerio de Relaciones Exteriores, *Memoria, 1958: Parte Expositiva y Anexos* (Panama, 1958), viii–ix.

50. Assistant Secretary of State, Department of State, to Bureau of the Budget, July 20, 1956, October 30, 1956; Panama Canal Company to Bureau of the Budget, June 17, 1957, Dwight Eisenhower Library, Abilene, KS.

51. Aquilino Boyd, speech, November 23, 1956, in *Ministerio de Relaciones Exteriores, Discursos pronunciados: Boyd* (Panama, 1956), 15–17.

52. *New York Times*, November 4, 1959.

53. *New York Times*, November 29–30, 1959.

54. Clymer, *Drawing the Line at the Big Ditch*, 5.

55. Lester Langley, "U.S.-Panamanian Relations Since 1941," *Journal of Interamerican Studies and World Affairs* 12, no. 3 (July 1970): 339–66, 353.

56. House Committee on Foreign Affairs, *Report on United States Relations with Panama*, 86th Cong., 2nd sess., 1960, H. Rep. 2218, 12–40.

57. *New York Times*, November 18, 1961.

58. Langley, "U. S.-Panamanian Relations since 1941," 357; Alan McPherson, "From 'Punks' to Geopoliticians: U. S. and Panamanian Teenagers and the 1964 Canal Zone Riots," *The Americas* 58, no. 3 (January 2002): 395–418.

59. "One witness said he saw one officer strike a soldier on the back of his neck to make him stop firing his weapon." Richard Eder, "Violence a Shock to Panama: Radio Continues Attacks on U.S.," *New York Times*, January 13, 1964, 14. This sort of action goes far beyond the range of normal U.S. military discipline, even during wartime.

60. Barger, *The Transportation Industries, 1889–1946*, 88.

61. Leon Cole, "Economic Ramifications of Panama Canal Control and Use: A Survey," Congressional Research Service, published in 94th Cong., 1st sess., 1975, *Department of Transportation and Related Agencies Appropriations for 1976*, 65–79, 74.

62. Ibid., 65–79, 73.

63. Ibid., 65–79, 75–76.

64. Ibid., 65–79, 73–74, 78.

65. Stephen R. Gibbs, "The Economic Value of the Panama Canal," *Water Resources Research* 14, no. 2 (April 1978): 185–89.

66. Data from National Bureau of Economic Research Macrohistory Database, chapter 3, "Transportation and Public Utilities," available at http://www.nber.org/databases/macrohistory/contents/chapter03.html; and Bureau of Transportation Statistics, *National Transportation Statistics*, chap. 3, "Transportation and the Economy," available at http://www.bts.gov/publications/national_transportation_statistics/.

67. We assume that exports from the United States (mostly grain and other agricultural products) originated from Chicago, and that the final market for imports was the New York metropolitan area.

68. Data from Cole, "Economic Ramifications," 70. International Research Associates calculated the effect on demand from a 25 percent and a 50 percent rise in canal tolls per ton of cargo. Their average result was a very low elasticity of 0.09 and 0.11. Canal tolls, however, made up only 7 percent of the estimated cost of the average transit through the Panama Canal. We, therefore, recalculated their elasticity estimates by using their estimate of the percentage decline in transits through the Panama Canal against the percentage increase in the total cost of shipping through the canal. The result of this calculation produced an average estimate of the elasticity of demand for shipping through the Panama Canal with respect to the total cost of shipping of 1.19 and 1.52.

69. Calculated from data in *Annual Reports* (selected years).

70. Cole, "Economic Ramifications," 69.

71. Calculated from data in Cole, "Economic Ramifications," 70.

72. The new Panamanian management did move away from the flat rates charged by the Americans. Average rates did not rise dramatically, but certain kinds of shipping paid much more, while others received rate cuts. See chapter 8.

73. Authors' calculations, based on data in Cole, "Economic Ramifications," 70, and the Panama Canal Company's report for 1975.

74. By 1975, almost none of the ships engaged in international trade were owned by American shipping lines. IRA estimated that shippers captured roughly 2 percent of the cost savings, and the rest were split roughly fifty-fifty between importers and exporters.

75. The Panama Canal Commission changed its depreciation schedule several times. We have adjusted for those changes.

76. Panama Canal Commission, *Annual Reports* (various years).

77. William Gardner Bell, ed., *Department of the Army Historical Summary: FY 1970*, (Washington, DC: Center of Military History, U.S. Army, 1973), 149; and Michael Murphy, "Anthrax Strike: The 1976 Outbreak of Labor Militancy in the Panama Canal Zone," IBEW Local Union 520, October 2005, 18.

78. Murphy, "Anthrax Strike," 21.

79. The PCC board needed to submit rate hikes to the president for approval. Alfred Osborne, "On the Economic Cost to Panama of Negotiating a Peaceful Solution to the Panama Canal Question," *Journal of Interamerican Studies and World Affairs* 19, no. 4 (November 1977): 509–21, 514; PANAMA CANAL COMPANY, *Petitioner, v. GRACE LINE, Inc., et al. GRACE LINE, Inc., Isbrandtsen Company, Inc., Luckenbach Steamship Company, Inc., et al., Petitioners, v. PANAMA CANAL COMPANY*, United States Supreme Court, April 28, 1958, 2 L.Ed.2d 788; 78 S.Ct. 752; 356 U.S. 309, http://www.altlaw.org/v1/cases/394413.

80. *Panama Canal Company Authorization for Fiscal Year 1995*, 103rd Cong., 2nd sess., March 1, 1995, 31.

81. Panama Canal Authority, "Walter P. Leber," http://www.pancanal.com/eng/history/biographies/leber.html.

82. Harry Truman, *Memoirs: Year of Decisions* (Garden City, NY: Doubleday, 1955), 1:377.

83. Major, *Prize* Possession, 376; and John Major, "The Panama Canal Zone, 1904–79," in *The Cambridge History of Latin America*, vol. 7, *Latin America since 1930: Mexico, Central America and the Caribbean*, ed. Leslie Bethell, 669 (Cambridge: Cambridge University Press, 1990).

84. Clymer, *Drawing the Line at the Big Ditch*, 7.

85. Congressional Research Service, *Background Documents Relating to the Panama Canal* (Washington, DC: GPO, 1977), 1149–318.

86. Major, *Prize Possession*, 342.

87. "The Canal Zone: Panama and the United States," *Heritage Foundation Backgrounder* 31 (August 16, 1977).

88. Clymer, *Drawing the Line at the Big Ditch*, 14–15.

89. LeFeber, *Panama Canal*, 146–47.

90. Clymer, *Drawing the Line at the Big Ditch*, 44.

91. Major, *Prize Possession*, 346.

92. Clymer, *Drawing the Line at the Big Ditch*, 44.

93. Ibid., 61.

94. Ibid., 49–51, 85, 97–101.

95. Ibid., chap. 14 and 15.

EIGHT   Ditching the Ditch

1. William J. Jorden, *Panama Odyssey* (Austin: University of Texas Press, 1984), 480.

2. *Panamá en cifras*, various years (Panamá: Controloria general de la republica, Dirección de estadistica y censo).

3. Andrew S. Zimbalist and John Weeks, *Panama at the Crossroads: Economic Development and Political Change in the Twentieth Century* (Berkeley: University of California Press, 1991), 26.

4. Law 63 of 1917, December 5, 1917; Commercial Code of August 22, 1916; State Department 819.851/3, 7.11.1922.

5. This affected one-third of the American merchant marine fleet. Paul Maxwell Zeis, *American Shipping Policy* (Princeton, NJ: Princeton University Press, 1938), 15.

6. Darrell Hevenor Smith and Paul V. Betters, *The United States Shipping Board: Its History, Activities, and Organization* (Washington, DC: Brookings Institution, 1931), 99.

7. William S. Benson, *The Merchant Marine: "A Necessity in Time of War, a Source of Independence and Strength in Time of Peace"* (New York: Macmillan, 1923), 176–77.

8. Carlisle, *Sovereignty for Sale*, 6–9; McCain, *United States and Republic of Panama*, 206–7.

9. Carlisle, *Sovereignty for Sale*, 10–11.

10. *New York Herald*, October 1, 1922. Comyn is better known for his experiments in developing cargo ships made from reinforced

concrete as a response to steel shortages. See "Big Concrete Ship Afloat in Pacific," *New York Times*, March 15, 1918.

11. Carlisle, *Sovereignty for Sale*, 19–21.

12. Carlisle, *Sovereignty for Sale*, 33.

13. Carlisle *Sovereignty for Sale*, 47–52. Carlisle notes, "Although ESSO's Marine Division . . . evidences some foresight in removing the vessels to Panama, that foresight apparently was based on evidence of Polish, not Nazi, difficulties."

14. Carlisle, *Sovereignty for Sale*, 59–61. The ships were registered through the Panamanian firm of Arias, Fabrega and Fabrega. See Erling D. Naess, *Autobiography of a Shipping Man* (Colchester, UK: Seatrade Publications, 1977), 40–41.

15. Carlisle, *Sovereignty for Sale*, 62–65.

16. Carlisle, *Sovereignty for Sale*, 61. This was the *City of Panama*, originally the HMS *Mistletoe*, which operated as a Q-ship during World War I, as a warship decoyed as a freighter. After the war, the ship changed hands several times, working as an actual freighter in Mexico and Central America. As the *La Playa*, she operated as a gambling ship off Los Angeles. As the *City of Panama*, she started broadcasting as a pirate radio station, RXKR, whose programming was listed in the *Los Angeles Times*. After several colorful incidents, Panama withdrew its registry, and the ship was refitted as a fishing barge and floating nightclub as *The Star of Scotland*. Shortly after the start of World War Two, the *Star* foundered in Santa Monica Bay and sank, where it is currently an attraction for scuba divers. See Darren Douglass, *Guide to shipwreck diving. Southern California* (Houston, TX: Pisces Books, 1990), 53–56; James Schwoch, "The Influence of Local History on Popular Fiction: Gambling Ships in Los Angeles, 1933," *Journal of Popular Culture* 20, no. 4 (Spring 1987): 103–11; Andrew R. Yoder, *Pirate Radio Stations: Tuning in to Underground Broadcasts in the Air and Online* (New York: McGraw-Hill, 2002), 154–55.

17. Carlisle, *Sovereignty for Sale*, 73–78, 82–83.

18. Carlisle, *Sovereignty for Sale*, 110–11.

19. *International Historical Statistics: The Americas, 1750–2000* (New York: Palgrave Macmillan, 2003), 575.

20. Carlisle, *Sovereignty for Sale*, 115–24.

21. Carlisle, *Sovereignty for Sale*, 132.

22. Zimbalist and Weeks, *Panama at the Crossroads*, 64. By 2004, the ship registry generated approximately $255 million per year for the Panamanian government. "The Lawless Sea," *Frontline*, PBS, January 2004, http://www.pbs.org/frontlineworld/stories/spain/panama.html.

23. Interview with Oswaldo Heilbron, December 18, 2008.

24. Ibid.

25. Ibid.

26. René Goméz-Valladares, "The Development of the Colón Free Zone and Its Relationship to the Economy of Panama" (master's thesis, Southern Illinois University, 1971), 2; Roland Blair Reems, "The Colon Free Zone of Panama" (master's thesis, University of Florida, 1965), 26.

27. Reems, "Colon Free Zone," 28.

28. Milton C. Taylor, *Fiscal Survey of Panama: Problems and Proposals for Reform* (Baltimore, MD: Johns Hopkins Press, 1964), 186.

29. "Colon Free Zone 1952 Imports," *New York Times*, May 11, 1953.

30. Taylor, *Fiscal Survey of Panama*, 187.

31. "Trade Zone Opens U.S. Office," *New York Times*, April 25, 1956.

32. "Colon Free Zone Is Held Strategic," *New York Times*, July 18, 1956.

33. Taylor, *Fiscal Survey of Panama*, table 12.1, 191; John S. Radosta, "Colon Free Zone Gives Business Forward Base in Latin America," *New York Times*, April 1, 1957.

34. "Panama No-Duty Zone Busy," *New York Times*, June 29, 1969.

35. Taylor, *Fiscal Survey of Panama*, table 12.1, 191; David Hummels, "Have International Transport Costs Declined?" (working paper, University of Chicago, 1999).

36. Taylor, *Fiscal Survey of Panama*, 187.

37. "Colon Free Zone Seeks Industry," *New York Times*, November 14, 1958.

38. "Contract Is Signed to Give Panama a Textile Industry," *New York Times*, November 29, 1964.

39. Biesanz, "Economy of Panama," 19, which cites the *Annual Economic Report* of the American embassy in Panama, no. 90.

40. Data from *Panama en cifras* and the International Labor Organization, *Yearbook of Labor Statistics* (selected years).

41. Reems, "Colon Free Zone," 38.

42. Biesanz, "Economy of Panama," 14.

43. Taylor, *Fiscal Survey of Panama*, 93, table 6.1.

44. Taylor, *Fiscal Survey of Panama*, 6.

45. Zimbalist and Weeks, *Panama at the Crossroads*, 24.

46. Barletta, *Estrategia para el desarrollo nacional, 1970–1980*.

47. Luis H. Moreno Jr., *Panamá: Una vocación de servicio* (Panamá: Banco Nacional de Panamá, 1991), 21.

48. McCain, *United States and Republic of Panama*, 101.

49. Ibid., 101.

50. UN Economic Commission for Latin America, "The Economic Development of Panama," *Economic Bulletin for Latin America* 4 (October 1959): 48–59, 49.

51. Biesanz, "Economy of Panama," 21.

52. Phanor J. Eder, "Panama: Coded Bank Accounts," *American Journal of Comparative Law* 8, no. 3 (Summer 1959): 371–72.

53. Moreno, *Una vocación de servicio*, 21; Harry G. Johnson, "Panama as a Regional Financial Center: A Preliminary Analysis of Development Contribution," *Economic Development and Cultural Change* 24, no. 2 (January 1976): 261–86.

54. Moreno, *Una vocación de servicio*, 22; Zimbalist and Weeks, *Panama at the Crossroads*, 70–71.

55. Barney Warf, "Tailored for Panama: Offshore Banking at the Crossroads of the Americas," *Geografiska Annaler* 84 B(1) (2002): 33–47, 38.

56. Zimbalist and Weeks, *Panama at the Crossroads*, 70–71.

57. Warf, "Tailored for Panama," 38.

58. Moreno, *Una vocación de servicio*, 50.

59. Zimbalist and Weeks, *Panama at the Crossroads*, 70.

60. Steve C. Ropp, *Panamanian Politics: From Guarded Nation to National Guard* (New York: Praeger, 1982), 109.

61. Zimbalist and Weeks, *Panama at the Crossroads*, 64.

62. Zimbalist and Weeks, *Panama at the Crossroads*, 67, 72.

63. "Atlantic Richfield Obtains Core Sample from Test Well," *Wall Street Journal*, February 19, 1968, 11.

64. "Alaska Oil, Gas Find Is Potentially Vast, Consulting Firm Says," *Wall Street Journal*, July 19, 1968, 3.

65. "Atlantic Richfield Co. Opens 34.50 Higher After Halt in Trading," *Wall Street Journal*, July 23, 1968, 6.

66. John Abele, "North Slope: An Oil Bonanza—but the Problem Is to Get It Out," *New York Times*, September 21, 1969, E8.

67. "Alaska Oil Enters Canal," *Los Angeles Times*, August 31, 1977, 1.

68. See "Guatemala—East-West Pipe Link for Alaska Oil," *Chicago Tribune*, April 3, 1978; "Pipeline in Nicaragua Proposed as a Link in Moving Alaska Oil," *New York Times*, December 8, 1969; "Panama, Costa Rica Fight for Pipeline," *Chicago Tribune*, February 14, 1971; and "Costa Rica Weighs Sea-to-Sea Oil Pipe," *Chicago Tribune*, June 20, 1982.

69. "Panama Pipeline Job Is Award to Unit of Morrison-Knudsen," *Wall Street Journal*, March 18, 1981; Zimbalist and Weeks, *Panama at the Crossroads*, 62.

70. Zimbalist and Weeks, *Panama at the Crossroads*, 182, note 40.

71. Charlotte Elton, "Serving Foreigners," *NACLA Report on the Americas* 22, no. 4 (1988): 27–31.

72. Calculated from figures in Zimbalist and Weeks, *Panama at the Crossroads*, 63, and OxLAD.

73. Elton, "Serving Foreigners," 27–31.

74. *Annual Report* (various years).

75. Ropp, *Panamanian Politics*, 79–81.

76. Seymour Hersh, "Panama Strongman Said to Trade in Drugs, Arms and Illicit Money," *New York Times*, June 12, 1986, A1; Stephen Engelberg with Jeff Gerth, "Bush and Noriega: Examination of Their Ties," *New York Times*, September 27, 1989, A1.

77. Alan Riding, "A Troubled Dictator: The Canal Is Only One of Panama's Flash Points," *New York Times*, October 10, 1976.

78. As far back as *1918*, U.S. authorities considered the cocaine trade in Panama a menace to its troops garrisoned there. See *Panama Weekly News*, June 1, 1918, included in USNA State Department file 819.1151/18.

79. Pippin, *Remón Era*, 65–66.

80. Pippin, *Remón Era*, 127–29.

81. Robert J. Nieves, "Colombian Cocaine Cartels: Lessons from the Front," *Trends in Organized Crime* 3, no. 3 (1998): 13–29, 14–16.

82. Sandra W. Meditz and Dennis Michael Hanratty, *Panama: A Country Study* (Washington, DC: GPO, 1989), 150.

83. Elaine Sciolino, "Accountant Says Noriega Helped Launder Billions," *New York Times*, February 12, 1988.

84. Francisco E. Thoumi, "Illegal Drugs in Colombia: From Illegal Economic Boom to Social Crisis," *Annals of the American Academy of Political and Social Science* 582, no. 1 (2002): 102–16, 109.

85. Zimbalist and Weeks, *Panama at the Crossroads*, 77–78.

86. Sciolino, "Noriega Helped Launder Billions." It should be noted, however, many of these gains were held off the books within the Panamanian Defense Force or by close associates of Noriega. Dinges notes that estimates of Noriega's personal wealth shifted with American attitudes toward him: in 1986, Noriega's personal wealth in the *Miami Herald* was estimated as $16 million, by 1989, Deputy Secretary of State Lawrence Eagleburger was claiming $300 million. See Dinges, *Our Man In Panama*, 312, and 388 n. 312.

87. U.S. Senate, Committee on Foreign Relations, *Drugs, Law Enforcement, and Foreign Policy: Hearings before the Subcommittee on Terrorism, Narcotics, and International Communications and International Economic Policy, Trade, Oceans, and Environment of the Committee on Foreign Relations*, 100th Cong., 1st sess. (Washington, DC: GPO, 1988), 251.

88. Zimbalist and Weeks, *Panama at the Crossroads*, 139–40.

89. Ibid., 139–40.

90. Stephen Kinzer, "3-Time President Runs in Panama," *New York Times*, May 5, 1984, 5.

91. Dinges, *Our Man in Panama*, 186–87.

92. "Official Result of Vote in Panama Is Delayed," *New York Times*, May 9, 1984.

93. Stephen Kinzer, "1 Killed and 23 Hurt in Panama as Rivals Contest Vote Result," *New York Times*, May 8, 1984, A1.

94. Dinges, *Our Man in Panama*, 187–89.

95. Stephen Kinzer, "The Winner in Panama, Nicolas Ardito Barletta Vallarina," *New York Times*, May 18, 1984, A8.

96. Kevin Buckley, *Panama: The Whole Story* (New York: Simon and Schuster, 1991), 20.

97. Alan Riding, "Panamanian Doctor Listens for Another Call to Arms," *New York Times*, December 28, 1980, 3.

98. Buckley, *Panama*, 23.

99. Ibid., 27.

100. James LeMoyne, "Elements in Ouster of Panama Chief: Beheading and a Power Duel," *New York Times*, October 10, 1985, A12.

101. Buckley, *Panama*, 28.

102. Buckley, *Panama*, 33–36. Barletta originally believed the broadcast would be live.

103. Buckley, *Panama*, 34.

104. Buckley, *Panama*, 36.

105. Eytan Gilboa, "The Panama Invasion Revisited," *Political Science Quarterly* 110, no. 4 (1995–96): 539–62, 543.

106. Buckley, *Panama*, 47–48.

107. U.S. Senate, *Situation in Panama: Hearings before the Subcommittee on Western Hemisphere Affairs of the Committee on Foreign Relations*, 99th Cong., 2nd sess., March 10 and April 21, 1986, 52–54.

108. Buckley, *Panama*, 120.

109. LaFeber, *Panama Canal*, 204.

110. Gilboa, "Panama Invasion Revisited," 539–62, 544.

111. Ibid., 539–62, 545.

112. Philip Shenon, "Noriega Indicted by U.S. for Links to Illegal Drugs," *New York Times*, February 6, 1988, 1.

113. "Three Island Officials Indicted in Drug Case," *New York Times*, March 15, 1985.

114. Elaine Sciolino, "State Dept. Aide Hints at a Deal If Noriega Quits," *New York Times*, February 19, 1988, 1.

115. Elaine Sciolino, "Panama President Dismisses Noriega; Situation Unclear," *New York Times*, February 26, 1988, 1.

116. Buckley, *Panama*, 125.

117. Buckley, *Panama*, 129.

118. Buckley, *Panama*, 130; Douglas Martin and Sara Abruzzese, "William D. Rogers Is Dead at 80; Planned U.S. Policy in Latin America," *New York Times*, September 30, 2007.

119. Jorden, *Panama Odyssey*, 285–86, 561–63.

120. Zimbalist and Weeks, *Panama at the Crossroads*, 68; Russ Mackendrick, "Numismatics: Interesting Facts about the Coinage of Panama," *New York Times*, August 28, 1977. Panamanian historian Alonso Roy has a full description of the 1941 Arias balboa note issue at AlonsoRoy.com, "Política Nacional," http:// www.alonsoroy.com/pn/pn04.html.

121. Marjorie Williams, "The Panama File: A D.C. Attorney's 'Revolution by Litigation,'" *Washington Post*, March 22, 1988, D1.

122. Zimbalist and Weeks, *Panama at the Crossroads*, 81.

123. Williams, "The Panama File"; Zimbalist and Weeks, *Panama at the Crossroads*, 147.

124. Zimbalist and Weeks, *Panama at the Crossroads*, 69.

125. Zimbalist and Weeks, *Panama at the Crossroads*, 147.

126. Williams, "The Panama File."

127. Charlotte Elton, "Panama and Japan: Who Is Setting the Agenda?" MIT Japan Program publication 90-02 (1990), 21.

128. Williams, "The Panama File."

129. On April 8, 1988. Accessed via Public Papers of Ronald Reagan, April 1988, website at the University of Texas, http://www .reagan.utexas.edu/archives/speeches/1988/040888a.htm.

130. Robert Pear with Neil A. Lewis, "The Noriega Fiasco: What Went Wrong," *New York Times*, May 30, 1988, 1.

131. United States General Accounting Office document GAO/T-NSAID-89-44, "GAO Review of Economic Sanctions Imposed Against Panama," written statement to the House Western Hemisphere Affairs Subcommittee on International Economic Policy and Trade, Frank C. Conahan, assistant comptroller general, July 26, 1989, 19–20. Compare the range of 17 percent to 26 percent given in Zimbalist and Weeks, *Panama at the Crossroads*, 150.

132. Gary Clyde Hufbauer, Jeffrey J. Schott, and Kimberly Ann Elliott, *Economic Sanctions Reconsidered*, 2nd ed. (Washington, DC: Institute for International Economics, 1990), 87. Hufbauer, Schott, and Elliott calculate a direct 6 percent drop in GNP over three years for Panama. It should be noted, however, that they assume a multiplier effect of less than one (!) caused by the disruption of Panama's financial system, and that they fail to use proxies such as electricity consumption or industrial production to confirm their estimates. Pape critiques Hufbauer, noting that both Iran and Rhodesia are problematic instances of the success of sanctions; see Robert A. Pape, "Why Economic Sanctions Do Not Work," *International Security* 22, no. 2 (Autumn 1997): 90–136, 101. Oddly, Hufbauer, Schott, and Elliott's estimation of the relative success of Panamanian sanctions has increased with time, moving from a four on a scale from zero to sixteen in the second edition of 1990, to an eight in the third edition of 2008.

133. John D. Harbron, "Yankee Dollars Wanted," *Barron's Weekly*, July 31, 1978.

134. Zimbalist and Weeks, *Panama at the Crossroads*, 147. This is not as bizarre as it might first appear. Panama had a history of issuing commemorative coins on special occasions. See Mackendrick, "Numismatics."

135. Buckley, *Panama*, 133–34; Zimbalist and Weeks, *Panama at the Crossroads*, 82.

136. Zimbalist and Weeks, *Panama at the Crossroads*, 82.

137. Buckley, *Panama*, 134–35.

138. Dinges, *Our Man in Panama*, 298–300.

139. Elaine Sciolino, "As the Election Nears, Talk About Noriega Fades," *New York Times*, October 28, 1988, E6.

140. *Annual Report* (1988), 27.

141. John Goshko, "Panama Canal Official Says Harassment Growing," *Washington Post*, March 28, 1989, A12.

142. Ibid.

143. Bob Poos, "Gianelli Cites Frustrations in Panama Canal Resignation," *Traffic World* 218, no. 3 (April 17, 1989): 29.

144. William Branigin, "Noriega's Candidate Is Likely Victor," *Washington Post*, May 6, 1989, A1.

145. William Branigin, "Carter Accuses Noriega of Stealing Election," *Washington Post*, May 9, 1989, A1.

146. William Branigin, "Opposition Leaders Attacked," *Washington Post*, May 11, 1989, A1; Buckley, *Panama*, 180–83.

147. Bruce Vail, "Political Tension Hurts Canal Operations," *Journal of Commerce*, July 27, 1989, A1.

148. Larry Rohter, "Panamanian Runs the Canal: A First," *New York Times*, January 3, 1990.

149. Ronald H. Cole, *Operation Just Cause: The Planning and Execution of Joint Operations in Panama, February 1988–January 1990* (Washington, DC: Joint History Office, Office of the Chairman of the Joint Chiefs of Staff, 1995), 17–22.

150. Cole, *Operation Just Cause*, 27–30.

151. Ibid., 32, 38.

152. Ibid., 56.

153. Ibid., 63.

154. Ibid., 66–67.

155. Larry Rohter, "Panama and U.S. Strive to Settle on Death Toll," *New York Times*, April 1, 1990, 12.

156. Zimbalist and Weeks, *Panama at the Crossroads*, 200 n. 57.

157. *Annual Report* (1990), 13.

158. Rohter, "Panamanian Runs the Canal."

159. Jorden, *Panama Odyssey*, 684–85.

160. David Pitt, "Challenge for Panamanians: A Canal in Transition," *New York Times*, January 29, 1990.

161. Ibid.

162. Panama Canal Commission, *A Decade of Progress in Canal Operation and Treaty Implementation* (Panama City: PCC, 1989), 11–15.

163. *Report of the Panama Canal Commission*, selected years.

164. Panama Canal Commission, *A Decade of Progress in Canal Operation and Treaty Implementation*, 28; and Francisco Montero Llacer, "The Panama Canal: Operations and Traffic," *Marine Policy* 29 (2005): 223–34, 228–29.

165. Peter Sánchez, *Panama Lost? U.S. Hegemony, Democracy, and the Canal* (Gainesville: University Press of Florida, 2007), 177–78.

166. *Panama Canal Commission Authorization, Fiscal Year 1995*, 103rd Cong., 2nd sess., Serial No. 103-84, March 1, 1994 (Washington, DC: GPO), 8.

167. See Ley 23 de 1941 por la cual se crea la Caja de Seguro Social, March 23, 1941, accessed through the Panamanian legal database Legispan.

168. Ropp, *Panamanian Politics*, 79–81.

169. Buckley, *Panama*, 166.

170. The Arnulfista Party would change its name back to Panameñista in 2005.

171. Margaret E. Scranton, "Panama's First Post-Transition Election," *Journal of Interamerican Studies and World Affairs* 37, no. 1 (1995): 69–100; Howard French, "Democracy at Work: Under Shadow of Dictators," *New York Times*, February 21, 1994, A4.

172. Robert R. McMillan, *Global Passage: Transformation of Panama and the Panama Canal* ([North Charleston, SC]: BookSurge, 2006), p. 80.

173. Sánchez, *Panama Lost?* 180–81.

174. Larry Rohter, "Re-election Struggle in Panama Could Affect Transfer of Canal," *New York Times*, May 29, 1998, A4.

175. Mireya Navarro, "The Widow of Ex-Leader Wins Race in Panama," *New York Times*, May 3, 1999, A8.

176. Matthew M. Singer, "Presidential and Parliamentary Elections in Panama, May 2004," *Electoral Studies* 24 (2005): 531–37.

177. Panama Canal Commission, *Ten-Year Report: A Decade of Progress in Canal Operations and Treaty Implementation* (Balboa, Panama: Panama Canal Commission, 1989), 19.

178. Ibid.

179. In this context, "pre-tax" means Panama Canal profitability before any payments to the Panamanian government, save the $10 million charged to provide public services in the former Canal Zone, and the interest payments made to the U.S. Treasury.

180. Panama Canal Commission, *Ten-Year Report*, 11–13.

181. *Panama Canal Commission Authorization, Fiscal Year 1995*, 104th Cong., 2nd sess., March 5, 1996 (Washington, DC: GPO), 59.

182. Andrew Bounds, "The Profit Motive: Panama Canal, in Switch from U.S. Days, Seeks to Operate Like a Business," *Journal of Commerce*, May 13, 2002.

183. Data in Rodolfo Sabonge, "Expanding Capacity of the Panama Canal" (paper presented at the Transportation Research Board 2006 summer conference, La Jolla, CA, July 9–11, 2006).

184. Andrew Bounds, "The Profit Motive: Panama Canal, in Switch from US Days, Seeks to Operate Like a Business," *JoC Week*, May 13, 2002.

185. In point of fact, there is no simple conversion between TEU and long-tons. In 2007, the Panama Canal moved 13.8 million TEU of container traffic. The ACP registered those containers as the equivalent of 58.6 million long-tons, for a rough conversion factor of 4.2 long-tons per TEU. That conversion factor, if applied to all the cargo passing through the canal, would produce an estimate of 52.4 million TEU as the total amount of cargo moved through the Panama Canal in 2007.

See Diego Ferrer, "Freight Movement in Panama," Embassy of Panama in the United States, 2007.

186. Panama Canal Railway Company, http://www.panarail .com/en/cargo/index-02.html.

NINE   Concluding the Ditch

1. A good compendium of social saving estimates can be found in Nicholas F. R. Crafts, "Social Savings as a Measure of the Contribution of a New Technology to Economic Growth" (working paper 06/04, London School of Economics, 2004). Mexico: John H.

Coatsworth, "Indispensable Railroads in a Backward Economy: The Case of Mexico," *Journal of Economic History* 39, no. 4 (December 1979): 939–60; Brazil: W. R. Summerhill, *Order against Progress: Government, Foreign Investment and Railroads in Brazil, 1854–1913* (Stanford: Stanford University Press, 2003).

2. Hutchinson and Ungo, "Social Saving of the Panama Canal."

3. Ibid.

4. M. Ishaq Nadiri and Theofanis P. Mamuneas, "Contribution of Highway Capital to Industry and National Productivity Growth" (working paper, U.S. Department of Transportation, Federal Highway Administration, 1996).

5. J. A. Hobson, *Imperialism: A Study* (London: J. Nisbet, 1902).

6. V. I. Lenin, "Imperialism: The Highest Stage of Capitalism," in *Essential Works of Lenin: "What Is to Be Done?" and Other Writings* (New York: Dover, 1987), 267.

7. "Panama Canal Activities," *New York Times*, August 27, 1920, 26.

8. Interview with Stanley Motta, former head of the ARI (Autoridad de la Región Interoceánica), December 16, 2008.

9. Richard Koebner, "The Concept of Economic Imperialism," *Economic History Review*, n.s., 2, no. 1 (1949): 1–29. See also D. K. Fieldhouse, "'Imperialism': An Historiographical Revision," *Economic History Review*, n.s., 14, no. 2 (1961): 187–209.

10. Stanley Lebergott, "The Returns to U.S. Imperialism, 1890–1929," *Journal of Economic History* 40, no. 2 (1980): 229–52.

11. Avner Offer, "The British Empire, 1870–1914: A Waste of Money?" *Economic History Review* 46, no. 2 (1993): 215–38.

12. Robert Paul Thomas, "The Sugar Colonies of the Old Empire: Profit or Loss for Great Britain?" *Economic History Review* 21, no. 1 (1968): 30–45.

13. D. K. Fieldhouse, "The Metropolitan Economics of Empire," in *The Oxford History of the British Empire*, vol. 4, *The Twentieth Century*, ed. Judith M. Brown and William Roger Louis, 88–113 (Oxford: Oxford University Press, 1999).

14. Lance Edwin Davis and Robert A. Huttenback, *Mammon and the Pursuit of Empire: The Political Economy of British*

Imperialism, 1860–1912 (Cambridge: Cambridge University Press, 1986), 262–79.

15. D. K. Fieldhouse, "The Metropolitan Economics of Empire," in Brown, *Twentieth Century*, 111.

16. Michael Edelstein, "Imperialism: Cost and Benefit," chap. 8 in *The Economic History of Britain since 1700*, vol. 2, *1860–1939*, 2nd ed., ed. R. C. Floud and D. N. McCloskey (Cambridge: Cambridge University Press, 1994), 197–216. Edelstein also calculates a much higher gain of 5.7 percent to 6.8 percent for British GNP under his "strong non-imperialist" assumption, which posits that territories inside the empire had an additional 40 percent to 300 percent of commerce with Britain compared to counterfactual independent territories trading with Britain from outside the empire. This strikes us as perilously close to assuming one's conclusion.

17. Calculated from 1913 trade data found in Fieldhouse, "The Metropolitan Economics of Empire," 100.

18. It should be noted that the lion's share of the economic benefits to Britain from imperial trade came from the self-governing dominions of Canada, Australia, New Zealand, and South Africa, the first three of which were voluntarily associated with the United Kingdom and would have been unlikely to change trade policy (which they already controlled) had the Statute of Westminster been enacted in 1881 or 1913 rather than 1931. In other words, it is far from clear that the United Kingdom and its settler offshoots in North America and Australasia formed separate political communities before 1913, let alone that some unrecognized threat of U.K. sanctions kept their (rather protectionist, if not as much as the United States) trade policies in check.

19. Stanley L. Engerman and Kenneth L. Sokoloff, "Factor Endowments, Institutions, and Differential Paths of Growth Among New World Economies: A View from Economic Historians of the United States," in *How Latin America Fell Behind*, ed. Stephen Haber (Stanford: Stanford University Press, 1997).

20. Daron Acemoglu, Simon Johnson, and James A. Robinson, "The Colonial Origins of Comparative Development: An Empiri-

cal Investigation," *American Economic Review* 91, no. 5 (2001): 1369–401.

21. Ferguson and Schularick, "Empire Effect," 283–312.

22. Mitchener and Weidenmier, "Empire," 658–92.

23 Alfaro, Maurer, and Ahmed, "Gunboats and Vultures."

24. Robert L. Tignor, *Capitalism and Nationalism at the End of Empire: State and Business in Decolonizing Egypt, Nigeria and Kenya, 1945–1963* (Princeton, NJ: Princeton University Press, 1998), 120–21, 168.

INDEX

base gold, 14
Bastidas, Rodrigo de, 15
Bates, Robert H., 5
Battle of Guadalcanal, 219, 221–22
Battle of Midway, 219, 222
Battle of Palonegro, 77
Battle of the Coral Sea, 219, 222
Bay Area Rapid Transport system, 98
Bay of San Miguel, 16
Bay of the Honduras. *See* Gulf of Mexico
Beckel, Bob, 261
Belen Quezada (ship), 271
Benson, William, 270
Bethlehem Shipyards, 164
Bethlehem Steel, 164, 368n38
Biddle, Charles, 13, 33–35
Bidlack, Benjamin, 35
Bidlack-Mallarino Treaty, 35–36, 67, 69, 80–83
Big Dig, 98, 345n152, 357n4
Big Inch, 184
Bishop, Joseph, 191–92
black market, 195, 198
Blades, Ruben, 303
Blandy, W.H.P., 226
Blue Book of Panama, 189
Blue Spoon (military operation), 297
Bô, Marius, 75
Boeing, William, 179
Bogotá, 29, 32–36, 42, 59, 65, 68, 77–82, 128
Bolívar, Simón, 29–32, 189
Bosporus, 40–41
Boston (war ship), 84
bounty depression, 130
bourgeoisie, 317
Boyd, Aquilino, 236
Boyd, Federico, 85, 122
Brazil, 126, 206, 314
Brazil Maru (ship), 166
bribery, 39, 65, 292
bridges, 23–24, 44, 46, 49, 52
Bridgetown, 130–31, 134
British, the, 39, 139, 324; Cape Horn and, 30; Clayton-Bulwer Treaty and, 40–42, 67, 72; empire effect and, 201; Five-Power Treaty and, 168; imperialism and, 319–20; Lesseps and, 57; Mosquito Coast interests and, 35; Panama money and, 129–30; Potsdam Conference and, 228; ship registration and, 272; San Lorenzo

fort and, 26; Taft and, 146; Tehuantepec Railroad and, 52; toll controversy and, 146–47; Treaty of Balta-Liman and, 40–41; U.S. Diplomacy and, 14, 33, 72; Vanderbilt and, 40–41
Brooklyn, 73, 98, 100, 118, 275, 357n4
Brooklyn-Queens Expressway, 98
Brooklyn's Twelfth Congressional District, 275
Bryan, William Jennings, 147
Brzezinski, Zbigniew, 260
B-25 bombers, 221
Buchanan, James, 35
Buchanan, William, 201
Buenos Aires, 6
Bullard, Arthur, 131–32
Bunau-Varilla, Philippe, 79–80; Culebra Cut and, 61; fraud accusations against, 75; Hay–Bunau-Varilla Treaty and, 84, 87–92, 95, 193, 203, 211
Burgess, Harry, 194
Bush, George H. W., 296–97

Cáceres, Alonso de, 19
California: American conquest of, 6, 14, 36; gold rush of, 36–40; petroleum industry and, 179–88, 314–15; price-reduction effects and, 314–15; transcontinental pipeline and, 183–88
Calle de Santo Domingo, 17
Camino de Cruces, 17–18, 23–26
Camino Real, 17, 24–27
Canada, 54, 271, 320
Canal Area, 256
Canal Builders, The: Making America's Empire at the Panama Canal (Greene), 11
Canal Zone, 7, 10, 361n83, 375n39, 396n179; barriers to growth in, 273–75; birth of, 92–96; Boyd march and, 236–37; Colón Free Zone and, 269, 275–81, 311, 322, 387n26; colonial origins of comparative development and, 323–24; as comfortable sinecure, 326; Commissary and, 190–200 (*see also* Commissary); as corporate enterprise, 102; decolonization and, 325–31; defense of, 105–6, 167–73, 226–28; digging of Panama Canal and, 101–25; disappearance of, 264–65, 282–84, 287, 297, 303, 306; disease in, 97–98 (*see also* disease); empire effect and, 200–

208; flying of Panamanian flag and, 236–38; Frelinghuysen-Zavala Treaty and, 87; Hay–Bunau-Varilla Treaty and, 84–92, 95, 193, 203, 211; Hay-Concha Memorandum and, 79–80; Hull-Alfaro Treaty and, 208–11; labor strikes and, 112–14, 293, 323; market advantages of, 230–31; Merchant Marine and Fisheries Subcommittee and, 275; Panamanian economic development before 1977, 266–69; Panamanian flag and, 236–38, 262, 269, 322; private property rights in, 318–19; racial issues and, 115–20, 234–35 (*see also* racial issues); Remón-Eisenhower Treaty and, 231, 234–35, 277–78, 322; as settler colony, 321–22, 332; sliding irrelevancy of, 212–13, 226–31, 234–40, 247, 251, 255–57, 260–63; Thatcher plan and, 101–2; toll controversies and, 146–47, 246–48; United States Citizens Association (USCA) and, 235

Canary Islands, 16

Cape Horn, 30, 36–37, 49, 72, 140, 150, 214, 224, 245, 367n25

Cape of Good Hope, 141, 166, 243

Cárdenas, Adán, 66

Carlos V, 16, 321

Cartagena, 22, 26, 35, 44

Carter, Gilbert, 133–34

Carter, James Earl "Jimmy," 1–2, 262; decolonization and, 326–27; Neutrality Treaty and, 259–60; Noriega and, 296; Panama Canal Treaty and, 259–61, 287; political bravery of, 326–27; Rogers and, 292; Torrijos and, 9, 259–61, 298; vote trading by, 261

Casey, William, 287, 290

Castañeda, Francisco de, 20

Castilia del Oro, 16

cattle, 193

Central Intelligence Agency (CIA), 285, 287, 290

Central Pacific Railroad, 54, 66

Chagres, 16–17, 26, 34, 36, 42, 44, 99, 102, 108, 225

Chanís, Daniel, 229–30

Charco Azul, 282

Charles V. *See* Carlos V

Chase Manhattan Bank, 237

Chase National, 200

Chatsfield, Frederick, 41

Chiari, Roberto, 229–30

Chicago, Milwaukee, and St. Paul Railway, 174

Chicago Association of Commerce, 174

Chicago Sanitary and Ship Canal, 72

Childs, Orville, 37, 39

Chile, 206, 285; benefits of Panama Canal and, 140; iron and, 152, 162–64, 243, 315; nitrates and, 162–63; price reduction effects and, 314–15

Chinese, 31, 43, 110, 221, 303, 344n143

Chiriquí Grande, 282, 284

Chiriquí Railroad, 204

Chivela Pass, 53

Choate, Joseph, 147

Chuchures, 15

Churchill, Winston, 219

cigarettes, 108, 198

CitiBank, 279

City of Panama (ship), 386n16

Clark, Dick, 262

Clayton, John, 33, 40–41

Clayton-Bulwer Treaty, 40–42, 67, 72

Cleveland, Grover, 67–68, 70, 87

Clymer, Adam, 11

Coatzacoalcos, 52–53

cocaine, 285–86, 292, 375n39, 390n78

Cocoa Grove, 202

Cold War: Anti-Ballistic Missile Treaty and, 253, 255; Crittenberger plan and, 225–26; Panamanian riots and, 226; Río air base and, 226; sliding irrelevancy of Canal and, 223–27; spies and, 286; Strategic Arms Limitation Treaty and, 253

Colombia, 2, 5, 318; American negotiations with, 78–82; battle of Palonegro and, 77; Bogotá, 29, 32–36, 42, 59, 65, 68, 77–82, 128; Commissary and, 198–99; Concha and, 78–81, 85–86, 89; Fabian strategy of, 77; Hay–Bunau-Varilla Treaty and, 84, 87–92, 95, 193, 203, 211; Hay-Herrán Treaty and, 81–82, 86, 89, 162; Isthmian Canal Commission and, 76–77; Marroquín and, 77, 82; Martínez Silva and, 76–78; Neutrality Act and, 67; New Granada and, 32–36, 42–43, 46, 341n88; Núñez and, 67; Panamanian secession from, 56; Roosevelt's intervention and, 7,

economic issues (*cont.*)
390n86; naval spending and, 167–68; New Panama Canal Company and, 74–75; overruns and, 2, 44, 97–99, 102, 106, 140, 147, 344n148, 345n152, 357n4; Panama Canal Company productivity and, 249–51; Panama Canal Treaty and, 260; Panamanian development before 1977, 266–69; Panamanian's lack of financial skill and, 203–4; Panama's first peak (1150–1671) and, 21–22; patronage networks and, 265–67, 328–29; petroleum industry and, 179–88; price sensitivity of shippers and, 155–57; private-property rights and, 318–19; railroad losses and, 173–77 (*see also* railroads); Remón-Eisenhower Treaty and, 231; rents and, 7–8, 61, 95, 142, 190, 246, 258, 272, 281; sanctions and, 2, 5, 190, 206, 294–95, 328–29, 333n1, 393n132, 398n18; sanitation and, 128; shipbuilding and, 270–71; ship registration and, 270–73, 281; Silver Roll and, 111–15, 118, 191–92, 198, 274, 323; slavery and, 6, 18–24, 321; smuggling and, 20, 28–29, 267, 271–73, 285, 292, 298; social savings and, 5–6, 313–16 (*see also* social savings); Suez Canal and, 57–58, 349n11; tariffs and, 52, 69, 87, 94, 130, 191–94, 267–69, 278; taxes and, 22, 50, 57, 66–69, 80, 84, 87, 128, 160–61, 173, 190–93, 198, 204, 209, 231, 238, 267–73, 277–81, 295, 306, 314; Third Locks project and, 226–27; tolls and, 146–47 (*see also* tolls); *trajín* and, 23–30; transformation of Barbados and, 129–38; Trans-isthmian Pipeline and, 265, 281–84; transportation and, 212 (*see also* transportation); U.S. aid payments and, 9, 212–13, 230, 236–39, 248, 255–56, 262–63; U.S. costs of building Panama Canal, 98–100, 103–8, 114, 118, 128, 135–39; U.S. Department of Commerce and, 272, 275; U.S. Treasury and, 149, 153, 157, 160, 162, 172, 213, 218, 248, 260, 263, 325, 396n179; wage caps and, 112; Wyse Convention and, 81–82
Ecuador, 29, 32, 126, 235, 243
Edelstein, Michael, 3, 320, 398n16

Egypt, 4, 190, 348n3; indemnity payments and, 58; Nasser and, 328; Suez Canal and, 4, 55, 57–58, 141, 190, 243, 284, 328, 349n11
Eiffel, Alexandre Gustave, 62
Eisenhower, Dwight D., 225, 239, 256; Boyd march and, 237; Commissary and, 230–31; flying of Panamanian flag and, 236–38; Remón and, 228–31, 235–36, 255, 277–78, 285, 322
elitism, 33, 236, 267, 277, 284, 290, 311, 328
Elliott, Kimberly Ann, 393n132
El Niño, 308
El Salvador, 26
El Tofo iron ore deposit, 163–64
Emigration Act, 131
empire effect: British and, 201; fiscal agency and, 204–7; United States and, 201–7
Endara, Guillermo, 296, 299, 302–3
Engerman, Stanley, 323, 357n4, 398n19
Enterprise (aircraft carrier), 224
Erie Canal, 37, 98, 357n4
Espinosa, Gaspar de, 16–17
Essex-class carriers, 222–23
Esso oil tankers, 273
European Union, 4
Executive Order 12635, 293–94

Fábrega, José de, 29
Falmarc, Maurice, 31–32
Fascists, 229
Federal Bureau of Investigation (FBI), 234
Felipe II, 321
Ferguson, Niall, 3, 201, 324, 333n2
Fermín, Felipe, 81–82
Feuille, Frank, 102
Fieldhouse, D. K., 319–20
Finlay, Carlos, 123
First National City Bank of New York, 279
Five-Power Treaty, 168
flags: American, 143, 236, 238, 240; of convenience, 269–73, 322; Panamanian, 229, 236–38, 262, 269–73, 322; ship registration and, 158, 270–73
Fogel, Robert, 5–6, 148
Ford, Gerald, 258–59, 262, 292
Foreign Relations of the United States, 11
Foreign-Trade Zones Board, 275
Forrestal-class carriers, 224

Forty-niners, 37, 43
France Field, 106
Franck, Harry, 139
freight rates: Commissary and, 193–94; decreased, 141–45, 160, 241–45; Interstate Highway System and, 241; railroads and, 173–77, 193–94; World War II and, 216
Frelinghuysen, Frederick, 66
Frelinghuysen-Zavala Treaty, 87, 92, 162
French, the, 1, 277, 348n4, 359n52; attempts at Panama Canal construction by, 59–66, 69, 71, 75, 98–99, 110–11, 123, 187, 199; Colombia and, 77; Compagnie bond failure and, 63, 65; economic law and, 348n4; Eiffel design and, 62; Five-Power Treaty and, 168; imperial interests of, 35, 42, 47–48; Mendoza and, 120; New Granada concession rights and, 32; payroll systems and, 359n52; Potsdam Conference and, 228; Silver Roll and, 111; Suez Canal and, 55, 57–60; useless excavations of, 99; Wyse Concession and, 59, 78, 81–82, 86, 89, 92, 95, 162, 316

Gaddis, John, 333n1
Gaillard, David du Bose, 112
Gaillard Cut, 103. *See also* Culebra Cut
Galicia, 111
Galley, Daniel, 224
Garibaldi, Giuseppe, 57
Gaskin, Ed, 234–35
Gatún Dam, 214
Gatún lock, 306
Georgia Tech, 294
Gianelli, William, 295–96
Gibbs, Stephen R., 243, 247
Gilberts raid, 219, 222
Gillette Safety Razor Corporation, 275
Goethals, George Washington, 194, 321; authority of, 101–2; Canal Zone defense and, 106; Commissary and, 191–92; construction of Panama Canal and, 100–102, 106, 113, 115, 118, 121; and cuts of workday hours, 113; depopulation and, 115; Isthmian Canal Commission and, 100–102, 106, 113, 115, 118, 121; lock-canal plan and, 102–3, 105; Mendoza affair and, 121–22; personality of, 100–

101; racial issues and, 101, 115, 118; Thatcher plan and, 101–2
Goethe, Johann Wolfgang von, 32
gold: Argonauts and, 37, 44; Aspinwall and, 36–37; base, 14; California gold rush and, 36–40, 43; Forty-niners and, 37, 43; Vanderbilt and, 37, 39–40
Golden Gate Bridge, 46
Gold Roll, 111–12, 115, 118, 191–92, 198, 360n58
González Dávila, Gil, 18–19
Good Neighbor diplomacy, 209–10
Goodyear, 373n96
Gorgas, William Crawford, 118, 187; anti-malaria campaign of, 124–26; fumigation and, 123–24; size of operations of, 97–98; yellow fever campaign of, 123–24
Government Accountability Office (GAO), 275
Granada, 20
Gran Colombia, 32
Great Depression, 142, 175, 245, 331
Greene, Julie, 11
Greenwood Timber Company, 179
Greif, Avner, 5
Greytown. *See* San Juan del Norte (Greytown)
Guadalcanal, 219, 221–22
Guardia, Ricardo de la, 229
Guardia, Santiago de la, 121–22
Guardia Fabrega, Gilberto, 298, 303, 309
Guatemala, 239, 270
Guizado, José Ramón, 236, 274
Gulf of Mexico, 16, 166, 174, 345n155
Gulf of Nicoya, 20
Gulf of St. Michael. *See* Bay of San Miguel
gunboats, 84, 370n63, 376n43, 399n23

Haber-Bosch process, 162–63
Hague, The, 147
Hains, Peter C., 108, 167
Haiti, 173, 207
Hanna, Mark "Dollar," 75, 80
Harding, Chester, 114–15, 194
Harding, Warren, 202–3
Hardy, Thomas, 129
Hart, Charles, 78–79
Havana, 22
Hawaii, 56, 72, 93, 168, 222
Hay, John, 72, 81–85, 201

Hayakawa, Samuel, 212
Hay–Bunau-Varilla Treaty, 84, 95, 211; Commissary and, 193; transportation privileges under, 203; U.S. gains from, 87–92
Hay-Concha Memorandum, 79–80
Hay-Herrán Treaty, 81–82, 86, 89, 162
Hay-Pauncefote Treaty, 74, 146–47
Hayes, Rutherford, 66
health issues: Commissary and, 193; disease and, 8 (*see also* disease); infant mortality and, 119–20, 127, 130, 138; racial discrimination and, 118–20; sanitation and, 82, 84–85, 115, 122–28; Spadafora and, 288; UN Standard Minimum Rules for the Treatment of Prisoners and, 323; water purification and, 127–28
Heilbron, Oswaldo, 273–75
Helms, Jesse, 287, 290
Hernández de Córdoba, Francisco, 19
Herrán, Tomás, 81
Herrera, Balbina, 313
Herrera, Roberto Díaz, 290–91
Hitt, Reynolds, 121, 361n87
HMS *Bermuda*, 40–41
HMS *Express*, 40
Hobson, J. A., 317, 319
Holland, Henry, 235
Homestead Air Force Base, 298
Honduras, 26, 172, 270
Hong Kong, 303
Hoover Dam, 98, 357n4
Hornet (aircraft carrier), 219, 221
Hufbauer, Gary Clyde, 393n132
Hughes, Charles Evans, 195
Hull, Cordell, 209–10, 229
Hull-Alfaro Treaty, 231, 274, 322
Humboldt, Alexander von, 30–32, 53, 62, 340n74, 351n48
hurricanes, 130
Hutchinson, William, 10, 152–53, 314, 368n29
Hutchison Whampoa Limited, 303
Huttenback, Robert A., 3, 320

Iberian Union, 28
Iceland, 238
Idaho (battleship), 219
illegal drug trade, 285–86, 289–90, 292, 294
Immigration and Nationality Act, 315

imperialism, 1, 11–12, 95–96, 201, 313, 332; American consumer and, 7–8; American flag and, 240; bourgeoisie and, 317; British, 319–20, 398nn16,18; colonial administration and, 2–3; colonial origins of comparative development and, 323–24; economic issues and, 2–4, 56–57, 317–24, 398nn16,18; empire effect and, 200–208; end of empire and, 333n1; exploitative nature of, 317–18; fiscal agency and, 204–6; flying of Panamanian flag and, 236–38; formal, 2–4; Hobson and, 317, 319; informal, 2–4; large-N studies and, 3; Lebergott and, 319; Lenin and, 317, 319; literature on, 3–4; private-property rights and, 318–19; rent expropriations and, 7–8; Roosevelt and, 7; sovereignty issues and, 3; threat of force and, 7
Incas, 20
Independence-class carriers, 222–23
Indiana (battleship), 219
Indians, 15, 19, 39, 43
infant mortality, 119–20, 127, 130, 138
interest costs, 106, 149, 260, 325, 396n179
International Banking Center, 269, 280
international banking sector, 269, 278–81, 292–93
International Research Associates (IRA), 245, 247, 383nn68,74
Interstate Commerce Commission (ICC), 173–75, 185
Interstate Highway System, 212, 241, 315–16
Ionian Sea, 189
Iran, 239
Irish, the, 43
iron: American, 166; Chile and, 152, 162–64, 243, 315; Haber-Bosch process and, 162–63; pig, 368n38; shipping data and, 22, 174–75
Islas de Perlas, 14
Isthmian Canal Commission, 10, 131; Commissary and, 190–200, 208–11, 230–31, 260, 263, 279, 321–22; defense costs and, 105–6; Emigration Act and, 131; Goethals and, 100–102, 106, 113, 115, 118, 121; labor unrest and, 108–22; mismanagement of, 99–102; political infighting and, 100; preparing to con-

struct Canal and, 73–76; Roosevelt's sacking of, 100; sanitation crusade and, 122–28; supervision from Washington by, 99–100

Isthmus of Panama: Balboa's crossing of, 15; Clayton-Bulwer Treaty and, 40–41; first canal proposals and, 15–17; French private interests and, 1, 6–7, 13–14; gold rush of California and, 36–40; Humboldt and, 30–32; as major commercial center, 14; pre-Columbian trade across, 13–15; unique geographic location of, 1–2

Isthmus of Tehuantepec, 49–54

Italians, 111–13, 168

Jackson, Andrew, 34

Jamaicans, 43, 110, 130, 269

Japan, 164–66; attack on Panama Canal and, 213–15; Doolittle raid and, 219, 221; Five-Power Treaty and, 168; Pearl Harbor and, 218–19, 222; World War II and, 214–15, 218–22

Jewish refugees, 272

Jim Crow system, 97

Jiménez, Enrique Adolfo, 226, 229, 275

Johnson, Lyndon, 255–59, 262, 292

Johnson, Simon, 323, 398n20

Johnston, William, 60

Jones Act, 142–43

Juan Franco Racetrack, 231

Just Cause (military operation), 297–98

Kane, Theodore, 68

Kansas City Southern Railroad, 310

Kelley, Frederick, 66, 351n48

Kennedy, John F., 255, 262, 292

Keynesian stimulus, 331

Kinai Maru (ship), 166

King, Ernest, 219

Kissinger, Henry, 257–58

Kitty Hawk-class carriers, 224

Klein, Mathew, 42

Knox, Philander, 121–22, 362n95

Korean War, 227

labor, 318; accident rates and, 251; AFL-CIO and, 231, 234; American, 43; Barbados and, 98, 110, 113, 129–38, 323, 365n162; child, 130; Chinese, 43, 110,

344n143; Colón Free Zone (CFZ) and, 276–77; Commissary and, 190–92, 195; cost-of-living increases and, 113–14; Cuban, 110–11; demographics for, 108–10; discontents and, 108–22; disease and, 61, 97–98 (*see also* disease); Gold Roll and, 111–12, 115, 118, 191–92, 198, 360n58; humanitarianism and, 323; Irish, 43; Italian, 111–13; Jamaican, 43, 110; Jim Crow system and, 97; job force reduction and, 305–6; "laziness" and, 108, 110; mortality rates for, 61; Noriega and, 295–96; Panamanization of, 298–305; Panama Railroad and, 43–44; payroll issues and, 111–12; productivity and, 249–51; racial issues and, 115–22; Remón-Eisenhower Treaty and, 231, 234–35; repatriation costs and, 110; respect and, 113; road building and, 18–21; Silver Roll and, 111–15, 118, 191–92, 198, 274, 323; skilled, 111–12, 238, 276; slavery and, 6, 18–24, 321; social returns and, 147–55; Spanish, 110–13; strikes and, 112–14, 293, 323; suicide and, 43; unskilled, 43, 134, 276–77; UN Standard Minimum Rules for the Treatment of Prisoners and, 323; wage caps and, 112

LaFeber, Walter, 11

La Higuera, 163

Lake Gatún, 99, 103, 214, 308–9

Lake Nicaragua, 16, 37, 39, 70

Landes, David, 3–4

landslides, 98, 103, 168, 213

Laos, 238

large-N studies, 3

Las Cruces, 17

Leber, Walter, 253

Lebergott, Stanley, 10, 319

Lenin, Vladimir, 317

Lesseps, Charles de, 55

Lesseps, Ferdinand de, 46, 190, 316; background of, 57; Bunau-Varilla and, 75; Compagnie bond failure and, 63, 65; death of, 66; diplomatic service of, 57; fund-raising by, 59–60; Panama Canal and, 59–66, 75; Panama Railroad and, 60; reputation of, 59; sea-level Panama Canal attempt of, 60–66; Suez Canal and, 55, 57–58; tiered workforce and,

Lesseps, Ferdinand de (*cont.*)
    111; West Indian labor and, 115; Wyse
    Concession and, 59
Levi, Margaret, 5
Liberia, 273
Liberty ships, 274
Libro azul documents, 11
Libya, 291
Limón Bay, 99
Lloyd, John Augustus, 31–32, 341n85
lock-canal designs, 37, 70, 83, 100–105, 257
Loomis, Francis, 83–84
Lula da Silva, Luiz Inácio, 4
lumber industry, 177–79, 241, 371n76
Lyons, Thomas, 275, 276

McAuliffe, Dennis, 298, 305
McIntyre, Tom, 262
McKinley, William, 72–74, 370n55
McMillan, Robert, 303
macuquinas, 34–35
Madden Dam, 297
Mahan, Alfred Thayer, 167, 370n56
Maine (war ship), 84
Major, John, 11
malaria: health measures and, 55, 61, 97, 99,
    124–28, 322; mortality rates and, 124–
    26; mosquito transmission of, 124;
    sanitation crusade and, 124–28
Malucos. *See* Moluccas
Mamuneas, Theofanis P., 315, 397n4
Manfredo, Fernando, 298
Manzanillo Bay, 276
Marblehead (war ship), 84
marijuana, 292
Maritime Canal Company, 69–73, 87
markets: ancillary enterprises and, 310–11;
    antitrust laws and, 144–45; black, 195,
    198; Colón Free Zone and, 269, 275–81,
    311, 322, 387n26; cost savings through
    Panama Canal and, 140–45; illegal drug
    trade and, 285–86, 289–90, 292, 294;
    international banking sector and, 278–
    81, 292–93; Interstate Commerce Com-
    mission (ICC) and, 173–75, 185; lumber,
    177–79; money laundering and, 285–86,
    291–92, 294; petroleum, 179–88 (*see also*
    petroleum industry); price sensitivity of
    shippers and, 155–57; ship registration
    and, 270–73, 281; smuggling and, 20,

28–29, 267, 271–73, 285, 292, 298; tariffs
    and, 52, 69, 87, 94, 130, 191–94, 267–69,
    278; textile, 22, 166, 277, 339n47; *trajín*
    and, 23–30; transportation and, 212 (*see
    also* transportation)
Marroquín, José Manuel, 77, 82
Marsh, Richard, 121–22, 362n95
Martinelli, Ricardo, 313
Martínez Silva, Carlos, 76–78
Martinique, 80
Martyr, d'Anghiera, Peter, 18
Massachusetts Turnpike, 98
Maury, Matthew Fontaine, 46
Mayans, 15
Mayflower (war ship), 84
Medellín, 128, 285, 286
Mendoza, Carlos, 120–22
Menocal, Aniceto García, 69
Menocal Contract, 71, 87
Merchant Marines and Fisheries Subcom-
    mittee, 275
Mexican-American War, 36
Mexican Revolution, 106
Mexico, 141, 163, 386n16; American policy
    in, 147, 172; Díaz and, 50, 52; Eads and,
    50; Isthmus of Tehuantepec and, 14,
    49–54; mortality rates and, 126; mule
    transport and, 27; railroads and, 314;
    social savings and, 314
Miami Metrorail, 98
Mi-Jack Products, 310
military: Anti-Ballistic Missile Treaty and,
    253, 255; Blue Spoon and, 297; bourgeoi-
    sie and, 317; Canal Zone defense and,
    105–6; Crittenberger plan and, 225–26;
    defense benefits of Panama Canal and,
    167–73; Dignity Battalions and, 296, 302;
    Five-Power Treaty and, 168; ICBMs and,
    253; imperialism and, 202 (*see also* impe-
    rialism); labor strikes and, 114; Monroe
    Doctrine and, 172; naval spending and,
    167–68; Neutrality Treaty and, 260; Op-
    eration Just Cause and, 297–98; Panama
    Canal Treaty and, 260; Strategic Arms
    Limitation Treaty and, 253; suicide ships
    and, 213–15, 224; various U.S. interven-
    tions and, 172; War Department and,
    170–73; War Shipping Administration
    and, 216–18; Zonians' influence in, 258.
    See also specific conflict

Mindanao, 94
mining, 340n66; copper, 14, 163, 261; gold, 6, 14, 37, 59; iron, 152, 163–64, 243, 315; nitrate, 163; silver, 6, 13, 22, 28
Miraflores lock, 306
Miskito Indians, 39
Mississippi (battleship), 219
Mississippi River, 52
Mitchener, Kris James, 3, 324, 333n2
Mohammed, Saif, 141–42
Moluccas, 16
money laundering, 285–86, 291–92, 294, 390n86
Monroe Doctrine, 172
Morgan, Henry, 28
Morgan, John, 72–73, 75
Morgan, J. P., 85
Morison, Samuel Eliot, 11
Morris-Knudsen, 282
Morrow, Jay, 194
mortality rates, 8, 61, 119–20, 124–27, 130, 138, 148, 323
Moscoso, Mireya, 303–4
Mosquito Coast, 35, 40–41
Motta, Alberto, 273
Mount Hope reservoir, 127–28
Mount Pelée, 80
Movimiento Papa Egoró, 303
mud slides, 60–61
mules, 31, 39, 42; Acuapulco-to-Veracruz route and, 27; *trajín* and, 23–30, 246
Muslims, 93–94

Nadiri, M. Ishaq, 315, 397nj4
Napoleon III, 58
Nashville (battleship), 84
Nasser, Gamal Abdel, 328
National Aeronautics and Space Administration (NASA), 249
National City Bank, 200, 203–4
nationalism: American, 4, 9, 213, 228, 262, 375n43; Panamamian, 326
National Vote Counting Board, 288
Navy Bay, 42
Neutrality Act, 67, 272, 352n54
Neutrality Treaty, 259–60, 264–65, 286, 327, 332
New Cristóbal, 209
New Granada, 32–36, 42–43, 46, 341n88
New Jersey Turnpike, 249

New Mexico (aircraft carrier), 218–19
New Orleans, 36, 39, 166, 241
New Panama Canal Company: preparations for building Canal and, 65, 73–76, 79–81, 84, 89; U.S. purchase of, 99, 106
New Spain, 16
New York, 75, 275, 279, 289; Aspinwall and, 43; Biddle and, 34; Cleveland's dispatching of troops from, 68; Hay–Bunau-Varilla Treaty and, 85, 203–4; drugs and, 285; Lesseps and, 60; Panama Railroad and, 6, 83; Pan-American Exposition and, 73; petroleum industry and, 184–85; transportation from, 36, 39, 142, 145, 163, 216; textile industry and, 166; Vanderbilt and, 37; Wyse and, 48, 59
New York Herald, 271
New York Stock Exchange, 46, 281
New York Times, 99, 122, 192, 195, 226, 295
New York Tribune, 61
New Zealand, 320
Nicaragua, 14, 54, 162, 172–73, 207, 282; cattle and, 193; Frelinghuysen-Zavala Treaty and, 87; geography of, 56; Maritime Canal Company and, 69–73, 87; Menocal Contract and, 87; Mosquito Coast and, 35, 40–41; mule transport and, 26; Pedrarias and, 18–19; preparations for building Canal and, 66–82, 86–89, 95; Sandinistas and, 286–87, 291; San Juan River and, 16, 37, 39, 70, 83, 87; ship registration and, 270; slavery and, 6, 18–21, 24; spies and, 286; Vanderbilt and, 37–38; Zavala and, 66
Nicaraguan Canal Association, 69
Nicatlnauac, 18
Nicoya, 18
Nimitz-class carriers, 224
nitrates, 162–63
Nixon, Richard, M., 253, 256–58, 262
Nombre de Díos, 15–18, 200, 335nn5,10, 336n19, 339n45, 375n40
Nootka Sound, 31
Noriega, Manuel, 328–29, 390n86; Balladares and, 303; Barletta and, 289–90; Blue Spoon and, 297; Bush and, 296–97; calls for resignation of, 291; Carter and, 296; Casey and, 287, 290; Central Intelligence Agency (CIA) and, 285, 287, 290;

and, 9, 212–13, 230, 236–39, 248, 255–56, 262–63; U.S. Free Trade Agreement and, 313, 332; U.S. troops in, 56–57, 68, 77, 80–84, 203, 221, 325; water purification and, 127–28

Panama Canal: American commerce benefits and, 158–62; amount of excavated rock for, 103; ancillary enterprises and, 310–11; Article 10 and, 190; attack on, 218; budget overruns of, 97–99, 102, 106, 140, 147; changes in revenue sources for, 267–68; Chile's gain from, 162–64; Cold War era and, 223–27; concrete needed for, 103; Culebra Cut and, 61, 83, 103, 213–14, 279, 309; decrease of strategic position of, 226–27; defense issues of, 105–7, 167–73, 214, 224–25; discontents and, 108–10; distributional effects of, 173; Eiffel design and, 62; as engineering marvel, 97, 139; estimating economic value of, 139–40; fear of Panamanian mismanagement of, 248–55; Fogel method and, 5–6; freight rates and, 141–45 (*see also* freight rates); French attempts at, 59–66, 69, 71, 75, 98–99, 110–11, 123, 187, 199; French private interests and, 1, 6–7, 13–14; future of, 331–32; Goethals and, 100–102, 106, 113, 115, 118, 121; imperialism and, 1–4, 7–8, 11–12, 57, 95–96, 201, 313, 317–23, 332, 333n1; increased ship size and, 308–9; interest costs and, 106, 149, 260, 325, 396n179; internationalization of, 255; Japan's gain from, 164–66; Kissinger-Tack principles and, 257–58; labor unrest at, 110–15 (*see also* labor); landslides and, 98, 103, 168, 213; Lesseps and, 59–66, 75; as liability, 228; local canals and, 102–3; local treasury contributions of, 312; lock-canal designs and, 37, 70, 83, 100–105, 257; logistic effects of, 214–18; long-term profitability of, 305–12; management missteps of, 99–102, 248–55; Mendoza affair and, 120–22; modern assessment of, 55; national symbolism of, 228, 262, 264; oil tankers and, 180, 183, 272–73, 282; opens to civilian traffic, 98; palindrome about, 1; Panamanization of, 298–305; petroleum industry and, 179–88;

post-Panamax vessels and, 242–43, 245; price sensitivity of shippers and, 155–57; racial discrimination and, 115–20; rainfall and, 306–7; reservation system improvements and, 309–10; sanitation and, 122–28; sea-level design for, 60–66; shipper competition and, 143–44; social savings of, 147–55, 240–46; steel needed for, 103; supertankers and, 243; as symbol of American nationalism, 228, 262; Third Locks project and, 224–27; toll controversies and, 146–47, 246–48; Transisthmian Pipeline and, 265; transportation cost savings from, 140–45; U.S. costs of, 98–100, 103–8, 114, 118, 128, 135–39; U.S. lumber industry and, 177–79; U.S. railroad industry and, 173–77; U.S. returns from, 158–62; wage caps and, 112; World War II era and, 213–23; Wyse Concession and, 59, 78, 81–82, 86, 89, 92, 95, 162, 316

Panama Canal, The (LaFeber), 11

Panama Canal Act, 255; Commissary and, 192; Goethals and, 102; Panama Canal Company and, 248, 251; private-property rights and, 108; repeal of, 147; railroads and, 144; toll provisions of, 146; Wilson and, 146–47

Panama Canal Authority, 302–5, 308–11

Panama Canal Commission, 10, 260, 263, 384n75; Guardia and, 298, 303, 309; long-term profitability and, 305, 308–11; Noriega and, 284, 295–98; Panamanization of, 298–305; U.S. handover of Canal and, 264, 284, 295–305, 308–11

Panama Canal Company, 10, 382n50, 383n73, 384n79; accident rates and, 251; mismanagement and, 248–55; New Panama Canal Company and, 65, 73–76, 79–81, 84, 89, 99, 106; Panama Canal Act and, 248, 251; productivity and, 249–51; raising tolls and, 246–48; sliding irrelevancy of Canal and, 246–55, 260, 263; U.S. handover of Canal and, 274, 306

Panama Canal Treaty, 327; American public's reaction to, 264–65; long-term profitability and, 305–6; sliding irrelevancy of Canal and, 228, 256, 259–63; U.S. handover of Canal and, 287, 312

Panama Canal West Indian Employees Association, 234

Panama City, 209, 248, 344n141; American fiscal agent in, 190; declining revenue of, 269; founding of, 18; historical perspective on, 13, 17–18, 22–24, 27, 33, 36–37, 41–44; mortality rates and, 122–27; preparations for building Canal and, 61, 67–68, 77, 82–85; railroads and, 204; Remón assassination and, 231; riots in, 202–3, 237; Trans-Isthmian Highway and, 210, 276; U.S. construction of Canal and, 108, 114, 122–28; U.S. handover of Canal and, 274–79, 297–98

Panama Fortification Board, 105

Panamanian Defense Forces (PDF), 287

Panamanian flag, 229, 236–38, 262, 269–73, 322

Panamanian National Assembly, 204, 226, 238, 275, 279, 297

Panamanization, 298–305

Panama Railroad, 14, 36, 54, 141, 325, 344n146, 348n181, 350n24; amortization funding and, 63; Aspinwall and, 41–43; building of Canal and, 110–12, 115, 118, 127–28; budget of, 44–46, 344n148; Clayton-Bulwer Treaty and, 40–42; Commissary and, 191–94, 198–99; Compagnie Universelle du Canal Interocéanique and, 46–48; completion of, 44; construction of, 42–45; cut tracks of, 68; dividend payments and, 42; economic issues and, 44–47; fading of, 246; as feeder to Pacific shipping, 41–42; freight rates and, 193–94; groundbreaking ceremony of, 42–43; Hay–Bunau-Varilla Treaty and, 84; Hull-Alfaro Treaty and, 210–11; incorporation of, 42; increased business for, 61; labor issues and, 43–44; Lesseps and, 60; lignum vitae ties and, 44; Navy Bay and, 42; new contract of, 46; New Granada concession rights and, 42; Pacific Steam Navigation Company and, 49; preparation of Canal project and, 59–69, 79, 82–86; profits of, 6–7, 46–47; rehabilitation of, 99–100, 103, 105, 310–11; rising stock prices of, 47–48; sliding irrelevancy of Canal and, 231, 246; Stephens and, 42; surveying of, 42; Tehuan-

tepec Railroad and, 52–53; trucking competition and, 274; U.S. communications and, 41–42; U.S. handover of Canal and, 265, 274

Panameñista Party, 302–4

Pan-American Airlines, 203

Pan-American Exposition, 73–74

Park, Trenor, 59

Parke-Davis, 276

Parkinson, Constantine, 108

Partido Revolucionario Democrático (PRD), 284, 303–4, 313

Pasha, Sáid, 57

patronage networks, 265–67, 328–29

Pauncefote, Julian, 72, 74

Pearcy, Thomas L., 11

Pearl Harbor, 218–19, 222

pearls, 14, 26

Pearson, Weetman, 52–53, 347n178

Pérez Balladares, Ernesto, 303–4

Peru, 71, 243; illicit trade in, 28; oysters and, 15; Pizarro and, 19–20; ship technology and, 29; silver of, 6, 13–14, 22, 28; slavery and, 20, 24; Straits of Magellan and, 29

petroleum industry: Alaska and, 281–82; Big Inch and, 184; Cookenboo study and, 184, 372n93; crude oil prices and, 179–80; Goodyear and, 373n96; Noriega and, 295; oil tankers and, 180, 183, 185, 272–74, 282; Panama Canal effects on, 179–88; post-Panamax vessels and, 242–43; refining and, 182–83; social savings and, 314–15; Sumed Pipeline and, 284; supertankers and, 243; transcontinental pipeline and, 183–88; Transisthmian Pipeline and, 265, 281–84

Petroterminal de Panamá S.A., 282

Pfizer, 276

Philippines, 56, 93–95, 168, 173, 204, 207, 271, 321

Philippine War, 93–94

Pippin, Larry, 11, 381n36

pirate radio, 272, 386n16

pirates, 26, 81

Pizarro, Francisco, 19–20

politics: Alianza Democrática and, 303; Alianza Pueblo Unido and, 303; Article 136 (Panamanian constitution of 1904) and, 7, 85–86, 94, 121, 201–3, 210; autoc-

racy and, 266–67, 284; Cold War and, 223–27; Colón Free Zone and, 269, 275–81, 311, 322, 387n26; Communists and, 9, 228, 234; decolonization and, 325–31; elitism and, 33, 236, 267, 277, 284, 290, 311, 328; empire effect and, 200–208; Executive Order 12635 and, 293–94; Fascists and, 229; flying of Panamanian flag and, 236–38; Good Neighbor diplomacy and, 209–10; historical perspective on, 4; illegal drug trade and, 285–86, 289–90, 292, 294; imperialism and, 1–4, 7–8, 11–12, 57, 95–96, 201, 313, 317–23, 332, 333n1; Mendoza affair and, 120–22; Merchant Marine and Fisheries Subcommittee and, 275; Movimiento Papa Egoró and, 303; Neutrality Act and, 67, 272, 352n54; Noriega and, 9–10, 12, 265–66, 284–99, 302–5, 311, 328–29, 390n86; Panama Canal Act and, 102, 108, 144–47, 192, 248, 251, 255; Panamanian National Assembly and, 204, 226, 238, 275, 279, 297; Panameñista Party and, 302–4; Partido Revolucionario Democrático (PRD) and, 284, 303–4, 313; patronage networks and, 265–67, 328–29; populists and, 4, 266, 278, 287–88, 302; Progressive Era and, 321; Republic of Panama and, 2, 7, 56–57, 102, 189–90, 201, 211, 257, 263, 277, 306, 312; sanctions and, 2, 5, 190, 206, 294–95, 328–29, 333n1, 393n132, 398n18; ship registration and, 270–73, 281; sovereignty issues and, 2–5, 33, 36, 69, 78–83, 206, 209–11, 235–39, 257, 333n1, 386n16; tolls controversy and, 146–47, 246–48; Torrijos and, 9–10, 255–61, 265–66, 278, 282–88, 291, 297–98, 302–5, 327–28; U.S. Shipping Board and, 143–44, 270–71; vote competition and, 266; Watergate scandal and, 262. See also specific treaty
Ponce de León, Juan, 19
populism, 4, 266, 278, 287–88, 302
Porras, Belisario, 189, 202–4, 207, 376n54
Portobelo, 22, 26, 27–28, 339n45
Port Said, 190
post-Panamax vessels, 242–43, 245
potato raids, 130
Potsdam Conference, 228, 255

Prairie (war ship), 84
Prensa, La (newspaper), 287–88
Prestán, Pedro, 67–68
price sensitivity, 155–57
Prize Possession: The United States and the Panama Canal (Major), 11
Probyn, Leslie, 133–34
Progressive Era, 321
Prohibition, 209, 271
prostitution, 375n39
Prudhoe Bay, Alaska, 281
Puente del Rey, 23–24
Puerto Rico, 93–94, 201, 321
Putin, Vladimir, 4

Quechua, 15
Queens (borough of New York city), 98, 290, 357n4

racial issues, 321; Commissary and, 192; depopulation and, 115, 118; Goethals and, 101, 115, 118; health care and, 118–20; Jim Crow system and, 97; labor and, 115–22; Mendoza affair and, 120–22; payroll systems and, 111–12; wage caps and, 112
railroads: competition and, 145; containerization and, 241; dieselization and, 241; Eads and, 49–54; effects of Panama Canal on, 173–77; exports and, 241–42; Fogel method and, 5–6; freight rates and, 173–77, 193–94; grade issues and, 53; Hay–Bunau-Varilla Treaty and, 203; Interstate Commerce Commission (ICC) and, 173–75, 185; modernization and, 52–53; Panama Canal's effect on U.S. industry of, 173–77; social savings and, 314–16; transcontinental, 54; trucking competition and, 241; wind jets and, 53–54; World War II and, 215–18. *See also* specific railroad
Ranger (aircraft carrier), 223
Reagan, Ronald, 259, 262, 287–90, 296, 326–28
Reed, Walter, 123
Remón, José Antonio, 228, 231, 236, 285
Remón-Eisenhower Treaty, 231–35, 277–78, 322
rents, 7–8, 61, 95, 142, 190, 246, 258, 272, 281

Republic of Panama, 306, 312; Colón Free
Zone and, 277; economic opportuni-
ties in, 189–90; Panama Canal Act and,
102; Roosevelt's threats and, 7; sover-
eignty issues and, 257; as underdevel-
oped country, 2; U.S. Influence over, 7,
56–57, 189–90, 201, 211, 263
Reyes, Rafael, 68
Rhipicephalus annulatus tick, 193
Richardson, Bonham, 11
Río Abajo, 24
Río Hato air base, 226, 231
Rivas, 39, 70
Robinson, James A., 323, 398n20
Rockwell, John, 46
Rodriguez, Ramon Milian, 286
Rogers, William, 292–95
Rognoni, Mario, 294
Roman Catholic Church, 296–98
Roosevelt, Franklin Delano, 208–11, 219,
224
Roosevelt, Theodore, 1, 4, 291; Bunau-
Varilla and, 83; coercive diplomacy of,
82–96, 202; Colombia and, 82–92, 202;
defense spending and, 167–68, 170, 172;
and Goethals, 100; Gold Roll and, 112;
impatience of, 56; imperialism and, 7,
56–57, 321; interventionism and, 324;
Isthmian Commission and, 75–76, 100;
McKinley assassination and, 74; Monroe
Doctrine and, 172; on his greatest ac-
complishment, 97; Panamanian uprising
and, 83–92; Pan-American Exposition
and, 73; political infighting and, 100;
Progressive Party and, 146; rent expropriations and, 7; threat of force by, 7,
82–92; unrepentant nature of, 92–93
Roosevelt Corollary, 172
Root, Elihu, 147, 191, 200
Root-Arosemena Treaty, 191–92, 374n14
Rosenthal, Jean-Laurent, 5
Royal Navy, 28
rum-running, 271
Ruyz, Bartolomé, 15

Saavedra Cerón, Álvaro de, 16
Sai Baba, Satya, 291
Salina Cruz, 52, 53
salt, 14, 19, 34

sanctions, 2, 5, 190, 206, 294–95, 328–29,
333n1, 393n132, 398n18
Sandinistas, 286, 286–87, 291
sanitation: Barranquilla and, 128; building
of Panama Canal and, 122–28; crusade
for, 122–28; depopulation and, 115;
Hay–Bunau-Varilla Treaty and, 84–85;
Hay-Herrán Treaty and, 82; mortality
rates and, 122–27; U.S. technology and,
128
San Juan del Norte (Greytown), 39–41
San Juan River, 16, 37, 39, 70, 83, 87
San Lorenzo, 26
Santa Clara Mountains, 24
Santo Domingo, 19
Saratoga (aircraft carrier), 224
Sardá, José, 31, 31–32
Saunders, Norman, 292
Schley, Julian, 209–10
Schott, Jeffrey J., 393n132
Schularick, Moritz, 3, 201, 324
Sea Witch (ship), 43
Seybold, John, 275
shells, 14–15
shipbuilding, 270–71
ship registration, 270–73, 281
Shonts, Theodore, 110
Silver Roll, 111–15, 118, 191–92, 198, 274,
323
Singapore, 189
slavery, 6, 18–24, 321
Slifer, Hiram, 112
smuggling, 20, 28–29, 267, 271–73, 285,
292, 298
social savings: 396n1; cost analysis and, 147–
55; decline of, 240–46; decolonization
and, 325–31; decreased freight rates
and, 242–45; distribution changes and,
315–16; Fogel and, 148; global rate of,
313–14; gravity model for, 152–53; Immigration and Nationality Act and, 315;
internal rate of return and, 157; Interstate Highway System and, 315–16; petroleum industry and, 314–15; post-
Panamax vessels and, 242–43, 245; price
reduction effects and, 314–15; railroads
and, 148, 314, 315–16; rate of return on,
153–55
Social Security, 302

Sokoloff, Kenneth, 323
Solís, Manuel, 292
South Africa, 320
South Dakota (battleship), 219
Southern (yellow) pine, 177–78
sovereignty, 2–3, 33, 333n1, 386n16;
American flag and, 236, 240; Article 136
(Panamanian constitution of 1904) and,
7, 85–86, 94, 121, 201–3, 210; Bidlack-
Mallarino Treaty and, 35–36, 67, 69,
80–83; Boyd march and, 236–37; Colombia and, 78–79; empire effect and, 206;
flying of Panamanian flag and, 236–38,
262; Good Neighbor Policy and, 209–
10; Hay–Bunau-Varilla Treaty and, 211
(*see also* Hay–Bunau-Varilla Treaty); ir-
relevant position of Canal and, 235–39,
257; Westphalian, 4–5
Soviet Union: Anti-Ballistic Missile Treaty
and, 253, 255; ICBMs and, 253; ir-
relevant position of Canal and, 223–28;
Noriega and, 291; spies and, 286; Strategic Arms Limitation Treaty and, 253;
Strategic Rocket Forces and, 223
Spadafora, Hugo, 288–90
Spanish-American War, 56, 71, 172–73
spies, 286
Spondylus shells, 15
Spooner, John, 76, 79
Spooner Act, 80
steam power: shovels and, 103; steam en-
gines and, 58; steamships and, 34–44,
49, 53, 67–68, 71, 132, 140, 144, 148,
174, 214; Suez Canal and, 58; sugar
mills and, 129
steel, 49, 103, 163–64, 174–76, 183, 241,
243, 368n38, 372n93
Stephens, John, 42
Steuart, John, 33–34
Stevens, John, 99, 100, 110
Stevens, Simon, 49
Stimson, Henry, 212
Strait of Magellan, 13, 16, 150
Straits of Malacca, 189
Strategic Arms Limitation Treaty, 253
Suez Canal, 4, 349n10; closure of, 243; cost
of, 57–60, 349n11; French and, 55, 57–
60; indemnity payments and, 58; nation-
alization of, 328; opening of, 58; Port

Said and, 190; shipping and, 141; steam
power and, 58; Sumed Pipeline and, 284
sugar, 94, 113, 129–31, 134, 155, 166, 191
suicide, 43, 375n40
suicide ships, 214–15, 224, 226
Sumed Pipeline, 284
supertankers, 243
Svedberg, Peter, 3, 333n2
Sydney Morning Herald, 33

Tack, Juan Antonio, 257
Taft, William Howard, 101–2, 105, 122, 146,
158, 321, 362n96
taxes, 173, 238, 306, 314, 396n179; Article
10 and, 190; Cleveland and, 67; Colombia and, 80; Colón Free Zone and, 269,
275–81, 311, 322, 387n26; Commissary and, 190–94, 198; double taxation
and, 272; excise, 198, 209; exemptions
from, 50, 69, 190–94, 198, 273, 277;
Frelinghuysen-Zavala Treaty and, 87;
Hay–Bunau-Varilla Treaty and, 84, 193;
Hull-Alfaro Treaty and, 231; international banking sector and, 279–80; Nicaragua and, 66, 87; Noriega and, 295–96;
Panamanian revenue and, 270–73, 277–
81, 295; Peruvian mines and, 22; Prohibition and, 209; sanitation works and, 128;
social savings and, 160–61; subsidies
and, 57; tariffs and, 52, 69, 87, 94, 130,
191–94, 267–69, 278; trade, 267, 269,
278; United Fruit and, 204
Taylor, Zachary, 40–41
tehuano (wind), 53–54
Tehuantepec National Railroad Company,
52–53, 348n181
Tehuantepec Ship Railway, 49–54
Tennessee Valley Authority, 249
Terminales Panama trucking company, 273
Texaco, 295
Texas, 178, 182, 184, 188
textiles, 22, 166, 277, 339n47
Thatcher, Maurice, 101–2
Thierry, Charles de, 32–34
Third Locks project, 224–27
thorny oyster, 15
Thousand Days War, 76, 199–200
through-freight, 274
TIROS weather satellites, 315